# Leroy

*Hand of the Cau...*

*At the site of the future Ma<u>sh</u>riqu'l-A<u>dh</u>kár on Mt. Carmel, 1961*

# Leroy Ioas
*Hand of the Cause of God*

*by*

ANITA IOAS CHAPMAN

GEORGE RONALD
OXFORD

GEORGE RONALD, Publisher
46 High Street, Kidlington, Oxford OX5 2DN

*A catalogue record for this book is available from the British Library*

ISBN 0-85398-426-3

Typesetting by Leith Editorial Services, Abingdon, Oxon, UK
Printed and bound in Great Britain by Biddles Ltd, Guildford and King's Lynn

# CONTENTS

Foreword                                                          xi

1    Charles and Maria                                            1

2    Leroy and his Family                                         7

3    'Abdu'l-Bahá                                                 17

4    Change                                                       29

5    The Bahá'ís of the Bay Area                                 32

6    Settling In                                                  38

7    The Conference for World Unity                              45

8    The Geyserville Story                                       52

9    The First Decade                                            64

10   Race Unity                                                   75

11   The Teacher                                                  81

12   A Wider Field of Service                                    91

13   The First Seven Year Plan 1937-1944                         95

14   The Republics of the South                                 119

15   Family Life                                                125

16   The Last Years in San Francisco                            134

17   Return to Chicago                                          142

18   Appointment and Departure                                  153

19   Meeting the Guardian                                       160

20   At the World Centre                                        165

21   Forging Relationships                                      177

22   The Hands of the Cause in Haifa                            187

23   Representing the Guardian                                  198

24   Land                                                       205

25   The Queen of Carmel                                        217

26   Báb-i-Ioas                                                 229

27   Serving Quietly                                            233

28   The International Bahá'í Archives                              238
29   The Ten Year Crusade: The First Five Years                    248
30   Ella Bailey                                                   267
31   The Passing of Shoghi Effendi                                 271
32   The Beloved Guardian                                          284
33   The Custodians                                                292
34   The Universal House of Justice                                329
35   "You will, I am sure, persevere till the very end"            341

*Appendices*
  I   Statement signed by members of the International Bahá'í
      Council present in Haifa on 6 November 1957                  350
 II   Unanimous Proclamation of the twenty-seven Hands of
      the Cause of God                                             352
III   Resolution of the Hands of the Cause of God                 356
 IV   In Memoriam: Sylvia Ioas                                     358

Bibliography                                                       362
References                                                         367
Index                                                             376

# ILLUSTRATIONS

*Frontispiece*

At the site of the future Ma<u>sh</u>riqu'l-A<u>dh</u>kár on Mt. Carmel, 1961

*Between pages 82 and 83*

Charles and Maria Ioas
Leroy at two years old
Leroy as a high school student
First job
Young people at the Temple grounds in Wilmette
Leroy as a young married man
At Geyserville summer school, Leroy with a children's class
With Farrukh
At home
The first Regional Bahá'í Convention in California, San Francisco 1926
Early years in California
At Geyserville in the 1930s: In front of the Bosch house
John and Louise Bosch
John and Louise Bosch with Martha Root at Collins Hall
John Bosch and Leroy talking to Louise Caswell
Mark Tobey, George Latimer and Marion Holley at Collins Hall
Leroy at Geyserville
Leroy and Sylvia at the steps leading to Collins Hall
With Milly Collins and Harlan Ober in front of the Philanthropic Club
At the Temple grounds during National Convention
Upstairs in the House of Worship

*Between pages 114 and 115*

The National Spiritual Assembly, 1939, during the first Seven Year Plan
At the office

*Between pages 274 and 275*

With the Guardian at the funeral of Isfandiar, April 1957
Leroy at his desk
With Ugo Giachery in Jerusalem
Meeting officials
Kampala, Uganda, Intercontinental Conference 1953
Ten Hands of the Cause of God during the Conference
At the dedication of the British Ḥaẓíratu'l-Quds, January 1955
In Dublin with Adib Taherzadeh
Building the superstructure of the Shrine of the Báb
Báb-i-Ioas. The ninth door of the Shrine of the Báb
The Arc and the Archives building
At the funeral of Shoghi Effendi
At the beloved Guardian's resting-place, March 1958


*Between pages 306 and 307*

Leroy Ioas in the Ḥaram-i-Aqdas
Second Conclave of the Hands of the Cause, November 1958
Leroy with Sylvia at the Chicago International Conference, May 1958
Leroy with his daughter Anita
At the Singapore International Conference, September 1958
In Abadan, traveling to the Djakarta Intercontinental Conference, September 1958
In Djakarta with Hands of the Cause Agnes Alexander and Collis Featherstone, and Mrs. Featherstone
Hands of the Cause in Djakarta
In front of the Eastern Pilgrim house, 1960
The International Bahá'í Council, Bahjí, June 1961
Speaking at Kensington Central Library, London, September 8, 1961 at the Fiftieth Anniversary celebration of 'Abdu'l-Bahá's visit to England
At the Marian Anderson rose garden, at the Temple in Wilmette
With Joan and Ernest Gregory at the Irish Summer School, 1961
Leroy and Sylvia in Luxembourg, 1962
At Summer School in Finland, 1962

*Between pages 338 and 339*

Hands of the Cause of God on the steps of the Master's House just
    before the International Convention, April 1963

Leroy with his first granddaughter Catherine

Leroy and Sylvia on the balcony of their Haifa apartment

Last portraits taken in Spring 1964

Conclave of the Hands of the Cause of God, October 1964, Bahjí:
    The Universal House of Justice and the Hands of the Cause of
    God.

# FOREWORD

THIS is the story of one of the eminent American Bahá'ís of the formative age of the Bahá'í Faith. Leroy Ioas was the son of immigrants from Germany and carried in him the drive and pioneering spirit that had caused them to settle in a new country and take up a new and little known religion. They were a major influence in his life, and he grew up to share their belief in and devotion to Bahá'u'lláh, Prophet-Founder of the Bahá'í Faith. The seminal spiritual experience of his life was meeting 'Abdu'l-Bahá, the eldest son and designated successor of Bahá'u'lláh, on the occasion of 'Abdu'l-Bahá's historic trip in 1912 to bring His Father's teachings to the Western world. Leroy was a youth of sixteen at the time. He was to become a brilliant administrator and a gifted teacher.

With the death of 'Abdu'l-Bahá in 1921 and the appointment of His grandson Shoghi Effendi as the Guardian of the Bahá'í Faith and sole expounder of its scriptures, a new era opened, the formative age in Bahá'í history, when its institutions were formed, its laws and principles given application and its great teaching missions begun. This was the work to which Leroy gave his considerable talent and energy. Indeed, his life cannot be understood except in terms of his fidelity to Bahá'u'lláh and the dissemination of His teachings.

In late 1951, Shoghi Effendi activated the institution of the Hands of the Cause of God, described in 'Abdu'l-Bahá's Will and Testament as a body of spiritually eminent Bahá'ís who were to be engaged in service to the Guardian of the Faith. It was the highest appointive position in the Bahá'í world. Leroy was one of the twelve named in that year as Hands of the Cause; shortly thereafter he was invited to move to Haifa, site of the Bahá'í World Centre, to assist Shoghi Effendi in his multitudinous responsibilities. The five and a half years Leroy spent in service to the Guardian were the apogee of his life.

Following the passing of Shoghi Effendi in 1957, Leroy was one of nine Hands of the Cause elected, from among the full body of Hands, to act as Custodians at the World Centre, directing the Bahá'ís in the completion of the global Crusade begun in 1953. With the election in 1963 of the Universal House of Justice (the international governing body of the Bahá'ís) the institution of the Custodians ceased its function, although the individual Hands of the Cause continued, to the end of their lives, to discharge the specific duties of preserving and propagating the Word of God assigned to them by Bahá'u'lláh. Leroy lived and worked in Haifa for the remainder of his life.

The latter half of the book which details Leroy's work in Haifa is replete with notations of what the Guardian said. With the exception, however, of chapter 19, where the Guardian's words were taken down at table as he spoke, the other chapters give the words of the Guardian as Leroy remembered them and as he shared them with others. They have the weight of pilgrims' notes only, unless Shoghi Effendi had specifically asked him to convey certain information. Pilgrims' notes are just that: recollections of what people heard Bahá'u'lláh, 'Abdu'l-Bahá or the Guardian say. They have no weight as Bahá'í scripture.

This book is the result of many persons' efforts. Many years ago two daughters of Charles and Maria Ioas, Marguerite Ullrich and Viola Tuttle, compiled their mother's memories of the experiences of the Ioas family with 'Abdu'l-Bahá in Chicago in 1912. This proved invaluable as family history. It was augmented in 1978 with help from the other three surviving siblings of Leroy Ioas: Monroe, Paul and Joseph.

Several years after Leroy's death, his widow Sylvia began to collect remembrances of his life. A number of his friends and colleagues sent her stories of their association with him, which were the source of highly useful sketches of Leroy in action.

While working in Haifa from 1986 to 1988, Leroy's eldest granddaughter, Catherine, began, with the encouragement and knowledgeable help of Marion Hofman, to collect more material. She interviewed a number of his colleagues and wrote to many more. On her return to the United States, she traveled and gathered recollections from friends and family members.

To me fell the happy task of continuing the research and putting it all together, three wonderful years of dwelling in his life, being astonished at the scope of his accomplishments, and reliving our lives together as a family. Leroy was a letter writer and much of the material in the book comes from his letters and from tapes of his talks at Bahá'í summer schools and meetings. Sources of other material are given in the Reference section, as well as for all quotations from Shoghi Effendi's letters and cables. The Research Department at the Bahá'í World Centre sent materials and several photographs. Additional material and letters were found in the National Archives in Wilmette with the help of chief archivist Roger Dahl. I am grateful to editor May Hofman for putting the final polish on the text and for organizing its format and presentation.

But there is always a guiding spirit and in this case it was David Hofman, whose constant encouragement and comments on the text as it came into being, were the inspiration to continue. I am profoundly grateful for his help, given I know because of the depth of his admiration for Leroy, a man whose life left an imprint on the Bahá'í world.

# CHAPTER ONE

# Charles and Maria

THROUGHOUT the Protestant world of the nineteenth century there were small bands of people who courageously stepped out of the conventional mold of religious thinking and dared to speak of the Return, the time of the end, the coming of Christ. They were Biblical scholars whose convictions were strong and their intentions pure. Study of the texts had proved to their satisfaction that this was the time when the silent prayers of the centuries were to be answered.

They were called variously Adventists, Millerites, dreamers, even less flattering names. In Germany, in North America, in England, these groups were actively examining how to make ready for the great fulfillment, which they generally associated with the mid-1800s. William Miller in New York, founder of the Adventist sect, wrote that there were "one or two" in every quarter of the globe who "have proclaimed the news and agreed on the time – Wolff, of Asia; Irwin, late of England; Mason of Scotland; Davis of South Carolina; and quite a number in this region are or have been raising the cry." Leonard Heinrich Kelber of Stuttgart wrote: ". . . the year 1843 is the terminus, at which the great struggle between light and darkness will be finished, and the long expected reign of peace of our Lord Jesus will commence on earth." In England under the inspiration of Edward Irving, a group of clergymen and laymen met together every year for five years and "spent six full days in close and laborious examination of the Scriptures" in order to discover what the Bible revealed in regard to the anticipated coming of Christ.[1]

Throughout Christendom there were many souls deeply dissatisfied with what they had received as religion, frustrated that the single

message of Christ had been fragmented into ever narrower and more
rigid forms of belief. Religious faith seemed lost in disunifying theol-
ogy, no longer quenching their spiritual thirst with the life-giving
waters which Jesus had brought. So to the scholars awaiting prophetic
fulfillment were added the many spiritually-minded people who sought
a fulfilling religious life.

One of these spiritually-minded persons was a matron in Munich,
Germany, who looked around her at the divided churches and their
contentious relationships. She was restless and dissatisfied. Surely, she
felt within her, there had to be some new way, some new power that
would create a spiritual environment in which people could find joy.
She was Lutheran. She knew the Bible and the prophecies, and
although not a member of any such movement, she was like the
Adventists in feeling great certainty that this was the time Christ had
spoken of, the time of the Return.

This thoughtful, perceptive woman had a son and a daughter. In
this story we are concerned with her son, Karl Ioas, who as he grew up
took his mother's attitudes very much to heart. Indeed, they so
impressed him that the intellectual formation of school was only one
facet of his thinking and not the most essential.

Karl was of a questing intellect, that inborn quality that leads one
on to discovery. Very deeply within him lay the desire to explore and to
understand. His mother had planted the seeds, and as he matured the
questions that preoccupied her increasingly came to preoccupy him.
More than once she had told him there must be a new religion to unite
the unhappy quarrelling sects, and she had assured him that he would
live to see the return of Christ. It will be seen what harvest came of the
seeds she had planted.

Karl was a young man of brilliant mind, sharpened through the
curriculum of a European education. He spoke several languages and
could read Greek. As a profession he was attracted to the law which he
studied at the University of Munich. When he had completed his law
degree a well-to-do uncle offered him a trip to America as a graduation gift. The gift was accepted with alacrity. He was twenty-one years
old, filled with curiosity about the new world and its vigorous life. He
did not go alone, however, but travelled with the family of one of his
classmates from the university. The family included an orphaned

cousin, a young girl of quick intelligence who had been brought up with his classmate. Her name was Maria Reiser.

She had come to the family from Passau, Bavaria, where she and her twin sister, Ottilia, were orphaned early in life, the death of their father in the Franco-Prussian war having been followed two years later by the death of their mother. In the face of this double tragedy, the girls had to be separated. Maria was sent to live with her aunt and uncle in Munich, while her sister was adopted by a French woman in Munich who unfortunately, and against her promise, separated the girls by taking Ottilia to live in France.

The twin sisters were never to meet again. Maria grieved deeply at the absence of her twin and in the loneliness of her childhood surrounded herself with dolls, talking to them, and vowing to have twelve children so that none would ever be lonely.

By the time the visit to America was drawing to a close and while preparations were being made to return to Europe, an astonishing decision was announced: Karl and Maria had decided to marry and settle in America. She was very young, not yet sixteen, and although Karl had a good degree, he had no experience of work. Nonetheless they confidently went ahead with their plans. They were married on September 20, 1880. The page was turned on their former life. Karl thereafter always used the name Charles and spoke nothing but English at home. He often said, certainly foreshadowing the life he would help his children to build: "I am a citizen of the world."

In this new country he set about making his way in his chosen profession. They moved out to Russell, Kansas, where Charles was offered the opportunity to "read" law with a judge. This prepared him for the bar examination which he passed in 1886. The first four of their children were born in Kansas though the first-born, a son named Karl after his father, did not survive infancy.

As they moved about, from Kansas to Missouri and Arkansas and Illinois, Charles acquired a degree as a Chartered Public Accountant and worked for several years with the civil service. He was never highly successful in the practice of law and felt dissatisfied with his accomplishment. Perhaps, said one of his sons, he was more of a scholar than a realist. Maria contributed to the family income by her photographic skills which were sufficient to enable her to set up a studio in their various homes for portraiture work.

Charles continued his philosophic avocation with great zeal, little by little acquiring a library on Scriptural interpretation and seeking out people who shared his interest in the great themes of the Return. It should not be thought that he was alone in this quest; Maria's approach was more from the heart than the mind.

She had been raised in the Catholic tradition. But even as a child of ten, she recalled, "I rebelled against certain things in the church, such as telling of one's inmost thoughts to a strange person. Yet I loved to go to the big Catholic church. In the afternoon when no one was there I would just sit and meditate; there was such peace that I wished I could sit there all the time. Yet I made up my mind that when I could use my own will, I would never be a Catholic. I came to America, and we were married by a Methodist minister. Later we joined the Methodist church, but I was never satisfied." And so the years passed.

She and her husband were spiritually restless. Maria had prayed every day for seventeen years to find the truth that she felt existed somewhere. Often during her prayers she would sense a curtain separating her from that truth and she urgently wanted to pull the curtain aside to know what was on the other side. And then, just two years before she and Charles heard of the existence of Bahá'u'lláh, she had a strange experience. She was awakened during the night by heavy pressure on her chest. An angelic figure seemed to be leaning over her and saying twice: "I come again. I come again." And then the vision faded.

It was in April of 1898 that their path crossed the path of Paul Kingston Dealy, a Canadian-born engineer who was one of the first Bahá'ís in Chicago. They knew nothing of what he believed nor did they hear the word "Bahá'í" from him for several months.

But they had found one of the great early Bahá'í "teachers". Paul Dealy held classes in his home on the north side of Chicago; another early believer, Thornton Chase (the first North American Bahá'í) held the same type of class in the south of the city. They followed a pattern set by a Syrian Bahá'í who attracted many of the first believers to the Bahá'í Faith. The technique was to present a series of weekly classes based on explanations of Scripture concerning the coming of Christ, the signs of the times and the time of fulfillment. Mr. Dealy was a gifted and shrewd teacher. To encourage continued attendance he would sometimes, instead of fully answering a question, say they would take that up next week!

These strong-minded early Bahá'ís pursued a variety of reform ideas also. Thus toward 1900 Paul Dealy moved to Fairhope, Alabama, attempting with others to put into practice the principles of the Single Tax movement. His wife Addie and their four sons followed shortly and he remained there until his death in 1937, spreading the knowledge of Bahá'í teachings in that area. Leroy Ioas once described Dealy's book on prophecy as one of the best works written on the subject. Dealy was in touch with 'Abdu'l-Bahá, Who encouraged him in the work he was doing in Chicago. Shoghi Effendi paid tribute to him as one of those "whose names will ever remain associated with the first stirrings of the Faith of Bahá'u'lláh in the North American continent".[2]

Charles and Maria were attracted to Mr. Dealy's classes through a young friend who had been following his lectures. She was aflame with what she had heard and urged them to attend, and because of her sincerity and the friendship they felt for her, they decided to do so. It was to be the turning-point in their lives. Let Maria herself recount the story:

My husband never cared for, as he called them, "isms" and cults, but seeing our friend's enthusiasm, he promised he would go to hear Mr. Dealy, the gentleman who gave the lectures. The first lecture was on the soul, and Father was immediately impressed with it. We both went again and again, and at the third or fourth lesson, a prayer was given to each one of us to use every day. A certain line in that prayer ("And the curtains were torn asunder and the faithful hurried to the lights of their God, the Chosen One") seemed to be the direct answer to my prayer, tearing asunder the curtain which had veiled me for so many years from the things I was seeking.

Altogether we attended twelve lectures consisting of signs of the time, prophecies about the vineyard, etc. It took nearly three months, one lesson a week to go through the course. Mr. Dealy lived on the north side of the city, we on the west side, one hour's ride on the street car. As I was expecting a child, it was difficult some of the evenings to go, but the lessons were so interesting, and the longing to know what the next lesson would bring so great, that the urge to go was irresistible. So we didn't miss a lesson. And when at the twelfth lesson Mr. Dealy told us that God in His love and mercy for mankind had again manifested His Spirit on earth in a human temple in Bahá'u'lláh, there was a stillness in that room – it seemed as if everyone's breath had stopped. It seemed as if it was too much for our hearts to bear.

It was customary in the early days of the American Bahá'í community for those who grew to believe in the mission of Bahá'u'lláh to write a supplication to 'Abdu'l-Bahá, acknowledging their belief and asking for acceptance into the Bahá'í community. So, as Maria recalled: "Shortly before midnight on July 6, 1898, my husband and I wrote our letter to 'Abdu'l-Bahá, and then went home, so tired, but oh, so happy."

Only five years before, the name of Bahá'u'lláh had first been mentioned in America.* He was calling His people to Him.

---

* The Bahá'í teachings were first introduced into America on September 23, 1893 at the World Parliament of Religions in Chicago, in a paper written by a Christian missionary in Syria which quoted part of the statement made by Bahá'u'lláh to Dr. Edward Granville Browne of Cambridge University.

# CHAPTER TWO

# Leroy and his Family

MANY who join new movements waver or have doubts. This was not the case with Maria and Charles. Already in deciding to stay in America they had shown proof of their capacity to set a new course. The key they now held in their hands, the key to spiritual truths that had long eluded them, brought such joy that they freely opened their lives to what they confidently believed was a new revelation from God. A new life began for them, one which brought them confidence, serenity and assurance.

They quickly plunged into activity in the burgeoning Bahá'í community, numbering some three hundred persons, although Maria was kept close to home with their growing number of children. It was Charles who attended the meetings and shared everything in detail with the family. He began giving talks on the Faith, his years of study now blossoming into wisdom through exposure to the divine teachings. Whenever possible they went all together to the meetings in Chicago, which was the central gathering place for believers from a broad area. The meetings were often held in halls of the Masonic Temple and it was a long trip from where the Ioas family lived, a half-mile walk through the prairie, then a lengthy ride on the elevated train that took them to the city. But this did not discourage them. They began, too, to share their new-found Faith with those living around them, so that before long it became known in the neighborhood as "that Ioas religion".

The family had always gathered around the dining room table to read the Bible. But what new meaning the Book now had for them! Maria recalled: "Father had always been a Bible student, had read the Bible in Greek, and in the evenings we studied and took up prophecies, but what a difference in reading the Bible after we had the key and could understand – such wonderful evenings! He started a class and the children would sit and listen, so they just grew up with this great Faith." The children remember discussing whatever happened to them in the light of the teachings.

It was into this large and loving family that Leroy Ioas was born, the sixth of twelve children.* There were three older brothers, George, Rudolph and Arthur, and two older sisters, Pauline and Viola. His younger sister, Marguerite, was born shortly after Charles and Maria sent their petition to 'Abdu'l-Bahá and for some time she was called "the Dealy baby". Later came three younger brothers, Monroe, Paul and Joseph.

Leroy was born on February 15, 1896, during the family's stay in the small city of Wilmington, Illinois, some fifty miles southwest of Chicago. It is interesting that he was less than a month older than the Guardian of the Bahá'í Faith, Shoghi Effendi, whom he would much later in life serve with great distinction and all the love of his heart. Shortly after Leroy's birth the family settled permanently at 26th and Austin Boulevard in Clyde, a pleasant, multi-ethnic suburb west of Chicago. When his parents became Bahá'ís he was just two years old so that, as Maria said, he just grew up with this great Faith.

The family was a conventional one for the time, with most decisions made by the father. Yet Maria in her quiet way played an equally important role and had tremendous influence on her children. They remember her as always being serene and never raising her voice. One of the children described her as "the epitome of Bahá'í virtues, with something nice to say about everyone". Leroy often spoke of her pro-found wisdom, so that talking with her helped clarify one's problems. Throughout his life, he sought her counsel in important decisions.

Although in the above sense, they were an ordinary family, in another they were a most uncommon one. Leroy expressed it best when he described his parents as "pioneers and advance guards in the cause of spiritual democracy, who loved the principles of the Heavenly Civilization when the world at large did not realize their dynamic power". Charles and Maria had qualities found in most of the early believers: independence of mind and freedom of spirit.

---

* The first son and the second daughter died in infancy.

It was a family that lived modestly. They never had very much of material wealth – one early Chicago Bahá'í remembers the Ioases as "all those children and very little money". But if there were deprivations they were not aware of them, since they possessed a different kind of security. One helped the other, and they were curiously without jealousy. As the years passed, they rejoiced in one another's accomplishments and remained intensely close and loyal all their lives, as if they were magnetized to a center that held them together. In the beginning it was no doubt the strong parental bond; to that was later added their devotion to Bahá'u'lláh.

In 1900, two years after they had become Bahá'ís, a Tablet came to Charles Ioas from 'Abdu'l-Bahá:

> O thou who hast advanced toward God!
> By God, I rejoiced when reading thy letter which declares thy belief in the unity of God and thine acknowledgement of the appearance of the Kingdom of God. This is a matter whereby thy face shall brighten in the Supreme Concourse, and thy forehead shall sparkle among the people. Then know the worth of this gift, the lights of which shone forth unto all directions and indicate the attraction of the Concourse of El-Abhá, the Most Glorious. Then be firm in this Cause, and thou wilt behold thyself in a lofty station, having all that is in earth under its shadow, because this is verily that gift which is mentioned in the Gospel. O how good is this bounty in this day, when the commemoration of the true God is published and spread in all directions!

"This is that gift which is mentioned in the Gospel . . ." How well 'Abdu'l-Bahá knew the fervor of his search for the Return and lovingly assures him that he has found it. This message of love now connected them with 'Abdu'l-Bahá. They read it again and again, finding guidance in its promises ("thou wilt find thyself in a lofty station") and its exhortations ("then be firm in this Cause"). They shared it with the believers, as was the custom whenever anyone heard from 'Abdu'l-Bahá – this was, after all, their literature. A vivid memory of the Ioas children is of sitting on the floor listening raptly to the grownups reading and discussing these messages. What a remarkable grounding they received in this way!

It is difficult now to realize how little written material the early

Bahá'ís had on which to base their belief. They did indeed go forward on faith in the unseen and the unprinted. It was fully two years after Maria and Charles joined the Faith that an early teacher, Anton Haddad, translated the first work of Bahá'u'lláh into English, the "Surat-ul-Hykl" (Súriy-i-Haykal, Sura of the Temple); another four years before Dr. Ali-Kuli Khan's translation of the Kitáb-i-Íqán (the Book of Certitude) was published (this was begun in 'Akká at the request of 'Abdu'l-Bahá); and yet another five before a selection of 'Abdu'l-Bahá's Tablets was compiled and published by the House of Spirituality.*

Charles Ioas was a devoted member of the House of Spirituality, which had been organized with the assistance of Mírzá Asadu'lláh, one of several Persian teachers sent to America by 'Abdu'l-Bahá to deepen the Bahá'ís in the teachings. It was formed in 1901 with such stalwart believers as Arthur Agnew, Thornton Chase, Henry Goodale, George Lesch and Albert Windust, some ten members plus Mírzá Asadu'lláh. On the night that this fledgling institution received its first communication from 'Akká, Charles Ioas brought home a very small piece of envelope. It was from the Holy Land. The House of Spirituality had cut the envelope into portions and given one to each of the friends – "What a treasure!" Maria said, and always kept their piece.

A few years later, Maria received her own Tablet from the Master in which He sent the name Joseph for her last child. In that Tablet 'Abdu'l-Bahá told her:

> I am ever thoughtful concerning that family and ask the Lord of the Kingdom to confirm your household more and more each day. Thus may it serve the Cause of God, move according to its will, spread the Divine fragrances, educate the children, give life to souls and prove the cause of illumination to the world of humanity.

A grandiose project was forming in the minds of some of the Chicago Bahá'ís. Inspired by the efforts of the believers in 'Ishqábád, they longed to build a Mashriqu'l-Adhkár† in the West. Two Bahá'ís, Albert Windust and Charles Ioas, were chosen to draft a letter to 'Abdu'l-

---

* Chicago was to be the distribution center for Bahá'í publications to most parts of the world until a national secretariat was created in New York in 1924.

† The term used by Bahá'u'lláh to designate houses of worship; its meaning is "the dawning place of the remembrance of God".

Bahá, asking his blessing on the enterprise. Their petition was phrased in a poetic and spiritual language now rarely used except in prayer. It is quite moving:

> We were enkindled with the fire of the love of God that burnt and melted all other thoughts and desires into one great desire: That in these . . . regions there may arise a Mashriqu'l-Adhkár, built in the Name of the Glorious God, and that there may go forth from the shelter of its Beauty, rays of brilliant light, diffusing the fragrances of El Abhá over these wide and expectant lands.

'Abdu'l-Bahá's reply has been quoted in numerous statements concerning the Temple: ". . . Verily the greatest affair and the most important matter today is . . . to found a Temple from which the voices of praise may rise to the Kingdom . . ." "Some material things," He said, "have spiritual effect and the Mashriqu'l-Adhkár is a material thing that will have great effect upon the spirits of the people . . . not only upon those who build it, but upon the whole world." When 'Abdu'l-Bahá's approval was received, each member of the House of Spirituality pledged $100.00, a large sum at that time, and thus the first $1100.00 was raised. It was the beginning of a project that would absorb the talent and energies of the Bahá'ís for the next fifty years. (Ground boring was begun in 1920, the basement laid in 1922, the Temple itself begun in 1931 in the midst of the Depression; it was completed, other than for interior ornamentation and the gardens, and formally opened for public use in 1953 by Rúḥíyyih Khánum.*) 'Abdu'l-Bahá would Himself lay the cornerstone of the Temple on the first day of May in 1912, thus conferring on the House of Worship in Wilmette, on the shore of Lake Michigan, the inestimable honor of being the most sacred of all the Mashriqu'l-Adhkárs throughout the world, and a symbol of the high spiritual destiny of North America.†

To give impetus to the work, a "Mashriqu'l-Adhkár Convention" was held in 1907 with a small circle of Bahá'ís in attendance. On that

---

* Amatu'l-Bahá Rúḥíyyih Khánum was the wife of the Guardian and daughter of the distinguished early Bahá'í May Maxwell and her husband Sutherland Maxwell.

† It was while walking near the ocean in Santa Barbara, California, that French-Canadian architect Louis Bourgeois saw in his mind's eye the complete design of the House of Worship as it would be erected.

occasion a lovely site bordering Lake Michigan north of the city was
chosen as the site of the Temple. Then, at 'Abdu'l-Bahá's suggestion,
one person from each Bahá'í community was chosen to attend a
national convention at Naw-Rúz (the Bahá'í New Year, March 21, the
spring solstice) of 1909. This was done and the Bahá'í Temple Unity
was formed as an Illinois corporation, with full authority to carry out
the project of raising the great silent teacher of the Faith in North
America. It was the first Bahá'í institution in America whose responsibilities extended beyond the local level. In Haifa, on that same day,
'Abdu'l-Bahá was laying to rest the remains of the Báb on Mt.
Carmel.*

But to return to the subject of our story, Leroy Ioas. Of all the Ioas
children, he was closest to their father Charles. It could perhaps be
termed a philosophic closeness. They were both of combative mind
and enjoyed wrestling with problems. They also shared an abiding
interest in the subject of religion. Indeed for each it became the pre-
dominant interest of life. A sister remembers Leroy studying the Bahá'í
teachings every spare moment. So as he grew, his lively mind and
curiosity led him to benefit greatly from his father's knowledge. Leroy
and his father would go off for long walks together, Charles swinging
along with his cane, both lost in their discussion. In the friendly teasing
within the family circle, they were called the Kaiser and the crown
prince.

While the children were being trained in the Bahá'í teachings at
home, they also attended churches in the neighborhood, of their own
choosing. It was not unusual for the early Bahá'ís to participate in the
activities of the churches, whose Scriptures had led most of them to
Bahá'u'lláh, and it exposed the children to other views of religion.
This participation, however, did not usually extend to membership.†
The youngest son, Joseph, for instance, attended a Methodist church

---

* Siyyid 'Alí-Muḥammad, known in history as the Báb, appeared as the Promised One of
Islam, and as the Precursor announcing the appearance of Bahá'u'lláh. He was executed
in 1850 in Tabriz and His remains were held secretly in a number of localities before
being brought to the Holy Land where they were interred in the heart of Mt. Carmel. In
Bahá'í belief the Báb is a Manifestation of God with equal authority to those preceding
Him.

† Bahá'u'lláh enjoined upon Bahá'ís to "consort with the followers of all religions in a
spirit of friendliness and fellowship".

because two of his friends did so. When the minister one day tried to persuade him to join the church because his friends planned to do so, Joseph said no, he was a Bahá'í. The minister said he should bring his father to see their church and take part in its activity. So Joseph brought his father. When the minister politely asked him to "say something" to the congregation about his beliefs, his enthusiastic father stood up and talked for almost an hour about the Bahá'í teachings.

Leroy also attended church classes but it ended badly. While he thoroughly enjoyed discussion and debate, this did not endear him to those who organized the classes. He was constantly questioning and must have been an irritant when he would then question the answers given him. This was the way his mind, even at that age, dealt with issues: questioning, answering, then analyzing the answer to test the soundness of the reasoning, and so on. Inevitably the day came when they suggested it might be better for him not to attend any further classes. Thus his association with the church in Clyde ended.

Leroy was never to become reconciled to the church's attitude towards Jesus, the inferior status given His message as compared with the physical aspects of His life. Much later, during his years in Israel, he observed holy day celebrations in the land of Christ's birth. "The thing that impresses you most as a Bahá'í," he wrote to the family, "is the importance given in these great celebrations to procedure and ritual and ceremony; there isn't much said any more about the spirit of Jesus, Who came to give new life and always stressed the spiritual. Now more attention is paid to the physical form, to literal interpretation."

In these formative years, he already longed to become a Bahá'í teacher, and was trying to teach even before his teens. But he soon realized that to be a teacher one had to develop the ability to speak. Yet he was so self-conscious that he found it difficult even to sit and talk with people. So he made a plan. During high school he sought out occasions at least once a month when he could speak in public. When the principal asked why he was doing this he said he was determined to become a public speaker. "But I was so frightened when I got up," he recalled, "that I perspired all over and my knees shook. I thought if I spoke often enough, I would get over it. I never really did, but once you are under way, it is as if you were made for nothing else." He entered a Declamation Contest between the various high schools, though the public-speaking teacher warned him that he had little chance of winning. He worked diligently at his presentation, practising alone up in the attic of their house. Not only did he win at his own school but he took first place among all the schools in the district.

The incident showed how persistent he could be in pursuit of a goal, in spite of obstacles and in spite of the opinion of others. And the experience gave him confidence that he might actually one day "raise his voice in great assemblies".* Of course, as he often said, when the purpose of speaking is to teach the Faith, the Holy Spirit gives you power. He was to speak on innumerable occasions during his lifetime and to many large and important gatherings. After a particularly grand event, his daughter asked if he wasn't nervous on such occasions. He said, "Yes, always, but the nervousness changes. At first one is nervous about himself, his voice, his body, but later one is nervous that he will not reach people's hearts with the Message. That is the nervousness that never leaves you."

Leroy was a good student at school and a good athlete. Tall and slender, he was a competitive center at basketball and an excellent tennis player. After graduation in June, 1912, from the J. Sterling Morton High School – one of a class of 34 – he enrolled in a business course to prepare for work. Neither he nor his siblings had the option of attending college; they were not in a financial position to do so. Only later did he become sensitive to his lack of higher education, as he moved into spheres of endeavor which threw him with those whose easy confidence rested on such credentials. Each of the Ioas children went to work early and assisted the family, and he, as a middle child, felt particular responsibility for the younger ones.

We know little of his early working life – with the Monon Railroad – except that an older sister, Viola, worked near him and they went to and from the office together. Whichever arrived at the train first saved a seat for the other and they greeted each other warmly and talked all the way home. Only later did they learn that their fellow passengers thought them to be young lovers, so affectionate were they with one another. Viola inherited her mother's serene disposition and was a source of comfort and help to all the family. We mention her particularly because this lovely soul was to outlive all her sisters and brothers.

---

* From a prayer of 'Abdu'l-Bahá, which begins: "O Lord, my God and my Haven in my distress!" It was Leroy's favorite prayer.

A young people's group had formed in Chicago, probably through Leroy's initiative, certainly with his active participation. Notes that he left speak of "organizing the youth" and planning activities to bring them together. One can well imagine him giving this leadership, as throughout his life he was quite clear as to what he felt needed to be done in particular situations. This clarity of vision no doubt enabled him to accomplish all that he did, as his energy went directly into action. As an instance, when 'Abdu'l-Bahá said it was important to learn Esperanto, Leroy studied the language, mastering it sufficiently to give classes for young people in south Chicago. The renowned Bahá'í teacher, Marion Jack, was then living in the city and held general education classes for the children of that deprived area. Leroy felt proud to be a small part of her work.

The Temple land drew Bahá'ís to it. They would go there to walk and to pray. It provided the young people with an attractive setting for study classes, picnics, and occasional swimming in the nearby lake. (Leroy taught some of the classes, along with early Bahá'í Julia Sobel.) It also inspired the young people to adopt a teaching goal, the "Wilmette campaign" to attract to the Faith those living in the area. The campaign resulted in a half dozen new believers. When older teachers such as Albert Vail interested youth in the teachings, they sent them to the young people's group, Leroy at one point noting that "Mr Vail thinks the occasion of our outing on the Temple grounds on Decoration Day would be an opportunity to create deeper interest in his young people from the South Side." Shortly after leaving Chicago in 1919, Leroy wrote to his close friend Carl Scheffler, informing him of other teaching possibilities he knew of in the close vicinity of the city "if the young people desire to take hold and sponsor any more campaigns".

The young people also met in their own homes for discussion and social events, simple pleasures like singing around the piano and dancing. Occasionally, meetings and parties were held at the home of neighbors of the Ioas family who were showing interest in the teachings. It was in the home of this German-Czech couple with two charming daughters that Leroy, on meeting the older one, said to himself, now there is someone I could marry.

But let us go back to 1912 when Leroy, a serious and engaging young man, came into contact with the spirit and power of "the Master". At the time of 'Abdu'l-Bahá's first visit to Chicago Leroy was finishing high school. By the time of the Master's second and third visits, he was preparing to start his working life. He was sixteen years old.

Meeting 'Abdu'l-Bahá was the seminal experience of his life. It shaped his spiritual character and made him aware of the vast implications of the Faith. It caused him to dedicate his life to its service. This young man was just one of the numerous believers who journeyed from place to place in Chicago, from meeting to meeting, just to be in the presence of 'Abdu'l-Bahá, restless to be elsewhere than where He was.

CHAPTER THREE

# 'Abdu'l-Bahá

'ABDU'L-BAHÁ, the eldest son of Bahá'u'lláh, became aware at the age of eight of His father's unique destiny and from that time onward devoted His life to serving and protecting Bahá'u'lláh during His subsequent long life of exile and imprisonment.

'Abdu'l-Bahá shared that exile and imprisonment for thirty-nine years, first in Baghdad, then in Constantinople, Adrianople and 'Akká. Increasingly, as attacks and calumnies rained on Bahá'u'lláh, it was 'Abdu'l-Bahá who interceded with the authorities, organized the life of the exiles, and received visitors. On arriving in 'Akká, His final place of exile, Bahá'u'lláh is reported to have spoken the poignant words: "I have finished with the outer world",[1] and from then onward, He rarely received other than the believers.*

Outstanding in every aspect of His character and erudition, 'Abdu'l-Bahá became known among the Bahá'ís by the term which Bahá'u'lláh used in referring to Him: "Áqá" – the Master. By the peoples of 'Akká and Haifa, He was regarded as a saintly figure, a benefactor of the lowly, a wise philosopher. As the years passed, officials, judges, spiritual leaders, sought His wisdom and advice.

It was this eldest son whom Bahá'u'lláh appointed in His Will as His successor and the Interpreter of His teachings, as the Center to whom all Bahá'ís should turn after His ascension. It was a position without historical precedent.

The unique written appointment of a successor has made it impos-

---

* Professor Edward Granville Browne, famed orientalist of Cambridge University, was one of the few visitors to attain the presence of Bahá'u'lláh, and the only westerner.

sible for schisms to take root, even when the disaffection of former believers led them to attack the Faith and its leaders. Such persons "violate" the Covenant established by Bahá'u'lláh with His followers, yet the line of authority remains inviolate. 'Abdu'l-Bahá extended this center of unity through His subsequent appointment of His eldest grandson, Shoghi Effendi, as the Guardian of the Bahá'í Faith and sole Interpreter of its teachings.

In Chicago, where our story is now centered, 'Abdu'l-Bahá spoke often and forcefully to the Bahá'ís on the question of "violation" of the Covenant, something which was occurring then in America. On one such occasion He said the believers were united by strong bonds forged by Bahá'u'lláh Himself, Who because He "desired that there should not be any ground or reason for disagreement among the Bahá'ís" had left the Book of the Covenant (His Will) "addressing His relations and all peoples of the world", wherein He appointed Him Who "is informed of My purpose".[2] Leroy was present the night 'Abdu'l-Bahá spoke these words, in the home of an early Bahá'í, Corinne True, and he remembered the fire in His eyes, and suddenly understood what the Bible meant by the wrath of God. He felt he was witnessing it as 'Abdu'l-Bahá described what the Covenant-breakers had done to try to destroy the Cause of Bahá'u'lláh.

Many years later the Guardian noted that one of the purposes of 'Abdu'l-Bahá's visit to America was to make clear the question of His station, Who He was and Who He was not, as this had been the basis of the violation that had occurred in America. In New York City 'Abdu'l-Bahá clarified who He was: He was the Center of Bahá'u-'lláh's Covenant with the believers. In Chicago and the other cities He visited, He removed the widespread and erroneous teaching that He was the return of Christ.

It was in 1908 that 'Abdu'l-Bahá was released from imprisonment as a result of the Young Turk Revolution. His first act in His new-found freedom was to arrange for the interment of the remains of the Báb on Mt. Carmel according to the express instruction of Bahá'u'lláh.

Then in August of 1910, 'Abdu'l-Bahá, quite suddenly and without warning, left Haifa for Egypt. The departure was ostensibly for His health. But a Bahá'í historian observes that in retrospect it could be seen as 'Abdu'l-Bahá's first step in His plan to reach the western world with the Message of Bahá'u'lláh.[3]

By October the startling news of 'Abdu'l-Bahá's departure from the
Holy Land reached the American believers through the letter of an
American Bahá'í traveling in the Middle East, which appeared in the
newly-created *Bahá'í News*. It caused a great stir of excitement. Those
who had made the life-changing pilgrimage to 'Akká knew what the
presence of 'Abdu'l-Bahá meant, and they sent off messages pleading
with Him to come to America. It would be two years before He did so.

After passing one month in Port Said, 'Abdu'l-Bahá sailed for
Alexandria, intending to continue on to Europe. But the fatigue of His
forty years of suffering was so great that he remained in Egypt for the
winter, settling in Ramleh, a suburb of Alexandria. He remained in
Egypt a full year.

It was a year of personal triumph for 'Abdu'l-Bahá. Visitors came
from far and near to see Him, and high dignitaries sought His presence. The Egyptian press, always hostile in the past, wrote highly
laudatory articles concerning Him. Wellesley Tudor-Pole, an English-
man with close Bahá'í sympathies who visited Him in Ramleh, was
struck by the fact that 'Abdu'l-Bahá spoke at length of the work being
accomplished by the Bahá'ís in America.

In August of 1911 'Abdu'l-Bahá left Egypt for His first historic visit
to Europe; the historian H.M. Balyuzi has given a vivid word picture of
the encounter of this life-long prisoner with the western world:

> In His sixty-eighth year, in precarious health, He stepped into a crowded,
> demanding arena to proclaim to the Christian West the essential verities of
> the Faith of His Father. He addressed meeting after meeting; He met day
> after day, throughout the day, a stream of visitors; He sat patiently with
> press reporters; He talked with the eminent and the accomplished; He
> sought the poor and the underprivileged, and His love went out to them
> abundantly, as did His munificence. And He refused to curry favour with
> the powerful, the mighty, and the rich.[4]

'Abdu'l-Bahá returned to Egypt to rest from the rigors of the European visit, and then, at the end of March 1912, He at last set sail for
America.

Nearly half the American Bahá'í community at that time (which
included the few believers in Canada) lived in the Chicago-Great
Lakes area and excitement among them was intense. All conversation

turned on the subject of "the visit". How should it not, when among them were believers who had shared the moving and inspiring stories of their pilgrimage to 'Akká: Corinne True, Thornton Chase, Arthur Agnew.

Rooms had been engaged in Chicago for 'Abdu'l-Bahá and His party at a small but very comfortable hotel, the Plaza, just across the street from Lincoln Park. Flurries of arrangements were underway, flowers and fruits in the rooms, a greeting party. Much thought and planning were given to the organizations where 'Abdu'l-Bahá would appear, notably Jane Addams's Hull House, the fourth Annual Convention of the National Association for the Advancement of Colored People, the Theosophical Society, and several churches. Receptions, dinners and open houses were foreseen, though they knew it was 'Abdu'l-Bahá who would in the end make all decisions.

At the same time the Bahá'ís were laying plans for the fourth National Convention of the Bahá'í Temple Unity, which would take place during the last days of April. It was there that 'Abdu'l-Bahá would make his first appearance before the community of believers. A great tent had been ordered to be placed on the site of the projected Mashriqu'l-Adhkár, the Temple grounds as it was called, for the historic ceremony at which 'Abdu'l-Bahá would lay the cornerstone of the future edifice. This was planned for May 1st, His second day in Chicago.

Then one day near the end of April, 'Abdu'l-Bahá was actually among them. He had come.

A large group of expectant Bahá'ís waited as the train drew into the station, calling out "Yá-Bahá'u'l-Abhá".* They accompanied Him to the Plaza Hotel where He sat with them for some moments. He told them His visit to Washington D.C. had been fruitful, as it had brought together the black and the white races. But it was Chicago, He told them, that was especially dear to Him, for it was here that the call of Bahá'u'lláh had first been raised in America.

That fate-laden event had occurred fifteen years earlier, September 23, 1893, during the World Parliament of Religions. A paper from a Christian missionary in Syria was read; it closed with ten lines of Bahá'u'lláh spoken to Professor Edward Granville Browne, ending:

* An Arabic invocation to God: "O Thou the Glory of the Most Glorious."

". . . *Let not a man glory in this, that he loves his country; let him rather glory in this, that he loves his kind* . . ." The proceedings of the Congress were widely reported in the journals of the day. Thus both Thornton Chase and Lua Getsinger first set eyes on the name of Bahá'u'lláh, and followed where it led them.*

It was also the city where in 1894 the first Bahá'í community in North America had been formed through the highly successful teaching endeavors of a Syrian Bahá'í of Christian background. His knowledge of the teachings was incomplete and he planted in the minds of the believers a number of erroneous ideas of his own. In 1898 he was invited to travel to 'Akká with the first western pilgrims and there, when he met the majesty of 'Abdu'l-Bahá, his inner crisis began. By the turn of the century, unable to give up his own ideas or his position of authority as the first teacher in America, he had turned away from the Center of the Covenant and joined forces with members of Bahá'u'lláh's family who sought to destroy 'Abdu'l-Bahá. This man, who had succeeded brilliantly as long as his intentions were pure, was actually living in Chicago at the time of the Master's visits to the city. But he did not approach 'Abdu'l-Bahá. If his intentions had been pure, said 'Abdu'l-Bahá to one of the man's associates, he would have come in all sincerity, like everyone else, to visit the Master. Instead, he expected 'Abdu'l-Bahá to approach him and seek his favors.

The disaffection of this early teacher caused shock and consternation among the believers, some turning away forever. But the firm believers, such as Charles and Maria Ioas, felt only pity that one so blessed by his early accomplishments had chosen to leave the protection of the Covenant.

'Abdu'l-Bahá spent three weeks in Chicago, making three separate visits, in April, September and October. He spoke at more than a dozen public meetings and at innumerable large and small gatherings. Charles and Maria saw Him on a number of these occasions, always taking one or more of the children with them so that they too might have the bounty of meeting, and being in the presence of, the Master.

Leroy's experiences of the Master remained vivid and ever-fresh throughout his life. His deepest impression was of 'Abdu'l-Bahá's

---

* He became the first Bahá'í in America; both were outstanding personalities and teachers.

magnetism and majesty, the magnetism drawing one irresistibly toward
Him, the majesty forming an invisible barrier beyond which one could
not penetrate. Though he saw 'Abdu'l-Bahá often, Leroy "never knew
what He talked about". Perhaps he realized intuitively that it was not
on the plane of knowledge that one could meet the Master.

He recalled that he loved to watch the Master's eyes, "ever-chang-
ing, now stern, now loving, filled with all the pathos of the world and
then again, all its joy. Everything was revealed in His eyes, what one
saw depended entirely upon what the Master was thinking." Once,
while he listened to 'Abdu'l-Bahá, Leroy thought, Oh! how I wish
'Abdu'l-Bahá would look right into my eyes. And at that moment the
Master turned his head and looked directly at him. Leroy said: "It was
as if He looked through you, as if He saw your soul, before your beginning and beyond your ending."*

Leroy saw 'Abdu'l-Bahá for the first time outside the Plaza Hotel.
The Master had arrived the night before. As Leroy and his father
approached the hotel, Leroy was insistent that they hurry to the far
side of the building or they would miss the Master. His father wished
to enter the hotel. But Leroy said he knew 'Abdu'l-Bahá was leaving
the building by the other door because he could see the light that was
radiating from Him. And it was thus that in hurrying to the side
entrance, they found 'Abdu'l-Bahá preparing to leave for Hull House.
He stopped and motioned for them to come to Him. As they hesitated,
He beckoned again. Leroy was faint with the power he felt emanating
from the Master, and when he went forward to take His hand in greeting, he used both his hands to see if this luminous being had hands like
those of ordinary people. Leroy recalls: "As I looked at the Master, I
saw His physical form, but shining through it were flashes of light,
flashes of light, bright and shining. The spiritual power simply flooded
through Him and I was overcome."

Each person who met 'Abdu'l-Bahá, knowing something of His
spiritual station, had his own experience of that presence; this was
Leroy's.

The Hand of the Cause Horace Holley, in 1911 a writer and poet
living in Europe, recorded his first experience of the Master: "From

---

* A number of these reminiscences were given in a talk in Wilmette, March 8, 1952, on the
  eve of Leroy's departure for Haifa.

sheer happiness I wanted to cry – it seemed the most suitable form of self-expression at my command . . . I had entered the Master's presence and become the servant of a higher will for its own purpose. Even my memory of that temporary change of being bears strange authority over me."[5]

On another occasion when Leroy and his father were going to see 'Abdu'l-Bahá, Leroy stopped to buy a large bouquet of white carnations. But as they went into the hotel he decided not to give the flowers to the Master. His father said the Master loved flowers and would be pleased. "I know He does," Leroy replied. "but I'm not going to take them. I come to the Master offering Him my heart and I don't want Him to think I am currying favor. He knows the condition of a person's heart and that is all I have to offer." So his father presented the flowers to 'Abdu'l-Bahá and as the Master sat talking, He held them, touched them, in a typical gesture buried His face in them to smell the fragrance. When He finished speaking He stood up and shook hands with everyone; to each He gave one of the carnations. When there were only a few left Leroy thought, Oh! I wish he would turn around and shake hands with me before they are all gone! Just as he thought this, the Master turned and looked at him. Then He gave him a small red rose that He pulled from His coat. As He did so, it pricked the skin of His finger and Leroy received that precious rose with a bit of the Master's blood on it. In 1952 in his farewell talk, Leroy said "and I still have it".

This story recalls his mother's first encounter with 'Abdu'l-Bahá when He knew her unspoken wish too. Some years before the Master's visit, she had gone to say farewell to Arthur Agnew and his wife who were to visit 'Akká; she intended to ask them for a flower that 'Abdu'l-Bahá had held in His hand. But on the way into town she decided such a request was presumptuous and she said nothing. On one of the Master's first days in Chicago she took her small son Monroe and went to the hotel. They waited all afternoon for 'Abdu'l-Bahá to return from His engagements. When He arrived He greeted them with love and said come, come, as He went toward His rooms. Maria thought of His fatigue and did not move. But an interpreter said quietly: when 'Abdu'l-Bahá says come, you must come. So she went with two others to His reception room. As she recalls: "In a few minutes He came out of His bedroom with some roses. He walked over to where I was sitting and handed me a rose. He looked at me with those eyes that could read one's very heart. There was no need of His telling me 'This is the flower you have wished for so many years'. He then gave Monroe, Mrs. Getsinger and Mr. Mills a rose also."

Maria was always concerned with her lack of time to teach and with her lack of capacity. One day when in the presence of 'Abdu'l-Bahá she said, "'Abdu'l-Bahá, what can I do to serve the Faith?" He replied, "Teach, teach!" and she replied "'Abdu'l-Bahá, I can't teach." He said, "The earth brings forth nothing of itself, but God causes the sun to shine and rain to fall upon the earth, and it becomes fruitful. So you too can teach." Then He assured her that there are many ways of teaching the Faith, and one is to live the life of a true Bahá'í.

There are many stories of 'Abdu'l-Bahá's "knowing the hearts". Yet another that concerns Maria and her children is this. She taught her youngest child, Joseph, an evening prayer that said "Dear 'Abdu'l-Bahá, help me to be a good boy and make me a good man." When she took Joseph with her to the railroad station to say farewell to the Master, 'Abdu'l-Bahá patted him on the cheek and said: "He *is* a good boy, a very good boy, and he will be a very good man."

Stories, sometimes inaccurate or exaggerated, grew up quickly around statements made by the Master. One concerned the Ioas family and the "seed of Abraham". This is how it began. One day Leroy and his father went to see the Master. As they were ushered into 'Abdu'l-Bahá's room, Leroy noticed that some of the attendants seemed to bow quite low to his father and show him deference, one of them uttering something about Father Abraham. Later he asked his father what it meant. His father said the Master on the previous day had talked to him about the Faith, about the teaching work, and about his family. The Master mentioned that he had a wonderful family. Then He spoke of Abraham, that because Abraham remained firm in the Faith of God, God caused his seed to increase as the sands of the sea, and from them came great servants and great teachers. The Master said He hoped – and would pray – that all his family would be firm and grow in strength daily, and that his seed would prosper and from it arise many great teachers of the Faith and great servants of the Cause. 'Abdu'l-Bahá said through firmness and strong faith, this would be the case. Leroy wondered if this promise would come to pass.

On the second day of His sojourn in Chicago, 'Abdu'l-Bahá traveled out to the Temple land to lay the foundation stone of the House of Worship. The day was cold and blustery but Leroy was out on the grounds early. It was then just an open prairie with a few trees on it. The large tent was in place for the ceremony and Leroy "squeezed up in front and sat on the ground to be right next to what was going on". 'Abdu'l-Bahá spoke some words about the future Temple that would arise on the site and then seated Himself near to where the stone now rests within the Temple walls, while He called forward Bahá'ís of different cultures to turn over some of the soil. As everyone was leaving, Leroy and another young man, Charlie Greenleaf, rushed to get some of the soil 'Abdu'l-Bahá had dug from the ground with a special golden trowel, and young Greenleaf had his blessed by the Master. They later gave the soil to the Archives. On Leroy's last visit to the Temple, as a guest of the Convention in 1964, he prayed at the cornerstone, and said he felt the spirit of 'Abdu'l-Bahá as strongly as when he sat at His feet when He laid the cornerstone.

In later years when trying to describe 'Abdu'l-Bahá's presence for the believers, Leroy said "You have seen many pictures of the Master but what they don't show you is the vibrant spirit that was coursing through Him at all times. All day long, starting at dawn, people would come to Him. They would hover around, ask questions, then a larger group would gather in His sitting room and He would talk to them about the Cause. When they left another group would come. Always they had questions for 'Abdu'l-Bahá, questions of infinite importance to them, and His answers were given rapidly – in one second He would be deciding someone's destiny. It showed the power of the spirit that moved within Him every moment, every second."*

One brief incident that made a lasting impression on Leroy illustrates this power of the Master. It occurred one evening when 'Abdu'l-Bahá spoke at the Masonic Temple. More than a thousand people were present. The Ioas and Dealy families were very close, as it was through Paul Dealy that they had become Bahá'ís. The Ioases had brought Mrs. Dealy to the meeting, as she to her great distress was going blind. Following the Master's talk, as hundreds milled around

* In Bahá'í understanding, Bahá'u'lláh conferred certain powers upon 'Abdu'l-Bahá which enabled Him to demonstrate the highest degree of human perfections and endowed Him with the capacity to interpret His teachings. It is these conferred capacities of which Leroy was speaking.

Him, she told her son he should have an interpreter ask 'Abdu'l-Bahá
to speak to her. Leroy, who was sitting next to her, remembers the son
saying that would be impossible with all the people present. But she
insisted and he went to pass on her request. The interpreter indicated
she should sit on the aisle where 'Abdu'l-Bahá would leave. As the
Master went up the aisle He stopped and greeted her lovingly. She
reached for His hand and said "'Abdu'l-Bahá, please put your hand on
my forehead, and I *know* that I will see." "Yes, my daughter," He
answered, "you will see. But you will have to choose. You may have
your spiritual sight or your physical sight – which do you desire?" She
said with emotion: "'Abdu'l-Bahá, that is no choice! I would be blind a
thousand years before I would give up my spiritual sight!" "Well said,
my daughter, well said," replied the Master as He touched her shoulder and continued on His way out. Sitting next to her on that bench,
Leroy realized with a chill how in that moment she had decided on her
destiny. She was steadfast.

It is perhaps difficult for those who have not lived in the era of the
appointed Interpreters of Bahá'í Scripture to realize how greatly both
'Abdu'l-Bahá and the Guardian after Him influenced the lives of the
believers. In the days of 'Abdu'l-Bahá, as each new believer wrote to
Him, a spiritual association with the Center of the Covenant was
established. It was strengthened through study of His Tablets, then in
the extraordinary experience of meeting Him. As we have seen, Leroy
was just two years of age when his parents joined the Bahá'í Faith, and
his child's mind and imagination were certainly impregnated with
what he heard and sensed of the power of "the Master". So it is interesting to note that even as a small child he was several times aware of
the presence of 'Abdu'l-Bahá. While he rarely spoke of these experiences, they were precious to him.

When he was four or five years old, while playing in the back yard
of their home, he looked up and thought he saw 'Abdu'l-Bahá at the
upper rear window; the Master waved and motioned for him to come
into the house. On another occasion he felt the Master walking in their
house. Yet another time he came into the house to tell his mother
'Abdu'l-Bahá had been there and he wondered if the Master had
asked for him; he remembers thinking 'Abdu'l-Bahá might not care for
him. These are tender memories of a connection he felt with 'Abdu'l-
Bahá in his child's reality.

As he grew to maturity in the years following 'Abdu'l-Bahá's visit, Leroy had several dreams of the Master. In one of them, he was sitting under a tree, resting, when 'Abdu'l-Bahá came through the field, perspiring, and called out to him to get up. This is no time to rest, He said, speak on the Cause, talk, talk, whenever they ask you!

When he was 20 or 21 he had a vivid dream of going to a Feast given in Chicago by 'Abdu'l-Bahá. A long banquet table was spread with a dazzling white cloth, shining with a particular brilliance. But the air was filled with dark, oily soot, and as he watched, several of the Bahá'ís were catching it with their hands. One put it on the cloth, and tried to smear it in. He did this three or four times. But his gestures left no trace. 'Abdu'l-Bahá, who had come from another room to greet His guests, said to Leroy: "You see, it makes no difference what they do. They cannot hurt or damage the cloth." Leroy shared this dream with his close friend and fellow Hand of the Cause Milly Collins in February of 1958, just three months after the passing of the Guardian, when the Bahá'í world was left without a Guardian and without the future House of Justice to guide its affairs. It was a time of great anguish for the Hands of the Cause (of which we shall speak later) and Leroy told Milly that this dream had sustained him in previous days of uncertainty and he hoped it would do so now.

The first world war broke out within two years of 'Abdu'l-Bahá's visit to America. Communication with the Holy Land was gradually severed and with entry of the United States as a combatant, it was entirely cut off. As the British advanced on Palestine, there was evidence that 'Abdu'l-Bahá was in great danger from the crumbling Turkish forces. In the first letters to reach America from the Bahá'ís in 'Akká, the appalling scenes of the war years were described: the poverty, the misery, the hunger. Darkness, wrote one, ruled over the minds and hearts. When the British army finally entered Haifa on September 23, 1918, a joyous message was received by the American Bahá'ís via London: "Master well and protected. Notify friends."

Yet it was during this period of His life, care-worn from a lifetime of service and sorrow, and in danger, that 'Abdu'l-Bahá was preparing His great plan for the American Bahá'í community. He was moved, in the words of Shoghi Effendi, "to confer once again, and for the last time of His life, on the community of His American followers, a signal mark of His special favor by investing them, on the eve of the termination of His earthly ministry, through the revelation of the Tablets of the Divine Plan, with a world mission."[6]

The stupendous mandate given the North American Bahá'ís, to carry the name of Bahá'u'lláh from their homeland to the entire planet, was contained in fourteen Tablets or letters, revealed between Naw-Rúz and Riḍván* of 1916 and during February and March of 1917. Collectively known as the Tablets of the Divine Plan, they were, in the words of the Guardian, a key with which they, the North American Bahá'ís, would "unlock the doors leading them to fulfill their unimaginably glorious destiny."[7]

These historic documents, on which future plans for the growth and dissemination of the teachings would be based, were presented to the Bahá'ís in New York City in 1919, during the first annual Convention to be held after the war. There was an "unveiling" ceremony with the assistance of Bahá'í children and youth; Rúḥíyyih Khánum (then Mary Maxwell) was one of the youth. It was an astonishing panorama which 'Abdu'l-Bahá presented to the Bahá'ís of their future responsibilities and only a few realized its true import as a call to immediate action. One who did was Martha Root, who arose at that very moment, at age forty-seven, to begin her ceaseless travels in the interests of propagating the teachings. As noted in a Bahá'í history, this lone woman traveled "longer and farther than any single Bahá'í has ever done since its [the Faith's] inception . . ."[8]

Leroy was present at the ceremony in New York City, profoundly stirred by 'Abdu'l-Bahá's vision of the destiny of his fellow North American believers. With such a destiny, they would certainly be invincible, he felt, and divine confirmations would surround them from that moment onward in whatever they undertook in carrying out the Master's mandate. It was a conviction he never lost.

---

* Riḍván commemorates the twelve-day period, April 21 to May 1, which Bahá'u'lláh spent in the Garden of Riḍván in Baghdad, during which He revealed His Mission to His family and followers; it immediately preceded His second exile which took Him to the capital of the Turkish Empire.

# CHAPTER FOUR

# Change

A TERRIBLE blow befell the Ioas family in 1917. Charles Ioas, who had been ailing for some time, became seriously ill and passed away. He was just 58. All his ten children were gathered at his bedside, Leroy with a strong sense that his father's work was not yet done. For some time before his passing (as Leroy noted in a letter he wrote to 'Abdu'l-Bahá two years later) Charles Ioas "had been busily engaged in working out and writing certain things relative to the Cause, which he hoped to use for the diffusion of the knowledge of God".

The funeral was held in their home, as was customary in those days, with the family watching through the open doors from the large kitchen. The program closed with the playing of the "Benediction", a solemn and curiously moving hymn written by one of the early believers, Shahnaz Waite. 'Abdu'l-Bahá had said: "Sing this melody in all gatherings of love and harmony of the beloved of God." Joseph, aged ten, remembers his mother saying as the music began: "We'll all sing!" and then leading the family in the simple verse:

May God's love now hover o'er us, as a dove with outstretched wings,
While His peace that flows around us, to each heart sweet comfort brings.
May we now receive His spirit and its radiance shed afar,
Now and here in love abiding, in the realms of El-Abha.

How did this remarkable woman carry on after the death of her husband? Her children say she simply carried on. A woman teacher came to live at the home and those who were working certainly did more and gave more time to the younger ones. Leroy was twenty-one

when he lost his beloved father, the same age at which Charles Ioas
had married and cast his lot in the new world.

Less than two years later, in the momentous year of the reception of
the Divine Plan, 1919, Leroy was engaged in making two of the major
decisions of his life. The first of these was to marry the daughter of
their Czech-German neighbors, Sylvia Kuhlman. In the four or five
years that he had known her, his feelings for her had deepened and
were reciprocated. Sylvia was a dainty, sweet-natured, lively member
of the young people's group; indeed when there was a party, it was she
who played the piano for their dancing. Her younger sister Mayme was
also a member of the group.

Under Leroy's affectionate tutelage, and the loving care of such
older Bahá'ís as Albert Windust, Sylvia was drawn ever closer to the
teachings and became a Bahá'í. She had left the church years earlier,
alienated by the concept that newborns are born in sin. Both her sister
and father followed her into the Faith. Her mother, Marie Benes, who
came from a small town near Pilsen, Czechoslovakia, was hesitant,
fearful of being disloyal to Christ. That is, until one day, when as she
descended the staircase in their home, she saw 'Abdu'l-Bahá – or was it
the figure of Christ? – at the foot of the stairs. He was saying to her:
It's all right! It's all right! It was a confirmation that removed her
doubts. Sylvia's father, George Kuhlman, never cared for his well-born
Bavarian relatives; he dropped the "von" from his name and rarely
spoke of them. He loved working with his hands, and became a crafts-
man in wood and gilding.

At the end of March 1919, Leroy and Sylvia slipped away to Lake
County, Indiana, just south of Chicago, and were married by a Justice
of the Peace. One can speculate that they wished to be married simply
and quietly, with no bother to the family just two years after his father's
passing. Or more likely, a sense of modesty concerning a personal
matter – something Leroy always possessed – in the light of 'Abdu'l-
Bahá's mandate to the Americans. What we do know is that they
began a marriage of forty-six years which was sustained throughout by
their deep love for one another. Sylvia adored Leroy and had the
general feeling that he could do no wrong, while he found strength in
his arduous life from her uncompromising loyalty. When they married,
Leroy gave her a ring set with a stone blessed by 'Abdu'l-Bahá. They
were twenty-three.

It now seems a young age at which to marry. But Leroy's character was already well formed and he was seasoned to the working world. He accepted responsibility easily and had already developed strong friendships with like-minded people of all ages. Above all he was an activist, with enormous latent energy, and an in-born capacity for leadership. As many people learned, he had a strong temper, and was probably, even at that young age, very impatient. It was a trait he struggled with but never really overcame.

His shining characteristic was his devotion to all that concerned this new religious dispensation. The needs of the Faith were central, all else was accommodation to daily life. He was in a very true sense steadfast. The Bahá'ís might fail but never the Message.

Then came the second great decision of that year of 1919. Leroy and Sylvia went to distant San Francisco for their brief honeymoon. It was a place of great beauty. They were starting a new life. They saw the need of Bahá'ís in the west. Whatever it was that sparked their decision, in late summer of that year they left the familiar surroundings of Chicago and moved to California.

# CHAPTER FIVE

# The Bahá'ís of the Bay Area

IT was Lua Getsinger and her husband, Dr. Edward Getsinger, who brought the Bahá'í teachings to the west coast of America. Lua was a magnetic personality, as even a cursory reading of early Bahá'í history will indicate, one of the "hollow reeds" from which the pith of self had been blown. 'Abdu'l-Bahá named her a "herald of the Kingdom"; the Guardian called her the "mother teacher of the West". As a pebble dropped into a still pond, her visit to California produced results that rippled out and out, passing from person to person, touching some who became the giants of the early days of the Faith in the western states.

The year was 1898. Lua and her husband arrived in California and with audacity began searching for the ready souls. One of the first whom they found was Mrs. Phoebe Hearst, widow of the Senator and industrialist, who received the Getsingers in her country home and listened to the Bahá'í "message" as it was then called. A silent observer of their conversation was the butler who served Mrs. Hearst, Robert Turner, who became the first black Bahá'í in America. He was born in Virginia in 1855 but had migrated to the west coast and married there. He was confirmed forever in his faith through meeting 'Abdu'l-Bahá when he accompanied Mrs. Hearst and her party to 'Akká in 1898. Sylvia Ioas in later years told her daughters of this "wonderful man".

Deeply moved by what she heard from the Getsingers, Mrs. Hearst insisted that Lua give a series of talks for her friends. These took place in her San Francisco penthouse. One eager participant, so insistent to learn more that she went every day to study with Lua, was Phoebe Hearst's friend, Emogene Hoagg, who shortly became the first Bahá'í in the city, indeed the first Bahá'í in California. Helen Goodall, a well-to-do friend of Mrs. Hearst in Oakland (across the Bay from San Francisco) had a daughter Ella who also attended the classes. When Lua had to leave the area, the Goodalls traveled to New York seeking another teacher. They found the devoted Anton Haddad, a Bahá'í of Syrian origin, who was the cause of their confirmation. Ella shortly thereafter was invited by Mrs. Hearst to accompany her party on their pilgrimage to 'Akká. It was a history-making visit, the first time that westerners were able to penetrate the grim walled city where the Center of the Faith dwelt.[1]

Mrs. Goodall, who was not able to go with them, returned to California and began quietly spreading the Bahá'í teachings among her family and friends. There was such interest that within a short time she and Ella, after her return from the Holy Land, were holding regular meetings in their home in Oakland. No experienced teachers lived in the west at that time nor were there Bahá'í books available.

As the seeds were sown by Lua's first adepts, new believers came into the fold. Ramona Allen Brown and her mother were friends of Mrs. Hearst who heard of the Faith while having tea with her in 1904; Ramona, age 15, accepted immediately. Her mother and her well-known father, Dr. Woodson Allen, followed later. Ramona's aunt and uncle, the Latimers, lived in Portland, Oregon, and after accepting the Faith were the spearhead of the first community there. The Latimers' son George, a lawyer and investment counselor, became one of the most active Bahá'ís in the country, a member for many years of the National Spiritual Assembly, founded in 1925. After Ella Cooper's second pilgrimage, which took place in 1908, she started a youth group to study the teachings, made up of Ramona Allen and some of her young friends and relatives, and eventually the young men who clustered around them; Ramona's future husband, Joseph Bray, was one of them.

Another of that early group was Kanichi Yamamoto, the first Japanese Bahá'í in the world, who had become an adherent of the Faith in Hawaii six months before moving to California in 1902. He worked in Mrs. Goodall's home and was a source of warmth and joy at all the gatherings. He eventually had twelve children who grew up attending Bahá'í children's classes. During the second world war this entire family was forced to live in a relocation camp, where they were visited by Bay Area Bahá'ís. On one of those visits he said to Marion Carpenter Yazdi: "Bahá'u'lláh and 'Abdu'l-Bahá spent forty years as prisoners, so we can't mind this."

Ella Bailey, another of the early western Bahá'ís, was an elementary school teacher who learned of the Faith in 1904 through a lecture given to an audience of teachers in Berkeley where she lived; her Bahá'í study continued with Lua and with Mrs. Goodall. This saintly woman was much loved by 'Abdu'l-Bahá (see Chapter 30). Georgia Ralston, a childhood friend of Ella Goodall, became a Bahá'í in 1906 and was part of the San Francisco group. All of these early Bahá'ís were the fruit of the work begun by Lua Getsinger.

Others came to the Faith quite independently of Lua's efforts, such as John and Louise Bosch, a Swiss couple who had settled on a property north of San Francisco; it was Thornton Chase who led John to the Bahá'í Faith in 1905. On the opposite side of the continent, Louise was studying the teachings with Bahá'ís in New England and with May Maxwell, who took her to 'Akká in 1909. She and John met and married in 1914. Mary Rabb, a tenacious worker and one of the earliest compilers of Bahá'í Scripture, joined the Faith in 1906 in San Francisco. Still another of the early Bahá'ís was Dr. Ernest Rogers, founder of the Montezuma School for Boys in Los Gatos in the foothills south of San Francisco. His mother learned of Bahá'u'lláh's teachings through a letter from her friend Isabella Brittingham, an outstanding Bahá'í teacher of New York; they both accepted the new message. In 1900 Dr. Rogers received the first of a series of letters from 'Abdu'l-Bahá, in one of which 'Abdu'l-Bahá outlined the teaching methods which he should use in his school. When the Master spoke at Stanford University in 1912, Dr. Rogers brought thirty of his students to hear Him.

In 1901, an outstanding Irish-born physician, Dr. Frederick D'Evelyn, professor at the University of California and man of multiple civic interests and activities, became a staunch adherent of the Faith. He was one of the most gifted persons to be confirmed in the Faith, a former president of the California Academy of Sciences, of the Geographical Society of California and of the Audubon Society of the Pacific Coast. He served Bahá'u'lláh tirelessly through the ensuing years, engaging in a broad range of activities "motivated by his wide, active love", as his fellow Bahá'ís stated at his memorial meeting in 1932.

No organization or structure existed among the believers in those early days in California and they happily mixed friends and Bahá'ís together at all their meetings. They knew nothing of the community meetings called the Nineteen Day Feasts (when the believers meet on the first day of each Bahá'í month to consult on the affairs of the community) nor their purpose. But 'Abdu'l-Bahá was closely guiding the development of the American community, and soon they received the visit of Mrs. Isabella Brittingham, sent by the Master for the express purpose of "inaugurating" the holding of these consultative meetings in all the fledgling communities around the country.

When the first Nineteen Day Feast was held in the west, in the spacious home of Mrs. Goodall in 1908, Bahá'ís came from seven localities in the area to take part. It was a truly spiritual Feast as 'Abdu'l-Bahá had wished; Mrs. Goodall had filled every room of the house with flowers and lavished all her care and love on the preparations. This serene, determined woman was the recipient of warm praise from 'Abdu'l-Bahá, Who called her the "spiritual mother of this confirmed community" (northern California). When she and her daughter traveled to Chicago in 1912 to be with Him, He one day remarked that her value was not known at that time but would be in future. "God has certain treasures hidden in the world," He said, "which He reveals when the time comes. She is like one of these treasures."[2] On her last visit to 'Akká, He told her she had "done more than her share." Helen Goodall was to live to hear the tragic news of His passing in November 1921, and within a few months she, who had often said that when the Master left the world she hoped to do the same, died.

Thornton Chase was transferred by his company from Chicago to California in 1907. His work, which had previously kept him traveling in the states around Chicago, now required him to travel throughout the west, and the Bahá'í groups on the west coast had the full benefit of his irresistible spiritual enthusiasm. He was one of a number of itinerant Bahá'í teachers who were a lifeline to the small groups scattered from Seattle to San Diego. They visited as often as they could, bringing encouragement and fuller knowledge of the teachings. Prior to one of Thornton Chase's visits to Portland, a new Bahá'í, Rouhanieh Latimer, "had the nerve" as she recalls, "to call up every minister and ask them to please announce from their pulpits Sunday morning that this brilliant speaker had just returned from the Holy Land. All but one said they would. When Thornton heard what I had done he looked at me and said, 'My dear child, you have done what angels would fear to do'. Then he smiled." "Thornton's talks," she added, "were heavenly."[3]

Another of the travelers was English-born John Hyde Dunn, who became interested in the Faith through hearing a single phrase quoted from the writings of Bahá'u'lláh. He and his wife Clara were among the first to answer the call of 'Abdu'l-Bahá to arise and spread the teachings in other parts of the world. In 1918 they left San Francisco and moved to Australia, where they spent the rest of their lives. Both were later named Hands of the Cause.

Lua Getsinger returned to the west in 1911 for another teaching trip throughout California in preparation for 'Abdu'l-Bahá's hoped for visit. She found enormous response to the teachings: "A great wave of interest is sweeping over the country up and down this coast", she reported, "just as 'Abdu'l-Bahá said it would."[4]

During the period of her second visit the first Bahá'í Assembly of the west was formed in San Francisco. In honor of its formation 'Abdu'l-Bahá sent a Tablet through Mrs. Goodall, calling the new institution "the Assembly of 'Abdu'l-Bahá". He expressed the hope that it would become a magnet of confirmation and that the believers would remain firm and steadfast. "Report to me the services which are accomplished by this Assembly so that they may become the cause of spiritual happiness and joy to the heart."[5] The spirit was moving everywhere. Down in Santa Paula, in the southern part of California, a woman came to the door of the Carpenter family. She was selling a product, but she spoke to them about 'Abdu'l-Bahá, Whom they had read of two years earlier when He spoke at Stanford. Mrs. Elizabeth Carpenter, along with her daughter and son, subsequently became devoted Bahá'ís; Mr. Carpenter followed some years later. The daughter, Marion, was to marry Ali Yazdi, descendant of an illustrious Bahá'í family of Egypt[6] while the son, Howard, was to marry Marzieh Nabil, daughter of Dr. Ali-Kuli Khan, eminent teacher and translator of many of the early Bahá'í texts. Marion Carpenter had the distinction of being the first Bahá'í student at Stanford University, a seat of learning founded on sacrifice,* where 'Abdu'l-Bahá was received with

* When the Stanfords lost their only child during a trip to Italy they founded the Leland Stanford Jr. University in his memory.

great respect and honor; He praised it highly and remained in contact with its distinguished president, Dr. David Starr Jordan.

On one of Hyde Dunn's trips through the San Joaquin valley in 1912, he interested Mrs. Mollie Burland of Visalia in the Faith. Several years later after moving to San Francisco, she became a Bahá'í and her thoughts turned to founding a Bahá'í community in her home town. She persuaded Isabella Brittingham to include Visalia in her teaching trip of 1917, and it was then that the dynamic and outstanding Grace Holley immediately believed in the Faith. Grace Holley and another new Bahá'í, Anna Johnston, began sowing seeds in other hearts, but the soil in their conservative valley community seemed infertile. Grace Holley recalls that she "met with herself" for regular study on Tuesday evenings during many of the ensuing months. But the valley eventually proved fruitful and by the fall of 1924 great interest was being shown in the Faith. Grace Holley was one of the pillars of the Faith in California until her untimely illness in 1934. Her daughter Marion, brilliant student and Olympic athlete, was to become a shining light in the American national community.*

Another of the early Californian Bahá'ís migrated there from Chicago. Kathryn Frankland, a woman of force and energy, joined the Faith in 1902. She was instructed in a letter from 'Abdu'l-Bahá to "spread the Glad Tidings", so when her husband became a Bahá'í one year after her, they moved to the west where Bahá'ís were needed, settling near Oakland and later in Berkeley. She was to prove a very dynamo of activity. It was through working at her home that the second Japanese in the world became a Bahá'í in 1905. He was 'Abdu'l-Bahá's much-loved Saichiro Fujita whom the Master called His "Japanese Effendi". 'Abdu'l-Bahá invited Fujita to live in Haifa after he completed his education under the Master's guidance, studying matters that would be of use in the Holy Land. He was honored with serving both 'Abdu'l-Bahá and the Guardian.

This was the community, spread out in towns around the Bay Area and in cities along the Pacific coast, into which Leroy and Sylvia moved. These were the people who became their close friends, the collaborators with whom they worked in the ensuing years.

---

* In the 1940s she left the United States for England to marry David Hofman, outstanding Bahá'í teacher and writer, who was to serve for twenty-five years as a member of the Universal House of Justice.

# CHAPTER SIX

# Settling In

SYLVIA and Leroy loved their new home. They were stimulated by the natural beauty of the environment and the energetic optimism of the city. They stayed in the San Francisco area for twenty-eight years.

In comparison with the Chicago region, there were few Bahá'ís. But the very smallness of the community offered a wider field of initiative and from the start, as we will see later, Leroy was a pioneer in certain areas of the teaching work.

On December 7, 1919, within months of his arrival in the West, Leroy wrote an impassioned letter of devotion to 'Abdu'l-Bahá. He was inspired to do so by the visionary Plans received earlier in the year from 'Abdu'l-Bahá. He wrote:

> . . . one so weak as myself should not burden 'Abdu'l-Bahá, but . . . the confirmations that descended so intensely and uninterruptedly . . . have so filled my heart with desire to render some service in this great Cause, that I beg for continued confirmations and blessings to assist me therein.[1]

Ever the practical planner, he mentioned in the letter his study of Spanish and Esperanto, wondering how these might be used in the teaching work. He asks for 'Abdu'l-Bahá's blessings on his "dear wife" and any children that might bless their union.

How could avenues to "render some service" not have opened to him after such a plea to 'Abdu'l-Bahá!

The first year was a time of settling in for Sylvia and Leroy. During the first weeks they spent their evenings looking for a place to live. They finally found five rooms high on a hill above Chinatown, owned by a very spiritual woman who had recently been widowed. She was deeply interested in their views on life after death and the increased happiness of the departed one. Leroy gave her the *Paris Talks* and hoped some good might be accomplished through her. The day they moved in, she saw the picture of 'Abdu'l-Bahá on the wall, and went up to it slowly, gazing at it in an almost worshipful way. She said she had never before seen such a face and didn't wonder that they loved Him.

Sylvia and Leroy found a number of nice young people with whom they hoped to establish something similar to their group in Chicago. They missed the young people of Chicago and Leroy worried that such teaching projects as the Wilmette campaign would not be continued. He wrote at great length to his friend Carl Scheffler that the young people should be encouraged to undertake a teaching campaign in several towns situated around Indianapolis, where he and others had made contacts the previous summer. He even laid out a program of specific activities for the three towns.

But he and Sylvia were at first "rather inactive" by Leroy's account, feeling that as new arrivals they should not seem to intrude into the affairs of the San Francisco Bahá'ís. They decided the best way to begin their Bahá'í service was to invite people to their home for an enjoyable evening, and see if they responded and wished to continue the gatherings. Soon they were holding weekly meetings. Leroy writes enthusiastically to Carl of two seekers who were invited to the house, and the following week brought four of their friends. Another new person was a stranger who came to one of the Friday meetings held in the city. He wished to know more so they invited him to dinner, after which, Leroy writes to Carl, "we had a very interesting discussion of the teachings". Three years earlier, this man had heard a Bahá'í speaker at a Unitarian Church in Portland – Mr. Vail, no doubt, thought Leroy – and even then had wished to know more. "This again demonstrates", Leroy writes to Carl, "the infinite wisdom of 'Abdu'l-Bahá's instructions to sow the seeds and they would be watered by the heavenly water of life from the Kingdom." He also notes the need for Bahá'ís to establish centers in the large cities and let it be known that seekers can receive information there. "If a stranger came here," he writes, "he would never know there were any Bahá'ís, unless he accidentally ran into one." He asks Carl to take this question up with other Assemblies and "even with the Bahá'í Temple Unity".

About a year and a half after their arrival, Leroy was elected to the
Local Spiritual Assembly* and was drawn into close association with
Ella Goodall Cooper, who had married a prominent doctor and moved
to San Francisco from Oakland. "She is so wonderful," he wrote to
Carl. "She sizes up situations relative to the Cause more quickly than
anyone I've ever known, and in a sweet, spiritual way suggests a solution." Several months after his election it was she who telephoned him
with the terrible news of 'Abdu'l-Bahá's passing. Leroy had just completed a long letter to Albert Windust in Chicago, and he came back to
add a handwritten postscript: "Have just received the most terrible
news. Everyone here is broken and crushed and cannot believe the
Beloved of our hearts has gone. He has been the motive power of our
lives, our inspiration, and our real existence. Where will we turn now?
It is only through His increased confirmations that we will be able to
go forward. May we all become real standard-bearers!"

He redoubled his efforts to take on responsibility. He became head
of the Reception Committee, charged with greeting the new people
who attended meetings. He worked on the committee charged with
arranging speaking engagements and publicity for the visit to San
Francisco of the renowned teacher Jináb-i-Faḍíl (see page 47). He was
appointed Corresponding Secretary of the Assembly, with the interesting mandate to correspond with all new believers in the San Francisco
area and in other countries when they were known. This included
many persons in Australia where the Hyde Dunns were teaching, and
in South America where Martha Root had been traveling.

Thus in spite of his youth and inexperience, Leroy was drawn into
responsible tasks, and soon into public duties as well. He was chairman
of one of the public lectures held during the first Teaching Convention
of the western states in 1923, presenting such seasoned speakers as
George Latimer and Dr. Frederick D'Evelyn. And he himself began to
appear as a speaker at the regular public meetings, along with the
experienced teachers.

In 1920 their first child was born, a beautiful girl who was named
Mary Lorraine. But she also had a Persian name. Through a Chicago
Bahá'í who was to visit 'Akká, Leroy had requested a name for the

---

* According to provisions of Bahá'u'lláh's administrative order, each local Bahá'í community is governed by a nine-member body elected annually from among the believers.

baby. Some time later he received a small square of paper with the pencilled notation that 'Abdu'l-Bahá had named the baby Farrukh, "very joyous". From her earliest years she wished to be called nothing else. A second daughter, Anita, was born the following year and Sylvia, ever the caring mother, felt a home with a garden would be more suitable. They moved to Burlingame, a small community south of San Francisco sheltered from the fog of the city. But they remained there only a few years. Leroy's interests were centered in the city.

He had found work with the Southern Pacific railroad as a stenographer and shortly was appointed private secretary to the vice-president, E.O. McCormick. When this fine man died four years later Leroy was of such help and support to his widow that until her death years later she sent gifts each Christmas to his children. True to the tradition of that period, Leroy was to remain to make a career with the Southern Pacific in an era when elegant trains and great lines bound the country together and were part of the romance of settlement of the continent. He loved this service industry and the outstanding passenger service which he eventually headed.

In 1925, a large Victorian house at 2108 Scott Street had been made available for Bahá'í use by Ella Goodall Cooper. It was the first Bahá'í Center in San Francisco. Because it had to be occupied for insurance purposes, Sylvia and Leroy offered to move into it, though it meant leaving their home in Burlingame unattended.

For two years they kept it open as a Bahá'í Center. This meant they always had to be available: for the tea-time meetings each Wednesday, the firesides and public meetings, study classes, Assembly meetings, Bahá'í Holy Days, committee meetings and the Nineteen Day Feasts. By community decision, the Feasts were preceded by a dinner together. Sylvia remembers that with all this activity and hospitality at the Center, the Faith began to grow more rapidly.

But these things had to be planned for. Leroy was frequently called upon to substitute at the Friday night meetings if no one had been asked to speak or failed to appear; often Feast arrangements and other matters fell to the two of them.

At the same time he was working actively for the first of a series of world unity conferences in San Francisco. This was in addition to his own study classes, and overseeing the upkeep of the building. By the end of two years, it was all too much. Sylvia became worn and then ill.

A change was necessary, and they found a modest cozy house that looked out over the Pacific Ocean and moved. It was their home for most of their stay in San Francisco.

As both were extremely hospitable, this home also became a center of activity and accommodated numerous interesting houseguests. "They cultivated the new Bahá'ís," recalled Lottie Linfoot years later,* "making them feel a part of the Bahá'í family." Their children in retrospect realized how rich this life was for them, growing up listening in as gifted Bahá'í teachers discussed the future of the world around the dining room table. It was a wonderful Bahá'í home. "Bahá'í activity is what makes a house a home," Leroy wrote years later to a brother who had moved to a new area: "A home is where the spirit of unity and fellowship abide, whereas a house is simply a place to live."

In those years a remarkable teacher by the name of Orcella Rexford had arisen among the Bahá'ís. Shortly after being confirmed in the Faith through Dr. Getsinger, this spirited woman, who was a lecturer on health and related topics, found an original and highly successful method to reach the public. At the completion of a paid series of lectures she would announce to the audience a free lecture the following evening that would "bring them a knowledge that is beyond price". That talk concerned the advent of Bahá'u'lláh.

Invariably, she left a Bahá'í study class behind her, with dozens of participants who would be taught by local Bahá'ís. The success of this method became evident: in New York City alone there were some forty new Bahá'ís as a result of her efforts. Following Orcella's 1926 lectures in San Francisco and Oakland, Leroy took up the task of teaching her classes. Each initially numbered from 50 to 75 persons.

It is interesting to dwell a moment on the challenge these classes represented for him. There was no question but that he would accept to teach the classes. Yet this meant three study classes each week, one of them across the Bay in Oakland. He maintained this schedule for one and a half years; from it came the Oakland Assembly with a community of 35. Out of the San Francisco class came many new believers, including the long-time Assembly secretaries of Sacramento

---

* The Linfoot family became Bahá'ís through Leroy; Lottie (Charlotte) went on to serve on the National Teaching Committee and as Assistant Secretary of the National Assembly for many years.

and San Francisco. No bridges spanned the Bay between San Francisco and Oakland at that time; crossing was a half-hour ferry ride. And trolleys to and from home. Leroy looked around for help: where were the teachers who could assist him to seize this extraordinary opportunity?

It was an acutely discouraging time for him, as he found almost no one who would accept, or had the capacity, to direct these classes. And this, after the Faith had been established in the area for twenty-five years. "Here we were", he recalled years later, "with this great opportunity, yet there was no one who arose." Even more disheartening was the general lassitude toward teaching throughout the state, whereas he felt that doors were opening everywhere – in Central California, the San Joaquin valley, Southern California.

In the depth of his discouragement he "vowed to God that whenever I lived in an area for any length of time, Bahá'í teachers would be developed who would be able to take over classes, who would be able to carry on the teaching work, so that we would never again find ourselves in such a deplorable condition."

As he reached the point of deciding to curtail some of his activity, he had the same dream three times. He was addressing a large group of people and was earnestly expounding the teachings. As he reached the heart of his presentation, people would get up and leave, disturbing the meeting and distressing him greatly. He was about to announce that if anyone else left he would close the meeting, when 'Abdu'l-Bahá appeared in the background. He walked forward and said: "Continue to talk! Continue to speak about the Faith! Don't pay any attention to what the people do. In the end they will all wish to listen to you."

Leroy resolved that changes must be made. "By nature", he said later, "I have always faced a situation and then tried to figure out what was needed to solve the problem." Thus, during this period of intensive teaching and great stress, his mind began to work on solutions.

Three different teaching plans began to form in his mind. One was to organize – in this liberal western region – large conferences that would reach prominent people. Another was to create a teaching program to coordinate the work being done by individuals, so that greater result would be obtained from their efforts. The third question he was turning over in his mind was how to develop Bahá'í teachers.

Leroy was still a very young man, but vision has no age. He saw what needed to be done, and he was someone who made things happen. "A doer," Rúḥíyyih K͟hánum called him in a letter written to a friend one year after his arrival in Haifa in 1952, "and that is what Shoghi Effendi so desperately needs and so admires in him."

Let us look now at some of the activities initiated through his vision and efforts during his first decade in California.

CHAPTER SEVEN

# The Conference for World Unity

IN the 1920s a number of brilliantly successful conferences on the theme of world unity were sponsored by the Bahá'ís in the United States. The first, which was the inspiration for the others, was conceived and carried out in San Francisco in March of 1925. From there the idea spread across the country to other major cities.

It must be noted that Leroy had always thought the prominent people of the country, those in positions to influence policy and institutions, should know of Bahá'u'lláh's teachings concerning world order. They should know what the Faith stood for, they should espouse its principles if not its originating impulse, and they should be invited to take part in its activities.

Was there not a powerful precedent for this? Had not 'Abdu'l-Bahá spoken at the invitation of a wide range of organizations? If these were pertinent and life-giving teachings, should they not be announced to the leadership and offered for their consideration? Had not 'Abdu'l-Bahá called upon California to raise aloft the banner of world peace? And had He not directed Agnes Parsons* to organize a great race unity conference in the nation's capital, for which she called upon the participation of political and religious leaders?

But the insistent reason to plan such a conference was that 'Abdu'l-Bahá had specifically mentioned San Francisco in a Tablet to Mrs. Parsons concerning future amity conferences – a reference which

* An early Bahá'í of Washington D.C. of high social position and consummate devotion, at whose home 'Abdu'l-Bahá met each afternoon with a stream of officials and outstanding personalities of the capital.

Leroy considered a command. So it was to Mrs. Parsons that he turned in June of 1922 to seek her instructions and advice. Should it be a Bahá'í event, he wondered, or a gathering of sincere persons "from all avenues of uplift work" who sought amity among peoples? He noted their particular problem on the West Coast, the inharmony between Caucasian and Oriental, which imposed that question as a prominent issue of their conference. He shared 'Abdu'l-Bahá's instructions to Ella Cooper and Kathryn Frankland that they must be "most kind" to the Japanese. And every effort which had been made to show love to the Japanese, he told her, had met with "almost unaccountable" success.

But to Leroy's disappointment, when he proposed his idea for the conference to the Assembly, they did not think it timely to go ahead with the idea that year.

Leroy had been attending various functions in order to meet people and at one such event heard a speech given by Dr. Rudolph Coffee, Rabbi of Temple Sinai, the largest synagogue in the East Bay area, and the first Rabbi to be elected Chaplain of the California Senate. His talk that night was of such universality that Leroy immediately conceived of drawing Rabbi Coffee into a Bahá'í unity conference.

He again presented the idea to the San Francisco Assembly and was appointed a committee of one to study the possibilities. When a preliminary survey showed positive response to the idea, he asked the Assembly to appoint an official committee of Ella Goodall Cooper, himself and the resourceful Kathryn Frankland to act in the name of the Bahá'ís to develop the conference.

With this backing, they started to work. Leroy took his year's holiday to carry out the organizational work in all its myriad details – when necessary he was able to be both the conceptualizer and the one who coped with the drudgery of detail work.

A statement of purpose was drawn up as a basis of their approach to those whom they wished to invite as participants:

> The purpose of this Conference is to present to the public of the Bay Region, and those interested in the welfare of humanity, the spiritual facts concerning the beauty and harmony of the human family, the great unity in the diversity of human blessings, and this harmonizing of all elements of the body politic as the Pathway to Universal Peace.

The three day conference, convened for March 20, 21, and 22 of 1925, was to be free of any denominational sponsorship and to be "a gathering of public spirited people to further the spirit of brotherhood". No collections were to be taken "under any circumstances"; it was the San Francisco Bahá'í Assembly that assumed responsibility for all expenses. The conference was to be held at the dignified and prestigious Palace Hotel.

The committee's first great success was to interest the Chancellor Emeritus of Stanford University, Dr. David Starr Jordan, in serving as honorary chairman. He was a man of concern and vision, who over the years had evolved in his mind what he called the Essentials of a Peace Plan. He accepted to associate himself with the conference, but felt the title "Conference for World Unity" preferable to the word "amity" originally suggested by the Bahá'ís. This caused some negative reaction among Bahá'ís – and Leroy after the conference asked the National Assembly to comment on the question – but Mrs. Parsons made it clear that "amity" had been her choice of word and there was no necessity to follow it.

A number of personalities in the Bay area were enlisted as speakers, a list that should give pause to any who are cautious in planning. It included Dr. Aurelia Reinhardt, president of Mills College in Oakland; Clinton Howard, president of the World Peace Commission; Professor Kenneth Saunders of the Pacific School of Religion; Rabbi Rudolph Coffee of Temple Sinai; Rev. W.J.J. Byers of the AME Zion Church; Dean Wilmer Gresham of Grace Cathedral; Professors J.V. Breitwieser and G.M. Stratton of the University of California; Ng Poon Chew, editor of a large Chinese newspaper; Torao Kawasaki of the Consulate General of Japan; and the Rev. Charles Ramm of St. Mary's Cathedral.

To this prestigious list was added a very great Bahá'í speaker, Jináb-i-Faḍíl, erudite, humble, charming, a masterful teacher. 'Abdu'l-Bahá had sent this "ripened soul" to America in 1919 in order to strengthen and more fully educate the Bahá'ís in the teachings, and to proclaim the Faith to the public. His second visit, at the request of Shoghi Effendi, brought him to California in 1925, a fortuitous circumstance allowing him to take part in the World Unity Conference.

The planning committee, chaired by Dr. Coffee, rapidly approved the name, date, and place of the conference. They moved to hire a professional company, Western Organization Service, a firm accustomed to large campaigns and sympathetic to the work of the conference, to secure publicity; they appointed Mrs. Cooper with her many social contacts as the committee on patrons and patronesses and on music for the programs. They requested each speaker to prepare a 250-word summary of his presentation for publicity purposes. They worked expeditiously under their secretary, Leroy, and within some months were ready for the conference. As their vision was large, they also wrote to President Calvin Coolidge and the Honorable Herbert Hoover, Secretary of Commerce, to ask that a greeting in their name be sent to the conference.

An interesting detail is that the Esperanto Association of California declined to be a patron of the conference, stating it did not associate itself in any way with any religious movement. Leroy was very disappointed by this reaction. He wrote to them describing his ten year association with Esperantists and his work for the spread of a universal language, of his being vice-president for two years of the National Students Rondaro, and his close association with national and international Esperanto leaders (thinking no doubt of Martha Root among others). He expressed his profound regret to see them miss an opportunity to spread their message among such eminent persons as were taking part in, and would be attending, this conference.

During the three days of the conference, meetings were held each evening at eight o'clock, with three distinguished speakers on each program. On Friday night Dr. Saunders, a scholar of Eastern thought, spoke on India's contribution to world peace, Dr. Ng on China as a factor in world amity, and Dr. Jordan on the essentials of his own peace plan. The following evening, Saturday, Dr. Reinhardt spoke on knowledge as a basis of understanding, Dr. Byers on the Negro race and world peace, followed by Dr. Howard on the attainment of peace through the Prince of Peace. On the last evening, the Honorable Kawasaki outlined Japan's contribution to world peace conferences. Jináb-i-Faḍíl was the penultimate speaker (closing remarks being made by Rabbi Coffee on the birth and development of world unity) and in reporting on the conference Dr. Breitwieser described Faḍíl's address as a "fitting unification of the thoughts that had been gathered together in the conference."[1] Printed on each program were precepts of unity from the great cultures of the world, including the powerful statement of Bahá'u'lláh: *"This handful of dust, the world, is one home. Let it be in unity."*

Was it worth the effort that went into its planning? After the fact, it was obvious. Before the fact, it took audacity, determination, a formidable amount of work, and reliance on Bahá'u'lláh to open the doors. It was an event which galvanized the Bahá'ís, made them aware of what they could do and the power that would come to them if they dared to do great things.

Rabbi Coffee, obviously moved and stimulated by the event, wrote to ask Leroy what the next step should be; the three meetings had "splendidly brought out our strength and it should not be dissipated". He expressed the hope that conferences "of this kind" might be held every year and that an organization be maintained to define objectives and plans for the next meeting. Dr. Coffee was a very firm friend of the Faith from that time forward. In later years Leroy always attempted to put him in touch with leading Bahá'ís, telling them Dr. Coffee had proven himself to be the truest among the friends of the Bahá'ís.

Leroy had no ready answer to Dr. Coffee's question, but saw the ramifications of this work. "I am wondering," he wrote to the National Assembly, "if these world unity conferences cannot be developed into a national public activity, so that the Bahá'ís will be recognized as sponsors of real unity among the races, religions and peoples of the world." He affirmed that the sincere workers are willing to accept the leadership of the Bahá'ís in the work for peace "if we will step forward and show them the path, both by precept and by example". He felt there was no better way to raise the standing of the Cause in the eyes of the public and prove that it was more than a narrow, sectarian movement. As for the results locally if such events were held elsewhere, they would be as evident everywhere as they had been in San Francisco. "Many doors," he wrote, "have opened to us that were formerly closed, and would have remained closed."

But Leroy saw another, deeper significance to the conferences. Such efforts on behalf of unity acted as leaven to cause new life to stir among the people, unaware though they might be of its source. All believers, he frequently said, should bear this in mind and never become discouraged when they saw no immediate result from their efforts. They should work, and work diligently, knowing that through their efforts the power of Bahá'u'lláh was influencing people and events to move in the direction of the plan of God.

The National Assembly immediately saw the value of the conferences and asked its Teaching Committee to initiate a series of events similar to that which had been held in San Francisco. Within two years eighteen additional world unity conferences were held.

A report of the San Francisco conference was sent to Shoghi Effendi, very likely his first intimation of the scope of the work being done by the young man in San Francisco. The reply, written in October 1925, by Dr. John Esslemont,* who had moved to Haifa to assist the Guardian, noted: "Shoghi Effendi was much interested in the report of the Conference for World Unity in San Francisco, the arrangements for which seem to have been admirably carried through. He hopes that the Conference may bear much fruit and prove a starting point for further important developments."

Before going on to another important initiative in which Leroy played a key role, let us turn briefly to the story of David Starr Jordan and his offer to assist Leroy to attend Stanford University.

In their numerous meetings concerning the conference, Ella Cooper and Dr. Jordan must have discussed the evident qualities of the young man working with them in their conference planning, for within two weeks of the conference, Dr. Jordan wrote to her that if Leroy were serious about entering Stanford and would make the proper preliminary arrangements, it might be possible for him to obtain one of several scholarships offered to promising students at the University. He added that Leroy "seems to me a young man of marked promise who ought not to lose the advantages, which may be extremely real, of a college education."

Dr. Jordan, who himself had been obliged to work his way through Stanford, had observed with regret that many used the college for quite other ends: "While a certain number of boys take the institution to be a sort of exalted country club, these are not the ones for which the University lives, and at Stanford it is our habit 'to take them to the edge of the campus and drop them off' into seaside resorts."

Sylvia and Leroy had several long and serious talks about this offer. At 29, with two small children and no income but his salary, already deeply involved in all phases of the Bahá'í work in California, it was not feasible. He had to continue to educate himself, with 'Abdu'l-Bahá's texts as his teacher. That it was a successful schooling was

---

* Named posthumously as a Hand of the Cause.

shown in later years when several of his most successful talks in the Bay area were informal meetings given in Palo Alto for Stanford professors.

A close friend, Joyce Dahl, herself a Stanford graduate, remarked that Leroy "had been spared the clutter of lots of formal education" so that his mind went directly into understanding of the Faith. Professor Rogers of the Montezuma School said that Leroy had better than a university education, as he had learned the hard way, through constant study and experience in life.

Now let us look at another of his initiatives, the Bahá'í school at Geyserville, cherished in many hearts, and how it came into being.

# CHAPTER EIGHT

# The Geyserville Story

GEYSERVILLE in the mid-twenties consisted of a few stores and an ice cream parlor spread along the two-lane main highway running north from San Francisco through miles of fruit valleys. It was orchard country and its friendly but conservative citizens lived on farms scattered over the landscape. The hamlet of Geyserville became the site of the first Bahá'í summer school in North America.

We have noted how the teaching work in the Bay area expanded dramatically following Orcella Rexford's visit. But there were few trained teachers to take advantage of the opportunities she had created, a situation which made Leroy sick at heart and convinced him that a way must be found to train Bahá'ís systematically in the teachings. He felt that if a group of young, enthusiastic people, anxious to propagate the Faith, could meet together for a period of serious study, without outside distractions, from them some good public teachers could be developed. Furthermore if persons with serious interest in the teachings were included in the classes, no doubt a good percentage of them would be confirmed through such participation. It became evident that they must find a place where people could be brought together for one or two weeks. It is well to remember that nothing of the kind existed to answer such a need.

But how to do this? The first step came by chance, which works for those who have their objectives always in mind.

Leroy received a telephone call at his office one day in June of 1926 from Louise Bosch (see p. 34). She asked if he would come to Healdsburg, which was near their home in Geyserville, to conduct the funeral service of a prominent doctor whose wife was a Bahá'í and who had himself been studying the teachings. It was the sort of thing Leroy was frequently called upon to do and he agreed to take an early morning train.* They would lunch together under the "Big Tree" – a mighty Douglas fir under which a hundred and fifty people could sit – that stood on a clearing in front of their house.

Louise and her husband John were from St. Gallen in Switzerland. They had settled on a property of vineyards in Jack London's Valley of the Moon, through which the Russian River ran its course. Several years after becoming a Bahá'í John had closed the winery and planted fruit trees. At the time of which we write John was a man of seventy, white-haired and patriarchal, always spotlessly groomed, in summer clothed in a white suit and Panama hat. An observant Bahá'í described him as "a rare person – there was about him a continual inner happiness, a warmth, which was transmitted readily to others."[1]

In 1912, John had gone to New York to meet 'Abdu'l-Bahá, fearing that He would not make the long trip to California. As he waited outside the home where 'Abdu'l-Bahá was staying, he heard his name called: *Mr. Bosch! Mr. Bosch!* He went up to the Master, who had emerged from the house, and 'Abdu'l-Bahá patted him on the shoulder saying, "It's a fine strong shoulder." Then 'Abdu'l-Bahá indicated that John should accompany Him on a drive, during which the weary Master leaned his head on John's left shoulder and fell asleep. It was the same shoulder on which John, who was in 'Akká in 1921, carried the coffin of the Master up the hill of Mt. Carmel. (Preceded by dozens of dignitaries, there came "the sacred coffin, upraised on the shoulders of His loved ones" as Shoghi Effendi described the scene. Louise left a moving eye-witness account of the days after the Master's passing.) John had invited 'Abdu'l-Bahá to visit Geyserville, and even written the Master of his hope that the property might one day be used in service to the Faith: "May this simple place on the hills, directly west of Geyser Peak, be dedicated to the Universal Spirit of the Teachings of Bahá'u'lláh, combining the good of all the Messengers of God . . . that it may be a natural source of pure water for the believers to drink, and to flow out to all good hearts which are earnestly seeking enlightenment."

* Louise wrote to Sylvia that "he needed a rest instead of that mental effort, but some people had already inquired into the Truth since that memorable funeral."

After lunch with John and Louise, Leroy recalled, "we sat together, talking about the affairs of the Cause and the days of the Master. There was such a warm spiritual atmosphere pervading the place that I mentioned how wonderful it would be for the Bahá'ís to come together for a feast or party in this beautiful, scenic area." John mentioned his letter to 'Abdu'l-Bahá and said they, too, had hoped for this but it had never been arranged. So it was agreed that the Bahá'ís should be invited to Geyserville for the Feast of Kamál, August 2nd, 1926, one of the regular community meetings in the Bahá'í calendar. As this would be John's seventieth birthday, it seemed doubly appropriate for the Bahá'ís to gather "in this spot where there was such a strong feeling of peace and unity" to celebrate the two events. Leroy said he would take full responsibility for organizing it.

The San Francisco Assembly gave its backing and all the believers living nearby were invited, delighted with the idea and looking forward to meeting under the Big Tree. About one hundred were present that August day, from nine different communities. "It was a wonderful occasion," Leroy recalled, "full of happiness, full of unity, full of Bahá'í love, and above all full of enthusiasm." Various people spoke – John and Leroy among them – and plans were laid for a unified teaching effort throughout the area. By the end of the day, everyone had agreed that this celebration should be an annual event, something to look forward to each summer.

In the meantime Leroy had been trying to resolve the question of a venue where the Bahá'ís could meet for the training of teachers. He had discussed the concept with some of the "leading workers" on the Coast – Grace Holley in Visalia, Shahnaz Waite in Los Angeles, Ella Cooper, George Latimer, Ella Bailey and others. He also discussed it with John and Louise. They were enthusiastic – John shared with Leroy certain dreams of his in which he had seen the property being used as a haven of rest and comfort for the believers.

The three of them discussed whether the Bosches could receive the Bahá'ís for an extended period of time. There were a number of old buildings on the property where people could stay – the abandoned prune house and cook house, plus little wooden structures once used for keeping goats. The Bosches themselves lived in two different houses on the property and thought they could move to one house during the session.*

* An early Bahá'í visitor to the School, Joyce Dahl, remembers their home and its "cool lack of clutter and the lingering echo of their travel to the South Seas" in answer to the Tablets of the Divine Plan.

After much discussion, Leroy wrote to the National Assembly asking for approval to open a Bahá'í school on the Pacific Coast. The Assembly responded by appointing George Latimer, John Bosch and Leroy as a national committee, the Pacific Coast Summer School Committee, to investigate the entire project and submit recommendations for its implementation on an appropriate site. At that time there were other offers of property from Bahá'ís, some quite desirable, including land in Washington State, in Santa Cruz, in southern California and in Oregon.

They decided, however, to recommend the Bosch property. It seemed "spiritually ideal" because of the Bosches' long period of service and John's association with the Master.

The National Assembly gave its approval and arrangements were made to open the first Bahá'í summer school. It convened in Geyserville in 1927.[*] The school session was planned and conducted by the committee, Leroy from the very beginning thinking it extremely important to have such initiatives carried out through administrative channels.

They thought if a dozen people were attracted that first year, it would be a wonderful start. Forty people came, presenting serious housing problems. The visitors were dotted all over the property in makeshift arrangements, with the living room of the Bosch house serving as a classroom. During the early years, John and Louise were "hosts" to the school.[†]

Geyserville quickly developed a strong following. The setting was rustic but beautiful, with a redwood grove on the mountainside above the Big Tree for dawn prayers and discussion groups. It was a center of Bahá'í fellowship, of intense but leisurely discussions, of making friends "for life". To children, it was freedom in a spiritually enriching setting.[‡] One of the highlights each year was a "day off" spent at

[*] Greenacre opened as a Bahá'í summer school in 1929.

[†] Joyce Dahl, after her first visit before she became a Bahá'í: "One wrote to the Bosches at Box 101, Geyserville, that one hoped there would be a place for oneself at the summer school, and one always wrote a thank you letter for their hospitality."

[‡] Dwight Allen, Knight of Bahá'u'lláh to Greece, former member of the United States National Assembly, wrote to Leroy in 1953: "However many other schools I may be involved in, Geyserville will always be unique in my remembrances of childhood and youth."

nearby Griffith's Grove. Mr. Griffith had allowed ten acres of his property to remain in its natural state, trickling streams, pathways deep with fallen pine needles, miniature falls and springs, and a variety of California wild flowers which he had planted. He had also arranged a small amphitheater, where the theatrically gifted Bahá'ís appeared in clever skits of their own devising. Later there was singing around a bonfire. It was a day of enchantment for everyone.

Louise Bosch, hostess of the school, was a very special personality. One of the scenes none of the early visitors ever forgot was Louise making the rounds in the evening with her basket on one arm and her lantern on the other, to see if everyone was properly tucked in and happy. Leroy recalled: "One evening when I was very tired and not well she called to see how I was getting along. We were sleeping in the prune house with our bed along the window. She began to talk through the window about the Cause, the teachings and so on, and said she wondered what kind of wife God had. Since life in this world is propagated through male and female she felt sure God must have a wife in order to carry on this creation of His." And everyone remembered her little notes: *This door opens if you push with the handle and kick on the lower right hand corner.* They added whimsy and charm to the summer school setting and were avidly collected.

During the first few years the classes started immediately after the opening Unity Feast. But as the school expanded, first to four weeks and then to six, the Unity Feast was held at mid-point of the period. This made it possible for those leaving the first session and those arriving for the second to enjoy a day of fellowship and to see friends from the previous year.

While the school was thus developing, the Bosches were harboring certain doubts about giving up control of the property. They felt the National Assembly might sell the land or not conduct the school in accordance with certain theories they held concerning Bahá'í schools. So they proposed naming a very large board of directors, including some of their relatives in St. Gallen. But as Leroy pointed out to them, a large board for a small school, which was without funds or proper facilities, would cause its collapse. In any event the point was moot, he said, as only Bahá'ís could preside over a Bahá'í school. It was not easy to run the school under these uncertain conditions.

Indeed, as the fourth year of the school approached, Louise wrote to the committee that the session could not be held at Geyserville that year – the project they had begun was too big, the place was not equipped for it, and they should give it up. "We pointed out to her," Leroy noted, "that the school was an institution of the Faith, where it was held was a different question. In other words, the location might be anywhere, but the school and its purposes had to be carried forward as an institution of the Faith and could not under any circumstances be given up."

The committee began looking seriously at other locations. Professor Rogers of the Montezuma School for Boys had been urging use of his school facilities during the summer months. The owners of Asilomar on the Pacific ocean, an elaborate facility established by Phoebe Hearst for the Young Men's Christian Association, asked if the Bahá'ís would be interested in buying their property.

Then one evening Leroy and George Latimer had dinner with John and Louise in San Francisco. The matter of the property was discussed "quite vigorously". It happened that shortly before, a well-to-do Bahá'í, who intended leaving all his possessions to the Cause but put off making the arrangements, had suddenly been killed. His assets went to non-Bahá'í heirs. The Bosches were both well along in years, and if anything happened before their arrangements had been concluded, the intentions of a lifetime would be nullified.

As a result of that conversation, the property was turned over to the National Assembly, with provision of life tenancy for John and Louise. The deed was transferred at a ceremony during the ninth session of the school.

In the first two years, the curriculum of the school was very demanding. Lectures were given by well-known Bahá'í teachers: Helen Bishop, George Latimer, Amelia Collins, May Maxwell and Willard Hatch. Leroy took two days off to speak twice a day at the first session, on God's Plan for Man: Proofs of the Existence of God, Relation of God and Man, Evolution, and Immortality. Initially there were programs in the morning, afternoon and evening. While enormously enriching, it left little time for that leisurely discussion which is a large part of learning. So the program was modified. By the third year three sessions were held each morning six days of the week, with time for discussion groups, study of Esperanto, and other interests, in the afternoons.

An interesting feature of the early years was the use of professors who were "friends of the Faith". They included Professor John Meredith, Dean of the Montezuma School for Boys, and Professor George Hedley, archeologist and scholar of the Pacific School of Religions, who presented a week-long course on comparative religion. Use of such personalities was of benefit to the school in several ways: the Faith became better known and respected in intellectual circles, the Bahá'ís were stimulated in their thinking by the views of those outside the Faith, and the guest speakers could gain an experience of the Bahá'í way of life. In a letter to John and Louise Bosch in the fourth year of the school, the Guardian wrote (through his secretary) that the more such professors are brought in the better, for they "undoubtedly obtain just as much as they give to others."[2]

The Guardian obviously considered the school crucial in reaching a broader public, as he indicated in a letter to George Latimer that same year (through his secretary): "The Geyserville Summer School should be considered as one of the best means through which the public can be acquainted with the teachings and the principles of the Faith."[3]

As for its effect on the Bahá'ís, his secretary noted that "those who assemble there, then disperse throughout the Western states with a new spirit and added determination to spread the Cause."[4] Indeed, the first pioneers under the Seven Year Plan* went forth with the inspiration of this school. But most importantly it was a source of that "confirmation of souls" which had been one of Leroy's hopes, as those seeking spiritual life experienced the love and unity that Bahá'u'lláh was creating among His followers. Leroy often quoted a statement made by the Guardian to John Bosch in a letter concerning the spirit that should animate the school. The Guardian said that the principles of Bahá'u'lláh would civilize the world, but only the *spirit* of Bahá'u'lláh would quicken the world. And what the world needed now was quickening.

It was evident that the Guardian followed the work of the school with keen interest and was guiding its development. In the fifth year of the school he wrote to Leroy through his secretary that in the programming "special stress [should] be put on the history of the Movement as well as on the guiding principles of Bahá'í Administration. For on

---

* In 1937 the Guardian launched the North American Bahá'ís on their first teaching crusade, called the Seven Year Plan. See Chapter 13.

these two points most of the believers are not adequately informed."[5]*

That same year, a letter from Shoghi Effendi caused the committee to rethink the format of the school. "Lectures are very important," wrote the Guardian's secretary, "for they give a wonderful picture of the subject matter. But it is not sufficient to have a picture, the friends should deepen their knowledge and this can be achieved if together with the lectures there are study classes and seminar work carried on by the same lecturer . . . Should the friends desire to take the lead in informing the world, they should start by educating themselves and understand what the troubles and problems really are which baffle the minds of men."[6]

Several of the courses presented in Geyserville, carefully researched and prepared, became the basis for articles in *World Order* magazine;† in fact as Horace Holley, its editor, wrote to Leroy: "The summer schools are becoming our best source of material."

Amelia Collins, a frequent visitor and speaker at the summer school, became interested in providing better facilities on the school property. The sessions had quickly outgrown the Bosch living room and classes were held at the Oddfellows Hall in the village, with public meetings taking place at the local High School. The need for a proper meeting place became evident. Mrs. Collins commissioned an architect to draw up plans for an attractive large hall of rustic redwood; construction began during the ninth year of the school. At the same time she and her husband, Thomas Collins, offered the school a simple but modern dormitory building that could house fifty persons. Mr. Collins, a generous friend of the Faith, passed away in Europe shortly after the impressive dedication of Bahá'í Hall on July 12, 1936. It was during that ceremony that the Geyserville property was officially transferred to the National Spiritual Assembly. Later the Library of the school was named Collins Library in memory of Mr. Collins.

---

* Shoghi Effendi adds in his own hand one of his first warm appreciations of Leroy's work: "Your letters, replete with evidences of a vigorous spirit of determination, of ceaseless activity, and of noble enthusiasm, are a source of strength and inspiration to me in my arduous task."

† A monthly publication begun in 1935 as an amalgam of *Star of the West* and *World Unity*. *World Unity* was a review born of the world order conferences held throughout the country in the late 1920s. Horace Holley served as its editor, a function he continued with *World Order* magazine.

"Milly" Collins had become one of Leroy's closest friends. Their devotion to the Faith was so similar that they were like minded on most issues. He valued her wise judgment and knew she would do anything that would further the interests of the Faith. She admired his life of unstinting service. As the school developed and matured, certain Bahá'ís decided to build small houses on the hill overlooking the school. Leroy was one of them. Milly felt strongly that those who were essential to the work of the school should be assured of quarters on the property. She even envisaged building a few larger rooms in the dormitory for this purpose.

When that could not be done, she wrote to Leroy that she wished to help him build his "cottage" on the hill. When she mentioned this wish to Tom, he said, Do it at once. "You are always saying they are so sacrificial in serving the Cause, and this is the time for you to show them your love and appreciation." When she asked Leroy if she might do this, she wrote – and it is so typical of her whole life of giving – "It is not a matter of dollars – God forbid! Bahá'u'lláh has used me as His instrument. He knows how I am longing to be of service, and each must arise in the way he can. Bury it in your hearts, and we shall hold it as something sacred between us – and what a precious secret it is!"[7] Already in 1928 Millie had asked Leroy to be a co-executor of her estate. Tom Collins had made a fortune in metals in Alaska and Arizona, and much that was done in the Bahá'í world came through the silent outpouring of Milly Collins's generosity. The Guardian called her the "outstanding benefactress" of the Faith.

Sylvia's and Leroy's cottage became a most inviting and spiritually attractive place. Many close friends stayed there. Martha Root planted saplings outside it. Honor Kempton went from there to her new life in Alaska. There Marion Holley lay down one afternoon to "think about the Guardian", a remark which added new dimension to the spiritual life of one of Leroy's daughters. And there Isobel Locke Sabri became a Bahá'í. That is a story worth telling.

Isobel had been studying the Faith with her fellow student at Stanford, Leroy's daughter Farrukh. She had listened one night in her room as Farrukh, during four hours, poured out the story of the Faith, starting with the Shaykhís and ending with the World Order. Isobel knew it was the truth and it struck her with the force of lightning; she could only compare it with the experience of Mullá Ḥusayn, the first disciple of the Báb. She began cutting classes to read Bahá'í texts; her grades went down. Then one day during summer break she invited Farrukh to lunch to say she wished to become a Bahá'í. You should study more, Farrukh replied, come to Geyserville! Isobel, who knew she must work all summer to earn money for college, was in a quandary. Then she realized that what she wanted was at Geyserville and not at the university. The day after making that decision, she received a letter from Stanford offering a full scholarship for her final year. Many years later she realized she had met her first spiritual test.

Isobel was staying at the Ioas cottage. As a friend of Farrukh's she was a member of the family. After lunch one day as she and Leroy crossed on the path leading from the house to the clearing where they lunched, he asked her how her study of the teachings was coming. Well, she said half in jest, I want to become a Bahá'í but your daughter won't let me. That afternoon Leroy assembled a "representative group" of Bahá'ís and welcomed Isobel to the Faith. He asked if she had any questions. She said she wanted to learn about prayer; he designated Amelia Bowman* to help her. What he knew from long experience was that the soul is ready at a certain moment for this great step. If the step is not taken, life can intervene and the person may drift away, never to return. When the history of Geyserville is written, many such stories will form a part of it.

During the first decade or so of the school's existence, how did the people of Geyserville react to this growing invasion of their village each summer? When the school opened in 1927, they were mainly opposed to it, and even tried warning people against the Bahá'ís and their "pernicious teachings". The Bahá'ís were unable to counter such remarks other than to show friendship, and invite the citizens to their gatherings. But as a result of the warning, some in the area investigated the Faith and a few became believers. As the local citizenry took more part in the activities of the school, Shoghi Effendi noted that "they must be greatly impressed by the unity, love and enthusiasm animating the believers, and by the spirit of wide tolerance and appreciation with which they welcome the non-Bahá'í visitors to the school."[8] Finally, as the school flourished, the local people came to take pride in it. When Collins Hall was dedicated at the ninth session, these

* A pioneer to Norway in the second Seven Year Plan, and effective member of the National Teaching Committee.

once-suspicious people sent large bouquets of flowers for the occasion. They realized the school had brought fame to Geyserville, had made Geyserville known in every country and community where Bahá'ís lived, and had brought visitors to their small town from every corner of the globe.

The Guardian spoke to Milly Collins several times over the years about the conduct of the Bahá'ís at the school. Their conduct must be an example to the world, he said, a demonstration of the Bahá'í way of life. In a letter written to Shoghi Effendi in August 1936, Fred Schopflocher* painted for the Guardian a vivid picture of what was happening. "The work done there is most remarkable, and the little assistance I could give these last two years has resulted in a happiness which I experienced only in Haifa and the communities of Egypt. Out there we have solved the social phase of the Cause to an extent that the friends constitute one large family. There happiness reigns – the crust and fear of criticism have been replaced by mutual confidence and appreciation. The teaching work under these conditions is making great strides forward, as speakers and new teachers are being developed. There is so much harmony, so much encouragement, that even the most timid approach the platform with assurance to give talks and lectures, the spirit of which cannot be surpassed. They all leave Geyserville with the firm resolution to serve the Cause, and the assurance that they can do as well in their own communities after this unique experience. There is not a drone on the place, everyone is a contributor." Leroy sent a copy of this letter to John Bosch and Ella Cooper. He added: "I asked Fred if he would be here next summer. He said 'Try and keep me away'."

As long as Leroy lived in California the school remained where it was, growing each year in strength and enrollment. For a number of years he remained on the school committee until strong new Bahá'ís arose in the Bay area who could relieve him of the work. It was a prodigious job that John, George and Leroy, whom Sylvia called the Three Musketeers, did in founding the school and carrying it through its first decade. Yet in spite of the work it entailed, Leroy looked on Geyserville only with joy. Years later he said "the happiest days of my

* Siegfried Schopflocher served for fifteen years on the National Spiritual Assembly of the United States and Canada, then from 1948 until his death in 1953 as a member of the independent Canadian national body; he was named a Hand of the Cause in 1952.

life were spent in Geyserville, back in the days of building the summer school". He was breaking new ground and working with like-minded people to fulfill a vital need . . . it was satisfying work where he could see the result of his efforts.

The State took over much of the summer school property in 1972 in order to build a major highway. Gone was the redwood grove that had been named for Leroy after his passing;* gone were the cottages and the orchards. The school moved to the hills above Santa Cruz and re-opened as the Bosch Bahá'í School, thus perpetuating the memory of John and Louise. Shortly thereafter the same plaque was placed in the clearing of a stand of redwoods on the new school property, naming the grove in Leroy's memory.

Leroy felt the school would never have developed its powerful spiritual influence without the presence of the Bosches. In a tribute to them he called them unique: "Their integrity, their honor, their devotion, their service, their sweetness, and their effectiveness in presenting the teachings, have lent a spirit that cannot be duplicated. This, added to the dynamics underlying the entire program, has helped to establish an institution which bids fair to fulfill the Guardian's hopes that this school and others like it should in time become great Bahá'í institutions of learning."

It is fitting to end this discussion of Geyserville with Shoghi Effendi's words to John Bosch in 1932: "Your constant and magnificent services to the Cause, so devotedly and unostentatiously rendered, are a source of profound joy and strength to my heart."

And he added: "The Summer School at Geyserville is the object of my constant prayers."[9]

---

* The plaque stated: Leroy Ioas Memorial Grove, Beloved Hand of the Cause, Dedicated July 30, 1967.

# CHAPTER NINE

# The First Decade

LEROY was quietly becoming a pillar of the Faith in the west. He attracted activity to him as he sought ways to advance the interests of the Faith, and the number and variety of endeavors in which he was engaged during his first dozen years in San Francisco is prodigious.

The common denominator of his activities was the teaching work, in which he played his part on many fronts: speaker and class leader, administrator, organizer, and provider of spiritual sustenance.

"Leroy was always in the forefront of things," commented a friend, "large meetings, Geyserville, helping people, looking after them – in spite of all his duties". An intense power of concentration blocked out extraneous concerns. "There was a certain universality about the way he was oblivious of his environment," said another friend. "He did not allow it to interfere in any way with his services to the Faith. He just served in the way he knew; he did what he felt needed to be done." In a letter to Haifa in 1929, he asked a friend there to convey his deepest love to Shoghi Effendi. "What I particularly want him to know," he writes, "is that I am endeavoring to devote my life to this Cause, and to serve it as wisely as possible."

Already by the age of twenty-four he had entered the administrative field through election to the San Francisco Assembly, an association that lasted more than twenty years. Shortly thereafter he was elected for the first time as a delegate (from northern California) to the National Convention, though for some years, even when elected, he did not actually attend the Convention. He felt the limited energy and resources which he and Sylvia possessed were better spent on their short teaching trips than on attendance at the national meeting. That opinion changed as he took up services which required discussion in a national forum.

The San Francisco Bahá'í Assembly at the time of their arrival was the only one in the area, and it acted as a nerve center in generating activities not only up and down the West Coast but inland to states where there were no believers. The authority of the Assembly was not confined to the city – Bahá'í jurisdictions in those years did not follow civil boundaries – and therefore the community "of San Francisco" loosely comprised people of all the immediate region.

Several interesting initiatives were begun in the late twenties by the San Francisco Assembly, to which Leroy was already giving energetic leadership. One was to open a library and reading room in an attractive center located on the ground level of a downtown building. "This new center," he wrote to Ruhi Afnan* in 1929, "should be the nucleus for enlarged service and for putting into practice more of the principles of the Cause."

One of the principles being "put into practice" was that of racial unity, through the Assembly's active collaboration with black organizations of the city. Under the guidance of the Bahá'ís, a permanent Inter-Racial Amity Committee was established, which met once each month and whose officers were leaders of both black and white groups. It was an endeavor which Leroy felt opened an unlimited field to Bahá'í service. In a letter written at the time (1928) he commented that in America "there has been so much altruistic talk, with no . . . sincerity behind it, that the greatest force to teach the Cause in this particular field is service rather than speech."

The San Francisco community also initiated a series of world unity dinners, patterned after the large and successful International Fellowship dinners of the Portland Bahá'ís: Leroy had asked George Latimer of that city for specific information as to how they were planned and carried out. The first was to be a Chinese dinner, through which they hoped to reach out in fellowship to the one-sixth of the city that was of Chinese descent. Leroy loved to tell the story of another unity dinner, when two recent Bahá'ís, a German professor and his wife, wanted to attend the dinner after an all-day conference at the Bahá'í Library. But after leaving the Library they realized they didn't know which hotel the

---

* A cousin of Shoghi Effendi, living and serving the Guardian in Haifa, whom Leroy accompanied on a teaching trip in California in 1928.

dinner was being held at. Driving along, they saw a carfull of happy, radiant faces and decided to follow it and soon found themselves among the Bahá'ís and their friends at the dinner. This is how Bahá'ís should appear to others, Leroy would say.

Another innovative idea of the Assembly, which Leroy was asked to implement as one of his first tasks on arriving in the city, was to correspond with new believers elsewhere in the world who had been taught by San Franciscans such as the Hyde Dunns. This wonderful initiative created a bond between San Francisco and other parts of the Bahá'í world. A year later the Assembly established a Bahá'í Secretarial Bureau as an adjunct to its teaching committee, to organize the detailed advance work and follow-up work related to the visits of traveling teachers. This greatly diminished the stress associated with teaching campaigns. These various projects indicate the very practical and logical approach which the Assembly was taking to its work.

As we have noted, Leroy joined the distinguished Ella Goodall Cooper on the Assembly, she who as a young woman had visited 'Akká in the party of Phoebe Hearst and made two later pilgrimages with her mother. How enriching a friendship this was for him, and what a constant source of strength she was in the many teaching programs they undertook together! It was to her that Leroy initially turned for support with the idea of a world amity conference, and through her was able to gather the roster of outstanding personalities who brought public attention to the conference.

Fifteen years later, as a tribute to her outstanding life, he and Sylvia organized a surprise party on her seventieth birthday. Bahá'ís gathered from everywhere, eager to honor her. She herself later described in her flowing language what the evening had meant to her: "Beginning with the reading of the marvelous cablegram from our Guardian, we seemed to be, in an instant, transported to Haifa and the Holy Shrines . . . and we did not descend from those exalted heights during the entire evening. Then, when the gorgeous great cake was brought in, the spiritual thoughts that you, Leroy, were inspired to express regarding the light and the seventy candles, together with the reading of the Creative Word by you, Sylvia, and our dear Milly Collins, all conspired to bring a reverent hush over the gathering, a hush that was pregnant with meaning – we all, as one soul, suddenly knew, beyond the shadow of a doubt, that the Cause of God is invincible . . ."

As for his own personal teaching efforts, Leroy was always alert for openings to speak of the Faith, though not in the pushy aggressive manner of someone who intends to tell you something. That was not his style nor did he admire it or think it either wise or dignified. He was sensitive to what was appropriate. As an instance, if he mentioned some aspect of the teachings in his office, it went no further unless there was some sign of interest. As a Bahá'í friend described it, since he himself used the same technique, you ran the flag up the flagpole to see if anyone saluted. If there was response, he immediately followed up. In a letter to Carl Scheffler he gives a lengthy description of his conversation with a railroad official who was to pass through Chicago; would Carl please make a special effort to meet him and sustain his interest?

Leroy had a strong intuition as to the capacity of individuals. And when he sensed real potential, he went to great lengths to develop it and put it to use. One person in whom he sensed such capacity was Valera Allen.* She came to her first Bahá'í meeting in 1925 when he and Sylvia were living at the Bahá'í Center. She was then studying at a Methodist training school, and Leroy urged her to write a paper on the Bahá'í Faith for her school, knowing she would have to research the teachings to do so. (It was later published as an article in the Bahá'í journal, *Star of the West*.) After a period of study and association with the Bahá'ís, she heard there was to be a National Convention in San Francisco and wondered if she should attend. There was no formal declaration of membership then, and Leroy said, Well, if you consider yourself a Bahá'í, you should go, and if not, perhaps it's time you did something about that. His acceptance of the legitimacy of her attendance at the Convention, said her son Dwight, acted as a consolidation of her Bahá'í identity.

Another young woman whom we have already met (see p. 60–61) whose great capacity he recognized was Isobel Locke (later Sabri), and he took great pains with her spiritual development. One incident remained vivid in her mind. During her last year of college she decided to read everything in the university library on the Bahá'í Faith, not realizing that she might find books by Covenant-breakers. A brand new Bahá'í, she knew little of the Covenant and nothing of Covenant-

* John and Valera Allen moved to Swaziland in 1953, at the start of the Ten Year Crusade, and remained there for the rest of their lives.

breaking. The author of one such book lived nearby and Isobel determined to visit her to explain the wrongness of her views. When Leroy
heard of this, he immediately phoned Isobel to stay "right where you
are", that he was coming down to see her, a drive of some thirty miles.
"So he sat me down and talked to me about the Covenant of God and
the great importance of staying away from Covenant-breakers, that it
was a disease and if you associate with lepers you will eventually have
leprosy. It not only taught me the significance of the Covenant, it
impressed on me the seriousness with which Bahá'ís regard their
Faith . . . for a man of his position to leave his office in the middle of
the week and travel by car to see a humble university student who was
making a decision to see a Covenant-breaker! . . . it greatly impressed
me with how serious he considered the matter and that other things
were of less consequence."

Later when she was planning to move to Great Britain as a pioneer,
he invited her to attend a class on Bahá'í administration. She missed
the third class and had a call from him the next morning. Where were
you last night? It was the last class she missed, as she realized he had set
up that class for her benefit, to prepare her to be an effective pioneer
and to build sound Bahá'í institutions and communities.

We have seen the care he took in developing the new Bahá'ís in
Oakland following Orcella Rexford's visit, going there every week for a
year and a half to conduct study classes. When they were ready to
form their Assembly in 1925, he wrote to the national secretary, Horace
Holley, describing how active they were, having organized a circulating
library and found a meeting place in the Business Women's Club.
Then he suggested that a word of welcome into the fold from the
National Assembly would be an inspiration to their further development. At the same time he wrote to Haifa, asking if there might be a
word of welcome from someone there. Shoghi Effendi responded with
a cablegram ("Oakland Bahá'ís welcome to fold, assure California
friends affectionate prayers, Shoghi") These documents certainly constitute a precious legacy for that community.

The believers often turned to Leroy when a speaker was needed or
an event required someone of dignity and acumen, so that his presentation skills developed rapidly. His regular study of the Writings meant
that he was constantly acquiring a more profound understanding of
the Revelation. He was drawn in particular to the rational expositions

found in 'Abdu'l-Bahá's talks in the West, which Leroy frequently cited as the "textbooks" for those wishing to teach. Through constant reading of the Guardian's writings he caught Shoghi Effendi's vision of the application of the teachings to world problems. This wide reading made him an impressive speaker – he knew what he was talking about – and as a friend commented, his attractive and conciliatory manner made one want to listen to him.

Part of Leroy's charm as a speaker was his ability to tell stories. His lively sense of humor was one of his special characteristics and he had the story-teller's gift for finding an appropriate story for every occasion. He exhibited this talent more freely as he came into his own as a maturing adult, and learned, as has every public speaker, that one story will reinforce a point more quickly than a dozen explanations.

The San Francisco Bahá'ís actively sought association with other organizations and Leroy found himself taking part in affairs sponsored by a number of different interest groups. At a benefit concert of the Filipino Association, of which he had become a member (there was a very large Filipino community in the city), he acted as one of three judges of the annual oratorical contest. He and Dr. D'Evelyn both spoke at meetings of the Rosicrucian Fellowship, sometimes on topics concerning animal life in which Dr. D'Evelyn had particular interest. One night Leroy's subject was the evolution of animal life . . . a curious topic perhaps, but an opening into another group in the kaleidoscopic life of the city. He represented the Bahá'ís on many ecumenical panels and took part with great enthusiasm in such programs as the Symposium of Living Religions organized by Dr. George Hedley of the Pacific School of Religion.

These efforts sometimes had far-reaching consequences. One in particular gave Leroy immense satisfaction, as he felt it led to the opening of an entire country to the Faith. He had been invited, because of his work for the World Unity Conference, to speak to the Americanization Department of the Women's Christian Temperance Union. The WCTU had some forty departments covering various avenues of public welfare; their Americanization centers were in reality international centers. Ella Cooper and another Bahá'í had joined this "great organization of praying women" with just such a purpose in mind. It was a large meeting held for the benefit of immigrants, among them Filipinos. One of the Filipinos, a recent graduate of Stanford, was a rice expert returning to work for his government. He became so enamored of the Bahá'í teachings that after brief study with Leroy he accepted the Faith before returning to Manila, where he intended to gather his friends together to begin spreading the teachings there. He wrote back that formerly it had been "my Lord Jesus Christ", now it was "my Lord Jesus Christ, 'Abdu'l-Bahá and Bahá'u'lláh". Leroy wrote to the Guardian and asked him to pray for this radiant young man.

Leroy was speaking at innumerable Bahá'í-sponsored events as well. One example alone shows the extent of his commitment. At the request of the Oakland Bahá'í Assembly he accepted to travel across the Bay on nine consecutive Fridays, to speak at a series of public meetings arranged by the Assembly. His topics were a challenge in themselves, beginning with the influence of Christ and ending with the goal of a new world order. These took place in February and March of 1934 when he could be publicized in his new role as a member of the Bahá'í National Spiritual Assembly.

Along with his activities in and near San Francisco, he was travelling to outlying, even distant, areas to hold study classes and give public talks. Through such endeavor by him and other traveling teachers, both the Phoenix and Santa Barbara Assemblies were formed.

A noted Bahá'í teacher, Elizabeth Greenleaf, had settled in Phoenix and Leroy would assist with her teaching efforts whenever he went through on a business trip. He reports to George Latimer on a typical visit: "Sylvia and I went to Phoenix on December 12th and had quite a wonderful day with the new group there. They met us when the train came in at 6:00 a.m. We were not yet up, and they stayed with us until the train left at 11:30 p.m. In fact we looked like a bridal couple returning to the train, as they had given Sylvia a large bouquet, and they joked about throwing rice at us! Two meetings were held, one in the afternoon and another in the evening. In all, there are about fifteen or eighteen whom I would say are confirmed believers and Elizabeth agrees with that assessment . . . the group will be organized into an Assembly on April 21st."

On another trip to Phoenix John Bosch was with him, and Elizabeth, who had a lively sense of humor, seeing the two come in together, the one so white-haired, the other so young, said: "Ah! here come Father Time and Happy New Year himself!" John was with him on another trip, an intensive four-day circuit through the great San Joaquin and Santa Clara valleys of California. He was particularly pleased with this trip, which covered much the same itinerary he had followed the year before with Ruhi Afnan. He wrote to Ruhi: "I feel this trip one of the most beneficial to the Cause that I have ever made . . . each meeting seemed to be confirmed by the Master."

When the Santa Barbara community grew to Assembly status, Henrietta Wagner wrote to "dear friends throughout the world" of how blessed they had been in their development by the visits and inspiration of many traveling teachers – Albert Vail, Horace Holley, Ali-Kuli Khan, others. "Our brother Leroy", she notes, "has been most faithful, making numerous trips from San Francisco to spend a Sunday with us . . . he must pass two nights in a Pullman car in order to have a Sunday with us. This gifted young man was a schoolboy when 'Abdu'l-Bahá came in 1912. The seeds our Beloved sowed at that time have borne abundant fruit in the life of this devoted servant. He is one of our most capable Western speakers, fluent and logical and his message goes direct to the hearts."

Leroy wrote to May Maxwell in December 1926 – he is twenty-nine years old – that he and Sylvia will endeavor to go to Vancouver after the new year and see if they cannot be of some help to "the diligent souls there" . . . to which Mrs. Maxwell in her warm and loving way replied: "I am simply overjoyed at the prospect of your both going to Vancouver . . . I can imagine nothing which would bring greater confirmation, growth and new life to that faithful little group of ten or fifteen souls who are struggling up into the light without any other teacher save God and His Creative Utterance."

He went often to Visalia where Grace Holley lived, and to Fresno, Santa Maria, Reno – in fact, according to Sylvia, he really did "pioneering" work throughout the area. He would go anywhere where the Bahá'ís thought they could bring together an audience. In September of 1929 he writes to John Bosch that the Berkeley youth had interested some college people and "asked me to give a series of talks – so the next three Thursdays I will be doing so". Of course, at times there was little or no audience to compensate the effort. One rainy night he and the chairman arrived to find only one person in the audience. But Leroy went ahead with his talk and at the end said he was very happy to come to speak of Bahá'u'lláh, even if there was only one person who wished to listen. At that, the man got up and said, "Well I'm the custodian of the building, and when you have finished, we can both go home".

In 1928 he received a request from May Maxwell for suggestions as to how the teaching work on the West Coast should be coordinated. His analysis, which he had submitted to several friends for comment, is interesting. It begins with a statement of the two-fold purpose of the Geyserville summer school: to develop competent teachers and to confirm newly-attracted persons. He then goes on: "The teaching work on the Coast should be coordinated with the work of the summer school committee, so that new study groups formed during the fall and winter may have as their goal attendance at the summer school, where the students will become confirmed. The program committee of the summer school might well be utilized by the National Teaching Committee as its representative on the Coast, or as a subcommittee. Thus the two elements of teaching in this territory would be more or less under the same direction – and continuity certainly produces results."

The result was that he found himself on the first Pacific Coast Teaching Committee, a sub-committee of the National Teaching Committee. Its membership was composed of the Geyserville program committee and several other strong Bahá'ís. He had suggested for appointment to the committee a new Bahá'í of Los Angeles, Sara Witt, whom he described to May Maxwell as a "young, enthusiastic Bahá'í who is very energetic, and whose enthusiasm will do much to aid the development of the work in Southern California" – a typical example of his getting new talent into the field of activity.

But being a Bahá'í is not a profession and Leroy had another life, which centered on his demanding job. As we have noted, he spent his entire working life with the Southern Pacific railroad. Advancement was slow during the long years of the economic depression and he was unable to move forward at the pace which his ability clearly warranted. Only in 1942 did the dam break, when he was appointed assistant to the Vice-President. Others were promoted at the same time, men with whom he had long worked and with whom he had developed a true camaraderie; the new Vice-President was one of them. Leroy was in Chicago when the new position was publicly announced, and he sent a copy of the announcement to Sylvia with the notation "this makes it official". For both of them it meant much greater financial freedom. It also meant membership in the best clubs of the city, which gave him valuable contacts and standing in his Bahá'í work.

Leroy was able through his work to assist the Faith in numerous ways. As he was required to travel frequently he combined this whenever possible with short teaching trips, thus helping to fill the great need for traveling teachers.

In difficult economic times his position enabled him to help individual Baha'is, like his young friend Ali Yazdi, who found his first job through Southern Pacific, which took him to Sacramento as the first resident Bahá'í in that city which had been visited by 'Abdu'l-Bahá. Leroy was able to find employment for other Bahá'ís, from work at railroad hotels to guard duty on trains that transported illegal aliens. More importantly, during the war years when travel was strictly controlled, his railroad connections enabled him to assist a number of pioneers to reach their posts in various parts of the continent.

Over the years, as he spent long hours riding the trains, he developed a useful habit. It began with his trip west with Sylvia in 1919 when he wrote the first of his lengthy "train letters". Thereafter throughout his life he was to seize the opportunity of train journeys to maintain his large correspondence.

Being in charge of the passenger service gave him a certain freedom of action. An instance: when a well-known theologian traveled west to speak at a Stanford lecture series, Arthur Dahl telephoned Leroy to ask how they were going to "get to him" with the Message. Leroy said he had "already taken care of it". He had simply made sure that a small selection of Bahá'í books was placed in the theologian's compartment for the return trip east.

Leroy and Arthur, an investment broker, had a shared interest in reaching people of prominence with the teachings, and both were particularly interested in attracting business executives, realizing the value of practical executive minds in the Faith. In the later years of his career, Leroy's work stature certainly inspired confidence in the Faith in this segment of society which, at that time, was conspicuously under-represented in the Bahá'í community. As Arthur Dahl put it, business men saw in Leroy a successful, well-rounded man, which led them to feel that if "this" is something he is a part of, there must be something to it.

Another small example of how he used his work in the interests of the Faith: he wrote a letter to the then chairman of the National Spiritual Assembly, Allen McDaniel, a distinguished architectural engineer who was actively associated for thirty years with construction of the House of Worship, concerning shipment of the concrete casts for the Temple. "Can you let me know," he asks Allen, "how the casts are being shipped to Chicago, and how many carloads are involved. It may help in cementing contacts with our railroad friends here, and in providing an opportunity to tell someone else of the Temple and the Cause it symbolizes."

# CHAPTER TEN

# Race Unity

THE crux of all Bahá'u'lláh's teachings is the oneness of the human race. Leroy had been brought up with this conviction, and it underlay all his attitudes and his approach to and treatment of people. In his work life, he was given unique opportunity to demonstrate this radical and unifying principle of his Faith.

The most important use he could make of his business life in this regard was in helping the Black employees of Southern Pacific railroad. They were numerous. In those days travelers were surrounded by help on the long train journeys, and work on the railroads as porters and waiters was a step up in dignity; it was important work which led eventually to the formation of the Union of Sleeping Car Porters organized by the great civil rights figure A. Phillip Randolph.

Leroy became president of the Southern Pacific Employees' Club in 1925. This gave him stature to negotiate wage problems and better working conditions and as one employee put it, Mr. Ioas "did a lot" for the Black employees. He never failed to shake hands with Black employees whom he knew, even when he was with a group of executives inspecting the trains; perhaps the Black employee was a Bahá'í, perhaps just someone he knew, but there were always startled looks from the other executives. This was the reality of life in the 1920s and 30s. He experienced opposition many times over the years as he stood firm on the race issue but he felt many victories were won.

Leroy was still in Chicago during the race riots in the summer of 1919. He himself was able to save from the rioters a Black woman stranded on a bridge, and he and several other Bahá'ís went immediately to the home of a prominent Black believer, Mrs. Mary Clark, to offer assistance when the house was attacked by white people. By chance the Executive Secretary of the Chicago branch of the National Association for the Advancement of Colored People was visiting her. Leroy found that pregnant with meaning, as he wrote to her later: "The fact that the Executive Secretary should have been visiting your home at the time of the attack, and was able to see with his own eyes the desire of the Bahá'ís to overcome this race prejudice, is, I feel, really providential and will no doubt be the means of attracting many to the Cause." He suggests ("knowing that you are as anxious as I am to do anything that will further the Glad Tidings of the Appearance of Bahá'u'lláh") that she might write an article for the *Crisis*, official organ of the NAACP, telling of the principles for which Bahá'ís stand and the efforts being made to live up to them, "using the fact that while the colored people were being persecuted by most of the whites in Chicago, the Bahá'ís did all they possibly could to assist their brothers and sisters".

He and the well-known Bahá'í teacher Albert Vail were both members of the NAACP and when he accompanied Vail in the spring of that year to meetings called at the Black YMCA in Indianapolis, they made excellent contacts, including the Secretary of the local NAACP. Many doors seemed to be opening, and on his way to California he wrote a series of letters: to the Minister who invited them in Indianapolis, to the NAACP secretary, to a woman attending the meetings who asked for information, to a Bahá'í who could follow up on their work – all with the goal of continuing the entry that had been made into this community. "The terrible race riots", he writes to the YMCA director, "have demonstrated more than anything else the need of some Divine Power to overcome the animosity which has been bred into the hearts and minds of the people, both colored and white. Certain hatreds can be overcome by training but the feeling of hatred which is in the hearts, and which is really the cause of these outbursts, can only be overcome by a power that has influence over the hearts of men. This power is none other than the 'Power of the Love of God'. The Bahá'ís are endeavoring in every conceivable manner of demonstration and teaching to inculcate into their white and colored friends the Absolute Oneness of the world of humanity . . . every force for good should now exert itself to create this harmony and union, and these forces should unite their efforts and show a united force to the world for the upliftment of mankind." Leroy was twenty-three when he carried on such correspondence.

One of the reasons he urged Bahá'ís into close cooperation with workers in this field is that he had found Black organizations welcomed leadership from the Bahá'ís. In a 1929 report of the Pacific Coast Teaching Committee he noted that all the minority groups ("but particularly the Negroes") are seeking a pathway toward the brotherhood of man. Yet in their struggles they find that "a limited vision of the goal, with stunted leaders, down a darkened path, are greatly handicapping the work. Therefore they welcome the leadership of the Bahá'ís in harmonizing the races and in assisting in the diffusion of these ideals." Some months earlier he had written to friends in Vancouver that the Negroes "wish to work with the Bahá'ís in establishing a permanent inter-racial amity committee".

Many years later, on Leroy's last teaching trip to America, he spoke passionately on the subject of racism and related it to the impotence of Christianity. The greatest proof of the "utter failure of the churches", he said, "is that in 1964 they should be arguing in Washington as to whether a whole section of the population should be given their civil rights".

After moving to California, he urged the San Francisco Bahá'ís to enter into associative activity with the NAACP, so as to increase entry of the Faith into the important segment of the city served by the Association. He himself joined the San Francisco branch, which eventually gave him occasion to speak at several NAACP meetings. He well knew that 'Abdu'l-Bahá had rendered the Association historic by speaking at its fourth annual meeting during His first visit to Chicago.

Leroy was able to make use of stories even at emotion-laden moments, one of which occurred at an NAACP meeting after some distressing events had occurred in the city. He told a long story of a black man who moved to a town and went to the church of his denomination nearest him. There were some glances in his direction. He goes back the next week and again people look at him. The third week the minister comes and says you should go to "your" church on the other side of town, it only causes confusion if you come here. The man goes out, very distressed, thinking how he had been baptized with the blood of the Lamb – when was the Kingdom of God coming? As he walks along, God comes to him and asks why he is so distraught. He says, for three weeks I've been trying to get into that church. God says, three weeks! Why, that church was built forty years ago and I'm *still* trying to get into it! Leroy then drew some spiritual comfort from the story and did not neglect to comment on the coming of the Kingdom. He became the first white life member of the organization, which was a cause of much pride to him.

There was at the time a social club in San Francisco called the Cosmos Club. Its members were Black Americans of prominence. Leroy had become known to them through his defense of employees at the railroad, and was, as another Bahá'í observed, "very much revered" by the people running the club. They made him an honorary member, a tribute not just to him but to the stand of the Faith on the issue of race. At a black-tie musicale and ball in early 1944, with the famed tenor Roland Hayes as the featured artist, Leroy was the guest of honor. He asked to invite some of his Bahá'í friends and included Anthony and Mamie Seto, a Caucasian-Chinese couple,* the Dahls, Jamaican Rosa Shaw and her husband, and a few other believers. He was also invited to speak at some of their gatherings; in 1946 one member, a Minister, said he was going to make the "Ioas talk" the subject of his sermon the following Sunday.

An early student at Geyserville, who watched the school develop over the years, feels that one of Leroy's legacies to race unity was the growth of the school from being simply a teacher training institute to being a living example of Bahá'í fellowship. "The fruit of the Cause", Leroy wrote to Horace Holley in a 1930 report on the summer school, "is the realization of that ideal condition when the different elements of the human family live together happily, peaceably and enthusiastically . . . Only when Bahá'í community life develops into a radiant working body is the Cause functioning properly. In the summer school," he adds, "we have been endeavoring to develop this very thing, that is, that the spirit of unity in fellowship and happiness should be augmented, and a conscious, spiritualized conduct on the part of the friends be realized . . . Then the hearts of all who contact us may find the path to a mode of life they have not before known. If this spirit becomes as strong as the Master wishes, it will be a power of attraction for all who come under its influence." We have seen Fred

---

* Mamie Seto was for several years a member of the National Assembly, from which she resigned in order to settle with her husband in Hong Kong during the Ten Year Crusade.

Schopflocher's comparison of the spirit of Geyserville with that of Haifa. Geyserville became an oasis of unity where guests found a new dimension to the concept of unity.

One guest at the school who felt this attraction was from quite another background, a young Russian doctor whose strong belief in brotherhood was based, not on his atheistic upbringing, but on logical and scientific concepts. "He came to the summer school for a day or two," Leroy reports, "but the friendship of the friends was so warm that he stayed not only through that week but through the entire session. When he left, he wept, saying that never in his life had he experienced such a true oneness and harmony among people, and that he felt more intimately associated with the Bahá'ís than with his own family."

It is evident that Leroy was always reaching out and speaking on the principle of oneness, and that he longed to see more diversity in the Bahá'í communities. "We should not be concerned", he wrote to Dr. Sarah Pereira (chairman of the Inter-Racial Teaching Committee) in 1953, "with the attitudes of non-Bahá'ís, either white or black, but should carry forward our work according to the teachings of Bahá'u-'lláh, and the example of 'Abdu'l-Bahá, with audacity and wisdom."

As Leroy observed the extraordinary results of Louis Gregory's* teaching trips in raising up a whole generation of outstanding Black Bahá'ís, he urged Louis to concentrate exclusively on teaching. He felt such a great and empowered teacher – empowered by 'Abdu'l-Bahá – should not waste time on administrative matters. It was a much misunderstood opinion. Yet in 1953 Leroy was quoting the Guardian, in a letter to a San Francisco friend, to the effect that if many of the distinguished leaders of the Faith would arise and devote their energies exclusively to teaching and pioneering, the administrative aspect of the Faith would not suffer.

His sense of the urgency of reaching Black Americans was certainly confirmed by the Guardian. In a talk in Washington DC in 1963, Leroy recalled that one of the sorrows of Shoghi Effendi's life had been that there were not more Black Bahá'ís in the United States – after sixty

* A member of the National Assembly and one of the foremost teachers of the Faith, who was posthumously named a Hand of the Cause. A biography of his life, *To Move the World*, by Gayle Morrison, was published in 1982 by the U.S. Bahá'í Publishing Trust, Wilmette, Ill.

years, only a handful. Shoghi Effendi had said that if they were brought into the Faith, *they* would teach the white people. "Concentrate," said the Guardian, "on these people who are seeking justice!"

"Bind ye the broken with the hands of justice and crush the oppressor . . . with the rod of the commandments of your Lord," was the task laid by Bahá'u'lláh upon the rulers of America.

The initiatives described in the last few chapters were all begun within a dozen years of Leroy's arrival in California. In a later chapter we will consider another activity into which he was drawn during those years, which would be of historic significance. But first a look at how Leroy became a gifted and influential teacher.

# CHAPTER ELEVEN

# The Teacher

"TEACHING was always the dearest thing in the world to the heart of dear Leroy. It was his life," wrote Hand of the Cause William Sears to the National Spiritual Assembly Secretary, David Ruhe, a few months after Leroy's passing. "He was perhaps the most gifted of all teachers I have known at answering the questions of seekers at fireside meetings."

It is interesting to try to analyze *why* Leroy was so effective as a teacher. What were the qualities which he possessed or developed that constituted his "gift" of teaching?

Leroy taught on the basis of the authoritative Writings, which he was constantly engaged in studying. His daughter remembers one of the rare occasions when he stayed at home for several days because of illness. He spent the entire day wrapped in a warm shawl, with the sun on his back, reading and reading, and talking to himself under his breath with a far-away look in his eyes, as he went over 'Abdu'l-Bahá's argumentation of some complex subject. By contrast, that which was a pure gift, not derived from study, was his fertile and inventive mind, so that talking with him or listening to him was a creative experience. His views were refreshing and original and when applied to the teachings caught and held the attention of the seeker.

The teachings were not an intellectual exercise for him. He lived what he talked about and this caused the seeker to take what he said seriously. Jack McCants, a pioneer to the South Pacific and later a member of the U.S. National Spiritual Assembly, summed it up: "A man seeking truth does not like being fed theories or ideas which have not been digested by the teacher himself. I find it very hard to accept those people who are quick to urge some devoted soul to sacrificial service and would be the last to go and do it themselves. Leroy talked about what he knew from his own experience."

He certainly knew sacrifice from his own experience. We have noted some of the sacrifices he made for his Faith, from standing up for principle – in itself a sacrifice of caring what people think of you – to expending the last ounce of energy to go out and do what is needed. On one occasion when Marion Holley was ill and unable to speak at a large public meeting in Reno, another Bahá'í was asked to go but could not. However, he noted in his diary that "dear Leroy, burdened as he is, has agreed to do it". A minor incident typical of the constant calls to which he responded. The important thing for him was that the teaching work go forward and not that he was fatigued or overburdened.

Dwight Allen recalls that Leroy was always the symbol of sacrifice to the Allen family, even if it was only to attend the National Assembly meetings. The west coast was far more isolated in the thirties, propeller planes were both slow and unpressurized. Leroy regularly had to take oxygen to make the trip.

Leroy had a profound respect for each human being. He remembered their names and what interested them. They were important to him and their spiritual life was of concern to him. And they knew it. William Sears remembered serving on the San Francisco Assembly with him: "I was the greenest of fresh wide-eyed believers in those days, and Leroy was the kindest and most helpful of those who encouraged us on our way."

"He always seemed to be interested in me as a person," said one of the pioneers. "That was a very important trait of his: he made people feel that he cared about them and he was able to stir them on to greater service as a result of this caring and sharing. And he always had time for conversation – trivial or profound, he was always willing to share." Another close friend commented: "He would never talk down to people. He talked as if you understood what he was saying – which was one of the things that made him a great teacher."

He imparted a vision: "He tended to bring one up to his own level of devotion and his own eagerness to spread the teachings of the Faith," recalls a much younger Bahá'í. "He spoke to me as an equal and gave my questions serious and meaningful thought. I recall vividly how good this made me feel and it prepared me to fully ponder his

*Charles and Maria Ioas, Leroy's father and mother*

*Leroy at two years old. His parents became Bahá'ís at this time*

*Leroy as a high school student*

*First job*

*Young people at the Temple grounds in Wilmette: Sylvia far left, Leroy standing*

*Leroy as a young married man*

*At Geyserville summer school, Leroy with a children's class. His daughters are on either side of him, Farrukh at his right, Anita left*

*With Farrukh*                    *At home*

*The first Regional Bahá'í Convention in California, San Francisco 1926*

*Early years in California. Clockwise from top left: with John Bosch and Elizabeth Greenleaf (front centre), helping to form the Bahá'í community in Phoenix, Arizona; At Geyserville with Shahnaz Waite; and with Martha Root; with John Bosch and Fred Schopflocher; at the office*

*At Geyserville in the 1930s: In front of Bosch house. Back row from left: Mountfort Mills, Leroy Ioas, Stanley Kemp, Horace Holley, Alfred Lunt.*
*Middle row: Bijou Straun, Kevah Munson, Mr. French, Nellie French, Louise Bosch, Harry Munson, John Bosch.*
*Kneeling: Sylvia Ioas, George Latimer, Evelyn Kemp*

*At Geyserville. Top from left: John and Louise Bosch; John and Louise Bosch with Martha Root at Collins Hall. Center: John Bosch and Leroy talking to Louise Caswell. Bottom: Break between classes at Collins Hall: Mark Tobey, George Latimer and Marion Holley; Leroy; Leroy and Sylvia at the steps leading to Collins Hall*

*With Milly Collins and Harlan Ober in front of the Philanthropic Club, February 1939*

*At the Temple grounds during National Convention*

*Upstairs in the House of Worship, with stonework to be affixed to the building*

answers and treasure their worth." A niece and her husband visited him at his sister's house when he was convalescing from heart trouble. "We had been warned not to excite him by asking about his work," they said. "But when we did bring it up, he became very animated, rose up in his chair and discussed the importance for our generation of arising to teach the Faith. It is our legacy, he said. It was like electricity in the air."

Many persons of stature were drawn to the Faith through his answers to the question – posed in various ways – what does all this have to do with the real world? "He would find in newspapers, magazines, whatever," Isobel Sabri recalls, "those things of significance to the teachings, those things that accorded with the way the Faith explains current affairs or history or economics or whatever. His capacity to apply the teachings to the affairs of life, and to explain the teachings in terms of the trends that were taking place in the world, was really outstanding."

"He was neither effusive nor charismatic," remembers another colleague, "in the sense of attracting people by emotion. He attracted them through his great depth of knowledge and his understanding of the teachings. He had a great breadth of vision of where the Faith was going and where the teachings were taking us and what their implications were in terms of the affairs of the world." Another friend commented: "He had a grasp of the problems of the world and was in a way a futurist, in that he had a good idea of what would happen if things continued in the projection they were taking and why the Faith was needed to put us in the right direction. More than most people, he merged these two needs, the practical and the metaphysical."

We have mentioned five attributes which contributed to his success as a teacher: basing his teachings on Scripture and not on opinion; living the teachings, not just speaking of them; respecting each human being; elevating people to a new vision; and showing the relevance of the teachings to world problems. Now we turn to the most important quality, one which assured that his teaching efforts would be fruitful: he was centered in the Covenant, he was in contact, mental, physical and spiritual, with the center of the Covenant on earth.

We have seen how, as a newly married young man just arrived in the West, he wrote to 'Abdu'l-Bahá, expressing his desire to serve Bahá'u'lláh. He wrote to Shoghi Effendi shortly after the Guardian's return from several months of solitude in Switzerland: "Although only one of [Bahá'u'lláh's] many humble servants in this far away country, may I offer you my utmost loyalty and my pledge of active coopera- tion. May our deeds show forth the degree of our sincerity." The Guardian answered on February 24, 1923. "His thoughts go out in tender love," his secretary wrote, "to his dear friends in the west who have so faithfully laboured for the promulgation of the Cause during his period of retirement. . . . What gave him still greater joy was to know that unity and harmony prevail throughout all your activities." It was an impersonal letter, written to someone the Guardian did not know. But it reflected that loving friendship which Shoghi Effendi extended to all those who expressed fidelity to the Cause.

In the ensuing years, Leroy continued to turn to the Guardian. In 1925 he is reporting on the World Unity Conference, on the new Assembly in Oakland, on the many new Bahá'ís resulting from a study group of thirty-five. Dr. Esslemont replied for the Guardian with the hope that "you may all become pure and willing channels for the descent of the Holy Spirit and that through you many souls may be quickened to new life".

The third letter Leroy sent the Guardian, in 1927, was for the purpose of sending an article in the *San Francisco Examiner* sympathetic to the recent martyrdoms in Persia. In the letter Leroy also shared with Shoghi Effendi news of successful endeavors in race unity work in Santa Barbara; he reported on a meeting he addressed at the "Truth Center"; and he asked for the Guardian's prayers for the spiritual advancement of the Oakland Assembly. He included the names of the persons involved in these activities. Ethel Rosenberg,* in replying for the Guardian, said Shoghi Effendi was greatly encouraged to see the Bahá'ís carrying out the "commands and counsels" of the Master in regard to the race issue, and that he took "special note of the names you mention". As an addendum to the third letter, Shoghi Effendi for the first time adds a postscript in his own handwriting, with the tender signature: Your true brother, Shoghi.

---

* The first Englishwoman to become a Bahá'í in England; she spent some months in Haifa assisting the Guardian in his work. See Robert Weinberg's biography *Ethel Jenner Rosenberg: The Life and Times of England's Outstanding Bahá'í Pioneer Worker* (Oxford: George Ronald, 1995).

From this time onward, Leroy's communications with Haifa increased steadily and his thinking was ever more deeply imbued with the Guardian's vision. His letters always contained "enclosures" – clippings, photographs, Geyserville programs, later, detailed reports of progress in accomplishing the Seven Year Plan. His letters posed many questions: he wonders about the meaning of the Bahá'í cycle and Dispensation and about other Prophets coming under the "shadow" of Bahá'u'lláh, what constitutes Bahá'í marriage in the light of 'Abdu'l-Bahá's comments on the Aqdas, what emphasis should be given to world order as a social aspect of the Faith, would the Guardian comment on Leroy's understanding of the means for establishing the Lesser Peace, should pioneers receive support and should gifted teachers be put "on budget", what are the functions of the Hands of the Cause of God. This latter question was posed in a letter of 1935, to which the Guardian replied: ". . . They are numerous and varied, and include teaching as well as administrative work, and such activities as the Guardian may choose to ask them to perform. Their number has not been fixed by the Master. But as to their relationship to the Guardian, the Will is quite clear . . ." From the Guardian's answers (we do not have Leroy's letters) it is easy to trace Leroy's preoccupations at any given time – issues of teaching, National Assembly discussions, the proper functioning of national committees, and so forth.

We mention this communication with Haifa because it indicates how Leroy, like other Bahá'ís, turned to the source of guidance, and was himself sustained by contact with the designated Interpreter of the Word of God. In this way also the Guardian, in addition to his assiduous study of national reports and the news brought him by visitors, learned of those who were carrying on the affairs of the Faith. For instance, while Shoghi Effendi knew of Leroy's steady participation in the Geyserville school it was not until he later read a history of the school that he learned of Leroy's preeminent role in its creation. It is touching indeed to see the gratitude expressed by the Sign of God on Earth* in his letters to those who arose to assist in lightening his burdens. He knew who they were; he was closely following their work. Already in 1935 Shoghi Effendi noted in a postscript to Leroy: "I am well aware of the part you have played and the share you have had in

---

* A title used in 'Abdu'l-Bahá's Will to refer to Shoghi Effendi.

clarifying, in promoting and in enforcing the challenging and distin-
guishing principles of the Faith of God in this Day."

But Leroy was not only a speaker. Another aspect of his teaching
was the stream of letters which came from his pen. We could call these
his "teaching letters". There were many hundreds of them.

Because the teaching work meant more to him than any other
service, so the pioneers, those who put that work above home and
comfort, were particularly dear to him. He took great pains to help
them and to encourage them.

A simple example is the care he gave to the request of a young
Swiss pioneer, René Steiner – whom Leroy considered "an outstanding
young man with a great future in the Faith" – for his suggestions on
improving a slide program concerning religions in the Holy Land.
Leroy went through the program, slide by slide, suggested removing
some and substituting others, offered to find a few slides in Haifa to
illustrate the life of Christ, then suggested changes in the text to render
it more understandable to the listener. This was done in Haifa in 1962,
in the midst of daily meetings and just six months prior to the election
of the House of Justice. With it he sent warm words of encouragement: "Your bearing, your persuasive presentation of the Faith, and
the dynamic spirit with which your words are charged, all tend to win
souls to the Cause of God. This is a rare gift and I hope it will increase
as your days of service in the Cause of God go forward."

In a letter of 1965 to pioneers Ellsworth and Ruth Blackwell in
Haiti, he writes ". . . you have indeed fulfilled the Guardian's highest
wishes. He said repeatedly how he wished those who went pioneering
would look at their post as their home, and plan to remain. . . . This
you two devoted souls have done and have thus become an example to
many of the Bahá'ís of the world – at least you are to me." Then he
shared a story of Fujita and 'Abdu'l-Bahá, who had gone to Tiberias so
that the Master could take the baths, as He suffered all His life with
frozen feet from the time of banishment from Baghdad to Constantinople. It was the Master's habit to look at the accommodations given
his retinue and He saw that Fujita was given a very small room. He
asked Fujita if it were large enough and Fujita answered that anything
was good, as long as he was with the Master. 'Abdu'l-Bahá replied to
the effect that here on earth, Fujita, they may give you a small room
but I guarantee that in heaven, you will have a mansion. Then Leroy

added the point of the story: "You two are building your mansions in heaven!"

To "Mother Fisher", the elderly mother of Valera Allen, who joined her family in pioneering to Swaziland during the Ten Year Crusade, Leroy found the time to write this loving note: "Your action will become an example to many, many Bahá'ís – for when they see how you, at your advanced age, have gone forth to teach the Faith, they will wish to do likewise."

To pioneers from Goteberg who had been on pilgrimage, he sent a message of affection and explained why the Bahá'ís feel so close to one another: "It was so good to be with you while you were here, and to get to know you better, and to love you more . . . This is the great mystery of the Faith, that association in service deepens the love of the friends and makes them all closer to the Holy Spirit."

Louise Caswell, one of his friends from the early years in Geyserville, turned her steps southward and lived the remainder of her life as a pioneer in Latin America. She recalled the great influence he had on her life, because he was the one who asked her to go to Panama. And she went. "When I arrived in Panama," she wrote to Sylvia some years later, "there were two letters waiting to welcome me. One was from Shoghi Effendi and the other from Leroy. What a blessing!"

Sometimes his advice was very practical. To a relative in a pioneer post, frustrated and depressed because of disunity on the National Assembly due to an ambitious personality, he counsels that she concentrate solely on teaching the indigenous people, while avoiding controversy but standing firm on questions of principle. People of this ambitious type, he adds, need opposition to thrive, and when you remove the opposition, they sooner or later change or leave the field of battle. In teaching the local people, he cautions, "don't try to make them perfect Bahá'ís or perfect in their understanding of the Cause. In countries like America, too much attention is paid to book learning and not enough to the spirit which animates a human being. In the mass conversion areas they win the people to Bahá'u'lláh and His love, and when immersed in that love, their hearts are truly affected. In India, where large groups become Bahá'ís, they sometimes don't know who the Báb and 'Abdu'l-Bahá are. But they recognize that Bahá'u'lláh is the return of Krishna."

Another letter is addressed to a pioneer in a newly-opened capital city. There had been misunderstandings on the new Assembly, and Leroy's response is five pages long. First he praises at some length their unique blessing to be on the first Assembly in a virgin territory, then explains the origin and purpose of the administrative order, the spirit that must animate them in consultation. He cites the pages and paragraphs of the Guardian's writings to which they should turn. This was written in the mid years of the first Seven Year Plan, and no effort was too much to sustain and support the victory their Assembly status represented.

One last letter should be mentioned. It was sent to a pioneer teacher whose purity and self-sacrifice touched Leroy deeply, Rudolfo Duna. They had met in South Africa. Rudolfo had written on a scrap of paper from Mozambique, giving news of new believers in Mocuba and Quilima – five believers now! four indigenous and one Portuguese pioneer! He signs himself "in service to the Beloved Guardian". Within a week Leroy answers him, assuring him that they are praying for him at the Shrines: "It was such a joy to receive your letter and to learn that you are actively serving. God will surely bless you for all your services and guide and confirm your steps in His path."

Another type of teaching letter was sent in reply to questions. Many people wrote to him with inquiries concerning the teachings and he took great pains to share his understanding with them. Sometimes without realizing it he would adopt a formal manner as if addressing an audience, intent only on his line of reasoning. We have one such letter written to his own mother in 1935. She asks the meaning of a passage in the Gleanings. "It might be well," he writes, "for someone to ask Shoghi Effendi just what is meant by this, as it might seem somewhat obscure and lead one to think we believe in reincarnation in some way. On the other hand, it seems clear to me that there might be two or three different meanings to the statement." He then sets out in some detail his thoughts on the possible meaning of the passage.

In 1934 he is writing to Dr. H. Tsao of Shanghai. Mark Tobey, recently returned from China, had described Dr. Tsao's efforts on behalf of the Bahá'í community there and passed on Tsao's request for a compilation of the teachings on economics. Leroy immediately responds. "The Guardian has recently stated", he writes, "that these statements of Bahá'u'lláh and 'Abdu'l-Bahá are principles of economic stability, and not arbitrary parts of a program. In other words, the spirit of economics, as enunciated by Bahá'u'lláh, will have to be applied to situations existing in various parts of the world, until finally world conditions develop to the point where the full economic structure contemplated in the Bahá'í teachings can be established."

An old friend, Sally Sanor, wrote for clarification of 'Abdu'l-Bahá's statements in *Some Answered Questions* on composition. He answers: "As to the subject of creative composition, apparently you are not quoting 'Abdu'l-Bahá correctly. There are three kinds of composition and they should never be confused." In failing health, he nonetheless found the strength to write two pages of explanation and ends: "I hope this will clarify this very important matter." The letter was written just a few months before his death.

On another occasion he writes in response to questions that are troubling some of the Bahá'ís in regard to a future cataclysm. "The Guardian does not discuss these matters very much," he writes. "He has been definite in his statements that we should not dwell on this, but that we should redouble our efforts in the prosecution of our Plan, and that will in itself mitigate the difficulties. Why people should worry about these things and make them a major consideration in their thinking and way of life, I don't know. God surely is able to direct and assist His chosen ones in all circumstances, and to think of running away, or speculating on the punishment of humanity, is wrong. It is a Christian residue, stemming from the belief that the world would be destroyed, the chosen would be lifted up above the earth while the destruction takes place, and then return here to enjoy what is left."

Even the short notes he wrote were used as a means for praising, encouraging, drawing lessons, opening up spiritual meaning – depending on the recipient. He thanks friends for taking Sylvia and him sight-seeing in Scandinavia: "How the people of old built palaces of material splendor, forgetting the things of the spirit – no wonder the world is in the condition it is!" He praises two pioneers who use their money to serve: "You two have demonstrated that funds coming into your hands increase your service to the Faith rather than decrease it. In so many cases, money causes individuals to lessen their Bahá'í service until finally they serve the funds rather than letting the funds aid them in serving the Faith." In comforting a sick friend: "It is sad that so many of the active Bahá'ís have physical problems to overcome in their labors for the Faith. But on the other hand, the sacrifice and determination needed to continue, bring greater confirmations and blessings." Encouraging someone to go out and found a new Assembly: "The days of dreaming and hoping are over. The day of action has come and those who do not act, stagnate, as there is no such thing in the spiritual realm as quiescence."

A last "teaching letter" follows, though the recipient of this one without any doubt did not view it as such. In 1954 the famous columnist Herb Caen of the *San Francisco Examiner* carried an item concerning three Bahá'ís who had left the city to become Bahá'í "missionaries": Leroy, John Allen, and Sara Kenny, wife of the former Attorney General of California. It contains a number of loaded phrases – "slightly mystical Oriental sect", "going to Africa to work among the oppressed natives", "preaching Bahaism in Israel" – and is free with misstatements of fact. Many Bahá'ís would have sent off an angry reply to the paper, bought by many readers just for Caen's column. But Leroy quietly answered it from Haifa, without reprimand, without emotion, weaving his former position, his work in Israel, and a statement of his current duties (as drawn up for the press), with the information that "with the Bahá'í Faith established in 229 countries of the world, you can see how the international administrative work would develop in great volume". Informational, corrective, judicious, a wise reply to a skeptical journalist who ends his column: "You might argue with their judgment – but you must salute them for their courage."

In the final analysis, each of the great Bahá'í teachers is unique, with unique and inborn qualities. May Maxwell, herself far above our praise as a teacher, observed Leroy's gift with her beautiful comment: "There is a quality in your nature which is rare and precious and which, I believe, belongs only to the lovers of Bahá'u'lláh. It gives life and significance to all that you utter in the way of teaching and imparts a new spirit to the dead."

CHAPTER TWELVE

# A Wider Field of Service

PRIOR to 1929, Leroy's services to the Bahá'í Faith were centered in activities on the Pacific Coast. But in that year he and four other westerners were appointed to an enlarged National Teaching Committee. It was his first national assignment. Then, three years later, he was elected one of the nine members of the National Spiritual Assembly of the United States and Canada, the governing board of the North American Bahá'í community.

He was 36, the youngest person to serve on the national body. But he was not unknown on the national scene; his services had brought him to the notice of his fellow believers. With fair regularity he wrote to the National Secretary, Horace Holley, giving his thoughts and recommendations concerning the development of the national community. And as a delegate to the Convention, he had already established close working friendships with most of the other "active" Bahá'ís of the country. By the time of the 1931 Convention, the year before his election, his name figured high among those whom the delegates viewed as material for the national body. At the close of that Convention, Corinne True remarked to his mother how wonderful it was that Leroy, whom she dearly loved, had received so many votes. "It won't be long," she told Maria, "before he'll be on."

But for Leroy, it was a shock to find himself suddenly a peer of people whose stature as national leaders he had admired and respected.* Shortly after the election he wrote to Fred Schopflocher: "I

---

* Some of the other members were Siegfried Schopflocher, Alfred Lunt, Nellie French, Amelia Collins, Roy Wilhelm, Horace Holley, Allen McDaniel.

feel out of place with the responsibilities that have come to me . . . but realize that the kindly interest of the other members will help me to measure up. It is a privilege to be able to serve with the old true servants of the Cause. You have always been such a good friend of mine and helped me so much – I hope that relationship may continue in even greater degree because of our close association in service. May we all be confirmed in our humble efforts and produce constructive results in keeping with Shoghi Effendi's expectations of us."

To his close friend Milly Collins he confides that he feels very keenly his incapacity for this service and hopes for her assistance as their work goes forward. In reply, she shares an intimate experience with him: "When the call came seven years ago for me to attend my first N.S.A. meeting, I suffered agonies that only 'Abdu'l-Bahá knew. After much prayer I fell asleep and this is what I saw: the nine members were seated and suddenly we began to rise toward the ceiling and all that was left was a huge ball of light, the members submerged. That is the way God wanted me to enter the Council Chamber. I was so inexperienced and stood in awe of the older members, but I can say absolutely truthfully that after a meeting opens I am never conscious of the individuals. That vision was my gift and has been a great strength."

The greatest honor for Leroy was to hear, through the Guardian's secretary, that Shoghi Effendi "was very glad to see your name among the members of the National Assembly, because it shows that new blood is entering the administrative work . . . Your election to the N.S.A. answers fully your desire to have some guidance as to the form of service you ought to render the Cause [about which Leroy had obviously written the Guardian]. Administrative work and teaching do not exclude each other. Even though you will find yourself forced to give more time to the former, Shoghi Effendi hopes you will keep up the latter form of service and continue to draw new souls into the Movement . . . Even though you are the youngest member of that group he hopes you will be a source of inspiration to them and an example of servitude to the friends."

We have noted that Leroy's wish was to teach. Yet he found himself drawn, through the electoral process, into administrative work and of course accepted it, and served with efficiency and devotion. But he often spoke of the "over-administration" of the Faith in America, the multiplication of committees, sapping the initiative and burdening the spirit of the individual believer, on whom "in the final analysis" all teaching work depends. One evening in Haifa he remarked to Shoghi Effendi that the number of committees in America could probably be cut by half, to which the Guardian replied: "Oh, at least that!"

The Guardian added a postscript to the letter cited above that was so meaningful to Leroy that we quote it in full:

> I wish to add a few words in order to reaffirm my deep sense of satisfaction at your having been elected a member of the National Assembly – a position which, I feel confident, you will fill with ability and distinction. May Bahá'u'lláh guide and sustain you in your responsible task and enable you to lend a fresh impetus, by your advice and executive ability, to the work that the Assembly has arisen to accomplish. Your activities in the teaching field are worthy of the highest praise, and I trust that your administrative services will be no less enduring and remarkable.

In his next letter the Guardian addresses Leroy as "dear and precious co-worker" and three months later writes: "I will pray for the extension of your invaluable activities, which I consider an asset to be prized and cherished by every sincere lover and promoter of the Cause of God." Then Shoghi Effendi gives this loving advice to the increasingly burdened recipient of his letter: "Persevere, be happy and confident!"

Two years later the Guardian is writing through his secretary: "It gives him much pleasure to realize how effectively you are teaching the Cause and how actively you are engaged in extending and consolidating the basis of its new-born administrative institutions . . . To vindicate the truth of this Revelation is, indeed, a task which only those who have been truly reborn can claim to achieve. And it is for young, energetic and loyal Bahá'ís like yourself, who are alive to the manifold duties and responsibilities which the Faith has laid upon them, to arise and contribute their share. . . ." Shoghi Effendi adds in his own handwriting: ". . . as a member of the highest Bahá'í administrative institution in your land you have rendered and are rendering services that are truly notable and praiseworthy."

Through such constant outpouring of his love and encouragement did Shoghi Effendi give the direction, provide the inspiration, and impel each servant forward along the path of service. It was thus a very intense personal relationship that developed between him and his fellow Bahá'ís. Leroy gave the Guardian an unquestioning loyalty and devotion; he wished no more than to do exactly what the Guardian in his wisdom asked of him.

# CHAPTER THIRTEEN

# The First Seven Year Plan 1937–1944

ONE of the great endeavors with which Leroy's name will always be associated is the first Seven Year Plan, which marked a turning point in the history of the Faith, as it launched the North American Bahá'ís on the "world mission" given them by 'Abdu'l-Bahá. It was carried out under the close guidance and supervision of the Guardian but its implementation was put in the hands of the National Teaching Committee, the "right hand" of the National Spiritual Assembly of the United States and Canada.

Shoghi Effendi concentrated on the "home front" of North America in this first plan, where Assemblies were to be established in every state and province of the continent, and many new areas to be opened to the Bahá'í teachings. At the time, there were whole regions whose Bahá'í population was either sparse or non-existent. But in addition to such challenging goals in the northern hemisphere, the Guardian asked the Bahá'ís to look "beyond the confines of their native land". . . and implant the name of Bahá'u'lláh in the immense reaches of Latin America. The scope of the plan was vast, and it appeared daunting to the handful of Bahá'ís who would have to fulfill it.[1]

But let us go back to trace the emergence of the powerful committee that carried out the North American component of the plan, and Leroy's association with it.

Until 'Abdu'l-Bahá came to America in 1912, there was little organized teaching on the continent. Believers who felt moved to share the message of Bahá'u'lláh's coming, and they were no doubt the majority, did so in ways that seemed best to them. Some, like Thornton Chase, moved about the States because of their business interests. Others spent their holidays in places where they left new "believers" or journeyed to other parts of the country for the express purpose of sharing with friends and relatives what they called the "glad tidings". Through these efforts nascent centers arose here and there in a random pattern.

There were no committees to coordinate any of this activity or give direction to the affairs of the existing communities. In Chicago the House of Spirituality had been formed, but its principal purpose was to assist in the erection of the House of Worship. New York City established a Board of Council, while several other communities appointed service committees or working committees which gave a modicum of guidance to community efforts. In general, however, the Faith was administered by individuals who showed the natural inclination and ability to do so.

An entirely new spiritual awareness was born with the historic visit to America of 'Abdu'l-Bahá. Now all the believers experienced for themselves what the pilgrims to 'Akká had learned: the greatness of their Faith and its claim on their thoughts and on their actions. They set out consciously to nurture the seeds planted during 'Abdu'l-Bahá's passage among them, using the advice He had given them.

The result was a more systematic approach to the teaching work. The believers turned increasingly from home meetings to accessible public halls. A start was even made to purchase properties that could eventually become Bahá'í Centers.

The gifted traveling teachers, who were numerous in certain specific areas, made efforts to visit, encourage and deepen the newborn Bahá'í groups. Some even went beyond the confines of the continent to become the first North American settlers and traveling teachers in other lands – Alaska, Hawaii, India, and Persia.

Stable family units unable to travel, such as that of Maria and Charles Ioas in Chicago, played their role as vigorous supporters of the teaching work in their local community. The annual Convention of the Bahá'í Temple Unity, while primarily focused on the needs of the House of Worship, soon developed into a forum for consultation on teaching. The delegates returned home with a larger vision of the Faith as well as with new ideas, gleaned from their fellow conferees, for disseminating its teachings.

Then 'Abdu'l-Bahá began to lay the foundation for His own teaching plan, which He composed during World War I and sent to America for implementation. Within several years of His visit He informed the believers that the time was ripe to establish Spiritual Assemblies, one of whose primary tasks would be the "diffusion of the fragrances of God and the exaltation of His Holy Word"[2] – in other words, teaching. To ensure that the purpose of the new institutions was clearly understood and that they would be built on a sound foundation, 'Abdu'l-Bahá sent the gifted Jináb-i-Faḍíl to instruct the believers in their formation. There were no textbooks as to how this was to be done.

In 1920, one year before the passing of 'Abdu'l-Bahá, a National Teaching Committee was appointed for the first time. This was an immense and significant step forward in the teaching work. Now an instrument existed that could channel the enthusiasm of the believers into collectively accepted goals. Not only was a national committee appointed but also a series of regional and local committees to serve as support units.

It is interesting to follow the effort on such a vast continent to find a workable solution to the problem of consultation. As one formula was tested and found unworkable, another would be tried.

This first National Teaching Committee divided the continent into five sections: the northeast, central, southern, and western states, and the Dominion of Canada. The committee itself was composed of nineteen members plus the supporting committees. Within two years, this structure proved much too unwieldy. It was abandoned in favor of a committee of five members all of whom lived on the east coast.

Under the auspices of the second Teaching Committee, regional conferences were held for the first time in North America. It was hoped that by bringing Bahá'ís of a whole area together to discuss the nation-wide programs in progress, they would be inspired to support them vigorously. One of the conferences took place in San Francisco, an exciting event attended by individuals from the coastal and Rocky Mountain states, the Hawaiian Islands and British Columbia. (The very first Bahá'ís had just been confirmed on the west coast of Canada, so that Canada now had Bahá'í settlements in the extreme east, namely Montreal, and the extreme west, Vancouver. Between, there was at most a handful of Bahá'ís.)

The following year a major pillar of the administrative order, foreseen in 'Abdu'l-Bahá's Will and Testament, came into being. It was the

National Spiritual Assembly of the Bahá'ís of the United States and Canada, elected in 1925 under Shoghi Effendi's direction. (It replaced the Bahá'í Temple Unity.) This new institution, as one of its first initiatives, issued a call to forty-five of the continent's "thoroughly informed, capable, experienced and distinguished Bahá'ís" to "make a supreme effort" to spread the teachings throughout the continent.[3] The call was addressed to such souls as May Maxwell, Martha Root, and Mountford Mills.* If the Bahá'í community had had only three such outstanding persons it would have been rich indeed.

The National Assembly once again restructured its National Teaching Committee, this time appointing one member from each of the five originally designated divisions of the country, whose work would be coordinated by a chairman and secretary. But shortly the need was felt for greater geographical concentration, and an equal number of members was appointed in the east and west, with a chairman on one coast and vice-chairman on the other.

It was at the time of this change, in 1929, that Leroy stepped on to the national teaching scene. In a letter to "all Assemblies, teachers, and friends" the distinguished May Maxwell, secretary of the National Teaching Committee, wrote: "Our beloved National Spiritual Assembly has graciously extended the sphere of the National Teaching Committee by the addition of five members from the Pacific Coast, Mrs. Ella Cooper, Mrs. Louise [Shahnaz] Waite, Mr. Leroy Ioas, Mr. George Latimer and Mr. Stanley Kemp† giving it additional strength by making Mr. Leroy Ioas Vice-Chairman."[4]

Leroy took up the national teaching work in 1929 with his full energy and resourcefulness. In that year definite plans were laid to reach out to specialized audiences all over the country, to share with them the Bahá'í teachings on social problems and to hold a series of Inter-Assembly teaching conferences to strengthen the efforts of individual Assemblies.

Within a few years of his membership on the committee, Leroy was named its chairman and Charlotte Linfoot of Oakland its secretary. It

---

* Martha Root, a journalist from Pittsburgh, circled the globe six times in her international teaching work, taking the Bahá'í teachings to many heads of state and royal personages. Mountfort Mills, an early Bahá'í of New York, was a distinguished international lawyer who worked to return the House of Bahá'u'lláh in Baghdad to Bahá'í hands.

† He and his wife Evelyn were among the first Bahá'ís in Vancouver.

was the start of their lengthy collaboration. Still another modification resulted in a committee centered on the Pacific Coast. It was this lean committee, able to meet frequently and work with efficiency, that led the country through the momentous Seven Year Plan. It is of interest to note that in 1959, in a letter from Haifa to all National Assemblies on the subject of their unmet goals under the Ten Year Crusade, the Hands of the Cause in the Holy Land wrote: "Experience has proven that a strong national teaching committee, with a membership largely centered in one locality, is the best instrument through which a National Assembly can work to carry a teaching plan through to a successful conclusion."

In 1931 the committee issued a thought-provoking two-page document that caused individuals and Assemblies to re-think what they might do in the teaching field. It was a list of nineteen methods for presenting the Faith, simple ideas on which the Bahá'ís could easily act, and it proved invaluable in encouraging new initiatives. The committee also put out a generic talk on the Faith, a logical sequence of points which could be used by any Bahá'í in preparing a talk. This was Leroy's work, part of his constant endeavor to produce teachers. The talk concerned the influence of religion on society and consisted of eleven points, what is religion, the common basis of religions, and so forth.

The following year a "reconstructed" teaching program was approved by the National Assembly, a program which concentrated all activities and agencies of the Faith on the one objective of teaching. The purpose was "to release a new creative spirit within each individual that would cause him to rise to new heights of sacrificial teaching service; to reinforce the pioneer teachers with not only the spiritual and moral, but also the organized material strength of the entire community . . . Thus individual acts of heroism would be reinforced by the united effort of all the Bahá'ís, and the pioneer teacher would become a strong outpost of the new world order of Bahá'u'lláh."[5]

Shoghi Effendi was highly appreciative of the plan. He called on the Bahá'ís to turn to the Dawn-breakers (the first followers of the Báb, Forerunner of Bahá'u'lláh) as their inspiration in teaching. Nabíl's narrative, that infinitely precious gift of the Guardian, had only recently been published in English, making it available for the first time (1932) to western readers. Titled *The Dawn-Breakers, Nabíl's Narrative of the Early*

*Years of the Bahá'í Revelation,* it is an eye-witness account of the birth of the Faith and the persecutions it suffered in its early years. "Feel impelled," the Guardian cabled, "appeal entire body American believers to henceforth regard Nabíl's soul-stirring Narrative as essential adjunct to reconstructed Teaching program."[6]

Bahá'ís answered the earnest request of the National Assembly and its teaching committee and set off on tours of the country. They also formed groups to travel together, which proved highly effective. Typical of how the teaching committee worked was this letter from Leroy to Fanny Knobloch.* "Can you not arrange a teaching circuit," he asks her, "beginning about the middle of January and extending for a month or six weeks . . . We are hoping to launch this teaching effort all over America . . . If you can do this, I will start at once with the Local Assemblies where you will teach, so they may make openings, appointments, etc." The impressive list of some of those participating included Martha Root, May Maxwell, Keith Ransom-Kehler, Elizabeth Greenleaf, Orcella Rexford, Susan Moody, William Randall, Mabel and Howard Ives, Ali-Kuli Khan, Howard MacNutt and Mason Remey.

Another feature of the plan was to diversify the venues of National Assembly meetings, so that newly-opened cities could organize public events using members of the Assembly as speakers. One such meeting, in Nashville, Tennessee in 1935, was an historic event for the south, as it was the first time an audience of black and white came together in such a public event.

During the 1930s the Bahá'ís were slowly acquiring a deeper understanding of the purpose of their administrative order, and realizing that the institutions of the Faith were their most effective instrument for teaching. The consultative wisdom of the friends functioned through them and the individual efforts of the Bahá'ís were coordinated through them; the result was unity and strength in the community's work.

It was becoming evident that in addition to all the itinerant move-

---

* One of three Knobloch sisters; Alma Knobloch settled as a Bahá'í teacher in Germany before the first world war; Fanny went to South Africa as one of the first pioneers; the third sister Pauline married Joseph Hannen of Washington DC. Through study with them Louis Gregory became a Bahá'í.

ment, settlement by Bahá'ís was needed if lasting results were to be achieved in the teaching field. Already in 1932 the Guardian was writing (through his secretary) to Leroy that traveling teachers should remain long enough in one place to be effective: "Shoghi Effendi has seen, through the experience of the international teachers who keep him informed regarding their activities, that intensive work is ultimately of a more lasting nature. It has proven to be far better that a teacher should spend a month or two in one center and wait until a group is formed, than to cover a larger area and not stay long enough . . . to help the progress of those interested to the stage that they would feel themselves able to embrace the Cause and identify themselves with it."[7]

In 1935 the National Teaching Committee, for two years already under Leroy's chairmanship, conducted a survey of the continent and found twelve states in the U.S. without a single Bahá'í. It laid out detailed plans to bring these states into the fold of the Faith. The Guardian, on being apprised of the plan, wrote through his secretary to Leroy: "With regard to your committee's plan for the introduction of the Faith into the twelve states of the USA where there are as yet no believers, the Guardian wishes me to assure you that he fully and gladly endorses such a plan which, he hopes, when carried out, will inaugurate a new era of teaching activity throughout the States."[8] The Guardian then launched the first appeal he had ever made to the believers to go forth to "settle and teach"[9] in those areas. "The time for lectures on the philosophy of the Faith has passed," he said. "The Cause is not a system of philosophy, it is essentially a way of life, a religious Faith that seeks to win all people on a common basis of mutual understanding and love, and in a common devotion to God."[10]

Shoghi Effendi's appeal challenged the Bahá'ís to pass into action. A special fund was established, to which the Guardian made the initial contribution of thirty thousand dollars, as always setting the example for others to follow. Thus the foundation was laid for the Seven Year Plan that was shortly to be announced.

For the first time Shoghi Effendi used the word "pioneer", in a now famous passage in the same letter to Leroy: "What the Cause now requires is not so much a group of highly-cultured and intellectual people who can adequately present the Teachings, but a number of devoted, sincere and loyal supporters who, in utter disregard of their own weaknesses and limitations, and with hearts afire with the love of

God, forsake their all for the sake of spreading and establishing the Faith. In other words, what is mostly needed nowadays is a Bahá'í pioneer, and not so much a Bahá'í philosopher or scholar."[11]

In this same letter Shoghi Effendi commends Leroy on the work of the National Teaching Committee: "You have indeed discharged your duties and responsibilities as chairman of the Committee and have displayed such an intense interest in and zeal for the cause of teaching that many of your co-workers in that field might do well to follow your example."

Then, on May 1, 1936, came a brief, momentous cable to the assembled delegates at the National Convention. The Guardian called on them to ponder the historic appeal of 'Abdu'l-Bahá in the Tablets of the Divine Plan. "Humanity," he wrote in an unforgettable passage, "entering outer fringes most perilous stage existence." And then the fateful words: "Would to God every State within American Republic every Republic American continent might ere termination this glorious century [the Bahá'í century ending in 1944] embrace light Faith Bahá'u'lláh establish structural basis His World Order."[12] He was launching the North American Bahá'ís on their world mission.

A month later Shoghi Effendi outlined the exact goals to be pursued by the National Assembly: "A systematic, carefully conceived, and well-established plan should be devised . . ." with its immediate objective "the permanent establishment of at least one center in every state of the American Republic and in every Republic of the American continent not yet enlisted under the banner of His Faith." "The field is immense," the Guardian adds, "the task gigantic, the privilege immeasurably precious. Time is short . . ."[13]

His sense of urgency is confirmed when a brief two months later he writes to the National Assembly: "I am eagerly awaiting the news of the progress of the activities . . ." "The Tablets of the Divine Plan," he reminds them, "invest your Assembly with unique and grave responsibilities . . . The present opportunity is unutterably precious. It may not recur again."[14]

Conditions in the world were very troubled: a devastating war was to break out within three years. And it was against that background of conflagration, of restricted movement and funds, that the Seven Year Plan would have to be won.

The Guardian associated the teaching goals of the Seven Year Plan

with another goal whose achievement he said would release great spiritual power into the world. That goal was completion of the exterior
ornamentation of the Mother Temple of the west, which was yet to be
sheathed in the lacy envelope envisioned by its architect. Shoghi
Effendi cabled the Convention of 1937 that "no triumph can more
befittingly signalize termination first century Bahá'í era than accomplishment this twofold task".[15]

The members of the National Teaching Committee at the outset of
the Seven Year Plan were colleagues of many previous endeavors.
George Latimer had played a major role in the founding of the Geyserville school and he, Leroy and Milly Collins were co-workers on the
National Assembly; Lottie Linfoot proved an invaluable asset to the
committee through her masterful organizational skills; Dr. Forsythe
Ward, a Berkeley professor, brought his brilliant mind to the work;*
and Joyce Lyon Dahl, who served until the birth of her first child.
Before long, Marion Holley joined the committee.

Marion recalls that the committee met at first in Leroy's office, so as
he worked his way up – and during the years of the Seven Year Plan he
was advancing rapidly in his professional life – their meeting place "got
better and better". At first they met around his desk in an open area,
then in an enclosed office, then in his large private office. As the plan
developed and the work grew apace, they would meet for all day sessions at Leroy and Sylvia's home, sitting around a card table in the
living room with maps and papers spread out. Sylvia kept the house
quiet, sifted out the telephone calls, and relieved their intensive work
periods with lunch and refreshments.

Both Marion and Joyce remember Leroy as the motor, the driving
force, behind the teaching committee. It was not a consulting committee, they said, its purpose was winning goals. Joyce said: "He could see
nationally. He was like a general with his map, moving his pieces. His
resources were money and people." At the outset the committee had to
decide whether to begin its work with the U.S. or with Canada. They
had to decide which area was best suited to which person. As the
choice of unopened areas was large, it was practical to take into
account each person's professional and health needs, so as to facilitate

---

* He and his wife Janet, in Haifa on their way to pioneer in Africa, were asked to remain as
  custodians of Bahá'u'lláh's Tomb. Forsythe died on the grounds of Bahjí some years
  later.

permanent settlement. They needed bodies – pioneers; they needed subsidies. The teaching committee had to decide all this, and it was Leroy in his decisive way who proposed many of the solutions.

It is important to mention the question of funding. Settlement was a new concept to most of the Bahá'ís; it necessitated giving up jobs with whatever that entailed of loss, and it meant having the means to live until work could be found in a new area. Many of the cities without Bahá'ís were places of small population or comparatively simple economies, where finding work was not guaranteed. Yet the pioneers must fill the goals. Therefore subsidies were sometimes required; it was a practice known already from travel teaching, when some of the best teachers might not be able to finance their teaching trips. Persons who could not themselves become settlers could deputize others: the Guardian himself approved of such assistance in view of the circumstances under which the Plan was launched. An interesting facet of Leroy's thinking, which became the operating principle of the committee, was that decisions should not be made on the basis of the availability of funds. The committee knew that if the friends caught the vision and became involved in the teaching plans, they would support the work financially. This was the way they worked, first the vision, then the funds. Leroy felt that Bahá'ís who did nothing because they lacked funds were placing far too much reliance on money.

The initial goal of the committee was to settle one Bahá'í in the capital of each state and province, targeting both the Canadian and American cities at the same time. During their meetings, they would lay out the map and plan where the pioneers should go. But as the process continued there would be frustrations as someone changed his mind, and Leroy would become upset and at times very impatient when plans fell through. Yet when it came to writing to the person, Joyce recalls, he would be the "essence of kindliness". He understood the human side, the fallible side. He also felt Bahá'ís should be absolutely faithful to their intentions and promises.

Milly Collins and George Latimer were not always present at the meetings because they had to travel from other states, but their ideas and support were invaluable. The working committee narrowed down to the group geographically close. Lottie Linfoot became Leroy's right arm on the committee. When Marion joined the committee, it acquired another powerful personality. She was a dynamo of energy, highly capable, very energetic and very enthusiastic. "She, like Leroy," someone commented, "had a very practical, activist, get-it-done kind of approach to every thing she undertook, and this was exactly what was needed to get the Plan won."

Marion and Leroy developed a wonderful working relationship and a close lifelong friendship. He cherished her presence and yet, when it came time for her to move to England and marry, he was the first to want her to do so, in spite of the terrible loss her departure represented. To dwell one moment on this close relationship: a number of years later she wrote to him in Haifa of her deep gratitude for their association, especially on the National Teaching Committee, which she noted "taught me most of what I have learned of value". And he, writing from Haifa in 1957, recalls some of their frustrations during the Seven Year Plan: "I have read the report of the teaching work [in England] with intense interest. It reminded me of the difficult but happy times we had in America during the first seven year plan. . . . The friends in the British Isles merit the admiration of all the Bahá'ís as they are doing so much with so little. You will recall that during the first and second seven year plans I always felt the Bahá'ís in England were sacrificing much more than those in America. There we had so much and did so little." When in later life ill health settled in on him, it was to her he turned and one day in Switzerland asked if she would write his obituary. Sylvia was devastated to hear him say this, then realized he was dealing with the reality of his situation and wished to be remembered through the pen of someone who knew him well and loved him.*

A number of people have said that if you want to know how to win a teaching plan, go back and study the history of that first Seven Year Plan. The teaching committee evolved and developed the techniques for winning teaching plans. The technique is described by Isobel Sabri, who when she moved as a pioneer to England in 1945, benefitted from its application there:† "The technique was one of very, very close and constant contact with the pioneers in the goal towns. When you want

---

* See *The Bahá'í World*, vol. xiv, p. 291 for Marion Hofman's memorial.

† Marion Holley, who had by then moved to England, was secretary of the National Teaching Committee of the British Isles. The Guardian had suggested that her experience on the teaching committee of America might be invaluable to the sister body of the British Isles.

to open a country and you want to form a certain number of Assemblies, you choose the places where you're going to form them and you don't leave it to happenstance . . . Then you concentrate on them, you put pioneers in there, you send literature, you send traveling teachers, you do everything you can to support the pioneers, and this includes an absolutely steady stream of correspondence flowing from you to the pioneer and therefore from the pioneer back. It's an intensely personalized kind of work."

William Sears was to write to Leroy many years later, during the days of the Custodians:* "I remember what a green baby Bahá'í I was in the days of that national teaching committee, when the pattern was set for the teaching around the world." An "intensely personalized kind of work", yet in the early stages of the plan only a handful of people were involved in directing this pioneering and settlement work.

The Seven Year Plan started with a surge of energy as the Bahá'ís realized they were, at long last, starting on the road to fulfilling the wishes of 'Abdu'l-Bahá. As the first year opened, there were thirty-four "virgin" states and provinces – the definition being an area with no Assembly – ten of them without a single Bahá'í. In that first year twenty permanent settlers left their homes to relocate in the unopened areas, and an additional twenty-eight set out as traveling teachers to cover as much of the targeted territory as possible. By the end of the year, four of the areas had achieved Assembly status: Kansas and Oklahoma, and the Canadian provinces of New Brunswick and Ontario.

An interesting prophecy of 'Abdu'l-Bahá came to fulfillment during the first year of the plan. The Master had once said that in the near future there would be an insufficient number of teachers. Already in the first year, the teaching committee was unable to meet the demand for Bahá'í teachers. Studying the challenge, it asked all Bahá'í committees to ponder the question of how they could help meet the challenge. Out of this came three experimental courses created in an effort to establish some basic principles on which to build a national program for the rapid and effective development of teachers.

By the second year of the plan there were still thirty virgin states and provinces, nine with no Bahá'ís. Then came a new surge of

* An interim period of six years between the passing of the Guardian and the election of the Universal House of Justice. See Chapter 33.

pioneer effort, in direct response to the Guardian's cable of January 1939, calling for "nine holy souls" to "promptly fearlessly volunteer forsake their homes cast away their attachments definitely settle these territories lay firm anchorage Administrative Order this undefeatable Faith." Pioneer activity, said the Guardian, is the crying need of this fateful hour, and in a touching statement says he is "proud of the privilege to pledge nine hundred pounds" to assist the permanent settlement of pioneers in the nine unsettled areas.[16]

One of the nine holy souls who arose in response to his call was the valiant and fearless Honor Kempton, a comparatively new Bahá'í. Because hers is typical of the kind of effort that won the Seven Year Plan, we will tell something of her story. Honor offered to settle in the vast territory of Alaska, visited by Marion Jack and Orcella Rexford in earlier years. This cultivated Englishwoman had heard of the Faith in Chicago and her heart, which had been sore tried by losses in her life, responded. On moving to San Francisco she wrote to Sylvia and Leroy and was immediately caught up in Bahá'í activities. Her home was the locale for some of Leroy's finest classes, his technique being as always to find a nucleus of serious students and insist that they study and deepen regularly each week. These were superb classes from which came strong new Bahá'ís, including Honor. Leroy immediately put her talents to use on committees and in the summer school programs, and she was elected to the San Francisco Assembly.

Within three months of the Guardian's cable, she left for the capital city of Juneau, with Shoghi Effendi's assurance that his prayers would accompany her on her "great and historic adventure". But she disliked this small city built on a mountainside tumbling down into the ocean, and when she re-read the Guardian's cable, one word leapt out of the text at her. She asked and received permission to move, and settled happily in Anchorage, to build the Faith there on a permanent basis.

Honor had a particularly radiant personality and a childlike eagerness of spirit which caused people to want to help her, so that she soon found friends. Never having done more than nursing and office work, she nonetheless opened her own business, a bookstore called the Book Cache. The name had Alaskan roots – it referred to the food caches built high on poles along the wilderness routes for the unlucky traveler who lost his way. Her business flourished; a former governor called the Book Cache the cultural center of Alaska. Certainly hundreds of soldiers passing through Anchorage found quiet refuge and conversation there . . . and knowledge of the Faith. Thus her influence spread widely. The first to accept the Faith was a displaced New Yorker, and soon other pioneers arrived to join her. The winters were rigorous, the bears plentiful, and the almost total lack of fresh food permanently damaged her teeth. But she loved the magnificent grandeur of the state and she had found her lasting joy in pioneering. To achieve an Assembly would take long years of struggle. It was only toward the end of the sixth year of the plan that one happy evening, the women dressed in long dresses to honor the occasion, the first Bahá'í institution of Alaska was formed.

At the start of the second Seven Year Plan, when the Guardian turned his attention to the "war-torn, spiritually-famished"[17] continent of Europe, Honor followed, and was a pioneer teacher in Europe for the remainder of her life. She was one of the heroines of American Bahá'í history, the "mother" of two vigorous communities, Alaska and Luxembourg.

As a result of the Guardian's cable in 1939, not only nine offered to pioneer, but nine times nine. But as the committee had found, uprooting one's life involved many complicated questions, and the committee insisted that the settlement work be done in a way that would have sound results. So while "nine holy souls" did indeed move from their homes during the second year to the remaining territories without Bahá'ís, only six additional ones were able to fulfill their pledge. Nonetheless the year was highly successful, because for the first time every state and province was "illumined by the light of Bahá'u'lláh" through the settlement of at least one Bahá'í.[18]

It should be recalled that the Guardian at times referred to these lone pioneers as lighthouses, shedding the light of Bahá'u'lláh over an entire region and acting as the channel for the Holy Spirit to reach people. But to grow to group status, then Assembly status, to build a firmly-grounded community, took much more than the lone pioneer; it took many pioneers. Some of those who went out were forced to return home because of family or health problems; there had to be substitutes found for them, so that pioneers were needed until the very end of the plan.

One night in Haifa many years later, the Guardian, in speaking of the teaching work in general, made the observation that there should be at least nineteen Bahá'ís in a locality in order to have a sound community. Leroy mentioned to the Guardian that the national teaching committee during the first Seven Year Plan had taken that exact figure as their goal for a viable community. Their slogan had been nine for an Assembly, nineteen for a community. The Guardian commented that the committee must have been inspired in its work.

During the third year of the plan, a tremendous movement of settlers took place into the virgin areas, some forty-eight Bahá'ís picking up and moving. This pioneering spirit manifested itself in activity at home also, so that the entire third year of the plan was marked by an enthusiasm for service that had not been evident to the same degree before.

In this same year the Guardian issued another of his great appeals. It seemed that whenever Shoghi Effendi felt momentum building among the believers and saw response from the Bahá'ís, he would direct their energies toward a still higher goal. Now he called upon them to form one hundred Assemblies on the continent by the end of the year.[19]

The response was immediate. The believers concentrated on the new goal and formed one hundred and two Assemblies. Of greatest import for the plan was that three of them were in virgin areas: Nebraska, Utah and South Carolina. We think now of South Carolina as a state where there are many Bahá'ís, but at the opening of the Seven Year Plan six of the sixteen southern states possessed no Bahá'ís whatever, and in all of the south, there were only eight Assemblies, two groups, and forty-six isolated believers. As the National Assembly knew, 'Abdu'l-Bahá Himself had drawn attention to the lack of movement in the southern states. The teaching committee now devised a new strategy for teaching in the south, under which swifter progress was made. By the end of the year, one additional Assembly was formed, twelve groups established and the number of isolated Bahá'ís had doubled to ninety.

In Canada also, real progress was seen as a result of the Guardian's appeal. At the start of the plan, Assemblies existed only in Montreal and Vancouver, there were no groups and only four isolated Bahá'ís across that immense stretch of land. Yet in this third year – 1939–1940 – the Faith spread through the prairie provinces with great momentum, both through public proclamation – large meetings, publicity, radio – and the settlement of pioneers. By the end of the year there were Bahá'ís in every province and the number of Assemblies had risen to four, with two groups, and nineteen isolated believers.

This was the mid-point of the Seven Year Plan, and the Guardian, who was watching and guiding its every step, expressed satisfaction with what had been accomplished and the manner in which the task was carried forward. It is of the work of the National Teaching Committee that he writes, on the first page of *The Advent of Divine Justice* addressed in 1939 to the Bahá'ís of the United States and Canada: ". . . the extremely heartening progress recorded in the successive reports of their National Teaching Committee, attest, beyond the shadow of a doubt, the fidelity, the vigor, and the thoroughness with which you are conducting the manifold operations which the evolution of the Seven Year Plan must necessarily involve . . . it is being prosecuted with exemplary regularity and precision, with undiminished efficiency, and commendable dispatch."

And in a letter to Leroy on March 14, 1939, the Guardian comments: "The magnificent work you are accomplishing in the National Teaching Committee no less than on the National Assembly, are indeed remarkable and highly praiseworthy. The energy, judgment, zeal and fidelity that characterize your incessant and ever-multiplying activities are assets for which I am deeply and truly thankful. Persevere in your meritorious labours and be always assured that you are in my thoughts and prayers. May He, Whose Cause you promote with such diligence and distinction, reward you a thousand fold and fulfill the dearest wish of your heart."[20]

During the fourth year of the plan, several new developments took place. When the plan was launched, ten regional teaching committees were functioning. They worked in areas where Local Assemblies already existed – that is to say, areas quite outside the goals of the plan. This meant that settlement of the goal areas, as well as all arrangements for pioneers, had to be dealt with entirely by the National Teaching Committee. The committee finally recommended that regional committees be appointed in every area of the continent, and it transferred to them some of the volume of work involved in maintaining contact with the pioneers and giving them support. Indeed, the regional committees took on many responsibilities, publishing bulletins, sponsoring the teacher training courses, and maintaining contact with hundreds of groups and isolated believers. For the future it was important that some three hundred and fifty persons had the valuable experience of working on these regional committees.

At the start of the fourth year of the plan, there were still twenty-six virgin areas, the only gain from the previous year being the two Assemblies in Canada. Then came a challenge: the Guardian felt that henceforth Assemblies should be formed only of persons living within the civil limits of a city.[21] This meant a loss of seven Assemblies. From one hundred and two, the number fell to ninety-five. The positive side of the change was that a number of new groups were formed from the remnants of the former Assembly area. In this entire fourth year – the year that saw the United States drawn into the second world war in which Canada had already been embroiled for two years – only one person could be settled in a goal city. Life was tightening for everyone; Canada did not want U.S. "missionaries" – and the bulk of the Bahá'í population of North America lay in the U.S. – entering their territory in war time. Some Canadian cities needing settlement were crowded with servicemen from the Commonwealth being trained for war. Leroy reported the situation to the Guardian: they are endeavoring to move the pioneer settlers to their posts as rapidly as possible, but transportation is becoming very difficult and people are being urged not to travel. They are being "frozen" in their jobs and not allowed to give up positions important to the war effort, and as the war momentum increases, conditions for free movement will become more difficult, as everything is being subordinated to the total war effort. (At one point there was even question of Leroy himself being put into uniform and sent to Washington as a transportation expert; Southern Pacific had the longest lines in the country and carried the largest volume of troops and material.)

It was at this uncertain point that the Guardian expanded the goals of the Seven Year Plan. No longer was it sufficient to form only a strong nucleus of believers in each state and province, but elected institutions of the Faith must be established.[22] Because three of the Assemblies lost in the redistricting were in the important "virgin" areas, the number of goals had actually risen as the fifth year opened. Through dint of hard work, some of the lost ground was won back, twelve pioneers were settled and fourteen Assemblies formed, five of them in virgin areas. By the end of the year there were again more than one hundred Assemblies in North America, and the virgin areas fell to the lowest number since the start of the plan.

The second major goal (in North America) of the Seven Year Plan, completion of the exterior ornamentation of the House of Worship, had now been accomplished. With this goal behind them, the Bahá'ís were free to focus their full attention on the teaching work.

The National Teaching Committee, feeling the pressure of time, made a survey of its available resources and of the teaching initiatives throughout the continent. It prepared detailed studies of each virgin area. It asked regional committees to concentrate all their efforts to help form an Assembly in each area. It asked all Assemblies to try to provide settlers and traveling teachers. It called for more pioneers, and for renewal of the spirit of the third year of the plan when one hundred and two Assemblies had been formed. It was a discouraging period when results were simply not forthcoming – indeed, it was the lowest ebb of the seven year period. Only ten virgin areas had been won in the entire first five years of the plan and only two years remained in which to found Assemblies in the remaining twenty-four. Shoghi Effendi cabled the Convention of 1942: "Upon crucial years ahead hinge fortunes this historic crusade."[23]

Time was pressing. The committee again surveyed the unfinished tasks. The National Assembly and the teaching committee sent out urgent appeals. They called twelve large conferences in January touching all parts of the continent, seeking to awaken the spirit of devotion needed to achieve the goals. The Guardian made clear that the supreme requirement in the sixth year of the plan was the "increase in the number of pioneers of every class, race, age and outlook," regardless of qualifications, "whether newly enrolled or of old standing in the Faith."[24] "Speed," he said, "should be your motto."[25] Speed, Leroy said to himself, in the face of increasing restrictions on travel, resources and above all, manpower. In his city alone twelve of the strongest members of the community had left for pioneering posts.

In a letter to Leroy, the Guardian's secretary repeated the urgency of Shoghi Effendi's message: "He wishes to stress the importance of sending out the volunteers for pioneer teaching and settlement as quickly as possible: he does not feel that this is the time to be exacting about the qualifications of the people who volunteer. The time is too short and the stake too great to consider these secondary points; once the precious goal is won, all adjustments necessary can be considered and made." In his own handwriting, Shoghi Effendi sent another encouraging postscript to Leroy: "I admire the spirit that animates you, marvel at your stupendous efforts, and greatly rejoice at the success you and your collaborators in the teaching field are achieving. Persevere in your historic and all-important task. . . ."[26]

The sixth year was to see the greatest achievements of the plan. During this penultimate year more pioneers went out to settle in virgin areas than in the first five years combined. More Assemblies were created in that one year (1942–3) than ever before in the history of the Faith in America. There were many sacrifices, but the fact alone that the pioneers were all able to become financially independent was an indication of how the doors opened for them. Some indication of the overall vitality of the campaign, in spite of periods of quiescence, was the youthfulness of many of the pioneers – at least fifteen were in their early 20s. In the report he later wrote on the Seven Year Plan, Leroy noted that "the history of these months is rich with the devotion and sacrifice of the friends. With little or no regard for their own affairs, our pioneers and settlers hastened to take up their posts."[27]

By this date the make-up of the National Teaching Committee had changed somewhat. In addition to the oldtimers, Leroy Ioas, Lottie Linfoot, George Latimer, Milly Collins, and Marion Holley, were added Sara Kenny, wife of the former Attorney General of California, and the staunch Amelia Bowman; both were to pioneer to Europe under the second Seven Year Plan. As for the National Assembly, it had among its members during most of these years of the Seven Year Plan, seven persons who would in future be named Hands of the Cause: Louis Gregory, Horace Holley, Milly Collins, Dorothy Baker, Roy Wilhelm, Siegfried Schopflocher and Leroy.

Although Shoghi Effendi was constantly informed of the progress of the Seven Year Plan, the National Assembly and the committee did not wish to burden him unduly with facts and figures. But the Guardian wanted them all. In a letter written on behalf of Shoghi Effendi, Leroy is urged to continue sending detailed reports: "He enjoys very much receiving actual figures and details of how the Plan is progressing, and appreciates your having sent him this data at length. The number of pioneers already placed since Convention of 1942 is truly imposing, and, although he follows closely all reports in *Bahá'í*

*News*, minutes of the N.S.A., etc., he had not realized that so large a number had gone forth in less than a year, and this information truly rejoices his often heavily burdened heart! . . . Such letters, far from burdening him, make his work easier, as they give him a more complete picture of what is going on and encourage him."[28] In that same year Rúhíyyih Khánum writes to Leroy: "The wonderful work which you and the National Teaching Committee are doing thrills me, though I have had no chance to tell you so. And better than anything, it makes the Guardian happy and helps lighten his often over-burdened heart – surely that one thing makes it blessed in the sight of Bahá'u'lláh."

Only seven virgin areas (there was at this stage of the plan a new definition of the term: it now meant places settled by Bahá'ís but as yet without an Assembly) remained as the last year of the plan opened. They were Nebraska, North and South Dakota, South Carolina, Alaska, Saskatchewan and Prince Edward Island. The momentum must continue. To form the basic nine-member Assemblies in the remaining virgin areas would at that point require a minimum of twenty-six pioneers. In answer to the many appeals, volunteers continued to arise. Sixty-nine moved into these areas, strengthening the new communities by their numbers. This movement was greatly stimulated when the Guardian wrote that during the last year of the plan new Assemblies could be formed at any time that the requisite nine members were available. (Bahá'í institutions are usually formed only on April 21 during the Riḍván period.)[29]

And yet there were sudden wrenching setbacks. A pioneer would decide to leave his post – a goal won would be lost. Writing for the Guardian, Rúhíyyih Khánum notes in December of 1943, just five months before the end of the plan, that "he is very anxious to have it impressed on the minds of the pioneers that they should not, by carelessly leaving their posts at such a critical moment, jeopardize the labors of hundreds of their fellow-believers over a period of seven long years of devoted self-sacrifice and effort. It seems almost silly to think that one or two people could, at the last moment, blemish the perfection of this vast concerted enterprise of the American friends and deprive the whole Bahá'í world of a victory the completeness of which alone can befittingly crown our first Bahá'í century – such a century of light and heroic sacrifice!"

But, she adds, "ultimately all the battle of life is within the individ-

*The National Spiritual Assembly, 1939, during the first Seven Year Plan.*

*From left: Louis Gregory, Harlan Ober, Dorothy Baker, Leroy Ioas, Fred Schopflocher, Horace Holley, Amelia Collins, Roy Wilhelm, Allen McDaniel. Seven future Hands of the Cause served on this Assembly*

*At the office*

ual. No amount of organization can solve the inner problems or produce or prevent victory or failure at a crucial moment. In such times as these particularly, individuals are torn by great forces at large in the world, and we see some weak ones suddenly become miraculously strong, and strong ones fail – we can only try, through loving advice, as your Committee has done, to bring about the act on the part of the believer which will be for the highest good of the Cause."[30] Leroy wrote to the Guardian: "You may be sure the members of the teaching committee one and all will leave no stone unturned to gain complete and final victory, *even* if they all find it necessary at the last moment to move to virgin areas to do so."

As the consummation of the plan approached – timed to coincide with the centenary of the founding of the Faith – the Guardian called for a great proclamation campaign to celebrate the historic occasion befittingly. It came in his message of March 1943: "An unprecedented, a carefully conceived, efficiently co-ordinated, nation-wide campaign, aiming at the proclamation of the Message of Bahá'u'lláh, through speeches, articles in the press, and radio broadcasts, should be promptly initiated and vigorously prosecuted."[31]

The National Teaching Committee had hoped to accomplish the goals of the Seven Year Plan rapidly so that much of the Bahá'í year might be devoted to the proclamation campaign. This did not happen. But the committee nonetheless went ahead to formulate a program, approved by the National Spiritual Assembly, that would integrate all the resources of the community in a mighty centennial effort. The remainder of the Bahá'í year was divided into five periods of two months each. During each two month period public meetings, publicity, radio programs and other teaching activities would revolve around a given theme. The five themes chosen were race unity, religious unity, world order, the Manifestation, and the Bahá'í centenary. This program reached into every nook and cranny of the community of believers and became the most widespread proclamation effort in the history of the Faith in America.

While plans for the campaign were going forward, the goals of the Seven Year Plan still had to be achieved. The sacrifices of the past six years would be meaningless if the remaining Assemblies could not be established. In the fall and the spring of 1943–44 the necessary contingent of settlers had reached their posts. But it was not until the night of

March 28, 1944 that the final three Assemblies were formed, all in a single night, to complete the goals of the Seven Year Plan.

The story is told by Marion Holley that the committee members were huddled together on that evening in a lobby of the Palace Hotel in San Francisco, where one of the large proclamation events was about to start. Marion said the last Canadian Assembly had decided not to form because, although they were nine, they thought they were not sufficiently deepened in the teachings to form an Assembly. She said Leroy took off to a telephone, got them on the line and in her words "gave 'em hell". It is not difficult to imagine – six years of work and sacrifice to be lost because they felt they were not strong enough! They agreed to form the Assembly that night, and the committee went in to the meeting and made a public announcement of the completion of the Seven Year Plan.

That was March 28th. On the 29th, Leroy received a cable from Horace Holley, secretary of the National Assembly:

HAVE CABLED GUARDIAN AS FOLLOWS QUOTE: FORMATION ASSEMBLIES REGINA CHARLOTTETOWN MONCTON MARCH 28 COMPLETES REQUIREMENTS SEVEN YEAR PLAN NORTH AMERICA ACCLAIM SPIRITUAL VICTORY ENTIRE BAHA'I COMMUNITY AND EXTRAORDINARY ACHIEVEMENT NATIONAL AND REGIONAL TEACHING COMMITTEES. END QUOTE. MEMBERS OF NATIONAL ASSEMBLY WOULD SURELY WISH EXTEND PERSONAL CONGRATULATIONS TO ALL MEMBERS YOUR COMMITTEE.

On April 2nd Leroy received a cablegram from Haifa:

OVERJOYED SUCCESSFUL CONCLUSION HISTORIC TASK STOP ASSURE MEMBERS NATIONAL TEACHING COMMITTEE ABIDING GRATITUDE CONSUMMATION PROFOUND ADMIRATION BRILLIANT EXPLOITS STOP TRANSMIT REGIONAL COMMITTEES EXPRESSION LOVING APPRECIATION INVALUABLE ASSISTANCE. SHOGHI RABBANI[32]

A copy of this was sent by Leroy to every pioneer in the field.

When Leroy looked back on the plan it was evident to him that its success was due primarily to two things: the appeals of the Guardian and the sacrifices of the pioneers. Every surge of energy over those seven years he saw as the response of the Bahá'ís to the fervent calls of the Guardian for greater effort, more sacrifice, perseverance, holding their posts, rising to the standard of the Dawn-breakers whose spiritual heirs, he assured them, they were. The Guardian sounded the call, and they offered themselves as the troops who answered the call. Pioneering was a thrilling service that focused the soul. Many years later in Haifa, when the Guardian outlined the goals of the Ten Year Crusade and asked those present which of the goals they thought would be achieved most quickly, Leroy immediately said: the pioneering goals, because that is what excites the Bahá'ís.

In the first Seven Year Plan two hundred and ninety-three believers went out to render this service. Their common experience was that they were confirmed in everything they attempted to do, and that God did indeed assist all those who arose to serve Him. Little wonder that the Guardian had challenged the Bahá'ís: "Let the doubter arise and himself verify the truth of such assertions."[33]

"What will the future say", Leroy wrote in a report, "of men and women, who, in the midst of an unparalleled depression, forsook their positions and security and established their independence anew, often in areas of underprivileged and low economic level? Who can estimate the obstacles which beset them in all the aspects of life, as they found new homes, sought work, built friendships, adjusted the relationships of their children, carried the responsibilities of the Faith, and held 'aloft and undimmed the torch of Divine Guidance'? How fully do we appreciate the arduous labors of the pioneers to establish and organize administrative institutions, often with little or no experience, learning as they taught, helping new friends to mature . . . what will humanity conclude when, looking back on this darkest period and appalled by the problems and agonies of war, it discovers these 'stalwart warriors' of God, who pursued their undeviating course, while the nations crumbled, erecting the foundation of the coming world?"[34]

In the first forty-three years of Bahá'í history in North America, 1894 to 1937, seventy-two local institutions of the Faith were established. In the short span of the Seven Year Plan, the number rose to one hundred and thirty-six.

"My heart," the Guardian told the believers, "is filled with joy, love, pride and gratitude at the contemplation of the stupendous shining deed immortalizing the valiant prosecutors of the greatest collective enterprise ever launched in the course of the history of the Faith of Bahá'u'lláh."[35]

The reader will say, but we have sent out thousands of pioneers, all over the world, to many more difficult places. Yes, but this was the great experiment, the birth of the process envisioned by 'Abdu'l-Bahá and given life by the Guardian, the first organized endeavor to achieve the Divine Plan of the Master, Who certainly watched over its progress and aided its accomplishment. That was its unique quality, that it was a laboratory to determine the techniques and to forge the pattern to be followed in the future.

Over it all hovered the Guardian. This was *his* plan, he shaped its goals and he inspired the friends to pursue and accomplish them. Yet he never mentioned himself or his role in accomplishing it. After the Guardian's passing Leroy often spoke of how Shoghi Effendi would refer to the time of the Báb, the time of Bahá'u'lláh, the time of 'Abdu'l-Bahá, and then, the Formative Age. Therefore let us turn to the word picture left by Rúḥíyyih Khánum of his role during this momentous endeavor:

> If we view aright what happened in 1937 at the beginning of the first Seven Year Plan, we see that Shoghi Effendi, now in his fortieth year, stepped out as the general leading an army – the North American Bahá'ís – and marched off to the spiritual conquest of the Western Hemisphere. While other generals, famous in the eyes of the world, were leading vast armies to destruction all over the planet, fighting battles of unprecedented horror in Europe, Asia and Africa, this unknown general, unrecognized and unsung, was devising and prosecuting a campaign more vital and far-reaching than anything they could ever do . . . They fought for . . . the past order of things. He fought for the future, with its radiant age of peace and unity, a world society and the Kingdom of God on earth. Their names and battles are slowly being forgotten, but Shoghi Effendi's name and fame is rising steadily, and his victories rise in greatness with him, never to be forgotten.[36]

That Leroy should have been one of the soldiers in that army is the sole reason we tell his story.

# CHAPTER FOURTEEN

# The Republics of the South

THE story of the first Seven Year Plan would be incomplete if the pioneering endeavors in Central and South America were not mentioned. Though not directly related to our theme, the work in Latin America was one to which Leroy gave several years of effort as a member of the Inter-America Committee which had been charged with fulfilling the goals of the Plan in the southern hemisphere. He served only three years on the committee, 1937 to 1940, as he was at the same time chairing the National Teaching Committee and serving on the National Assembly.

In 1936, a year before the start of the Seven Year Plan, Shoghi Effendi had already, as we have seen, formulated one of its goals: the establishment by the end of the first Bahá'í century (1944) of a permanent settlement in every republic of Central and South America. The Inter-America Committee was formed in response to that message and drew up plans to send traveling teachers to visit the cities of the southern hemisphere. One year later when the Seven Year Plan was launched, Leroy was added to the committee, serving in a sense as a consultant because of his experience in planning teaching campaigns. Also named to the committee as an associate member was a very new Bahá'í of Latin America, Pedro Espinosa of Mexico City. The story of the opening of Latin America to the teachings of Bahá'u'lláh is one of high adventure, which is told befittingly elsewhere.[1]

The land mass to the south of the United States, stretching some six thousand miles in length, was almost totally devoid of Bahá'ís in 1936. A few North American Bahá'ís lived there: two women who had settled in Bahia, Brazil in the 1920s because of the significance

'Abdu'l-Bahá attached to that name in the Tablets of the Divine Plan, another who lived in Peru because of her husband's work, and one who was discovered in São Paulo by a Bahá'í traveler.

The countries of Latin America, as the Guardian had pointed out, were a composite of all the native peoples of the Americas plus varying strains of Europeans and even Asians. There was no uniform life pattern, but quite distinct social and political structures. And one of the great challenges in approaching the people of the southern continent was that the bearers of the Message of Bahá'u'lláh were persons coming from the north. Latin Americans were to be asked to accept a new Faith from the hands of North Americans, whose motives were almost universally mistrusted. It is a tribute to the sincerity of spirit of the Latin Americans that they responded with warmth and interest to the Bahá'í teachers.

The first Bahá'í to venture into the southern hemisphere was Kathryn Franklin who visited Mexico in 1912 at the request of 'Abdu'l-Bahá. But it was Martha Root who, obeying 'Abdu'l-Bahá's directive to her ("*Go thou to South America*"), set out on her dramatic trip of 1919 and first implanted the teachings in a number of the major cities of that continent. There was at the time but one small pamphlet in the Spanish language.

In the early 1930s spasmodic trips to South America were undertaken by a group of independent spirits who did the preparatory spade work for what was later to become an organized program of settlement. Among these traveling teachers were Frances Benedict Stewart, Nellie French of California, who later became the backbone of the Inter-America Committee, and Loulie and Edward Mathews who at the request of Shoghi Effendi visited the major countries of South America in 1935. They traveled through the territory, organizing and giving lectures, meeting journalists, calling on people. They went wherever the doors opened to them. A typical example of how they worked: Frances Stewart in 1936 attended a People's Peace Conference called in Buenos Aires as a symbol of resistance to the war mood in Europe. She was astonished at the warm response her remarks on the Bahá'í teachings engendered at the conference, and immediately decided to remain several additional months, teaching in the major countries: Brazil, Argentina and Chile. Another traveler was Orcella

Rexford, whom we have met in a previous chapter, who set out with Beatrice Irwin on a lecture tour of Mexico.

There were many spiritual adventures as these early travelers were led to the waiting souls. During the Mathews's second trip to the region, they followed a dauntingly difficult path through the Andes, crossing the lakes in winter and finding, on the deserted shore of Lake Llanquihue (Lake of All Saints) a German couple long established in South America, who had been searching for such a message of unity. While the Mathews awaited the boat that would take them across the lake, the German woman translated the whole of Shoghi Effendi's *The Goal of a New World Order* into Spanish. (It was a notable feature of the work in South America that the new believers immediately began the task of translation.) In some places the travelers founded study groups and in one, an entire Spiritual Assembly. Frances Stewart has left a description of how this first Assembly in Latin America was formed:

In Mexico City, while speaking to a Woman's Club on the subject of "Peace in a New World Order", and quoting from the Writings quite freely, I noticed the deep interest of a lady not far from me. After the meeting she hurried to beg me to go with her that evening to the home of a friend where a group met weekly for study and discussion . . . I went with [her] to meet nine Mexican people . . . My friend explained that for several years this group of seekers had met regularly to discuss spiritual questions and to study the increasing turmoil in the world . . . they asked me to repeat the message I had given at the club in the afternoon. I then asked if I might tell them of the Bahá'í Message.

Way into the morning hours they listened and asked questions about the Cause and asked that I meet with them often and they would bring to the circle all of their group. After three such meetings with an ever larger group, the leader told me that they had for some time been convinced that somewhere in the world a New Manifestation had appeared to give the Truth for the New Era. So convinced had they been that they had sent their leader, Mr. Espinosa, to the United States, where he traveled from New York City to California in search of evidence of this New Manifestation. He did not find it but returned to Mexico . . . They had continued their regular studies and when they heard the Bahá'í Message, they were convinced it was the Truth they had long sought. At this meeting Mr. Espinosa handed me a paper on which were written the

names of the nine I had first met saying they wished to be received as
Believers of the Bahá'í Faith and would become the center for spreading
the Message throughout Mexico.[2]

Several of the new Mexican believers journeyed to Wilmette the following year to attend the National Convention, the first time the
continents of North and South America had been joined in Bahá'í
activity and a harbinger of the unity that was steadily to grow between
the Bahá'ís of North and South America.

These trips were described as "apostolic" journeys by a Bahá'í
writer, Dr. Garreta Busey.[3] They mark the first phase of the work in the
southern hemisphere.

But the Guardian wanted more than traveling teachers passing
through a country or remaining a short time. He was calling for permanent settlement that would permit a "systematic penetration" of the
continent.[4] This opened a new phase in the work of the Inter-America
Committee, that of finding settlers for both the more conservative and
difficult countries of Central America and for the rapidly developing
new communities left in the wake of the itinerant travelers in South
America. The committee looked first at Central America, where the
populations were entrenched in traditional thought and habits. This
was the most difficult phase of the work but also the most significant,
marking as it did the first step of the North Americans on their world
mission outside their own borders.

Settlement in these countries was not easy. Work, language,
customs, religious tradition, all were barriers to easy accommodation
for the Bahá'í settlers. And yet people rose up with excitement and
determination and the Inter-America Committee backed up the settlers in every way possible. One of their creative steps was to institute
special training courses for those going to Latin America. Loulie
Mathews and her husband offered their ranch in Colorado for use as a
training school. She relinquished chairmanship of the committee to
devote herself to organizing the International School, as it was called.
It held its first session in 1940. The committee also actively promoted
the indispensable work of translating Bahá'í materials into Spanish
and Portuguese, and into French for the island of Haiti. But getting the
materials to the new centers proved extremely complicated due to
customs barriers and certain types of censorship. When a publishing

and distribution center was established in Buenos Aires toward the end of the plan, this task was greatly simplified.

At the mid-point of the teaching campaign in Latin America, an unexpected and dramatic event, the death of an outstanding Bahá'í, bound the two continents inextricably together. This sacrifice of life cemented, in the words of Shoghi Effendi, the "spiritual union of the Americas". Setting out in poor health to take the spirit of 'Abdu'l-Bahá and of the Guardian to the new believers of South America was the preeminent Bahá'í teacher, May Maxwell, the mother of the French and Canadian communities. Barely had she arrived at her destination, the city of Buenos Aires, when she was stricken with a fatal heart attack. At her memorial, there gathered together many newly enrolled believers, a number of Mrs. Maxwell's colleagues from North America, and many of the pioneers to the central and southern republics. The Guardian lauded this extraordinary woman: ". . . she set her face towards the southern outpost of the Faith in the New World, and laid down her life in such a spirit of consecration and self-sacrifice as has truly merited the crown of martyrdom."[5] She was the second American martyr, following in the footsteps of Keith Ransom-Kehler, who died of smallpox in Isfahan while on a mission for the Guardian.

Following this spiritual sacrifice, the work gained momentum everywhere. Numerous pioneers arose in answer to the Guardian's appeals – strong and devoted Bahá'ís – and the new believers themselves were arising to do the work. Individuals outside the capital cities, without the help of resident pioneers, started their own study classes, which turned into groups, and then Assemblies. There was a sense of vitality in the teaching work everywhere, from the Caribbean to Panama and through all the republics to the south. Even Haiti, the most resistant to the efforts of its devoted pioneers, beginning with Louis Gregory and his wife, at last yielded some fruit: by April of 1942 there were nine Spiritual Assemblies.

The last two years of the plan were passed with the war raging everywhere and affecting all areas of the continent. It became more difficult to send out pioneers; the voyage to the south was dangerous. And yet, as has so often happened in the history of the Faith, the fledgling groups thrived in spite of the turmoil surrounding them. Typical of the growth was that of Santiago, Chile. "With astounding rapidity,"

writes Dr. Busey, "the Cause in Santiago ran through phases of development which had required in many North American communities a
range of years: the growth from isolated believer to group, the development of wide publicity, the testing of the believers whereby they were
trained in unity among themselves, the beginning of extension work,
and finally, in 1943, the organization of an assembly."[6]

The key to such rapid growth lay in the rapidity with which the new
believers themselves accepted to shoulder the work of spreading the
teachings. These newly-enrolled Bahá'ís plunged into the translating
work, they sought effective publicity, they audaciously went beyond the
borders of their own land to assist other countries, they set up children's classes and youth groups, and they put their own knowledge of
their countries at the disposal of the pioneers.

In 1943 a victory – dear to the heart of the Guardian – was
achieved when Mrs. Stewart went at his request to Magallanes, the
southernmost tip of the western hemisphere. She was the first Bahá'í
to set foot there and she remained until she could leave a group of
Bahá'ís.

Already several months before the end of the Seven Year Plan, the
Inter-America Committee reported that the goals in Central and
South America were assured of accomplishment. No Latin American
country, it wrote, is without a group of believers. From Magallanes to
Alaska, Bahá'u'lláh is known, and believers throughout the Americas
stand ready for new tasks in a new Bahá'í century.

In mid-April of 1944 the first All-American Bahá'í Convention was
held in Wilmette. The Guardian sent a powerful message to the Convention, addressed to the "elected representatives of all the
communities of the New World". It was surely a recompense for all the
effort and sacrifice that had been made. In it he wrote:

> I, on my own behalf, as well as in the name of all Bahá'í Communities
> sharing with them, at this great turning point in the history of our Faith,
> the joys and triumphs of this solemn hour, feel moved to convey the
> expression of our loving admiration, our joy and our gratitude for the bril-
> liant conclusion of what posterity will no doubt acclaim as one of the
> most stirring episodes in the history of the Formative Age of the Faith of
> Bahá'u'lláh. . . .[7]

CHAPTER FIFTEEN

# Family Life

IT was within the circle of his family, and in particular in his relation to Sylvia, that Leroy found refuge from the stress of activity that swirled around him.

Though it was evident that he was the dominant partner of the two, it was she who provided much of his emotional support and they were both aware of this. Sylvia knew she had married a man of special capacity and she spent an increasing amount of time trying to ease his burdens. In fact as the years passed, she came to speak among close friends of a "they" who expected too much of him, who asked him to do too many things, who turned to him for everything.

They lived a very simple personal life, carrying out their roles of spouse and parent under the dominion of the interest that shaped their lives. As they were both of stable families they brought to their own marriage a strong sense of the ties of family. Leroy was delighted when Sylvia's parents moved to California shortly after they themselves had done so, and pleased that his brother Arthur decided to move west with his family. It was normal to him that Sylvia's widowed mother would later come to live with them for some years, just as he expected his brothers and sisters who lived near their mother to make a home for her when she was not able to live alone.

What might surprise some readers is the balance which they achieved between a public, dominant partner and a second who was fulfilled in her domain of assisting, maintaining the family and aiding the work of her husband. And yet so it was. Sylvia loved her role as mother and homemaker and as companion to Leroy's endeavors, all of which gave her pleasure and satisfaction.

From the start of their marriage, Sylvia was an energetic teammate, creating a home wherever they lived, serving in whatever capacity she could in the affairs of the community. She did innumerable jobs for "Roy" as she always called him, and gradually took on more and larger tasks as she grew in experience and confidence. (In a letter to Vancouver in the late 20s, Leroy says he will send along a report on the Geyserville classes as soon as it is ready: "Sylvia is now making a copy and inasmuch as it is nineteen pages long, single space, you will realize it may take a few days." There were of course no photocopying machines at the time.) When they lived in Burlingame with two small babies, she was nonetheless able to arrange a large luncheon meeting for the visiting Bahá'í, Jináb-i-Faḍíl, at the prestigious Exchange Club that was composed of leading business people of the area. We have noted her services at the first Bahá'í Center in San Francisco which she continued until the work adversely affected her health. She then had more time to play one of her favorite roles: that of welcoming hostess. As we saw at the start of their marriage, they were of like mind on the question of hospitality,* viewing it as one of the sure ways to make friends and establish close bonds with others.

They were an effective team in another way. Sylvia took a very personal interest in each individual and what he was doing, and therefore drew to her many of those who might be intimidated by Leroy's mental prowess and the leadership aura which he projected. Isobel Sabri remarked on how rarely one found a person like Sylvia who took joy in the accomplishments of others, and this seemed to be her special role in the Bahá'í community: to recognize the services of the most humble and let them know they were of value. These factors were all building blocks in creating a strong community in San Francisco.

Their tests as a married couple came principally from Leroy's constant involvement in activities that kept him away from home. At a certain point after they moved to their own house in San Francisco and Sylvia was confined with young children, she became deeply saddened that she almost never saw him. It was one of her many sacrifices for the furtherance of the Bahá'í work.

---

* David Hofman said they embodied what is known as American hospitality. When the Hofmans came to America with one-year-old May, Leroy and Sylvia, who were called out of town, left the keys to their house and car for the Hofmans and told them to make themselves at home.

Someone of Leroy's forceful character inevitably attracted a certain amount of criticism. It was sometimes personal, perhaps jealousy from those of more ambitious personality than him. Sometimes it resulted from his riding too roughshod over people's opinions, shortcircuiting discussion to get things done. A colleague said he was "not a great consulter". Yet William Sears remembered how patient Leroy was with him when he served as a new Bahá'í on the San Francisco Assembly. Marion Holley also remembered his patience with her as a new Bahá'í on that same Assembly. Here is an interesting contrast. Where he could be a teacher, with new, capable Bahá'ís serving with him, his patience was endless. But he could simply turn away from those who did not grasp something quickly enough to get a job done. Impatience was the great weakness in his character; he knew it; he tried to control it, sometimes succeeding but many times not. In a letter written to his cherished friend Eunice Braun some months before his death – in which he expresses irritation with a local workman – he says "patience is a virtue – but I wonder where and why?" Then as he reads the letter over before signing it, he puts in the margin "not to be quoted".

But the criticisms hurt because he knew that his motives were pure. As his friend Sally Sanor commented, Leroy had no axe to grind, or if he was grinding an axe, he openly said so. He once wrote to Roy Wilhelm, who had himself been the object at one period of continuous criticism: "What certain ones can accomplish by attacking the hardworking, faithful Bahá'ís, I don't know. If there is a hell, it is such situations that firm believers have to go through!"

Leroy was a man of complex character and certain traits of his character did not live peacefully with others. As a corporate executive he possessed attributes which in the American business world assure that one will accomplish what one sets out to do. He was practical, hard-headed, aggressive, a top manager and administrator, decisive, impatient. In the business world, his impatience was an asset.

On the other hand, he was spiritually minded, captive of inner thoughts and forces which people in his everyday life might never suspect. This side of him was tender, thoughtful, immensely kind, a teacher of infinite patience, a warm companion.

He was both assured and insecure. He developed great certainty as to what he was capable of doing, yet lived with some personal insecurities. He knew he was not one of the "team" who were academically brilliant and socially confident. Here he felt vulnerable, and even after repeated experiences of success still occasionally spoke of how hard he had had to work to compensate for that side of him which he had never had the opportunity to develop. In the very act of traveling to Haifa to serve Shoghi Effendi, he wrestled with whether the Guardian would like him, this Guardian whose life was touched by God, whose careful education was directed by 'Abdu'l-Bahá, whose mind was of a startling brilliance. Would he be good enough to serve him?

It is important to note that with all his impatience, Leroy never failed to praise where praise was due. Close friends who were pioneering in one of the western states learned a lesson when he passed through their city. A well known traveling teacher had come through and they were full of critical comment about her, recounting what she had done that they *knew* was wrong. He listened, and then asked how many Bahá'ís they had made in their time there. None, they replied, surprised. Well, he said, this teacher has made hundreds of Bahá'ís all over the United States. When you two have made as many Bahá'ís, then you may criticize.

It was also as a father that Leroy's tender faculties came into play. He was a caring parent, with a deep sense of responsibility toward his children, though he rarely had much free time to be with them. In an early letter to Chicago, he says he has just been playing with little Farrukh, but had to stop to write letters. In another he says our little one is getting big and a little sassy because of too much petting on our trip home. And he notes her "very joyous" disposition – the meaning of the name 'Abdu'l-Bahá had given her. He took Farrukh and Anita to children's classes and he and Sylvia established their own class in Burlingame to which the neighbors' children were invited. On the visit mentioned above of Jináb-i-Faḍíl, Ella Cooper brought Faḍíl down from San Francisco to visit with the children of "Sylvia's Garden" and later to speak with fifteen or twenty of the parents who came over for the evening.

As they grew up, his children easily accepted his active life. They simply knew that their father was often busy and frequently away on trips. One of their indelible, and, in retrospect, sad memories is of falling asleep with the sound of his typing in an adjacent room until late into the night and of hearing him groan with fatigue as he woke up in the morning.

But when he had time, there were family outings, sometimes to visit Sylvia's family or his brother Arthur. He liked to combine things – inspecting the service on a train while taking the family on a trip. This was high adventure indeed for the girls: trips in winter through the Sierras – two engines to pull the train and a snowplow to clear the tracks – to reach Lake Tahoe, then a pristine site with one rambling lodge for guests. There another thrill awaited them: sleigh rides with "Scotty" Allen, the famous Alaskan who brought his huskies to winter at Tahoe. There were trips to Santa Catalina Island and the Rose Bowl parade; whenever the children could be included they were.

As they grew older and the Guardian encouraged meetings of Bahá'í youth – then a new concept – Leroy asked Joyce Dahl to teach a class in their home for the older Bahá'í children and their friends. It was typical of the way he gave responsibility to people of capacity. Joyce was nervous about doing it but found it less difficult than she had feared, as Leroy would often sit in and casually expound on the subject under discussion. These meetings continued for several years, gradually becoming quite large and serving as a social occasion also for the young people. Years later Leroy recalled the time he first realized he was getting old. It was when his children were arranging a meeting of the young people and as he listened, he became very enthusiastic and said we'll do this and we'll do that. Then one of them said: Now listen, daddy, this is for the *young* people.

The girls loved to be part of Bahá'í activities when they could contribute something. One to which the entire family gave many exciting hours was manning the Bahá'í booth at the Golden Gate International Exposition during the summers of 1939 and 1940. Leroy had been active in planning the award-winning Bahá'í booth (a report says it "stirred the admiration of every advertising and display expert who has viewed it") which featured a model of the Temple woven structurally into the design. The Bahá'í exhibit was a tremendous success; Leroy wrote to Horace Holley that "it is developing into a much more important teaching venture than I had hoped for". One of those who stopped and spoke with Leroy's daughter was Dr. Rustum Vambéry of Budapest, the son of Arminius Vambéry, the well-known Orientalist, who welcomed 'Abdu'l-Bahá to Budapest in 1913 and felt deep friendship for Him; he considered the Bahá'í Faith "the perfect religion" and translated *Bahá'u'lláh and the New Era* into Hungarian. This son was a writer and editor interested in international cooperation; he was on his way to New York and was put in touch with Horace Holley there.

Leroy had also worked closely with Rabbi Rudolph Coffee, whom we have met in previous pages, who conceived the idea of a Temple of Religion and Tower of Peace on the fairgrounds, that would show the ways in which religion has contributed to human welfare. So the Bahá'ís had not only their own booth in one part of the fairgrounds but access to the impressive Temple of Religion. On the occasion of a "Bahá'í Day", designated as such on the official program of the exposition, the Bahá'ís sponsored a Religious Unity Service at the Temple of Religion; many of the students at Geyserville made the 75-mile journey to attend the meeting and return the same day to the school. When in October the National Assembly met in San Francisco, a "Bahá'í Day" was again designated and an afternoon Vesper Service was planned in addition to an evening meeting, both with speakers from the National Assembly.

Leroy was proud of his children. He was proud that they both went to Stanford, Farrukh the more diligent student graduating cum laude and Phi Beta Kappa. Both the girls were accepted at Stanford but had to be deferred for one year, as the university, unbelievable as it may now seem, permitted three boys to enter for every one girl. True to the immigrant tradition, all the Ioas family of their generation went to college as a matter of course. He was proud that they both spent some years pioneering. His younger daughter was very similar to him in character, and understood his moods and his reactions. Over the years they sometimes just exchanged glances and then laughed or shook their head, as they reacted in the same way to the same thing. It was an intuitive bond that Anita cherished. They had wonderful deep talks together and he even at times sought her opinion. Perhaps because Farrukh spent more time at home she tended to understand Sylvia's problems better than her sister. Leroy knew Farrukh needed him more than her sister did and he made special efforts to protect her.

The health of their elder daughter was to cause Sylvia and Leroy great sorrow. She was an outgoing personality, always in the thick of activity as a child and young person. But as a teenager she was struck with infantile paralysis which affected her back; most people who knew her later were not even aware of this difficulty. But the treatment prescribed for her at age seventeen caused a change in her personality.

The doctor advised that she defer college and spend a year lying on a hard bed in the hope of arresting the effects of the polio. The long year spent reading and listening to music made her more withdrawn and dependent than she had been. Then when she could get up the doctor ordered a cast put on her torso, and with this she started junior college. Leroy had written to the Guardian and asked for prayers "for her health and protection". Finally, energetic and optimistic friends from Australia, Doctors Marietta and Stanley Bolton,* removed her from this afflictive situation by taking her away to chiropractic head-quarters in Iowa and nursing her through several months of joyful freedom and treatment.

With her keen and thoughtful mind, Farrukh was a superb teacher. In later years she made circuit teaching trips in the Southwest, travel-ing each week between Houston, San Antonio and Dallas to give study courses on which she spent hours of preparation, so similar to her father's habit when he gave classes. The travel was very trying, overnight between each city, but she continued the circuit even after she fell and broke her ankle. At one time she worked closely with Eunice Braun[†] in the Publishing Trust and hosted a classical music series on an Evanston radio station. She lived with Sylvia and Leroy in Wilmette and later went to France and Italy to help in the work of the Bahá'í communities there. While in Paris she worked day and night to strengthen the communities in preparation for the formation of the first National Spiritual Assembly in 1958. And she did it through the steady attacks on her endeavors from an American who lived in France, and who later became a Covenant-breaker, closely linked to Mason Remey. Leroy wrote her a long letter of consolation, saying "it seems the lot of some of us to serve without proper consideration . . . I have seen that you too have this lot. One must serve for the Faith alone, the appreciation and reward come from God and from Him alone." It was in France that she developed cancer and was persuaded to return to live with her sister in Washington. During her last year, and suspect-ing how sick she was, she nonetheless answered the call of the Hands of the Cause for pioneers, telling Anita: "I have no excuse not to go."

* Stalwart early Bahá'ís of Australia whose farm, Yerrinbool, became the site of the Aus-tralian Bahá'í summer school; Stanley Bolton served for eighteen years on the National Spiritual Assembly.

† who was asked by Leroy and Sylvia to write her obituary, *Bahá'í World*, vol. XIII, p. 919.

She left the security of her sister's affection to return to Italy. There the cancer recurred and within a few months she passed away in Washington with her family gathered around her.

It was a traumatic event for Sylvia and Leroy. But toward the end, knowing the disease had spread widely, Leroy wanted her to be released, saying oh, why doesn't 'Abdu'l-Bahá let her go! He wrote to David and Marion Hofman after her passing that "the Hands in the Holy Land were praying for Farrukh at the Holy Shrines, so we know it was not in the plan of things for her to get well. But it is hard for us to become reconciled to the fact that we will not see Farrukh's smiling face again in the physical form . . ."

Milly Collins told Leroy and Sylvia she thought Farrukh the most spiritually mature person she had ever met; Leroy said if this were so, no doubt she had to move on to the spiritual world. Valera Allen wrote to them that without a doubt "there will be many . . . who will rise up and call her blessed." After her passing, Sylvia and Leroy deputized a number of Bahá'í teachers in Africa and one in Italy in her memory, and donated parts of her excellent library to the French National Center, the Geyserville School and personal friends.

A last note concerning that difficult period of April 1960. An honored guest at her funeral was the then Hand of the Cause Mason Remey, who even at that moment had sent off his pronouncement to the U.S. National Spiritual Assembly with the astounding claim to be the second Guardian and requesting the allegiance of the Bahá'ís to his person. Thus, within days of Farrukh's passing, Leroy was galvanized into action by this news and left Washington immediately for Wilmette where the National Convention was convening. In some curious way, his younger daughter was grateful that at least his thoughts were diverted away from his grief and into protection of the Faith.

In the next year Leroy and Sylvia were given a new and joyful role to play, that of grandparent. When they learned the first grandchild was expected, they went to the Shrines and prayed for the new soul. In June when Catherine was born, Sylvia slipped the cablegram announcing her birth in to Leroy, who was attending a meeting of the Hands of the Cause, and all stopped to pray for her. Leroy wrote to his daughter: "The evolution of life is one of the great miracles of God, and it will be a continuing joy and happiness to you both, as the child grows and becomes more and more a part of your lives. Her happiness will become your happiness and her accomplishments your accomplishments." When they learned that a second child was expected, Leroy again took the long philosophic view: "It is better when a child has brothers or sisters so they do not have to grow up alone. It gives companionship and an appreciation of the views, hopes and aspirations of others." It was a boy, Hillary, who was born the next August and Leroy often looked at his picture and said, he has a fine head. He kept their picture next to his bed always. They were but three and four when he passed away; his second granddaughter, Jennifer, was born six months later.

# CHAPTER SIXTEEN

# The Last Years in San Francisco

THE few years Leroy was still to spend in San Francisco passed in a steady flow of activity and more personal pleasure than he had previously had time to savor. The worst struggles were behind him. He had achieved position in his professional life and his Bahá'í activities were crowned with success. It was a time of fruition.

He was to remain on the National Teaching Committee only one more year. On July 31, 1945, Lottie Linfoot, secretary of the committee, sent out letters: "This evening concludes the term of office of all the members of the National Teaching Committee except Mrs. Amelia Collins, and in bidding you an official farewell, we wish to express our deepest appreciation . . ." For all of them who had worked so closely together, an era had closed.

In 1946 Leroy was not elected to the National Assembly, the first break from this service in fourteen years. During the previous year he had found it difficult to absent himself several days at a time from work, so that he had missed a number of meetings; in a note to Roy Wilhelm he joked that he was away so much they were starting to dock his pay.

It was a change of pace to be neither on the National Assembly nor on the national committee which was in the forefront of activity. Rúḥíyyih Khánum writes to him in a note in July 1946: "After all the wonderful work you did during the Seven Year Plan you must feel empty handed at present . . ."

However, while he was still a member of both bodies, there came another challenge – unexpected, exciting, historic. Let us look at that now.

It was March of 1945: the war was not yet over but the Allied leaders had for several years been laying plans for the post-war peace.

Marion Holley left her office one day after work and had not gone a half block before she heard newspaper boys yelling: Extra! Extra! The three Allied leaders meeting in Yalta had agreed that San Francisco would be the site for the convening of an international conference to create an organization to preserve the peace.

She rushed home to telephone Leroy and they immediately agreed that the Bahá'ís must take some action in response to this opportunity. An emergency meeting of the San Francisco Assembly was called, followed by a meeting of all the area Assemblies. It was evident this would be an occasion to proclaim Bahá'u'lláh's peace program to the government leaders and the world media who would be present.

As news of the conference spread, Bahá'ís everywhere were struck with wonder as they remembered the words spoken by 'Abdu'l-Bahá in 1912 in Sacramento, the capital of California: "I hope that advocates of peace may daily increase among [you] until the whole population shall stand for that beneficent outcome. . . . May the first flag of international peace be upraised in this state."[1] A Peace Plan Committee was appointed by the National Assembly on March 19, 1945 with Leroy, Marion and eight others. Their mandate was to "bring the Bahá'í teachings on peace to the attention of the delegates and the general public, but to emphasize the spiritual aspects of peace and the larger implications of the World Order of Bahá'u'lláh". The National Assembly cautioned that the teachings should be offered as a gift, and "not be associated in the public mind with the forms of sectarian pressure that were bound to be exerted during the Conference".

The Conference was to open on April 25, in little more than one month. It was therefore necessary to act swiftly and efficiently. As if in answer to the historic need, a wealth of Bahá'í talent had grown up in the area and an extraordinary variety of strong Bahá'ís was available to work on this significant endeavor.

In that brief time, and with the assistance of a number of sub-committees, they were able to produce the prestigious pamphlet *The Bahá'í Peace Program*, which was presented to all delegates and officials at the Conference, to deliver a series of radio broadcasts during the two months of the Conference, to create displays and exhibits, and to secure local and national press coverage. The crowning endeavor was

to host a banquet and large public meeting to which a number of delegates were invited. Particular mention should be made here of Dr.
Rudolf Holsti, former Minister of Foreign Affairs of Finland and
refugee professor at Stanford, who rendered valuable services to the
committee through advising them in the selection and approach to be
made to the delegates invited for this occasion. Dr. Holsti had taught
Bahá'í students at Stanford, attended Bahá'í meetings in Palo Alto,
and was one of the speakers at this public meeting.

The city bustled with activity in preparation for the United Nations
Conference.* Roosevelt had suggested this name for the organization
three years earlier and Churchill had agreed and quoted Byron to
him.[†] It was a time of expectation and hope. The new President,
Harry Truman, opened the Conference, speaking from Washington:
"Justice remains the greatest power on earth. To that tremendous
power alone will we submit . . . with Divine guidance, friendly cooperation and hard work we shall find an answer . . ."

Two months later, on June 26, Truman came to San Francisco to
sign the Charter of the United Nations in concert with the statesmen
of other nations. The United Nations had been born.

Two impressions are of interest. One is that of a Stanford student
who was attending her first Bahá'í meeting:

> The Bahá'ís had organized a large public meeting which was attended by
> 500 people. Leroy and Dorothy Baker were the Bahá'í speakers, and a
> Professor Holsti from Stanford. Marion Holley was the chairman. I
> remember very distinctly how impressive the entire occasion was. And
> then after the meeting, Leroy invited a group of about twenty of us to go
> out for ice cream. Dorothy Baker was there, and Marion Holley, and
> perhaps Firuz and Amin.[‡] We had a lovely, lovely evening, sitting until
> late, talking about the Faith and the wonderfully successful meeting.
> Everyone was very, very happy. Leroy had such a capacity for enthusiasm

---

* For a brilliant word picture of the city and the Conference see "California – Host to the
Nations" by Marzieh Gail, *The Bahá'í World*, vol x, p. 679.

† Lord Byron, *Childe Harold's Pilgrimage*: "Here, where the sword United Nations drew, Our
countrymen were warring on that day! And this is much – and all – which will not pass
away."

‡ Firuz Kazemzadeh and Amin Banani, Stanford students at the time, later professors at
Yale University and the University of California at Los Angeles.

and happiness about the successes of the Faith! . . . that meeting had been preceded by a banquet for some of the delegates, about thirty had been invited, and the delegates sat on the platform during the meeting. It was an outstanding public relations activity for the Faith."[2]

The other is that of one of the chief delegates, Sir A. Ramaswami Mudaliar of India:

It was in San Francisco in 1945 that I first had the privilege of meeting the followers of the Bahá'í Faith and learning something of the teachings of their great Prophet. I had spoken at the Plenary Session and had pointed out that it was not the independence of nations but their inter-dependence that had to be emphasized. . . . the distinctions of race and religion, of color and creed, are but superficial. A small group of Bahá'ís who were at the conference congratulated me afterwards on having given expression on that world platform to some of the beliefs that they held dear. . . . *"You are the fruits of one tree and the leaves of one branch"* says the Prophet. Again and again I have come across such sayings which have forcibly reminded me of the teachings of the Vedas. "Whenever virtue subsides and vice triumphs, then am I reborn to redeem mankind.". . . The Bahá'ís try to quicken the noble impulses of the true followers of every religion with the spirit of catholicity and fraternalism. How much the world needs such a spirit today . . . how far we are from that one far off divine event to which the whole creation is destined to move . . . the Fatherhood of God and the Brotherhood of man.[3]

A last memoir of this historic occasion. An early California Bahá'í, Ramona Allen Brown, had been with 'Abdu'l-Bahá during His visit to Sacramento, and was also present at the final United Nations ceremony, about which she wrote: "The setting on the stage was most unusual. On the curtain at the back was a large gold seal of the United Nations, and in a semicircle on the stage were the faintly waving flags of many, many nations. President Truman presided at a large oval table. After addresses by several important statesmen, the time came for the signing of the Charter. Then, in the most thrilling moment, a flag was brought onto the stage: the flag of the United Nations . . . I saw the fulfillment of prophecy: the wish of 'Abdu'l-Bahá had come true! The flag of international peace was unfurled in California."[4]

The National Assembly wrote to the Peace Committee: how providential it was that "at the very time the nations were convening this Congress, we had such outstanding Bahá'í workers to represent the Cause at the hour of the birth of the Lesser Peace . . .* Please convey the loving best wishes of the National Assembly to all members of the committee and the following excerpt from a message received from the Guardian: 'I rejoice in the success of the high endeavors of the Peace Committee in San Francisco.'"[5]

Dorothy Baker, one of the banquet speakers, went on to Wilmette and later wrote to the committee: "I'm afraid that I bragged about you at the Feast in Wilmette, for all I could think of was the wonderful group I had just left. The theme of radio was especially well received, and I passed around the newspaper publicity, and they oh'd and ah'd very much, as they realized how hard you had been working from April 25 on. Horace made it especially good when he told of a call from someone, not a Bahá'í, who had just come from San Francisco and said: "Mr. Holley, the Bahá'í Faith is very strong in the West, isn't it? It is in the papers and on the radio all the time, and a great many people were talking about it."

Within two years, the National Assembly of the United States and Canada was granted observer status as a national non-governmental organization. Application was then made for the much more important recognition of the Faith as an international NGO. All existing National Assemblies ceded authority to the Assembly of the U.S. and Canada to act in their behalf, and, under the name Bahá'í International Community, the Faith was recognized as an international NGO. The Guardian hailed this as a step that would have favorable reactions on the work of the Cause everywhere, and especially "in those parts of the world where it is still persecuted, belittled, or scorned".[6] The foundation for this relationship was laid by Shoghi Effendi himself in 1947 when he wrote a summary of the origin, teachings and institutions of the Bahá'í Faith at the specific request of the United Nations Special Palestine Committee. The Bahá'ís were first represented at an international United Nations conference in Geneva in 1948, when Mildred Mottahedeh, Ugo Giachery and Mason Remey took part in an NGO

* Bahá'u'lláh had warned the rulers in His messages He sent them in 1867 to "cling to the Lesser Peace", a political truce called from exhaustion with war, now that they had refused the Most Great Peace which was offered them in His teachings.

conference on human rights. Leroy and Marion Holley were also appointed as delegates but were unable to attend. The Guardian during this year of 1945–46 was preparing the Bahá'í world for a new challenge: "The cessation of hostilities on the continent of Europe, the prospect of an early termination of the bloody conflict raging in the Far East, invest the members of the world Bahá'í community, and particularly its standard-bearers in the great Republic of the West, with a great, a unique, and inescapable responsibility."[7]

Increasingly the Guardian speaks of the continent of Europe and the work to be done there when conditions permit and when the goals of the Seven Year Plan have been "adequately safeguarded".[8] Six months after cessation of hostilities in Europe, he appeals for assistance to the German Bahá'í community, so "dearly loved, highly honored by 'Abdu'l-Bahá". Funds and literature must start to flow immediately to alleviate their distress and rehabilitate their Bahá'í communities: "Particularly in the heart of the European continent . . . must the American believers contribute the major share in the work of rehabilitation which the followers of Bahá'u'lláh must arise to perform."[9]

It is impressive to remember how Bahá'í soldiers, caught up as everyone else in a devastating war, nonetheless reached across the barriers to carry out the imperatives of their faith. Two examples come to mind; there are no doubt many others. Two of the first U.S. soldiers among the occupation troops in Germany were young Bahá'ís. Through their access to post exchanges they were able, by paying hungry German workers with food, to facilitate the restoration of the building in central Frankfurt which became the national headquarters of the German Bahá'ís. Another story takes one into Nazi-occupied Warsaw, where the son of one of the early German Bahá'ís was posted as an ambulance driver. He found his way into the ghetto where half a million Jews had been imprisoned, and searched for Lidia Zamenhof.* There he found his fellow Bahá'í, but it was too late: she refused to try to escape and later died at the Treblinka concentration camp. The young German soldier was himself killed two years later as Russian troops fought their way into Poland.

Three months after his appeal for assistance to the German Bahá'ís,

---

* Daughter of Dr. Ludwik Zamenhof, creator of Esperanto; she translated into Polish *Bahá'u'lláh and the New Era*, the *Hidden Words*, *Some Answered Questions*.

Shoghi Effendi cabled: "Overjoyed, profoundly thankful for munifi-
cent donation made by American Bahá'í community for international
relief. Urge establishment communication with German believers and
careful consultation with their representatives . . ."[10] In the same cablegram the Guardian issues this significant directive: "Advise address
special immediate appeal American believers insure large representative attendance approaching Convention owing momentous historic
decisions to be disclosed assembled representatives ever-victorious
increasingly blessed spiritually maturing American Bahá'í community." It was evident that something of great import was coming.

At the National Convention of 1946 they learned what it was. The
two year respite which the Guardian had given the American Bahá'ís
was now at an end. "Hosts on high", he writes in his Convention
message, "are sounding the signal for inauguration second Seven Year
Plan designed to culminate first Centennial of the year Nine marking
the mystic birth of Bahá'u'lláh's prophetic mission in Síyáh-Chál at
Ṭihrán."[11]

The fourth objective of the Plan was the one that riveted attention:
". . . the initiation of systematic teaching activity in war-torn, spiritually famished European continent, cradle of world-famed civilizations,
twice-blest by 'Abdu'l-Bahá's visits, whose rulers Bahá'u'lláh specifically and collectively addressed, aiming at establishment of Assemblies
in Iberian Peninsula, the Low Countries, the Scandinavian states, and
Italy."[12] In a later message the Guardian added Switzerland and the
Grand Duchy of Luxembourg to the list, ten nations in all. "The challenge offered by virgin fields of Europe," the Guardian writes,
"outweighs momentous character of task already confronting American Bahá'í community in the Americas."*[13]

This new Seven Year Plan, the Guardian informs the American
believers, is the second stage of "the world mission entrusted by
'Abdu'l-Bahá to the apostles of His Father's Faith in the western
world".[14] The plan had other great goals in addition to the European
settlement. Among them was the formation of three new National
Assemblies – in Central America, in South America and in the Domin-

---

* Paris possessed a Bahá'í community from the turn of the century. Germany was the
  largest Bahá'í community on the continent at the outbreak of the second world war; it
  had established its National Assembly in 1923. All Bahá'í activity of any kind was banned
  in Germany well before the war; Bahá'í libraries and archives were demolished.

ion of Canada; completion of the interior ornamentation of the Mashriqu'l-Adhkár in North America, and consolidation of the victories already won throughout the Americas.

The Guardian called for nine capable teachers to initiate the work in Europe, and the first pioneers arose, a number of them native to the countries they settled in. Soon they were followed by others and the first small communities were born. The people among whom they settled were described in the Guardian's insistent messages as the "sorrow-stricken, war-lacerated, sorely bewildered nations and peoples of the European continent" – the "sorely-tried, war-ravaged European continent" – the "most afflicted, impoverished and agitated continent of the globe" – a continent that "stands in dire need of the ennobling, the reinvigorating, and spiritualizing influence of a world-redeeming faith". He draws attention to the heavy responsibility of North American Bahá'ís because of their protection from the "horrors of invasion and all the evils and miseries attendant upon it".[15]

Leroy's attention was strongly drawn to the work in Europe, his interest stimulated whenever new fields opened up to Bahá'í activity. But during the fate-laden year of 1946 when the new plan was launched he did not hold a directive office on the national scene. He was, in fact, at a point in his life when a major change was coming. Officials of the Southern Pacific wished him to take on more extensive responsibilities which would require his move to Chicago. After a period of hesitation he turned to the Guardian for advice. Shoghi Effendi indicated that it would be desirable for him to be closer to the heart of the national work: "Move to Chicago highly meritorious." Therefore in December, twenty-eight years after arriving in California, he and Sylvia left the scene of so much accomplishment and so much struggle, and returned to the city where they had grown up, met and married. Before leaving, he dug up the tall calla lilies that grew all around their garden and took them to the home of a Bahá'í colleague, Dr. Mildred Nichols, where they bloomed for many summers.

Years later, he looked back with satisfaction and fondness to the San Francisco years of his life. He considered them the "most productive" of his Bahá'í service, when he was able to give his energies to what he called the creative aspects of the development of the Faith. This evaluation was made prior to his move to Haifa; in the long context of history, nothing was "more productive" than his services there.

# CHAPTER SEVENTEEN

# Return to Chicago

THE five years Leroy now passed in Chicago, from late 1946 to early 1952, witnessed a series of historic events in the Bahá'í world.

In April of 1946 Shoghi Effendi had initiated the second great teaching plan for the North American Bahá'ís, again a plan of seven years' duration, due to culminate in 1953 with celebration of the centenary of the prophetic Mission of Bahá'u'lláh.* Two years later, in 1948, the State of Israel came into being, and was immediately plunged into war. For the first time in what the Guardian termed "twenty-century-long provincial status",[1] the land in which the World Centre was situated fell within the confines of a sovereign state. The very same year, long-deferred work was begun on the superstructure designed to embellish the Shrine of the Báb. Within yet another two and a half years, the Guardian announced to an astonished Bahá'í world the creation of an International Bahá'í Council, the precursor of the Universal House of Justice ordained by Bahá'u'lláh as the crown of His administrative order. Only ten months later Shoghi Effendi brought into active service the institution of the Hands of the Cause by appointing the first contingent of twelve living Hands of the Cause. In the same message he announced the inauguration of the intercontinental stage of Bahá'í activity through a series of four conferences that would embrace the National Assemblies in all continents.†[2] Events

---

* Bahá'u'lláh received the intimation of His Mission while held under severe and degrading conditions in the prison known as Síyáh-Chál in central Teheran; Shoghi Effendi named October 1952 to October 1953 a Holy Year to mark this central event of Bahá'í history.

† In the United States the National Assembly immediately appointed an intercontinental

(continued on p. 143)

were moving with astonishing rapidity and the individual Bahá'í, excited but overwhelmed by their magnitude, could only ponder what his role would be in the evolving process.

For the subject of our story, these five years were a period of continued flowering in both his professional and personal life. He and Sylvia bought the largest home they had ever owned, situated just two blocks from the Bahá'í Temple on Sheridan Road in Wilmette.* They were pleased that their younger daughter was in the pioneering field in Europe and that their older daughter, when not away on teaching trips, could be with them. The family circle also included Sylvia's widowed mother who had come from California to make her home with them.

Relieved of much detailed committee work and for a brief period of National Assembly duties, Leroy had more time to devote to personal teaching work, and he relished that. He was a frequent speaker in both the United States and Canada, took part in teaching campaigns, and became involved with the work of the European teaching committee. Edna True, daughter of early Chicago Bahá'í Corinne True,† was the key figure in this work.

When re-elected to the National Assembly he was able to contribute in a different, more consistent manner, to its work. He and Horace Holley had from the start of their collaboration worked closely together, both being of similarly strong character and desirous of seeing results, so that their combined influence on the Assembly had always been considerable. Leroy was called on to serve for several years as its treasurer, during a period of tremendous financial obligation when, as we will see, ever greater demands were made on the U.S. community. Being in close proximity to the Temple permitted him also to assist with the work of its interior ornamentation and landscaping – both goals of the new Seven Year Plan. As a youth he had watched 'Abdu'l-Bahá lay the cornerstone of the building; now within five years

---

teaching committee to prepare an agenda for the Wilmette conference two years hence and to study how the Assembly might assist the conferences held in other countries. Leroy, Edna True and Dorothy Baker were the initial members of this committee.

* The house has since become the Graduate Center for Reading of the National Louis University and its large garden has been turned into a parking area.

† Named by the Guardian a Hand of the Cause in the second contingent of appointments.

he expected to see it completed, formally dedicated and opened to public worship.

The new position that had brought him to Chicago was both prestigious and satisfying, and as he was a "clubby" man he enjoyed the business and social activities that surrounded it. Over the years he had brought many innovative ideas to railroading, and during his tenure in Chicago as head of the passenger services, Southern Pacific achieved wide recognition as the outstanding railroad in America in this field. Leroy accepted an award given the company at a formal dinner in Chicago's Palmer House, with General Mark Clark as speaker. These last years of his career were years of professional recognition and he enjoyed them thoroughly.

The company, however, seemed to be giving increasing attention to the frequency with which his name appeared in public announcements of Bahá'í events and he was cautioned to discontinue wide use of his name for this purpose. Given the uncompromising nature of his character where questions of principle were concerned, he tended to view this as "religious persecution". It was evident the company was considering him for ever more senior echelons of the railroad, as within two years of his arrival in Chicago he was offered a higher position in San Francisco – headquarters of the railroad – with a later promotion in view that would necessitate his remaining in California. He cabled the Guardian with this news, adding "New position prevents attendance many national assembly national committee meetings. Later future promotion will necessitate living San Francisco. Appreciate cable whether remain Chicago or accept offer." The Guardian's answer: "Advise remain Chicago presence highly desirable loving appreciation."[3]

He and Sylvia stayed at first with his sister Viola in Riverside, a suburb northwest of the city, where the three of them comprised the entire Bahá'í community. It was their first such experience and they considered it a pioneering post and set about trying to form an Assembly. They began meeting with the Bahá'ís of nearby townships on Bahá'í feast days and organized a series of public meetings. The response delighted them. As Sylvia notes in a letter to Joyce Dahl: "We were thrilled to have about thirty interested people at each meeting and we have continued with discussion evenings, hoping these will develop into a study class. There is some fine response, particularly from the young people. Roy has been giving all the talks!"

While his work was in Chicago, they gave no thought to settling in the city itself. The Guardian was insistently asking Bahá'ís from the "long established leading strongholds" of the Faith – Chicago was mentioned by name – to move out of the cities to assist in forming the one hundred and seventy-five new Assemblies needed in North America under the new plan.[4] It was because the Temple was a magnet to both of them that they looked for a home in that area and moved to Wilmette. He and Sylvia were now frequently traveling together, as he continued his practice of combining business trips with speaking engagements.

Leroy, interested above all in new spiritual frontiers, was appointed to the European teaching committee soon after coming to Chicago. There had been what he termed an "extraordinarily vigorous" reaction to the teaching work in Europe, so much so that by the time of the National Convention in 1948, only two years after the plan was launched, seven Assemblies had already been formed. The pioneers had begun arriving only in late 1946.

The success was such that a Europe-wide teaching conference was called for the summer of 1948, with Leroy and Edna True as active participants. It was an occasion for the committee, the pioneers and the new Bahá'ís to meet one another, a time of intense consultation and friendship-building. Bahá'ís from the old established centers were also invited, persons such as Laura Dreyfus-Barney who was again living in Paris.* Thus the new and the old centers in Europe were brought together. The Guardian called the conference a landmark in the European campaign.

Its purpose was to deepen both the pioneers and the new believers in the significance of the Covenant and the administrative order, so that the Assemblies they were forming would be firmly grounded. Isobel Sabri, then a pioneer in England, attended the conference with Marion Hofman and recalls the activist point of view of the committee: "You have to bring new believers into the Faith, you have to train them in the Covenant and Administration, you have to form Assemblies based on that. And this is why it all succeeded so well – the work was pinpointed: it was very simple, very direct and very potent."

In 1948 Canada formed its own National Assembly, as foreseen

* She was the compiler of 'Abdu'l-Bahá's table talks in 'Akká, published in the book *Some Answered Questions*; her husband, Hippolyte Dreyfus, was the first French Bahá'í.

under the plan, and launched its own teaching plan, as did the National Assemblies on other continents. Thus it fell to what was now the National Assembly of the Bahá'ís of the United States to implement the provisions of the second Seven Year Plan. And its creative, dynamic and brilliant secretary was not in good health. Doris Holley recalled in later years how precious it had been for Horace to have Leroy living nearby. "It was a time", she said, "when Horace's health was beginning to be very bad and Leroy never refused to take people through the Temple, or see them, or do anything that he could, no matter how tired he was after a strenuous business day in Chicago. He was indeed a Bahá'í friend!" It is important to note that this Seven Year Plan now devolving on the National Assembly of the United States was fundamentally different from the plans adopted by other National Assemblies. As Shoghi Effendi himself said: the other plans were regional in nature, whereas the mission entrusted to "the community of the champion builders of the World Order of Bahá'u'lláh" was world-embracing in its scope.[5]

When Leroy was again elected to the National Assembly, one of the new members was its treasurer, Phillip Sprague of New York City, whose illness would lead Leroy into one of the tasks for which he felt least suited. As Sprague's health worsened, Leroy offered to assist with his work and was then elected to the newly-created post of assistant treasurer. The following spring Phillip Sprague was not elected to the Assembly and Leroy found himself the national treasurer. He set his mind to the task he had been assigned, though it was not one he would have chosen.

The financial burdens of the American community became a preoccupying factor in the following four years. Completion of the Temple alone would require one million dollars from the numerically small American community, dollars that were six times the worth of current dollars. The National Assembly outlined the challenge to the Bahá'ís: "A careful study of the costs and building conditions shows that construction of the interior of the Temple, once begun, must be completed without interruption. This means a schedule aiming at completion early in 1951, with costs running up to $300,000 in 1949 and up to $250,000 in 1950! Never have we had such a spiritual and financial obligation."[6] These amounts were over and above expenses for all other activities.

"The House of Worship", the National Assembly secretary writes, "will not be built of steel and stone alone. It will be built out of the heart's blood of every Bahá'í. Not one of us", the passionate appeal continues, "has become the hero or heroine Bahá'u'lláh intends us to be!" It was the start of a two year period of the most rigorous austerity, touching all aspects of Bahá'í life.

The Guardian encouraged the Bahá'ís by reminding them that in the past also, periods of acute distress had been linked to "signal acts of accomplishment": the loss of 'Abdu'l-Bahá as the building of the administrative order was undertaken; the great depression while the erection of the Temple was progressing; the winning of the Seven Year Plan during a horrendous war, the revelation of the Tablets of the Divine Plan in the midst of an earlier war, steady achievement of victories even as all parts of the world were under threat of invasion and encirclement.

Sacrifice became the watchword of the Bahá'ís, as solemn pledges were made by well-to-do and poor alike in all parts of the country. Such sums of money had never before been either requested or raised by this comparatively small community. As pledges were honored, a steady stream of funds began flowing in, so much so that at the close of the first year of austerity, Leroy was able to write (in a note to Marion Hofman): "So far as the Temple is concerned, the interior construction work is on schedule. The main pillars have been finished up to the clerestory, the round columns on the main floor are completed, and some of the Bay ornamentation is being put in place. The funds are keeping up with the needs, and if we can maintain the sacrificial giving for one more year, we will achieve the goal by April of next year, two years ahead of schedule." He adds a highly significant comment: "Notwithstanding the austerity of the past year, we have had more new Bahá'ís than in any recent year."

Yet another call for funds came when contracts were signed for landscaping of the grounds surrounding the Temple. Leroy was chairman of the Temple Landscaping Committee which had recommended a design of Bahá'í landscape architect, Hilbert Dahl of Louisville. Mr. Dahl described his concept:

The gardens surrounding the Temple should be restrained and dignified in their simplicity, becoming a part of the structure in expressing the high purpose of the Temple: Ma<u>sh</u>riqu'l-A<u>dh</u>kár, the Dawning Place of Light. The path to the solution is carefully delineated by 'Abdu'l-Bahá in His many references to nine gardens – nine approaches – nine pools – nine fountains. It is *He* who is the landscape architect of the gardens! And He has indicated that the completion of the Temple will be accompanied by a surge of spiritual outpouring . . . When one views the record of achievement of the Bahá'í community in its sacrifice and unified action since 1909, when the Temple site was selected, there can be no doubt of its capacity now to win the final victory in arising collectively to complete the gardens during the coming year.

This was written in September 1951, when accomplishment of the most challenging of the tasks of the Seven Year Plan seemed to be in sight. The interior work on the Temple had indeed been completed two years ahead of schedule. Europe had established its Bahá'í Assemblies four years ahead of schedule. The National Assemblies of Central and South America were shortly to come into being (Leroy writes on April 21st of that year to Ella Cooper: "Four members of the National Assembly are now in the air, flying to Latin America – Paul Haney and Edna True to the Convention being held in Lima, Dorothy Baker and Horace Holley to Panama"). But Shoghi Effendi warned the American Bahá'ís that these successes did not mean that their vast responsibilities were over.

New and historic developments were occurring at the World Centre of the Faith, and the interest of the Bahá'ís was increasingly drawn to that sacred spot. As Bahá'í institutions had now been built on five continents and 'Abdu'l-Bahá's teaching mission for the North American Bahá'ís was set in motion with the two Seven Year Plans, it was time for the "third vast majestic fate-laden process" to begin, that is, the "gradual emergence of the manifold institutions" at the World Centre of the Faith.[7] Rúḥíyyih <u>Kh</u>ánum has written of how suddenly in November 1950 the Guardian sent cables inviting a small group of Bahá'ís to move to Haifa: Milly Collins, Dr. Lotfullah Hakim, Mason Remey, Jessie and Ethel Revell.[8] Several months later Shoghi Effendi released the news to the Bahá'ís "of East and West" of an "epoch-making decision": the formation of the first International Bahá'í Council, a body that would be the "forerunner of supreme administrative institution destined to emerge in fullness of time . . ."[9] Rúḥíyyih

Khánum and those invited to Haifa by the Guardian were to be its initial members. Its mandate would be, in the Guardian's words, to forge links with the authorities of the newly-emerged State, to assist him in building the Shrine of the Báb, and to conduct negotiations with the civil authorities on matters of personal status. At a later stage, he indicated, it would be an elected body.

On the slopes of Mt. Carmel the most sacred building project in the Bahá'í world was under way. For a number of years, the Guardian had been perfecting the plans conceived by Sutherland Maxwell, whom the Guardian referred to as the "immortal architect" of the Shrine,* that is, of the outer envelope that was to embellish the stone building housing the sacred Dust of the Báb. "The Shrine is not completed" had been 'Abdu'l-Bahá's frequent comment. Now work on the exquisite arcade section of the superstructure, begun in 1948, was well advanced in spite of the war devastation in Italy, where all the stone was carved and most components needed in the building were obtained,† and the turbulent conditions existing in the newborn State of Israel.

The Guardian did not anticipate the immediate completion of the superstructure because of the political situation and the limited funds available. But owing to changing conditions in both countries, contracts were signed in Italy for the full range of stone work and materials needed for completion of the Shrine of the Báb.

This work could not go forward without large sums in foreign exchange and the National Assembly in the United States appealed to the Bahá'ís for loans to be used to cover the contracted expenses. They also created a Shrine Fund so that individuals could feel a spiritual link with the Shrine through their gifts. Building the superstructure was an enterprise, in the words of the Guardian, "transcending any undertaking, whether national or local, embarked upon by the followers of the Faith of Bahá'u'lláh", and it "imposes an added obligation . . . on the already multitudinous duties assumed by a community wholly absorbed in the various tasks it shoulders".[10]

Shoghi Effendi called for a drastic reduction of national and local

* Distinguished Canadian architect, father of Rúḥíyyih Khánum, later named a Hand of the Cause, who lived in Haifa after the death of his wife May Maxwell.

† A superb account of this work in Italy is given in Hand of the Cause Ugo Giachery's book *Shoghi Effendi: Recollections*.

budgets; he himself suggested curtailing many activities, among them proclamation work, publications, and summer schools. He asked all National Assemblies of the world to designate substantial sums for the work of the Shrine, and appealed to individuals for sustained and direct giving to the "first international and incomparably holy enterprise" undertaken by the Bahá'ís of the world.

The Guardian further requested that the period of austerity in America be prolonged for another two years and that it be extended to include the rest of the Bahá'í world. Indeed, the Guardian calls such a period of rigorous sacrifice "supremely befitting" when the Bahá'ís recall, as he asks them to do, the holocaust visited upon their brethren only one century earlier.*[11] In many of his letters as national treasurer, Leroy uses this powerful theme of the Guardian: "We are now in our own way duplicating the terrible days of sacrifice of life, fortune, property, all, of those heroes one hundred years ago . . ." is the text of a typical letter Leroy sent out during that period.

The Guardian calls for nothing less than a "reorientation" of financial resources toward the building of the World Centre, and he uses the occasion of Milly Collins's visit to America to share his concerns with the National Assembly: "Our distinguished co-worker, Milly Collins, Vice-Chairman of the International Council," he writes, "is acquainting you with the pressing problems and the projected plans and the contracts afoot designed to accelerate the process initiated in the Holy Land for the furtherance of these supreme, momentous, highly meritorious objectives."[12]

Though she was now living in Haifa, Milly Collins was still actively participating as an American Bahá'í in the needs of the community. It was she who made one of the largest gifts to the Shrine Fund through cancellation of the very substantial loan which she had earlier made when the need was urgent and immediate. Leroy tried to find words to thank her in the name of the National Assembly: "There seems to be no end to your well-doing and you never weary in it. Your great sacrifices are an example to all . . . you have always come to our rescue when most needed." Leroy shared the news of her generosity with the Guardian whose secretary replied that the Guardian also "is very pleased at the way our dear Milly has arranged to go on, as you say,

* 1850–52: when the Báb was executed and the Bahá'ís attacked with genocidal fury by the leaders and mobs in Persia.

helping the fund there. She has been more than generous in her services, giving love, time, financial support – indeed everything she has – to the Cause. It is a great pity more do not reach this exalted height of service!"[13]

Leroy was still frequently in touch with the Guardian, transmitting material, budgets, questions, and from time to time being given special tasks. One will be noted as it gives a sense of the pressure of life in Haifa and the detailed nature of the tasks to which the Guardian was forced to give his attention. It concerns a pamphlet to be issued for the centenary of the martyrdom of the Báb. Rúhíyyih Khánum sends the material to Leroy for completion, proof-reading, design of a special cover, immediate printing and distribution to Haifa and all National Assemblies, all this to be done within five weeks. She writes: "As the Guardian has been passing through a severe crisis lately, and in addition has been very anxious about the health of my father who has been desperately ill for eight weeks – all of which has interfered with his correspondence with National Assemblies as well as individuals – he has not been able to devote sufficient time to the enclosed material."

We know in retrospect the anguish the Guardian was then suffering because of the growing disaffection and disloyalty of the family of 'Abdu'l-Bahá, including his own brothers and sisters. Some of these things Milly shared with Leroy and Sylvia during her visit, and through these intimate conversations Leroy learned to love the Guardian even more tenderly. But he was profoundly troubled by what he heard and could barely sleep after their discussions. "I was deeply moved, saddened and agitated," he wrote later to Shoghi Effendi. "Only once before have I felt more anguish, and that was when the beloved Master ascended to the glory of the realms beyond. The only relief then was the glorious word . . . that the Will and Testament of the Master created the Guardianship, assuring the strength and security of the Cause of God."

With increasing frequency there is mention of the Guardian's heavy burdens. In one letter to Leroy, Rúhíyyih Khánum comments: "Our beloved Guardian is feeling the strain of years of responsibility and over-work, and it is becoming so difficult for him to keep up with his correspondence!" Again a few months later: "As he is very busy these days, and really tired from over-work, I am making his letters as brief as possible, knowing the friends will understand the necessity for this."[14]

In September of 1951 Leroy received one of his last letters from Haifa, concerning a number of issues. But it was the last sentence that he re-read many times, pondering its significance. "The Guardian deeply values your own devoted work for the Cause," his secretary writes, "and hopes a time will come when you can devote more time to the work, and internationally as well as nationally."[15] Milly and Sylvia sat with him around the fireplace speaking of the possible implications of this statement. They wondered if there were any way that Leroy could assist in lifting some of the Guardian's burdens, while at the same time not abandoning his current responsibilities. Their conclusion was that he should give Milly a brief statement of his current status that she would take with her to Haifa, in case there were any discussion concerning his services.

As in earlier years of his life, Leroy wondered about new avenues of service. As in earlier years, the opportunity was to be given him.

# CHAPTER EIGHTEEN

# Appointment and Departure

THE "Hands of the Cause of God" comprise an institution created by Bahá'u'lláh that is quite distinct from the elected bodies which administer the affairs of the Bahá'ís throughout the world. The Hands of the Cause are an appointed body, designated by the head of the Faith and functioning under his direction and guidance. The specific responsibility of the Hands of the Cause is the propagation and the protection of the Bahá'í Faith, a mandate with many and varied ramifications.

Appointed on the basis of their demonstrated spiritual capacity and service, the Hands of the Cause possess an individual authority not shared by the elected bodies of the Faith, which have institutional but not personal authority. The Hands of the Cause are the highest officers of the Faith, having reached the "station of servitude". It is evidence of the spiritual vitality of the Bahá'í world that servitude should be the path to position and it is rare, though not unknown, that ambitious personalities reach some notoriety before disappearing into oblivion. 'Abdu'l-Bahá, to whom Bahá'ís look as the perfect exemplar of Bahá'u'lláh's teachings, carries the name "the Servant of Bahá".

During His lifetime Bahá'u'lláh designated four trusted companions whom He termed "the loved ones, the chosen ones, the pure in spirit" as Hands of the Cause.[1] 'Abdu'l-Bahá bestowed on four of His companions the title Hand of the Cause after their deaths. In His Will and Testament He further delineated the duties which the Hands of the Cause would in future be called upon to perform, such as the statement that nine of their number, elected from the full complement of Hands, were to be engaged at all times in service to the head of the Faith.

It was Shoghi Effendi who brought this unique institution into active service under his authority. During more than thirty years of his Guardianship, he had labored to build the administrative order and only when that order was established and functioning with vigor throughout the world, did he take the historic step of appointing living Hands of the Cause. The announcement of his decision was communicated to the Bahá'í world on December 24, 1951:

HOUR NOW RIPE TAKE LONG INEVITABLY DEFERRED STEP CONFORMITY PROVISIONS 'ABDU'L-BAHA'S TESTAMENT . . . THROUGH APPOINTMENT FIRST CONTINGENT OF HANDS OF CAUSE OF GOD, TWELVE IN NUMBER, EQUALLY ALLOCATED HOLY LAND, ASIATIC, AMERICAN, EUROPEAN CONTINENTS.[2]

It is difficult at this stage in the evolution of the Bahá'í world to appreciate the intensity of the joy that followed the Guardian's announcement. The majority of those who are now Bahá'ís have never known a time without the Hands of the Cause; they have sought them out and been deeply inspired by the example and the wisdom which the Hands of the Cause possess. But to see this institution come into being when there was nothing but the intimations of the Will and Testament of 'Abdu'l-Bahá was an electrifying experience, even more so as it followed so swiftly on the creation of the International Bahá'í Council. That which had been expected in a distant future was now coming to pass. "A mighty new day has dawned in the Faith of Bahá'u'lláh," was Agnes Alexander's comment in a letter to Leroy, ". . . the whole Bahá'í world is now stirring with new life."*

The Guardian had named Hands of the Cause previous to 1951 but with one exception the recognition had been bestowed posthumously. The sole exception was Milly Collins who was privately informed by the Guardian in 1946 of her elevation to that eminent position.[3] Each of the twelve thus honored received a similarly-worded cablegram from the Guardian, transmitted the same day as the public announcement that he sent to all National Assemblies.

Sylvia was alone when the cable arrived with the arresting news that her husband had been elevated to this rank. She went immedi-

---

* Agnes Alexander was appointed a Hand of the Cause in 1957 following the death of George Townshend.

ately to the telephone and read the message to Leroy. He was stunned, silent except for a formless exclamation of disbelief.

MOVED CONVEY GLADTIDINGS YOUR ELEVATION RANK HAND CAUSE STOP APPOINTMENT OFFICIALLY ANNOUNCED PUBLIC MESSAGE ADDRESSED ALL NATIONAL ASSEMBLIES STOP MAY SACRED FUNCTION ENABLE YOU ENRICH RECORD SERVICES ALREADY RENDERED FAITH BAHA'U'LLAH. SHOGHI[4]

Neither thought of much else that day, waiting for the evening when they could go with Farrukh to the House of Worship to pray, then to the cornerstone of the Temple to pray. Leroy felt quite unworthy of such high spiritual honor and conveyed as much to the Guardian in the cable which he sent within hours of Sylvia's call: "Dearly Beloved Guardian. Am completely overwhelmed your gracious appointment one so unworthy as myself as Hand Cause. Beg God for strength and capacity serve you humbly and well. Loving devotion."

He knew intuitively that this appointment would bring great changes in its wake, though their nature was impossible to discern. He remembered how the Guardian had termed his election to the National Assembly a "call to a wider field of service". Now this came to mind as he wondered what further and different types of service might come to him.

He was comforted to have near him another of those so honored, Horace Holley. They and Dorothy Baker were the three Hands of the Cause appointed in the American continent. His beloved friend Milly Collins was, along with Sutherland Maxwell and Mason Remey, appointed in the Holy Land; Ugo Giachery (with whose work for the Guardian Leroy was intimately acquainted), Hermann Grossmann and George Townshend in Europe; Valíyu'lláh Varqá, 'Alí-Akbar Furútan and Ṭarázu'lláh Samandarí in the cradle of the Faith.

Those so suddenly thrust into this position were advised to remain in their present posts and "continue discharge vital administrative, teaching duties pending assignment specific functions as need arises".[5] Six of the twelve were members of National Assemblies, including the three named in America.

The Guardian informed his newly-designated Hands that they were to attend as his representatives all four intercontinental conferences to be held during the Holy Year beginning in October of 1952, the first to be convened in Kampala in February by the National Assembly of the British Isles, the second in Wilmette in early spring by the National Assembly of the United States, the third in Stockholm during the summer by the European teaching committee, and the last in India to be convened in autumn by the National Assembly of India, Pakistan and Burma.

Leroy wrote immediately to Ugo, then to Milly, who was in Italy en route to Israel. She swiftly wrote back, thanking him for his expressions of love. "Ugo and I", she writes, "received our cables at the same time which was doubly precious . . . and Mason came on from Florence so the three of us could come together for prayers." Ugo wrote to Leroy from Rome: "Right after receiving your letter I learned of your appointment; it was like the most beautiful answer to my silent prayers, which I have recited for years, that a great bounty, a supernatural recompense should descend upon you for your sterling devotion to the Cause and the great services rendered to the Guardian . . . The appointment which the Guardian has so generously bestowed on me, has left me stunned and perplexed. I have had the news for nearly two weeks, but I am yet unable to adjust my heart and my mind to the reality of this tremendous happening."

Joy for the Guardian himself was one of the deepest emotions expressed in the many letters Leroy received. A typical remark was that of Honor Kempton: "How grateful we are that our beloved Guardian now has such steadfast souls – ready and waiting to serve him all the time. Never again will he be alone." "We feel deeply grateful to Bahá'u'lláh to see this spiritual support of the Guardian . . ." the National Assembly of the British Isles wrote to Leroy, ". . . our minds dwell continually on this wonderful event."

Harlan Ober remembered Sylvia's contribution: "Those who know, will appreciate how important a part Sylvia has played through the years, because without her complete and selfless cooperation not only in the matters of family life but in support of your far-flung activities, your splendid work could hardly have been carried forward." Leroy was touched by this tribute to Sylvia, for no one knew better than he just how significant had been her contribution to whatever he had been able to accomplish.

Leroy had always thought of his work for the Cause as being centered in America, and had felt no particular urge to go to the Holy

Land. But his lengthy and distressing talks with Milly Collins had fixed his mind on the needs of the Guardian, and he wrote to Shoghi Effendi offering his services in any way that might be of assistance. Being of practical mind he felt the need to temper his decisions to the heavy responsibilities he carried in his work, toward his family and in the Cause. But following his appointment as a Hand of the Cause these limitations on his thinking lessened, and he simply waited for whatever the Guardian might propose.

On February 4th the Guardian cabled: "Advise visit Shrines consultation affairs do not resign job. Love. Shoghi." This was followed two days later by a letter through his secretary advising Leroy to use his vacation time to stay as long as possible on this preliminary visit "to give you time to discuss the future with him in some detail. He is eagerly anticipating your arrival . . ."

On the 12th another cablegram arrived: "Make no plans visit. Writing. Shoghi." On the 15th, his secretary's letter followed: "In considering the entire situation here the Guardian has decided, as he cabled you, that it is not advisable to spend the time and money to merely come here for a few days' visit and consultation. What he needs, I might almost say desperately, is a capable, devoted believer to come and really take the work in hand here, relieve him of constant strain and details, and act as the secretary general of the International Bahá'í Council. If you will accept to do this it would be rendering him and the Faith an invaluable service." The letter makes clear that the Guardian needs him there as soon as possible as the various problems "are causing him the greatest anxiety, and if you are going to be able to come and accept this vital service, then the sooner you can arrange to do so, the better. If after some months of service here, you need to return to further arrange your affairs, this would be preferable to a long delay at this juncture." The letter was written on Leroy's fifty-sixth birthday.

Leroy cabled the Guardian: "Letter just received. Sylvia and I deeply moved privilege serve Beloved Guardian. If satisfactory I will arrive March tenth. Devoted love." A two-word cablegram came back: "Welcome. Love. Shoghi."[6]

These two months, December 24th to February 25th, were without doubt the most dramatic, the most moving and indeed, the most traumatic of Leroy's life. The experience of being called to the high endeavor of a Hand of the Cause was a deeply emotional event for him, as most certainly for the other Hands of the Cause, bringing feelings of awe that would have required a quiet time of adjustment. Then swiftly came the call to Haifa, so truly unexpected, and he faced relinquishment of position acquired in thirty years of work,* loss of much of his pension when he had responsibility for others, ridding himself of home and the assets of three decades of life.

There was a brief agonized hesitation as he turned the decision over and over in his mind thinking to find a way to adjust all the needs. It was Sylvia who cut through this and said simply: of course you'll go. As he had known he would, but it would be unrealistic not to note the emotional cost of the decision. He who had always been in control was now relinquishing all control and setting out into the unknown. *Are you interested in renunciation?* 'Abdu'l-Bahá had asked Howard Colby Ives.[7] In this hardest decision of his life Leroy was to learn new dimensions to renunciation.

In a letter of farewell to the National Assembly he wrote: "I am wending my way into a field I know little of, and into a spiritual atmosphere I aspire to but frankly am somewhat fearful of . . ." He paid tribute to Sylvia "who has been a spiritual lighthouse in this period of transition. Never have I realized her great spiritual strength and power as now." He wrote of Farrukh's "sweet grace of spiritual persuasion" which was a strong support to him. "My steps have faltered," he wrote to his brother Paul, "but Sylvia has been much stronger than I. How God ever gave me such a wonderful wife, I don't know, but I am grateful He did." The fact is that Sylvia and Leroy, like hundreds of other Bahá'ís, were caught up in the force of the Faith and allowed themselves to be its instrument.

The abruptness of his departure stunned everyone and made a profound impression on the Bahá'í community. Marion Hofman was to say later that she felt Leroy's obedience to the wishes of the Guardian prepared the American Bahá'ís for his call one year later for them to quit their homes and scatter to every country, island and territory of the earth under the Ten Year Crusade. A close friend who had studied the Faith with Leroy expressed pride that "the whole Bahá'í world may now know what we who have worked with you have long known – all

---

* Leroy was one of the few corporate executives in the North American Bahá'í community, in distinction to members of law and financial firms or owners of small business firms.

the strength and knowledge, the devotion, the undeviating justice, the broad vision and the gentle, personal understanding. Everyone whose life touches yours will retain some of these qualities which you mirror forth so constantly in your service." Then she adds her personal sense of loss: "When you left San Francisco for Chicago I cried, knowing what it would mean here without your strength and counsel. Today I am weeping in my heart – feeling the loss to America, to our National Assembly, to our teaching work, to our whole vision."[8]  At the large farewell gathering in Foundation Hall of the Temple, Leroy related a dream Albert Windust (an early Chicago Bahá'í and colleague of his father on the House of Spirituality) had had many years before. He saw 'Abdu'l-Bahá working very diligently, going to and fro, searching the ground, picking up a twig here, a few pieces of straw there, and finally with these bits and pieces making something with a little shape and form. Albert wrote to the Master asking the meaning of his dream and 'Abdu'l-Bahá replied: "I have been commanded to build the Temple of the Lord and I build it with what God gives me!"

Leroy concluded his talk: "Friends, you and I are those twigs, we are those stones, we are those scraps, and the Master is working to shape something out of us. Why should we, unknown and incapable, be quickened by the power of this great spirit and come alive in this day when millions are dying and deprived of spiritual insight? I don't know, and you don't know, but there is only one thing we can do in return for these great gifts and that is to dedicate our lives, purify our deeds, and allow ourselves to become dynamic vehicles which God can use to quicken society . . ."[9]

The next day Leroy departed for New York en route to the Holy Land. His plane stopped briefly at Ireland's Shannon airport, the time for him to telephone his fellow Hand of the Cause, George Townshend. Then he stopped in Paris to spend a few hours with his daughter Anita. During the time it took them to call on a friend, the car was broken into and some of Leroy's luggage stolen, including medications Dr. Katherine True had gathered for him, special glasses for his sensitive eyes, all the personal things. He said little, but then on the way to the airport spoke reflectively of the pioneers, some who lost everything, others who were robbed, arriving at their posts with empty hands to serve Bahá'u'lláh. With a toothbrush and razor purchased at the airport, Leroy left Paris for Haifa.

# CHAPTER NINETEEN

# Meeting the Guardian

FOR a Bahá'í, the arrival at Ben Gurion Airport is unlike any other
arrival, for it is the gateway to the Shrines of the Báb and Bahá'u'lláh,
to the Bahá'í World Centre, and in Leroy's time, to the presence of the
Guardian, "the priceless pearl branched from the two hallowed and
sacred Lote-Trees".*

The great experience into which Leroy was being projected was
entirely new. He had never lived outside the United States. He knew
little of dealing with people of the Middle East and he came not as a
pilgrim but as a settler. The flight to the Holy Land was filled with spiritual excitement and with deep anxiety. Would he be worthy of this
great task, would the Guardian be satisfied with him?

He arrived in Haifa around 2:00 in the afternoon, after going by
bus to Tel Aviv and then by taxi-bus to Haifa. There he found old
friends Milly Collins and Mason Remey who had moved to Haifa the
previous year. Everyone was fasting (a period of nineteen days which
immediately precedes the Bahá'í new year) and he spent a few quiet
hours settling into a room in one of the wings of the handsome building known as the Western Pilgrim House, no. 10 Haparsim Street,
preparing himself for the evening when the Guardian would come.

A little after six everyone gathered in the drawing room to break the
Fast with tea. Then after some time it was announced that the
Guardian had arrived. That was the signal to descend the stairs to the

---

* Citation from the Will and Testament of 'Abdu'l-Bahá which appointed Shoghi Effendi
as Guardian of the Bahá'í Faith; he was descended on his father's side from the family of
the Báb, on his mother's from Bahá'u'lláh.

ground floor dining room. Leroy, as the newly arrived guest, went down first.

The Guardian was seated, but rose upon seeing Leroy enter the room and came to embrace him warmly, saying they had been anticipating his coming and he was very welcome. The warmth and love of the Guardian enveloped him and put him as much at ease as was possible under the circumstances. For it was a deeply moving moment for him, to be actually in the presence of Shoghi Effendi, the person with whom his heart had for so long been in communion, whose thinking he had absorbed to such an extent that it dominated his actions for the Faith. He sat with his eyes going often to the Guardian's face, not wanting to stare yet longing to watch his expressive features, fascinated by the flow of his language, the clarity of his thought, the power emanating from his person.

As was customary the Guardian led the conversation, speaking of the Bahá'ís in America and the work of the National Assembly. He spoke of Leroy's family and of their services which he had followed closely. Leroy felt impelled to mention Sylvia's great strength in this move, to which the Guardian replied that they both had great spiritual strength, there was no question of it. Later he spoke of Leroy's appointment as a Hand of the Cause: how he had been active from the start of the teaching work in America in the first Seven Year Plan and had carried it to a successful conclusion, his intense activity since being in Chicago – which led Leroy to believe that all this may have been the reason for the appointment.

During the evening Shoghi Effendi told Leroy what his work in Haifa would be. "You have had a brilliant career in the Cause, now this is the climax of it. Your work was not only satisfactory, but brilliant. Now you are reaching another stage, at the international center of a World Faith. In your capacity as Hand of the Cause and member of the International Bahá'í Council, you will be at the very center – not at its circumference but at its very heart. Being its Secretary-General the work will revolve around you."* The Guardian spoke of the developments in Haifa, the Shrines, the International Council, the Hands of the Cause. He said, we are now building the international

* The statements of the Guardian cited in this chapter are his exact words, taken down by Jessie Revell as he spoke.

structure of the Faith, which is the most important development since the passing of the Master.

When the Guardian had left for the evening Leroy hastened to cable Sylvia: "Joyous meeting beloved Guardian who expressed hope you join us soon deepest love. Roy." Sleep was impossible that night as Leroy weighed all that he had heard. He wrote to Sylvia: It is clear that our destiny has been set here. Two days later Milly sent her own cable to Sylvia: "Rejoice Guardian now has helper adding more responsibilities honor Leroy's appointment dearest love. Milly."

During dinner the following evening the Guardian continued to outline the work that was needed. Leroy shared this with Sylvia:

> The next evening during dinner I asked if I might write to the National Assembly concerning comments of the Guardian in regard to the teaching work. Shoghi Effendi said yes, you will be writing to them often – and then he told me of a new development. [This is what Milly Collins spoke of in her cable to Sylvia.] He said that in addition to the work of the International Council, he had decided to appoint me Assistant Secretary to the Guardian, handling certain correspondence over my own signature on his stationery.* This would relieve him and would relieve Rúḥíyyih Khánum.
>
> He spoke of other work I would be doing. He said, you have cared for the Temple, now you will care for the finishing of the Shrine.† You have cared for the landscaping of the Temple, now you will care for the landscaping of the Shrine and the surroundings of Bahjí and the Shrine of Bahá'u'lláh. He said other things, but though I heard the words I could not seem to comprehend any more. I told him I was afraid I could not do all he wanted, that I did not have the capacity for it. He said, "I have been thinking of this for some time. I need help – Rúḥíyyih needs help – and you can do it." Well, it was all too much.

In Wilmette they read and re-read his first long letter and Sylvia quickly wrote back: "To have you speak of being in those sacred places

---

* Some months later Shoghi Effendi informed him that he would be responsible also for all correspondence concerning the Ten Year Crusade, the encouragement of the various National Assemblies, etc.

† The Shrine of the Báb, ordained by Bahá'u'lláh, its inner sanctum built by 'Abdu'l-Bahá and completed by Shoghi Effendi.

is so strange and so awe-inspiring . . . I can well imagine that you were overcome, but you must be able to do all this, or the Guardian would not have given it to you to do. I feel that your whole life has been one preparation after another just for this time."

That second evening the Guardian asked if Leroy had visited the Shrine of the Báb and Leroy said he had not, only the gardens, as the spirit was so strong he wished to approach it slowly. It was a measure of his spiritual turmoil that he had not plunged into this visit, wanting to know the Guardian's pleasure in the matter. Shoghi Effendi indicated that he should immediately visit the Shrine.* The next day he and Milly Collins went up and spent hours there in prayer. "I cannot describe," he writes to Sylvia, "the spirit in that Shrine, it is one I have never experienced; it lifts one to a realm above and beyond this existence." The next evening the Guardian asked if he had visited the Shrine of 'Abdu'l-Bahá. Again he said no, the spirit in the Shrine of the Báb was such that he could absorb no more. The Guardian said, Tomorrow, visit the Master. And there, from the moment of entering 'Abdu'l-Bahá's Shrine, he felt "all the warmth and embracing love" that he had known in the Master's presence on this earth. "It was as if 'Abdu'l-Bahá took me under His wing – and I seem now to have found calm and peace of mind . . ."

Shortly, he went over to Bahjí where he spent time in the Shrine of Bahá'u'lláh – a unique experience "where there descends on one that peace which surpasses understanding", as he later described it. In the Shrine of the Báb, the stirring vigor of the Dawn-breakers; with 'Abdu'l-Bahá, the comfort and love of the Master; in Bahá'u'lláh's Shrine, utter contentment of the soul.

In speaking of the Shrines in later years, Leroy would point out that they are not places of the dead, though they shelter the remains of the Manifestations of God. Rather they are places of dynamic life because the spirit of the age flows through them. One evening the Guardian remarked that when visiting the Shrine of the Báb one should remember that the spirits of all the Prophets of God are revolving around that Shrine. But what then of Bahá'u'lláh's Shrine? Leroy asked. The spirits of all the Prophets revolve around it, including that of the Báb, the Guardian replied.

* Shoghi Effendi frequently told pilgrims they must not think they come to Haifa to meet him; rather, they come to pay homage at the Shrines.

Leroy in later years told of the South American Ambassador, a devout Catholic, who asked to visit the Bahá'í holy places during an official visit to Israel. An official of the government accompanied him as Leroy took them to the Shrine of the Báb. The diplomat went up and knelt to pray, the official stood half way back and Leroy knelt in the back of the chamber. After a time he quietly left, as did the official. They waited outside for a time, then Leroy went in and observed the diplomat still in prayer. When he finally emerged he walked slowly to the Pilgrim House without speaking. Just before going in to tea, he turned to Leroy and said, "I want you to know that is the most profound spiritual experience I've ever had. And I've just come from Rome." Such is the living spirit of the Shrines.

After a few days Leroy settled into his work, rapidly taking up the tasks he had been given and figuring out how things were done in Haifa. And in Israel. The most important period of our lives, he told Sylvia, is now ahead of us.

His fellow Hand of the Cause, George Townshend, wrote these penetrating words to him in a letter received several weeks after his arrival: "I should think the experience of so much bestowed at once – the Guardian and the Holy Shrines and the Holy Places and the Holy Scenes one has read and heard so much about, and the Divine Atmosphere surrounding it all – must be bewildering and overcoming: one could not absorb it. But God tempers these things to us, and strengthens us to measure up to what is required of us. You must be so busy with all your work that your very activity will protect you and prevent you from meditating too much on the Celestial Forces that press all about you."

☆　☆　☆　☆　☆

*Thus far, we have been telling the story of Leroy's life. Now, however, the focus changes and is centered on the Guardian, his initiatives and his accomplishments. Leroy is now seen as one instrument among others placed in Shoghi Effendi's hands to assist him in his work at the World Centre.*

# CHAPTER TWENTY

# At the World Centre

THE fourth and final exile of Bahá'u'lláh led Him to the walled city of 'Akká in 1868. His Tomb outside 'Akká, on the property known as Bahjí (Delight), is the center toward which all Bahá'ís turn when they pray. From the time of Bahá'u'lláh's exile to this remote and pestilential prison-city of the old Turkish Empire, it has been the center of the Bahá'í world, whether governed by the Turks, the British, or the Israelis. (Shoghi Effendi once said: The Holy Land became the Most Holy Land after the coming of Bahá'u'lláh.)

On four occasions Bahá'u'lláh visited Haifa on the opposite side of the bay, remaining once for several months. During one of His sojourns, He indicated to 'Abdu'l-Bahá the site for the permanent interment of His Predecessor, the Báb, and revealed the Tablet of Carmel, where in mystic language He gave evidences that His World Order would encircle that Holy Dust on the slopes of Mt. Carmel. In this weighty Tablet Bahá'u'lláh states: "Ere long will God sail His Ark upon thee [Carmel], and will manifest the people of Bahá . . .",[1] the Ark being the Law of God, the people of Bahá, the Universal House of Justice.

It was thus that the twin cities of Haifa and 'Akká became the center of the Faith associated with His Name, and all the difficulties, all the problems of a rapidly-expanding world community flowed to it, requiring attention and resolution. At the heart of this nerve center, after the passing of 'Abdu'l-Bahá, was the figure of Shoghi Effendi, directing all activities, spending each day of his life in unceasing toil in the interests of the Cause.

Shoghi Effendi was a young man of twenty-four when he learned that 'Abdu'l-Bahá in His Will and Testament had appointed him Guardian of the Bahá'í Faith. The statements concerning him in the Will are powerful and definitive: he is the Center of the Cause of God to whom all Bahá'ís turn. He is the sign of God on earth. He is the expounder of the words of God. All are cautioned to be "lowly before him"[2] as he is the point through which divine guidance will flow to the peoples of the world.

Shoghi Effendi knew that 'Abdu'l-Bahá harbored a special love for him, but he felt it might be expressed through his being given the honor of calling the conclave that would elect the Universal House of Justice foretold by Bahá'u'lláh. When he learned of his appointment as Guardian of the Faith, he was not prepared for it, he didn't want it. He *knew* what it meant.

Feeling himself incapable of such a task, he went away for several months, and in the solitude of the mountains of Switzerland fought his battle with himself. He did not return until, in words he himself used, he had conquered himself and turned himself over to God. Then he returned to Haifa, knowing he could do what God wanted of him. Leroy often told of the struggle of this young man as he sought to accept his fate, and repeated over and over the message of the Guardian to the Bahá'ís: that every Bahá'í in the world must do exactly what he had done, whether he be a Hand of the Cause, a National Assembly member, a teacher, pioneer or administrator, whatever his role in the Cause, every Bahá'í must fight himself and conquer himself, and only then can he become a true instrument for service to the Faith.

When he became Guardian, Shoghi Effendi has said, he did not know what he was supposed to do as Guardian, and he searched the Writings for direction as to the course of his work. He knew he must complete the projects left unfinished by 'Abdu'l-Bahá, such as the Shrine of the Báb, the terraces on Mt. Carmel, extension of the gardens around the Shrine, and acquisition of land and properties around the Shrine of Bahá'u'lláh for the protection and future embellishment of that sacred spot.

In his study of the Writings he was able to discern his three primary missions. They would be to establish the administrative order of the Cause, to disseminate the teachings of Bahá'u'lláh throughout the world and to build the Bahá'í world center. The Guardian found mandates in the Writings for each of these undertakings. The Will and

Testament of the Master was the charter for building the administrative order, 'Abdu'l-Bahá's Tablets of the Divine Plan the charter for the teaching work, and the Tablet of Carmel the charter for development of the world center on Mt. Carmel.

These were the guidelines which he took for his work. But 'Abdu'l-Bahá had left no indication, no instructions, of how he should proceed. One evening at dinner, Leroy had ventured to remark that the Guardian's achievement in developing the administrative order in America was a work of genius, given the weak fabric of Bahá'í life in America in 1921. "Leroy," the Guardian replied, "did you think I had a blueprint to follow when I did this? Did you think that God had shown me a picture of how this was to evolve? No. When God guided me to do something, I did it, and then when He guided me to do something else, I did that, so that every step which has been taken has been taken under the direct and unfailing guidance of Bahá'u'lláh. As Guardian of the Bahá'í Faith, I have supreme confidence that God will inspire me to do whatever is necessary for the good of the Cause at the time it must be done." ('Abdu'l-Bahá had said in 1910 to one of His attendants in Egypt: ". . . I must always move according to the requirements of the Cause. Whatever the Cause requires for its promulgation, I will not delay in its accomplishment for one moment!"[3])

Shoghi Effendi realized that 'Abdu'l-Bahá's teaching plans could not be set in motion until an administrative structure had been erected that would ensure permanency to the efforts of the Bahá'ís. Almost nothing, he once remarked, remains of the work of such a great itinerant teacher as Martha Root, because there was nothing to follow up her work, no program, no coordination, no one to see that the seeds grew and developed – it was not the movement of the whole body of the Bahá'ís. And not until all the instruments of the Faith were acting in unison could the teachings be carried to the world. Shoghi Effendi was to spend twenty-five years painstakingly building the institutions that would serve as vehicles for the teaching work. Then, when both the believers and the institutions were sufficiently mature, he launched the first Seven Year Plan.

The Guardian spent thirty-six years in the role the Master designated for him, years that knew no respite from work. Starting in 1922 on his return to take up his duties, Shoghi Effendi himself opened every letter he received and answered each one through a secretary,

and to many of them he added a few words of praise or encouragement. Through such solicitude, he drew from the Bahá'ís greater deeds
of service than they knew they were capable of and made each one
feel he had the capacity to serve. But in Leroy's opinion the believers
often abused the Guardian's loving nature. They wrote to him frequently with questions that had been answered; some were reluctant to
take any step without consulting him; others asked him to comment on
issues properly addressed to the institutions. Whenever there were
problems they wrote to him, yet what he longed to hear was news of
their successes, as this lightened his burden. And then in order to guide
the institutions, the Guardian had to stay abreast of their work by
reading reports of the National Assemblies and major committees.
Leroy recalled one night when the Guardian commented that 770
pages of Minutes, letters and other material had come to him in that
single day. Indeed, his burden of work was such that, as Rúḥíyyih
Khánum tells us, even his holidays were simply a change of setting for
his continual work.

One evening Shoghi Effendi said he was so busy he had little time
to carry on the creative work that is necessary for the Guardian of the
Cause. "I have to consider the health of the Bahá'í world, I have to
consider the health of every country. I have to consider what can be
done to stimulate the Bahá'ís so they will go forward and win these
great victories. I have to consider the next step that should be taken in
these crusades. That is *my* work and those are the things I should be
engaged in doing."

In His Will and Testament the Master exhorted the "faithful loved
ones of 'Abdu'l-Bahá" to take the greatest care of Shoghi Effendi "that
no dust of despondency or sorrow may stain his radiant nature . . ."[4]
Rúḥíyyih Khánum shared a touching confidence with the Bahá'ís
gathered in Wilmette in 1953 at the Intercontinental Conference. It
was something Shoghi Effendi had said to her many times and which
wrung her heart: "Oh, 'Abdu'l-Bahá knew me so well when He said
'Make him happy'. He knew that if I was happy I could do so much
more for the Cause."

In speaking once of the Guardian, Leroy commented that to his
mind Shoghi Effendi was one of the saddest figures in the Faith, so
unable to delegate the problems coming to him in ever-increasing
number, so alone to withstand the attacks of the watchful enemies of

the Faith, and so "scarred" as Rúḥíyyih K͟hánum termed it, by the blows of those nearest and dearest. When Milly Collins moved to Haifa in 1951 she noted that "Shoghi Effendi's face was sad and we seldom saw him smile".[5] Arriving a few months later, Leroy saw the stress and sorrow of the Guardian, and yet, as he noted, it was under such conditions that Shoghi Effendi was inspired to launch his great endeavors and conceive the Ten Year Crusade.

A word should be said about the family of Bahá'u'lláh. Among its members were half-brothers of both Bahá'u'lláh and 'Abdu'l-Bahá who were weak of faith and strong of ambition, and the sufferings they and their descendants brought on Bahá'u'lláh, 'Abdu'l-Bahá, and the Guardian were intense. Their perfidy ranged from attempts to poison Bahá'u'lláh Himself to the many schemes to gain leadership and undermine the prestige of the Faith and its Head in the eyes of successive Turkish, British and Israeli governing bodies. 'Abdu'l-Bahá termed them Covenant-breakers, as they knew the Station of Bahá'u'lláh but through egotism turned against Him and His designated successors. 'Abdu'l-Bahá wrote in His Will and Testament of the "virus of violation" that had infected the family of Bahá'u'lláh and spread from generation to generation. Their renewed machinations were weighing heavily on the heart of the Guardian even as he was creating the International Bahá'í Council, and it became one of the duties of the Hands of the Cause on the Council to act for the Guardian in protecting the Faith against them.

As we know, Shoghi Effendi tried unsuccessfully in the early years of his Guardianship to attract highly capable and trustworthy Bahá'ís to assist him in Haifa. "How much I feel the need," he wrote to Horace Holley in 1926, "for a similar worker by my side, as competent, as thorough, as methodical, as alert as yourself. You cannot and should not leave your post for the present. Haifa will have to take care of itself." Although Ethel Rosenberg, the first Englishwoman to become a Bahá'í in England, made extended visits to Haifa, and some of Shoghi Effendi's early correspondence bears her signature, for one reason or another only Dr. Esslemont was able to move to the Holy Land, where he served as the Guardian's English-language secretary and assisted him in the translation of the Tablet of Aḥmad, the Hidden Words, and various passages from the Writings of Bahá'u'lláh. Such was the love Shoghi Effendi felt for John Esslemont, his friend from student days in

England and one of his chief consolers when 'Abdu'l-Bahá died, that he placed his own Bahá'í ring on Esslemont's finger for burial with him when he died one short year after coming to Haifa.* His loss was a grievous blow. We have the sorrowful picture left by Rúḥíyyih Khánum of the manner in which the Guardian faced his solitude:

> Shoghi Effendi came to grips with the harsh fact that he was to all intents and purposes alone and he placed increased reliance on himself. He set himself to do all the work and did it, using as secretaries various members of the Master's family, facing an ever-increasing spirit of disaffection on their part, resigning himself to the unending drudgery of petty tasks as well as major ones, accepting his fate with resignation, often with despair, always with loyalty and fortitude. It can truly be said of him that single-handed he effected the world-wide establishment of the Faith of his Divine Forefathers and proved that he belonged to that same sovereign caste.[6]

When he was ten years old Shoghi Effendi had received a Tablet from the Master which closed with the words: "At night pray and supplicate and in the day do what is required of you."

With the formation of the International Bahá'í Council Shoghi Effendi had that international secretariat he had always desired. In a lengthy cablegram to the Bahá'í world on March 8, 1952, he announced its enlargement and the structure he had conceived for it: "Present membership now comprises: Amatu'l-Bahá Rúḥíyyih, chosen liaison between me and the Council, Hands of the Cause, Mason Remey, Amelia Collins, Ugo Giachery, Leroy Ioas, President, Vice-President, member at large, Secretary-General, respectively. Jessie Revell, Ethel Revell, Lotfullah Hakim, Treasurer, Western and Eastern assistant Secretaries."[7] That the majority of its members should be drawn from the North American Bahá'í community was, the Guardian said, a unique bounty and blessing to the American believers. (In his announcement to the Eastern Bahá'ís his language is more intimate: "The Council will render assistance to this needy servant, who is submerged in an ocean of innumerable problems . . ."[8])

Leroy, who had been an executive accustomed to making decisions and giving orders, worked in Haifa as did the others, quietly doing

---

* Shoghi Effendi named him a Hand of the Cause posthumously.

exactly what the Guardian asked of him. One of the instructive lessons learned by the pilgrims who flowed through Haifa was the reverence demonstrated by the Hands of the Cause, each so independent and capable, in their relationship to the Guardian. "It was a wonderful thing to see," said Amin Banani, a pilgrim in 1955 who had known Leroy for many years, "like a facet of his character that was not visible before: this high-powered man who had put all his energy and vigor to the use of the Guardian yet could see his relationship to him in such a loving, adoring and reflecting fashion." As for Leroy, the Covenant was firmly in him and he worked with the conviction that if the Guardian wished something to be done, it would be done; his task was to remove the obstacles that stood in the way of its accomplishment. He early adopted the habit of speaking only of results to the Guardian, never of details of negotiations or of problems that arose. And this was exactly what Shoghi Effendi needed: workers who would hear what was needed and without any further word go and do it, even if it appeared impossible. In a later chapter we will describe a task that appeared impossible, but which was nonetheless accomplished (see Chapter 24). A number of times during the six years Leroy worked for him, the Guardian would refer to him as "my Hercules" because when he gave Leroy difficult things to do he would finally come back with them done. Once or twice Shoghi Effendi asked Sylvia how she liked being married to Hercules.

It was at the dinner table that the Council members, other than Rúḥíyyih Khánum, saw the Guardian and spoke with him. It was there amidst his conversations with the western pilgrims that Shoghi Effendi inquired as to their work, discussing the business of the Faith very openly with everyone; its affairs were never secret.* Leroy would report on the status of his work and the Guardian would indicate what should be done the next day – usually just a few words exchanged between them. At times the Guardian would ask him to do something in a way which seemed to his business mind complicated and lengthy. Yet obedient to the Guardian's instructions he would go from office to office,

---

* In 1924 May Maxwell made informal notes of her visit to Haifa: "Shoghi Effendi discusses the affairs and conditions of the Cause with astonishing openness and frankness; he does not like secrecy and told us many times that this openness, frankness and truthfulness among the friends constitutes one of the great remedies for many of our difficulties."

explaining to each official exactly what the Bahá'ís were doing on the matter in question and what their purpose was. Then he would come to an official who would say, here are the papers you need. Leroy soon realized the wisdom of the lengthy procedure. It was to inform a sufficient number of officials of the intentions of the Bahá'ís and when that knowledge was widely disseminated, the problem was quickly resolved.

Very rapidly Leroy found himself busy all day, every day. This was the rhythm of life in Haifa, set by the example of the Guardian. Rúḥíyyih Khánum shared a vivid picture of that life at the Wilmette Conference in 1953: "Haifa is a place where one thousand things happen every five minutes, without the slightest warning. You may be having your dinner and somebody dies in the next room. You may be trying quietly to attend to some particular thing and an important visitor arrives. Anything, anything can happen. All kinds of storms sweep over the World Centre in Haifa in about five minutes."

In later years Leroy would describe the Guardian's passion for action and accomplishment, how he worked rapidly and never spared himself, the manner in which he would assign a complicated task and the very next evening ask what progress had been made. Leroy learned to reply that he was "working on it". No sooner was one task completed, he wrote to his brother, than the Guardian would initiate two more – "and that is exactly what has kept the Faith moving steadily forward". One night Shoghi Effendi turned to him and said, "Leroy, I know you are very busy but I want you to set those things aside, as this takes precedence; I'd like you to do this first thing in the morning." It might be enough work for a month, Leroy later commented. When the Guardian was leaving in the summer of 1953 – the Ten Year Crusade had been launched and a strong appeal made for settlers – he told Leroy not to send him reports of *plans*, but when a pioneer arrived at his post, "let me know immediately".

After the evening meal, it became Leroy's privilege to escort the Guardian home, through the north door of the Pilgrim House, along the pathway and across Persian Street to the Master's house, and this he did each night. It was one of the rare times when he was alone with the Guardian other than the occasions when they would drive to visit a site or some work in progress. It also became Leroy's privilege to accompany the Guardian and Rúḥíyyih Khánum to and from the airport when they traveled abroad.

At first Leroy worked from eight in the morning until well after dinner at night, but he soon adopted a new rhythm of work, arising at five in the morning so as to have several quiet hours before appointments began; he found these the most productive hours, particularly as summer came on. When Sylvia arrived at the end of summer, she persuaded him to rest after lunch so as to cope with this lengthy day. This was the schedule seven days a week. And I still do not cope with the work, he wrote to friends.

The Bahá'ís at the World Centre learned to accommodate their work to the three days of rest of the other religious communities: the Jewish on Saturday, the Muslim on Friday and the Christian on Sunday. On Bahá'í Holy Days they spent the time in commemoration or celebration and one of the privileges of life in Haifa was to accompany the Guardian on the Holy Days as he led the way to the Shrine and intoned a chant "with such sweetness as cannot be expressed in words".* Sylvia spoke always of the tremendous longing expressed in the voice of the Guardian when he chanted.

Leroy undertook his work with a sense of urgency, beginning all the various tasks as quickly as feasible. He arrived during Ugo Giachery's first visit to Haifa, an extended pilgrimage which proved invaluable as they could discuss in detail the completion of the Shrine of the Báb which Leroy was expected to carry forward. Then he was drawn quickly into legal matters and negotiations for land which the Guardian wanted to buy. In addition there was a steady flow of correspondence directed to him to answer. Within several months he had called on many of the officials of the State of Israel, this being central to the work of the International Council.

It was a time of great austerity in Israel, when the four-year-old State had, above all, to preserve its independence and house the influx of immigrants. Foreign exchange was used for important purposes only so there were few consumer goods and the best foodstuffs were exported. Life in its outward manifestations was very simple indeed and the Bahá'ís lived modestly within that austere environment. This was but reinforced by the simplicity with which the Guardian was accustomed to live. Ugo Giachery paid tribute to Sylvia in this challenging

---

* Ugo Giachery in his memoir of Shoghi Effendi: "His voice rose and fell with varied degrees of tonality, expressing sorrow and joy, exaltation and hope."

life: "Very few persons who worked in Haifa in those austere years could display so much poise, dignity and wisdom as dear Sylvia . . . Her angelic presence in that Holy Spot made things better for everyone." (See Appendix 4.)

Nonetheless there were adjustments for westerners with their comfortable habits. There were spacious rooms but only one bathroom for all the inhabitants of the Pilgrim House, a communal kitchen, little heating in winter, no cooling devices in the extremely humid summers. Perhaps most trying for Leroy was the lack of accustomed telephones and automobile, so that he had at times to get about on foot and in buses and communal taxis to Jerusalem and Tel Aviv. And he was often quite alone in dealing with the new State and the new personalities. Following the election of the Universal House of Justice in 1963 he rejoiced at the changes which were instituted to facilitate its work, but it did make him think back to the conditions under which he labored and against which he struggled.

Sylvia often said of those early years that you cannot have heaven and everything else as well, and they had heaven because the beloved Guardian was with them. That beloved Guardian, grieved at the loss of his closest kin, had once said to those living in Haifa: "You are my family," a remark that was profoundly moving to them all.

Leroy and Sylvia were to live in what was then the Western Pilgrim House. Leroy described it to Sylvia as an extremely attractive Arab building, beautifully arranged and very comfortable, with high ceilings and many spacious rooms. "The sitting room where I am now writing this is some nineteen by twenty feet, and quite lovely with its rounded bay." As to the physical environment of their new country, Leroy noted immediately, and with a sense of belonging, the resemblance of the Holy Land to the coastal area of southern California – the eucalyptus trees, date palms, similar flowering plants, the sea. 'Abdu'l-Bahá, on His visit to the west coast of America, had Himself noted and remarked on this similarity.

In the five months that he was alone, while Sylvia was disposing of their house and furnishings and readying trunks for shipment to Haifa, he loved to cross the street to the room of Muḥammad Tabrízí in the house of 'Abdu'l-Bahá, and listen to his stories of the early days of the Faith in the Holy Land. This wonderful man was the uncle of Ali

Nakhjavani,* and was serving Shoghi Effendi when Leroy moved to Haifa, being in charge of the gardens around the Shrine of the Báb. It was a bounty for a western Bahá'í to hear these firsthand accounts of the days of Bahá'u'lláh and 'Abdu'l-Bahá.

In spite of his intense activity, or perhaps because of it, it was difficult for Leroy not to have Sylvia with him; he missed her greatly, the first time without her in thirty-three years. It was only in August that she was able to leave America. She traveled by boat, transshipping for her first taste of Israeli life to the Zim Line in Naples after spending several days with Anita on the island of Ischia, talking and sitting on the terrace of the hotel, just staring out over the Mediterranean, between two lives. She arrived in Haifa at the end of August, up at six in the morning and filled with anticipation as they neared land, searching for the Shrine of the Báb. At last she found it – the one familiar sight. As they came into dock she saw Leroy scanning the crowded deck for her. When she called to him he smiled broadly and rushed to meet her; his half had become a whole again; over and over, sometimes weeping, he told her how much he had missed her. She found him much thinner and very nervous, working much too hard she tells Anita, but "there are many, many problems and everything seems so hard to accomplish here". As Rúḥíyyih Khánum confided to her diary in 1949: everything here is done the hard way.[9]

The Guardian soon returned to Haifa, and Sylvia, quite nervous, found herself being presented to him. "The Guardian seated me across from him at table," she writes to Farrukh, "and I was trembling so that I could not eat. Here was the Guardian. I couldn't believe I was so near to him. One feels such an immediate and deep devotion to him, as he portrays the scope of things to come – not locally, not nationally, but on a global scale. The rest of the world just ceases to exist when you meet and watch and listen to the Guardian." Ugo Giachery described this phenomenon as "all contingent matters fading into nothingness".

In a thoughtful gesture Rúḥíyyih Khánum sent a note to Farrukh, alone now in Wilmette, saying everyone had told her what a fine woman Sylvia was, but no one had told her "how very sweet she is. We

---

* One of the first pioneers to East Africa, with his wife Violette and her mother and father, the Hand of the Cause Músá Banání. One of the original and current members of the Universal House of Justice. See also Chapter 23.

are going to get along wonderfully together, I feel sure, and I just love her." In Sylvia's words, Rúḥíyyih Khánum greeted her "with such warmth and love. She is so much like her mother – angelic."

It was the start of their thirteen years in Haifa, at the heart and center of their Faith yet so profoundly separated, as was every Bahá'í, from the person they had come to serve. So close to him, Leroy said, you could not be closer, yet so far that you could not be farther, as there was no association with the station of the Guardian.

What a great bounty it was to serve him, Leroy said years later. Nothing in the world equals the bounty for Sylvia and me of going to the Holy Land to serve him. He is the greatest figure the Cause will produce in the next thousand years.

# CHAPTER TWENTY-ONE

# Forging Relationships

THE principal task given the International Bahá'í Council at its inception was to represent the Guardian and the interests of the Bahá'í World Centre in relations with the Government of Israel. The backdrop to its work was the relationship developed by the Guardian with the governing authorities following the end of Turkish rule in Palestine.

When Shoghi Effendi acceded to the Guardianship in 1921, the Holy Land was governed by the British under a Mandate given it by the League of Nations after the first world war. With diligence and care the Guardian built a cordial understanding over the years between himself as Head of a world community and the British authorities, though the authorities may not have appreciated the import of what they termed the "movement" over which he presided. In a sense both the knighthood conferred by Great Britain upon 'Abdu'l-Bahá, and the time spent by the Guardian at one of England's renowned centers of learning, forged links of confidence and trust.

With the ending of the Mandate in May of 1948, the State of Israel was proclaimed. As was noted earlier, Haifa has been the site of the Bahá'í World Centre since 1868 when Bahá'u'lláh was banished to the neighboring fortress city of 'Akká, where He spent the remainder of His life. The new authorities, particularly in the higher echelons, knew what the Bahá'í Faith stood for and were aware that its Head remained quietly at work in Haifa despite the violence that led up to and followed the creation of the State and the exodus of many thousands of persons.

From the start, the Israelis were very correct in regard to the Faith. One of the early steps taken by the new government was to place markers on the property of Bahjí, isolated as it was, to protect it from entry or harm. This was but the first of many important evidences of their cooperative attitude toward the Bahá'ís. The Bahá'í commitment in funds and effort to its world center was visible to their eyes, as they watched, in the early years of the State, the majestic superstructure of the Shrine of the Báb take form despite conditions of unrest and social upheaval, an evidence of confidence in the future which was of significance to a struggling people. Within a brief time, all Bahá'í properties and Holy Places were exempted from taxation, and large shipments of construction materials, and objects of beautification for the buildings and gardens, were permitted into the State duty free. In all of this, the new government accepted the major concessions which Shoghi Effendi had won during the days of the Mandate. The authorities were grateful, moreover, that the Bahá'ís opened their Holy Places and gardens freely to the public; the year the International Bahá'í Council was established, more than one thousand persons visited the remote Mansion of Bahjí during Passover Week.

The International Bahá'í Council functioned in a very simple way. As we have noted, its discussions were conducted for the most part during dinner with the Guardian. Yet occasionally the Council did hold meetings as a body and when this occurred Minutes were kept of the proceedings. The Bahá'ís were curious about this, wanting to know if the Council functioned "like a National Assembly". Leroy explained that a National Assembly must hold continuous meetings, making its own decisions on matters that come before it, and then carrying out its own decisions. But the sole purpose of the Council was to assist the Guardian, so that matters coming before it were usually submitted verbally or in writing to Shoghi Effendi, who rendered his decisions which were then carried out. As time passed, the Guardian allotted more and more responsibilities to the Council and to the Hands of the Cause, both bodies working under his direct instructions.

The officers of the Council immediately began forging links with the authorities by making friendly contact with government officials, and to this end Milly Collins and Mason Remey, during the early months of the Council, paid calls on a number of dignitaries, among them the Minister for Religious Affairs and the Mayors of Haifa and 'Akká. (In the early years of the State any matter relating to the Bahá'í Faith came under the jurisdiction of the Minister for Islamic affairs, a situation which deeply upset the Guardian, who did not rest until a Bahá'í Department in the Ministry of Religious Affairs had been created.) After Leroy arrived in Haifa he set about calling on officials and within a few months had met a majority of them, a task he pursued until he had met all those whom he felt necessary to his work. As we shall see later, a court case pending when he arrived drew him and other Council members into immediate contact with a number of key officials.

As Leroy went everywhere for the Guardian, he rapidly grew to know many Israelis and he spoke quite openly to them about the Bahá'í Faith, cognizant that the time was ripe for the Faith and its activities to be known widely and favorably. Yet he was circumspect in his exchanges, aware that they were working out a millenia-long dream of establishing a Jewish homeland: all their effort and thought was focused on that. Bahá'ís sometimes asked Leroy why there was no teaching work in the Holy Land. It was a policy established by Bahá'u'lláh and maintained subsequently. In Leroy's opinion, even if it had been possible to teach, there would have been no result: both the Jewish people and the Bahá'ís were engaged in a building process, the one, their State, the other, their World Centre.

Similarly, the needs of the time dictated that access to the World Centre be limited to those Bahá'ís who came as pilgrims or by invitation. In the days of 'Abdu'l-Bahá no one approached the Holy Land without His permission; Shoghi Effendi continued this practice. The World Centre of the Faith, Leroy would explain to Bahá'ís who asked about this, is the most powerful place in the world; the strongest forces for good are operating there and by the same token, the most powerful forces for destruction, those forces which since the days of Bahá'u'lláh had sought to destroy the Faith or bring humiliation upon it. Rúḥíyyih Khánum calls this the principle of light and shadow, the more intense the light, the deeper the shadow it casts.[1] The protection of the Faith at its world center had precedence over any other consideration. When one lived in Haifa, as Leroy learned, one quickly became cognizant of the need to protect the Faith.

One of the services which the Council performed for the Guardian was to represent him at official functions. On the death of Dr. Chaim Weizmann, first President of the State of Israel, which occurred a few months before Leroy's arrival, the Guardian himself attended the ceremony in order to honor this historic figure. But Shoghi Effendi rarely attended any public function, as he feared the Faith might not be given its due as the sole religion having both its spiritual and administrative center in Israel, with its Head therefore taking precedence among the religious leaders. The modesty and humility of the Guardian were such that this attitude toward his position had solely to do with the dignity owed to the Faith of which 'Abdu'l-Bahá had made him the Head.

The International Council soon gained recognition as the body publicly representing the Bahá'ís in the Holy Land, and in the wake of its formation there were numerous invitations for the officers of the Council to attend functions in the official and diplomatic life of the country. As Leroy knew he was to make friends for the Faith, he and Sylvia attended as many of these events as possible in the interest of meeting a wide spectrum of people.

The Council found appropriate ways to play its part in this official life. One was to invite officials to visit the Bahá'í properties, a use the Guardian had always made of the gardens and Holy Places, showing hospitality and at the same time keeping officialdom abreast of developments at the World Centre. (A random notation in Leroy's diary says "the Assistant Foreign Minister had lunch with some of us at Bahjí".) Then it initiated more formal receptions through means of its annual teas; the first was held at the Mansion of Bahjí in April of 1952, to which were invited the consular, religious and urban officials of Haifa and 'Akká, as well as notables from Jerusalem. The annual teas were highly successful and brought the Government into more intimate contact with the Bahá'í community, as the full Council attended. They had an unintended usefulness in that they generated "news", since they involved personalities of the Government and Bahá'ís with titles. Shoghi Effendi in naming the Council officers had given the world something to which it could relate, though as Rúḥíyyih Khánum has clearly stated, the Council members knew they were nothing, the Guardian was everything. Nonetheless the existence of the Council stirred journalistic interest – its formation had been reported in several foreign language newspapers in Israel – and resulted in articles on the World Centre and Bahá'í activities in Israel and abroad. Leroy's return from the Kampala Conference in 1953, where he represented the Guardian, inspired a profile in the English-language newspaper on him and on the work in Africa. Leroy, as the designated public contact person, noted the steady increase in calls and requests for interviews and information.

In seeking to foster relations with another important segment of Israeli life – business and civic leaders – Leroy turned to the club circuit that had grown up in the country. An Israeli businessman recalled that he was "very friendly, very much liked and held in high esteem" in club circles. He joined several, renewing membership in Rotary International which with its weekly luncheon meetings proved an excellent platform for speaking of the Faith. His first public talk in the Holy Land was given to the Rotary Club of Haifa just six months after his arrival; from that came other invitations. In the following year and a half he spoke before clubs in Nahariya, Nazareth, Natanya, Beersheba and 'Akká. When the Guardian heard of these he said, Excellent. Leroy was presented as the Secretary-General of the Council, but he generated interest also because he was American, had chosen to live in Israel, and had given up a good business career to do so.

Twice he was asked to speak in 'Akká and these two experiences brought him profound satisfaction. On the first occasion he appeared before the Rotary Club, the date being the opening of the Holy Year in 1952; it was the first time the Faith had been presented publicly in the fortress city. Several months later he was invited to speak at a widely advertised meeting at the Quaker Center. There was an audience of some hundred persons, Jews, Christians and Muslims. On that occasion, he chose to speak of Bahá'u'lláh and His sufferings – this at a site just two hundred yards from the house of Bahá'u'lláh and two short blocks from the prison where the Manifestation of God had been incarcerated. A poignant echo comes to mind of the words heard in Bahá'u'lláh's dream in the Síyáh-Chál: "Ere long will God raise up the treasures of the earth – men who will aid Thee through Thyself and through Thy Name . . ."[2]

But Shoghi Effendi said he would not be satisfied until Leroy had spoken of the Bahá'í Faith in Jerusalem. It struck Leroy as very interesting that shortly after the Guardian expressed this wish, a new person became president of the Jerusalem Rotary Club, a man known to the Council members because of his position as chief of cabinet of the President of Israel. Before long, he invited Leroy to speak before the club on the subject of world peace; one guest commented later that it

was the finest talk he had ever heard on the subject of peace and
brotherhood. It was through this same official that the first tentative
soundings were made which eventually led to the visit of President
Ben-Zvi to the World Centre. When Leroy mentioned such a visit to
the chief of cabinet he answered: Yes of course, why not?

In Israel the home was the center of socializing and Leroy, on his
visits to Jerusalem, was sometimes invited to the homes of the hospitable Israelis for coffee after the day's work. He enjoyed this,
especially for the quality of conversation among these highly intelli-
gent and verbal people. Some of the most important people he met in
Israel were encountered in one particular home, that of a former government official who was a good friend to the Bahá'ís. On one such
occasion, the host's orthodox relatives were present and excitedly discussing in Hebrew the coming of Messiah. The host turned to English
so as to include Leroy in the conversation. He said Jewish literature
contains two main proofs of the coming of Messiah: the Jews' return
to Israel and the establishment of universal peace. Now, said the host,
we are sitting here in Israel! and everywhere in the world people are
talking about peace, and it is certainly on its way. So you will all have to
find some other approach to discussing Messiah.

It was also fascinating when Leroy would discover traces of the
legacy of 'Abdu'l-Bahá among the local people. One evening he and
Sylvia attended a reception and as they declined the various drinks
offered and remarked that they did not drink alcohol, the host said, We
didn't know that. Tell us about your beliefs. A group was gathered
around and Leroy began speaking of the appearance of Bahá'u'lláh,
the unity of religion, the abolition of prejudice. Then someone asked –
as Leroy had noted they always did – what do you believe about the
Trinity? Before he could answer, a man who lived up the street from
them, a Roman Catholic Arab, said, I'm going to tell you what Bahá'ís
believe about the Trinity and I'm going to tell you about it exactly as
Abbas Effendi explained it to me. He went on to use 'Abdu'l-Bahá's
example of the sun and the ray and the perfect mirror. On more than
one occasion Leroy had the moving experience of listening to people
share the wisdom they had learned from 'Abdu'l-Bahá; the Master
seemed near indeed.

One of his most interesting encounters with a government digni-
tary occurred at a 1959 reception celebrating the founding of the

Knesset, an event to which the Bahá'ís were always invited. It was a lengthy conversation he had with Prime Minister David Ben-Gurion, then serving in that position for the second time. (Leroy had met the Prime Minister before moving to Israel, when Mr. Ben-Gurion received a delegation of National Assembly members during a visit to Chicago.) Sylvia and Leroy were mingling among the guests when Ben-Gurion, who found himself near Leroy, said, Mr. Ioas, I want to talk with you. Leroy immediately asked if he should come to his office. No, we'll talk right now.

You're an American, said Ben-Gurion. Bahá'u'lláh was a Persian (he pronounced the name perfectly). What is there in the writings of Bahá'u'lláh, a Persian, that makes you a Bahá'í and one of His followers? Leroy said he could answer in several ways but the simplest was to point out that the world today is seeking peace and conciliation, and certainly the one who has contributed the most profound concepts to the idea of peace, and whose writings include the clearest program for the establishment of world peace, is Bahá'u'lláh. As I have always been interested in working for universal peace, I am a Bahá'í.

Now listen, replied Ben-Gurion, that is a social program. What is it that makes you, an American, a follower of Bahá'u'lláh? Leroy said, I will tell you in another way. We believe that from time to time God chooses a certain individual to be the mirror of His Revelation. This person usually arises in one of the most decadent places in the world and he raises the people out of that decadence to found a great civilization. Leroy spoke of Egypt and Moses, of Jesus and Muhammad. So we, he continued, feel Bahá'u'lláh has now come to create a civilization based on oneness and unity. That is why I am a Bahá'í.

Moses, replied Ben-Gurion, took his own people, the Jews, and created a great civilization. Now if you tell me that Bahá'u'lláh is going to take the Persians and make a great civilization out of his own people, yes. But what is it that makes you, as an American, a follower of Bahá'u'lláh?

Leroy said, Mr. Ben-Gurion, I will explain it to you this way. The Bahá'ís believe the cause of the evolution of society is religion. And religion is renewed by the appearance of a divine man who is an expression of the Holy Spirit. Leroy continued by explaining the wider sphere of unity created by each such figure and again took as his example Moses. How did he create this great Jewish civilization?

Because he had the power of God flowing through him which quickened the minds and hearts so that the people aspired toward nobler ideals.

It was a long conversation, noted briefly here, and at the conclusion, the Prime Minister said, Well, we must talk some more. A few days later Leroy happened to meet the Prime Minister's executive aide and asked how it was that Mr. Ben-Gurion knew so much about the Bahá'í Faith, as he had asked very pointed questions a few nights earlier. His aide replied that Mr. Ben-Gurion had Bahá'í books in his personal library and what is more, he said, he has read them.

In the officers of the International Council the Guardian had at his service people of considerable competence who were able to establish and maintain the dignified and effective relations which he sought with the Government. There is little doubt that the high caliber of their work greatly facilitated his task of building the World Centre and gaining recognition for the Faith. Indeed, during one of Ugo Giachery's visits to Haifa, when the Guardian was speaking of the work of Ugo and Leroy, he said to those at table, "Two of the Hands are here at dinner tonight, one is a Titan and the other a Colossus – and you can decide which is which, I don't care". On more than one occasion the Guardian said that when history is written, it will tell of the assistance of the International Bahá'í Council to the Guardian at the World Centre.

In his Riḍván message of 1954 the Guardian enumerated some of the fruits of the relationship which had developed with the authorities:

"Contact has . . . been established with the President of Israel, its Prime Minister and five other Cabinet Ministers, as well as with the President of the Knesset, culminating in the establishment of a special Bahá'í Department in the Ministry of Religious Affairs, and in an official statement by the Head of this Ministry to Parliament emphasizing the international scope of the Faith and the importance of its World Centre . . ." The Guardian then revealed momentous news: that these steps had "paved the way for the forthcoming official visit, during the early days of the Riḍván period, of the President of Israel, himself, to the Báb's Sepulcher on Mt. Carmel".[3] It is to be noted that the Guardian did not say the visit was being made to him.

Several months earlier the President, Vice-President and Secretary-General of the International Bahá'í Council had asked to call on the

President of Israel to officially greet him and they were received by President Itzhak Ben-Zvi on February 1st. During that visit the President expressed the wish to visit His Eminence the Guardian of the Faith, as well as the Shrine and gardens on Mt. Carmel. Subsequently, Shoghi Effendi extended a cordial invitation to the President, which was accepted for the date of April 26.

It was an historic day, marking "the first official visit paid by the Head of a sovereign independent State to the Sepulchers of the Martyr-Prophet of the Faith and the Center of Bahá'u'lláh's Covenant"[4] ('Abdu'l-Bahá is buried in the Shrine of the Báb), and to the head of the Bahá'í Faith. It is arresting to contrast this visit with the long history of persecution of the Faith in the land of its birth and in the countries of Bahá'u'lláh's exiles.

On the morning of that day, Leroy and Mason Remey went to greet the President and his wife at the Megiddo Hotel and found them finishing breakfast. The two Council members were invited to have coffee with them and their military aide, which they did. At nine o'clock they drove to the home of 'Abdu'l-Bahá, where they were warmly received by the Guardian and Rúḥíyyih Khánum, who "surrounded them with gracious hospitality". During the friendly and informal discussion which followed, the Guardian outlined the aims and objectives of the Bahá'í teachings and the friendship of the Bahá'ís for Israel.

The President remarked that the Faith was not unknown to him. When he and Mrs. Ben-Zvi were married they were very poor but wished to see all of the Holy Land, and set out to hike the length and breadth of the country. They came one day to the property of Bahjí. There at the Shrine they met Abbas Effendi who was very kind and courteous to them, taking them in to the Shrine of Bahá'u'lláh and then to His tea house where He served them tea. That visit with the Master (extraordinary in retrospect) had been their first contact with the Bahá'í Faith.

Persian tea and sweets were served and to commemorate the occasion, Shoghi Effendi presented a beautiful hand-wrought silver-bound album to the President containing colored views of the Bahá'í Holy Places in Israel.

The party then left for the gardens and Shrine. The Guardian led President and Mrs. Ben-Zvi through the gardens, fragrant at that season with the perfume of roses and lilies, showing them the view over Haifa to 'Akká in the distance. Then he escorted them to the Shrine of the Báb.

At this point Leroy, who was in attendance with the group, realized he would have to tell the President of the custom of removing one's shoes before entering the Shrine. When he did this the President turned and looked at him and said something in Hebrew. He asked if Leroy knew what he said. "I quoted to you what God said to Moses when He approached the Burning Bush: Put thy shoes from off thy feet, for the place whereon thou standest is holy ground."[5] Then the President said, "Of *course* I will take off my shoes. This custom originated with us, when God spoke to Moses."

The visitors were greatly impressed with the spirit of the sacred precincts and commented warmly on the beauty of the gardens. The President told Shoghi Effendi how grateful they were to have them and how proud they were that the World Centre of the Faith is in Israel.

On leaving, the President expressed his appreciation of the hospitality extended by the Guardian and of the work which the Bahá'ís were doing in Israel, and extended his best wishes for the success of the Bahá'í community throughout the world. Walking behind with one of the President's aides, Leroy said to him, Isn't this a good occasion to issue a press release? Yes, replied the aide, but I'm so busy today – why don't you write it? Leroy did so and sent it off to the papers.

On May 26, Shoghi Effendi and Rúḥíyyih Khánum traveled to Jerusalem to pay a return call on President Ben-Zvi, thus cementing the historic relationship.

# CHAPTER TWENTY-TWO

# The Hands of the Cause in Haifa

'ABDU'L-BAHÁ enjoined upon the Hands of the Cause to edify the souls of men, to spread the divine fragrances, to be the defenders of the Faith. Each of the Hands undertook these weighty spiritual responsibilities in his own manner. The work of the Hands of the Cause in Haifa, however, was dissimilar to that of their colleagues in other countries, as their sole function was to serve Shoghi Effendi.

Shoghi Effendi considered Leroy's work as his assistant secretary, charged with all correspondence concerning the global teaching campaign, to be part of his work as a Hand of the Cause. It was not the direct teaching that was implicit in 'Abdu'l-Bahá's words and which Leroy loved, but through it he could encourage the pioneers and keep the National Assemblies focused on the goals of the plan. (Masoud Khamsi recalls the letter Leroy wrote on behalf of the Guardian to the Bahá'ís in Iran; it said the friends should go pioneering "according to their own conscience". As he thought about this – and his wife was not then a Bahá'í – he decided to move to South America, a dramatic change in his life.)

As the Hands of the Cause in the Holy Land visited with officials of the Government in the interests of the World Centre, as they met the press, as they greeted dignitaries from abroad, they were by their very presence a living demonstration of Bahá'í standards, practices, and attitudes. This was surely an important part of their teaching function.

Those Hands who were members of the International Bahá'í Council were immediately drawn into the protective aspect of their work, specifically as it related to the Covenant-breakers. They lived at the very center of violation, where the enemies of the Faith could make common cause with the Covenant-breakers against the head of the Faith himself.

When Leroy arrived in Haifa, the Guardian was deeply preoccupied with such a matter, and it was causing him great concern. It involved a case brought against the Guardian by remnants of the Covenant-breakers in 'Akká. Starting with an insignificant incident it took on such dimensions that a deeper intent became evident on the part of those bringing suit, namely, to gain co-custodianship with the Guardian of the Shrine of Bahá'u'lláh, or to secure rooms for themselves in the Mansion of Bahjí, from which they had removed themselves so that the Guardian might repair the appalling deterioration that had occurred under their care. After its restoration the British High Commissioner had declared Bahjí a place of pilgrimage and not a personal residence, and the Guardian became its custodian. The court case is an example of the type of scheming with which Shoghi Effendi was forced to contend throughout his Guardianship.

The Guardian, ever intent on beautifying the surroundings of Bahá'u'lláh's Tomb, one day told the guard to tear down a dilapidated house of several rooms near the Tomb; the roof was falling in and the walls unstable. The Covenant-breakers living on the property of Bahjí, in a house leaning up against the Mansion, rushed to obtain an Order from the Haifa Court to halt the demolition because they had not been consulted and still held one-sixth of the deed to the Mansion. In fact the structure in question had been in Bahá'í hands since 1892 and in Shoghi Effendi's hands for more than twenty years.

Two of the Covenant-breakers and their lawyer met with Leroy, Mason Remey and the Guardian's lawyer with the intention of settling the question out of court. It was a fruitless meeting as sixty-year-old attacks on 'Abdu'l-Bahá were brought forward. So the case went to a hearing, scheduled to be held informally before a judge. After two ineffectual meetings with the judge, during which intense hostility was displayed on the part of the plaintiffs, the case was sent for a first hearing in Court.

Indicating the unchanging desire of the Covenant-breakers to humiliate the head of the Faith, they summoned Shoghi Effendi as a witness, an insulting act which caused the Guardian immense distress. "His great suffering," Ugo Giachery recalled, "was for the sacrilege being committed against this Institution of the Faith. It was so abhorrent to him that he felt physically ill, as if 'a thousand scorpions had bitten him'."[1]

The Guardian made the decision to appeal directly to the Government to lift the case out of the Civil Court and called Ugo Giachery from Rome to assist with the work that followed. The three Hands of the Cause called on the Attorney General, the Vice-Minister of Religions, and officials of the Foreign Office and the Prime Minister's office. The result was that the Attorney-General on instructions of the Vice-Minister informed the president of the Haifa Court that in accordance with a 1924 law, the case in question was a religious matter and not to be tried by a Civil Court. It would appear that the Guardian's initiatives had concluded the case.

But the clever and hostile lawyer of the Covenant-breakers challenged the finding on a technicality and made an appeal to the Supreme Court of Israel, in effect putting themselves in an adversarial position to the State. The Hands of the Cause again went forth to a series of interviews, and Shoghi Effendi made a personal appeal to the Prime Minister. There was an immediate reaction. The Prime Minister's legal adviser called to his office the Vice-Minister of Religions, the two lawyers and those they represented. The Bahá'ís refused to meet further with the Covenant-breakers and waited in another room of the building. The opposing lawyer made repeated claims, conveyed by the Guardian's lawyers to the Hands of the Cause, all of them rejected categorically. Finally the Prime Minister's adviser told the plaintiffs that they could continue their appeal if they wished but they should understand that their fight was now with the Government of Israel and what it had the authority to do. At this point they dropped the appeal and the case, and the authorities issued authorization to demolish the ruins. The Guardian cabled the Bahá'í world of the successful conclusion to the painful case inspired by what he termed the "blind, uncontrollable animosity" of the Covenant-breakers.

Within forty-eight hours the Guardian had levelled the house and sent over eight truckloads of plants and ornamental pieces to begin the beautification of the area. Leroy stayed in the Mansion to oversee the work. Within a week the Guardian had laid out a wide expanse of garden which appeared miraculously spread out before the eyes of the Bahá'ís in time for the commemoration of Bahá'u'lláh's Ascension.

The case had frustrated the Guardian's intentions from December through mid-May.

Leroy, who had initially found it difficult even to look at the Covenant-breakers, was told by the Guardian never to lower his eyes when dealing with them, but to look them "straight in the eye". Repugnant as he found it, he learned to deal with them because he was called on to do so, even at times alone when the Guardian was absent. Furthermore, as the Guardian felt Leroy might be called as a witness in this or future court cases with the Covenant-breakers, he clearly instructed him on an important issue about which he might be questioned. The Guardian said: When you are on the witness stand and these people ask you if the Will and Testament of Bahá'u'lláh appointed 'Abdu'l-Bahá as the Interpreter of the Word, the answer is no, He did not. There is nothing in the Will and Testament that says 'Abdu'l-Bahá is the Interpreter of the Word of Bahá'u'lláh. It states that He is the Head of the Faith, He is the successor, He is the Center of the Covenant, but it does not say He is the Interpreter. He becomes the Interpreter through the passage in the Aqdas which states: "When the Mystic Dove will have winged its flight from its Sanctuary of Praise and sought its far-off goal, its hidden habitation, refer ye whatsoever ye understand not in the Book to Him Who hath branched from this mighty stock."[2]

At times during his travels abroad, Leroy shared this with the Bahá'ís to warn them of the need for accuracy and clarity in their understanding of the Covenant, to prepare themselves for the attacks on the Faith which 'Abdu'l-Bahá promised them would come: "How great, how very great is the Cause! How very fierce the onslaught of all the peoples and kindreds of the earth . . . One and all, they shall arise with all their power to resist His Cause."[3]

Through this court case, occurring as it did shortly after the birth of the International Council, the Faith gained stature in the eyes of the most important government Ministries, as officials learned more of its history and purposes, dealt with its dignified emissaries, and noted its unified stand behind the head of the Faith, even as the plaintiffs revealed themselves as vengeful and vindictive.

We cite this case at some length to show the nature of the worries to which the Guardian was subjected at a time when he was being "pressed by the spirit" in Leroy's words, to establish the International

Council, bring into being the institution of the Hands of the Cause, inspire the Bahá'ís to meet the expenses of the House of Worship in Wilmette and the Shrine of the Báb in Haifa, and supervise on a daily basis the delicate and complicated construction work on the Shrine. It was of these things that Milly Collins had spoken to the National Assembly when visiting America in 1951, and which had brought such pain to Leroy's heart.

Shoghi Effendi's first appointment of Hands of the Cause in December 1951 was followed within two months by a second group of appointments, seven in number: Siegfried (Fred) Schopflocher and Corinne True in America, Zikrullah Khadem (Dhikru'lláh Khádim) and Shu'á'u'lláh 'Alá'í in Persia, Clara Dunn in Australia, Músá Banání in Africa and Adelbert Mühlschlegel in Germany. Five of his appointees died during the early years of the institution and Shoghi Effendi replaced each with another person singled out for this honor; thus were named Rúḥíyyih Khánum, Jalál Kházeh, Agnes Alexander, Paul Haney, and 'Alí Muḥammad Varqá. The Hands of the Cause, scattered as they were on all the continents, coordinated their work through the Hands in Haifa, who consulted the Guardian on their behalf and communicated his decisions to them. The Hands of the Cause never met as a body with the Guardian.

Shoghi Effendi had clearly indicated that the institution of the Hands of the Cause would develop rapidly and play an increasingly prominent role on the international scene, and we find him, one year after the initial appointments, calling upon four of the Hands of the Cause – "honored by direct association with the newly-initiated endeavors at the world center" – to represent him at the four conferences to be held during the Holy Year.

Milly Collins was to accompany Rúḥíyyih Khánum to the "most distinguished" of these conferences, called for Riḍván in Wilmette. This historic conference would mark not only the centenary of the birth of Bahá'u'lláh's Mission and the launching of the world crusade, but the dedication of the holiest House of Worship ever to be built. Leroy was designated to attend the first conference, in Kampala; Ugo Giachery the third, in Stockholm; and Mason Remey the fourth, in New Delhi. The Guardian's emissaries would have a four-fold mission: to deliver his message to the conference, outline the detailed plans of the world crusade and encourage the whole-hearted participation of the believers in achieving its goals. In addition, each of the Guardian's emissaries was entrusted by Shoghi Effendi with a "precious remembrance" of the co-Founder of the Faith, a reproduction of the portrait of the Báb. Wilmette was singled out for a special gift. In honor of the completion of the "consecrated edifice" of the Mother Temple, the Guardian sent a portrait of Bahá'u'lláh which was to rest thereafter beneath the dome of the Temple. The full complement of Hands of the Cause were invited to attend all four conferences, and indeed ten traveled to East Africa for the first conference.

As a further evidence of the growth of the institution of the Hands of the Cause, Shoghi Effendi called upon those living outside Haifa to represent him at National Conventions as each new pillar of the future House of Justice came into being. In this way the loving presence of the Guardian was brought to each new national community. During the period of the Ten Year Crusade, national and regional Assemblies came into being as quickly as the number and strength of local Assemblies permitted their creation: Panama, Alaska, Benelux, Iberia, Arabia, Southeast Asia, Japan, New Zealand, Pakistan, South America, Central America, the Greater Antilles and Scandinavia among them.

It was the Guardian's practice to send messages intended for the Bahá'í world to the United States for dissemination. After he implemented the institution of the Hands of the Cause his messages often begin or end with the phrase – so indicative of the honor he gave the institution – "Announce to Hands and all National Assemblies . . .", "Share announcement Hands of the Cause and all National Assemblies . . ."

Two years after his appointment of the Hands of the Cause, the Guardian instructed them to designate nine persons to act as an "auxiliary board" working under them in the "promotion of the interests" of the Ten Year Crusade. Thus was born an adjunct body to the Hands of the Cause, whose operation we are familiar with today. Toward the very end of his life, Shoghi Effendi, harassed again by the old enemies of the Faith, and foreseeing that the very success of the world crusade would alert those outside the fold of the Faith to what they might conceive as the danger of its powerful movement, called upon the Hands to assume more fully their role of protection of the Faith by appointing a second auxiliary board for the safeguarding of the Faith and the protection of the spiritual life of its communities. This released the first auxiliary board to address itself solely to the teaching goals of the Ten Year Crusade.

Near the end of his life the Guardian also felt moved to call for five intercontinental conferences to mark the halfway point of the great crusade which he had initiated in 1953. Again he turned to the Hands of the Cause who were members of the International Bahá'í Council to represent him in the widely-separated venues of these conferences: Djakarta, Wilmette, Sydney, Frankfurt, Kampala.

In his final communication to the Bahá'ís,[4] written one month before his passing, the Guardian appointed the last contingent of Hands of the Cause, giving to the Bahá'í world the youngest among them, Enoch Olinga. The final eight to be elevated to this rank were Enoch Olinga, John Robarts and William Sears in Africa, Hasan Balyuzi and John Ferraby in the British Isles, Collis Featherstone and Raḥmatu'lláh Muhájir in the Pacific and Abu'l-Qásim Faizi in the Arabian Peninsula. In naming them, the Guardian notes that they represent the Afnán (descendants of the family of the Báb), the black and white races, and Christian, Muslim, Jewish and Pagan backgrounds.

In this same message, the Guardian uses a designation for the Hands of the Cause which was shortly to have dramatic significance. He refers to them as the "Chief Stewards of Bahá'u'lláh's embryonic World Commonwealth". This designation was to form the basis of the period of the Custodians, lasting from 1957 to 1963. All of these developments came rapidly one upon another.

In retrospect it was seen how completely the Guardian through such decisions had protected all avenues of access to the Faith. As a crowning protection to the Faith, accomplished at the close of his life, there came the cleansing of the precincts of the Shrine of Bahá'u'lláh from the presence of those who had turned against His designated spiritual heir. The last service Leroy was able to perform for the Guardian was to assist him in this achievement.

For more than sixty years, disaffected members of the family of 'Abdu'l-Bahá had lived on the property of Bahjí, step by step being pushed back and restricted in their freedom of movement. But never in his lifetime was the Guardian able to visit the Shrine of his great-grandfather without their presence and their viewing of his acts of devotion. Whatever he did there was done under their unfriendly gaze.

Five years earlier, as we have seen, the Covenant-breakers had brought legal suit against the Guardian. A major result of those efforts had been recognition by the State of Israel of the Guardian as sole Custodian of the Bahá'í Holy Places, and the "irretrievable curtailment", in the words of Shoghi Effendi, "of long-standing privileges extended to the Covenant-breakers during the course of six decades".[5]

"It was a very dramatic story", Leroy said some years later of the sequence of events which led to the final departure of the Covenant-breakers from Bahjí, "and I remember when we started the process the Guardian said, 'Do you think it can be done?' I said, Shoghi Effendi, if the Guardian wants it done, it can be done. I did not know what I was getting into! The Covenant-breakers had been there for sixty-five years desecrating that sacred place and the Guardian said, it will be a miracle to get them out."

When Leroy was given this assignment, the Guardian said to him: "Everything you have done up to now, including your work on the Shrine of the Báb, is as silver, whereas removing the Covenant-breakers from Bahjí, and securing the buildings and lands for the Faith, will be as gold." It was to be the monumental victory which "crowned the beloved Guardian's life and filled his heart with profound joy, exultation and thankfulness . . ."[6]

The first step was taken on May 11, 1956 when lawyers representing the International Bahá'í Council applied for expropriation of the property owned by the Covenant-breakers within the Ḥaram-i-Aqdas, the outer Sanctuary of Bahá'u'lláh's Sepulcher, i.e. the consecrated grounds contiguous to the Shrine. This initiative was taken as a result of information Leroy gleaned from government officials responsible for questions of property ownership. The legal instrument was the Land Acquisition for Public Purposes Ordinance of 1943, permitting the Government to acquire land for purposes which it deemed public purposes, and to transfer that land to responsible authorities.

The Shrine and Mansion had been recognized as a Holy Place long years before by the Mandate authorities, a recognition confirmed by the Israeli Government in 1952. Its acquisition therefore on behalf of the Bahá'ís, so that it could be developed and maintained by them, was deemed by the Government to be a public purpose. (One of the arguments used by the Bahá'ís in urging expropriation was their intention to embellish and build on the Shrine of Bahá'u'lláh.) The Government issued an expropriation order which was published in the *Official Gazette* on December 20, 1956.

The expropriation order was immediately challenged by the Covenant-breakers, who appealed to the Supreme Court. They claimed that the expropriation (of their minimal shares of the property) constituted an interference in an internal dispute, an infringement of their spiritual and temporal rights, and discrimination against a minority group. The Bahá'ís appeared before the Court to answer what Leroy called "many of their nasty attacks against the Guardian and the Faith".

The case was heard by the Supreme Court in April of 1957 and judgment was given on May 31. The Court found against the Covenant-breakers, and in so doing found that the Government's purpose in acquiring the land was indeed a public purpose. The Court furthermore drew attention to the fact that the appellants had not contended the public purpose of the action and that the contentions which they had brought forward had no substance.

Following the judgment of the Supreme Court, the Bahá'ís proceeded with eviction orders against the Covenant-breakers. The Attorney General applied to the Haifa District Court for a dispossession order against them, but again they intervened, attempting to delay the court hearing. They were unsuccessful in this and judgment was given against them, resulting in orders that they quit the premises of Bahjí and relinquish whatever small holdings remained in their hands. The Supreme Court had set the amount of their recompense.

On June 3, Shoghi Effendi cabled the triumphant news that the expropriation order had been upheld, "enabling the civil authorities to enforce the original decision and proceed with the eviction of the wretched remnants of the once redoubtable adversaries . . ."[7]

Within three months, they were gone. The Ḥaram-i-Aqdas had been cleansed. The spiritual suffering inflicted on 'Abdu'l-Bahá and the Guardian by these enemies of the Faith had come to its end. Before leaving Haifa that summer, Shoghi Effendi had told Leroy that "just as soon as we acquire this house of the Covenant-breakers we will tear it down", so the moment they were gone – in late August – he cabled the Guardian asking if this should be done. The Guardian replied: "Postpone demolition until my return." He wished to supervise the work himself.

Two months before his passing, Shoghi Effendi again cabled the Bahá'í world (September 6, 1957):

ANNOUNCE TO HANDS AND ALL NATIONAL ASSEMBLIES THAT FOLLOWING LOSS OF THE APPEAL TO THE SUPREME COURT, THE GOVERNMENT EXPROPRIATION ORDER HAS BEEN IMPLEMENTED, RESULTING IN THE COMPLETE EVACUATION OF THE REMNANT OF COVENANT-BREAKERS AND THE TRANSFER OF ALL THEIR BELONGINGS FROM THE PRECINCTS OF THE MOST HOLY SHRINE, AND THE PURIFICATION, AFTER SIX LONG DECADES, OF THE HARAM-I-AQDAS FROM EVERY TRACE OF THEIR CONTAMINATION. MEASURES UNDER WAY TO EFFECT TRANSFER OF TITLE DEEDS OF THE EVACUATED PROPERTY TO THE TRIUMPHANT BAHA'I COMMUNITY.[8]

The legalities of the transfer took place in two stages. In October 1957 Leroy was able to cable the Guardian that the Bahá'ís had now acquired the properties, that "they are ours".

He left a Memorandum of the second occasion, when the transfer was completed, here briefly noted:

This morning, I joined our lawyer at the Land Registry in connection with the transfer of the properties at Bahjí to the Israel branch of the United States National Spiritual Assembly. We had a conference to review the details of my signing on behalf of the National Assembly, Israel Branch, in view of the fact that His Eminence Shoghi Rabbani had passed away.

It was demonstrated that the Power of Attorney which he had given me was not a Power of Attorney to act in his behalf, it was a Power of Attorney to act in behalf of the Israel Branch, and therefore his passing had no effect on the validity of my authority to sign. We likewise discussed the question of the local transfer tax of two per cent, inasmuch as I had brought from Jerusalem a letter waiving the government tax of four per cent. When it was learned that the property was definitely not within the city limits of 'Akká, it was stated that the two per cent would be waived.

We then proceeded with the transfer of the property. The Official Deeds of Sale were signed before the transfer agent. Thus there is concluded the complete purification of the Shrine area and the Ḥaram-i-Aqdas.

The historic day of the final transfer of properties was two days short of one month after the Guardian's passing, Monday, December 2, 1957. The Deeds for Bahjí – the Shrine, the Mansion, the house of the Covenant-breakers, and all small pieces of land which they held in 'Akká, were signed over to the Faith at 10:25 a.m. (It should be noted that until this date the Shrine itself was held by Covenant-breakers as part of their small percentage of property). Leroy was signatory for the Bahá'ís with Ugo Giachery and Sylvia as witnesses. The property was put in the name of the Israel Branch of the National Spiritual Assembly of the Bahá'ís of the United States. After Leroy's death, Sylvia found the pen with which he had signed the documents, left in the page of his diary at the date of December 2, 1957. On leaving Haifa, she gave it to the International Archives.

On Sunday, December 15, demolition of the house of the Covenant-breakers was begun. The Hands of the Cause in Haifa and the members of the International Bahá'í Council went over to Bahjí and took pictures of the event; the demolition was completed one week later.

# CHAPTER TWENTY-THREE

# Representing the Guardian

UGANDA, in 1953 a British Protectorate in East Africa, was destined to become the first area in the world where "entry by troops" became a reality, the start of that large-scale growth in the number of adherents to the Bahá'í Faith which had been anticipated with such longing by 'Abdu'l-Bahá and Shoghi Effendi.

Kampala, the capital, was the site chosen by the Guardian for the first of the four intercontinental conferences which he called to celebrate the Holy Year. It would be the venue for the initial presentation to the Bahá'ís of the world of his detailed plans for the Ten Year Crusade.

The Guardian often spoke of the purity of heart of the African people, their comparative freedom from "the evils of a gross, a rampant and cancerous materialism undermining the fabric of human society in the East and in the West . . ."[1] They were able to respond directly to the spirit of Bahá'u'lláh's message.

It was in 1950 that the Guardian called for the opening of the continent of Africa to the teachings of Bahá'u'lláh, and indicated that Bahá'í settlement there would be a major feature of a coming worldwide teaching campaign. He called for pioneers to leave their homes and settle in certain areas of Africa.

Among the first to arise and move to East Africa were Músá and Samíhih Banání. "I was in Teheran," he said later, "when the call of the Guardian came for pioneers for Africa, and I decided to go with Ali Nakhjavani [his son-in-law]. Overcoming many difficulties, both of us got our visas. I settled in Kampala where Ali joined me . . ."

The Guardian, who loved Músá Banání very much, spoke one

evening at dinner of how Mr. and Mrs. Banání were even then going up to the Kampala hills early in the morning and calling out the Greatest Name (Yá-Bahá'u'l-Abhá, O Thou Glory of Glories) over Africa and chanting prayers there. For some time they lived in a hotel and went out into the streets to teach until they could find a house in which to live. After several months of great discouragement they had two believers.

Then the Guardian permitted Mr. and Mrs. Banání to make the pilgrimage to Haifa. He gave them a number of instructions concerning the work in Africa and on the last day of their pilgrimage he informed Músá Banání of his appointment as a Hand of the Cause. Músá Banání wept and said he was unworthy, that Ali was the eloquent teacher. The Guardian said, It is your arising that has conquered the continent.

While they were away on pilgrimage, Ali had been living and teaching in the villages and the number of believers grew steadily. Músá Banání later spoke of those days: "There were three reasons for the great success of the teaching work in Uganda. First, the bounties and confirmations of Bahá'u'lláh. Second, the complete unity of the pioneers. Third, the exemplary way in which Ali Nakhjavani, one of the pioneers, conducted himself, with absolute freedom from prejudice.

"He went and lived with the Africans in the heart of the jungle. This was a new experience for the Africans, because at no time previously had any white man acted toward them as he did. In the past the Africans had heard many promises and many beautiful words from white men, but in actions they had always seen the opposite.

"When they saw that words and deeds were one in the person of Ali Nakhjavani they immediately warmed to the Faith and have received the Message of Bahá'u'lláh very eagerly and with exultation." By the time of the Kampala Conference, there were already a sizeable number of Spiritual Assemblies and several hundred new Bahá'ís. "I desire in particular", the Guardian stated in his message to the Conference, "to express to all those gathered at this Conference my feelings of abiding appreciation of the magnificent role played and of the remarkable prizes won by the small band of Persian, British and American pioneers . . . which is destined to exert an incalculable influence on the fortunes of the Faith throughout the world, and which may well have far-reaching repercussions among the two chief races in the North American continent." This latter statement is surely highly significant and thought-provoking.

Leroy went to Kampala as the Guardian's representative. "It was an unusual experience," he was quoted as saying in a *Jerusalem Post* interview on his return to Haifa, "to see Britishers and Africans mingle freely in a British Protectorate in the heart of Africa, without even a psychological color bar . . . Bahá'ís have as a basic tenet the equality of all men, irrespective of their color or race." One of the first things Leroy did in Kampala was to change hotels when he learned that in the major hotel where he had been booked he would not be able to meet with the African believers.

The new African Bahá'ís were a cause of such joy to the Guardian that he invited every one of them to attend the Kampala Conference as his guest, hoping they would constitute the majority of the participants. But when the time came for the Conference the villagers thought they would have to stay at home to help with the harvest. "Moreover," recalls Músá Banání, "their friends had told them that the white people would gather them in and sell them as slaves." Ali and another Bahá'í went to them and said, "Ali is not inviting you; Banání is not inviting you; but you will be the guests of the Guardian." Encouraged, many of them decided to attend, so that they were indeed a majority at the Conference, one hundred and forty out of two hundred and thirty-two participants. They represented some thirty tribes. "Moreover", Músá Banání reported, "when they went back to their villages their suspicious relatives were surprised to see them, and the fact that they returned hale and hearty and much happier after contact with the Bahá'ís resulted in fifty more coming into the Faith after the Conference."

Leroy had been charged by Shoghi Effendi to greet each and every one of the native believers on his behalf, to embrace the men and shake hands with the women. The Guardian himself greeted the African believers in his message to the Conference: "I welcome with open arms the unexpectedly large number of the representatives of the pure-hearted and the spiritually receptive Negro race, so dearly loved by 'Abdu'l-Bahá, for whose conversion to His Father's Faith He so deeply yearned and whose interests He so ardently championed in the course of His memorable visit to the North American continent . . ."

When Leroy arrived in Kampala, there among others to greet him was Isobel Sabri, who had settled in Dar-es-Salaam with her husband Hassan. He embraced her warmly and said, Isobel, did you ever think we would meet in the heart of Africa? Being cognizant that he must represent the Guardian with the utmost dignity, he asked Isobel to go down the lines of believers with him so he would be sure to distinguish the men from the women, as both wore their hair very short. As speaking was his natural mode of expression – but most of the new Bahá'ís did not know English – he realized the significance of the Guardian's instruction to greet each one individually in a way that demonstrated the Guardian's love. I have never, recalled Isobel, seen him express his love more directly than with the African believers; he was absolutely obedient to what the Guardian had asked him to do.

The Conference was held under a large canopy set on the grounds of the Ḥaẓíratu'l-Quds in Kampala; there was a rich mixture of people with none of the unease that might be expected when two such forcibly separated races came together. "They are so *proud* to be Bahá'ís," said one observer about the African believers, "they keep expressing their joy to be able to mingle and share with white people, and they all recognize the source of their joy – the beloved Guardian and Bahá'u'lláh. Bahá'u'lláh's name is so often on their lips." There were informal meetings each evening at which the new believers recounted with dignity and sincerity how they had become Bahá'ís. One of the new believers was named Enoch Olinga. Already an Assembly member and itinerant teacher, he would soon leave to pioneer to the Cameroons and attract others to the Faith who would in turn go out into the pioneering field (see p.258). Some of the new believers arose as pioneers right there at the Conference, saying "only give us transportation and don't worry about us – we will teach our people".

Ten Hands of the Cause attended the Conference, many meeting one another for the first time. The wisdom of the Guardian in asking the Hands of the Cause to attend as many of the four conferences as possible was evident, as the Bahá'í world came to know them and began to appreciate the special gifts and wisdom which the Guardian had recognized in them. Their presence greatly enhanced the important consultations which took place during the Conference and in the many informal gatherings. From Kampala some of the Hands would go on to teaching missions on the continent; Leroy was to return immediately to Haifa.

As the Guardian's representative, Leroy presented the powerful message sent by Shoghi Effendi to the Conference, in which he detailed his plans for the "divinely propelled and mysteriously unfolding collective enterprise" known henceforward as the Ten Year Crusade. The plans for Africa called for intensive teaching efforts to be carried out in fifty-seven territories of the continent by the six national bodies that had inaugurated the work in Africa, the National Assemblies of the Bahá'ís of the British Isles, Egypt and the Sudan, the United States, Persia, Iraq, and India, Pakistan and Burma. Leroy spoke to the Conference about the Knights of Bahá'u'lláh, who would accomplish the settlement goals. He shared with them the map of the crusade made by the Guardian, its lines of many colors criss-crossing the world to show the cooperative undertakings of the Bahá'í communities. He unveiled for their solemn viewing the precious gift of the Guardian, a reproduction of the portrait of the Báb, and presented for their keeping a second gift, a magnificent scroll with those portions of the Báb's Commentary on the Surih of Joseph* which prophesy the extension of the Faith of God to Africa.

Dorothy Baker was one of the Hands of the Cause in attendance. Whenever she spoke to the Conference she addressed her remarks almost entirely to the African Bahá'ís, showering them with her special radiance. She was also a speaker at one of the two meetings planned for the public, and her talk gave rise to a controversy which in its result showed the working of the powerful spirit of the Faith.

In her public talk Dorothy Baker had referred several times to the 'Revelation of God' which was understood by a reporter of the leading local newspaper as 'revolution'. It was learned that the paper intended the next day to print a report of her talk on the front page, under a bold headline, to the effect that if the people did not adopt the Bahá'í Faith, they had no alternative but rebellion. A meeting of the Hands and the British National Assembly (which had convened the Conference) resulted in the decision that immediate action should be taken by calling on the editor to ask him to withdraw the story.

Leroy and Ali Nakhjavani were the delegation sent to meet him.

---

* A commentary revealed to the Báb's first disciple on the night when He declared His mission.

They proceeded to the office of the paper, explained the purpose of their call and were received at once. Ali recalled that Leroy "eloquently" set forth the aims and purposes of the Faith, and appealed to the editor to give a fair account of Mrs. Baker's talk instead of a distorted one. The editor's response was "cool and negative". He trusted the integrity of the reporter and the accuracy of the report. A further attempt at clarification was of no avail and with some impatience in his manner the editor stood up and from behind his desk proffered his hand to Leroy, obviously intending to shake hands and bid him farewell. Ali continues the story:

Leroy was sitting cross-legged on our side of the desk. He hardly moved, and with a confident tone in his voice, he said: "I refuse to accept your hand, and we will not go from here until we are satisfied that you understand our position." I well remember the sense of discomfiture in the editor's face as he resumed his seat. Leroy went on expatiating on the extent of the spread of the Faith throughout the world, the recognition and respect its institutions had received from civil authorities in various lands, and its declared policy of non-interference in political affairs, and its aloofness from political controversies. If the article was to be published, the paper, which upheld fairness and justice, could not refuse our "letter to the Editor" refuting its report of what our speaker had said. The editor conceded and said he would publish such a letter but reserved for himself the right to add his own comments.

At this point Leroy decided to leave, and we shook hands and departed. When we came out Leroy told me to remember this man and his newspaper. No individual or institution which deliberately strove to misrepresent the Faith and its growth had ever met with good fortune. This man and this paper would be disgraced, he ventured to predict. The article came out, our letter was written and sent. He published it but added ungracious and offensive remarks in his comments.

About four years later a new daily paper was started in Kampala and much to our amazement, became so popular within the first few weeks of its appearance that the other paper had to close down. The shock was too much for the editor. He took to heavy drinking.

One morning in that same year, a few minutes before 8:00 a.m., I stood at the door of the Kampala Post Office waiting for it to open. I was the first to enter the Main Hall. In a corner was the emaciated figure of the once powerful editor of the paper, a broom in his shaking hands, completing his duty to sweep the floor of the Post Office before the morning business began. Our eyes met. I nodded, but he was too humiliated and debased to respond. He was on the verge of becoming an alcoholic, and he soon became one, lost that menial job, and died soon after.

When Leroy had spoken about the future disgrace to overtake the man and his paper, I could not believe that the "rod of divine chastisement" as the Guardian points out in his writings, would be so "rigorous", so "swift" and so "unsparing" in its visitation.

At the start of the East Africa teaching work, when the pioneers were greatly discouraged, the Guardian spoke with enthusiasm of the remarkable results that would ensue, the numbers of Africans who would embrace the Faith, the rapid spread of the Cause on that continent. Leroy, knowing the difficulties of breaking into a new field, sat there and said to himself, well, that's pretty ambitious. He wondered if the Guardian were not being too optimistic. But later as reports of success after success came in to Haifa, the Guardian would come to dinner holding cables in his hand, exuberant and joyful. One night he turned to Leroy and remarked that "some of you" thought I was being overly enthusiastic about the results we would achieve.

Accomplishment, he told them, depends on the efforts of the Bahá'ís, and you see, I *knew* the pioneers who went to East Africa, I *knew* how they would serve, I *knew* the sacrifices they would make for the Cause. Therefore I knew what the results would be.

# CHAPTER TWENTY-FOUR

# Land

THE Guardian considered the protection and embellishment of the Shrines of the Báb and Bahá'u'lláh one of the sacred tasks of his stewardship of the Faith. To this end he began, early in his ministry, to acquire parcels of land around the Shrine of the Báb. These holdings were steadily increased so that an irregular cordon was gradually built up within which the Shrine nestled. Ever present in his mind was the need of land at Bahjí to protect the Shrine of Bahá'u'lláh, but that was more difficult of acquisition.

In 1953, with the International Bahá'í Council now functioning, the Guardian asked that a survey be made of land needed for the development of the properties; thereafter every effort was made to purchase the necessary parcels. As land in Israel was extremely limited, the State had no desire to sell more of it than necessary. But due to the high repute in which the Guardian (and the Faith) was held by the various officials and organs of government, plots of land were gradually acquired.

From the time Leroy moved to Haifa he managed all questions of land acquisition, negotiating – when the Guardian felt the time propitious – for properties Shoghi Effendi wanted to purchase. He was able to buy more than one million dollars worth of land on Mt. Carmel (in 1955 dollars) to fill out the area desired by the Guardian, acquisitions that also provided protection against the constant threat of roads and construction that would interfere with development of the Shrine and the Arc.

Early in his ministry the Guardian conceived of a unique way to safeguard the properties that were being acquired, and at the same time establish the international character of the Faith. This was to create Israel Branches of the various National Assemblies, the first being the Israel Branch of the National Assembly of the United States and Canada. Thus, as the acquisition of land accelerated, new Israel Branches were created and various parts of the International Endowments – as the Guardian termed the properties of the Faith in the Holy Land – were held by them, "recognized formally", as Shoghi Effendi wrote in his Riḍván message of 1954, "as Religious Societies by the Israeli Civil Authorities, and empowered to hold without restriction title to immovable property in any part of the country on behalf of their parent Assemblies."[1] These legal entities had as their officers Shoghi Effendi as President and Leroy as Secretary-General, but the entire operation of the bodies, as Leroy noted in a memorandum of record, was under the control of the Guardian.

But the Guardian was forced to wait, often for many long years, to acquire property needed for his plans. One such piece of land covered a large area around the Shrine of Bahá'u'lláh.

The startling fact is that until 1952 the Bahá'ís held no land contiguous to the Shrine, thereby frustrating any hope of development or beautification. When Bahá'u'lláh ascended, the Mansion was surrounded by small buildings, dependencies of the Mansion itself, which were owned by various Bahá'ís: one of the believers made a gift of his home for the burial of Bahá'u'lláh. It was 'Abdu'l-Bahá's poignant desire to beautify the surroundings of the Shrine but all the property was owned by the Baydún family, Muslims who were close friends of the Covenant-breakers. They were determined that the Bahá'ís would never own an inch of their land, the parents binding the children in a promise never to sell land to the Bahá'ís. It is this family who built ditches around the Shrine and planted trees that would close the Shrine off from view.

'Abdu'l-Bahá and the friends would carry plants and flowers from 'Akká, arising at four in the morning so they would not be jeered at by the public and the enemies living on the property. They brought soil from nearby areas, 'Abdu'l-Bahá sometimes carrying it in his *abá*, and brought water from a distance to water the plants. Such was the tender care given by 'Abdu'l-Bahá to the very small garden which He was able to plant around the Shrine.

During the lifetime of Bahá'u'lláh, 'Abdu'l-Bahá had bought some properties at His direction near the Sea of Galilee and the Jordan River. In one of His Tablets Bahá'u'lláh, in referring to these properties, speaks of them as forerunners of "noble and imposing structures" to be dedicated "to the worship and service of the one true God".[2] One of the properties was an area of 140 dunams (a dunam being one fourth of an acre) registered in the name of Zikrullah (Dhikru'lláh), a descendant of Bahá'u'lláh's faithful brother Músá. 'Abdu'l-Bahá told him never to parcel out or sell this land because one day it would be a holy place. Zikrullah left the property to his eldest son, also a trusted Bahá'í.

During the war between Israel and the surrounding Arab states that followed the declaration of statehood, the Jewish forces were able to withstand the invading armies. When a truce resolution was adopted by the United Nations, more than half a million Arabs fled the land and settled outside Israel. Among those who fled was the Baydún family whose abandoned property eventually reverted to the State.

The Zikrullah property near Galilee happened to be on the immediate border of Syria with Transjordan in the demilitarized zone, and the State of Israel was very anxious to acquire that land. Officials approached the Zikrullah family to buy their property, but when the Guardian was asked, he said no, the Master told you to keep the land; it cannot be sold. Then someone had the idea of trading this property for the Baydún land around the Shrine of Bahá'u'lláh. The Guardian approved of this being done and Larry Hautz, the first American to come on pilgrimage after a ten year hiatus due to the troubled conditions in the country, remained in the Holy Land to begin the negotiations. On his departure, Leroy carried the lengthy transaction to its conclusion.

The trade of land was finally accomplished, the Bahá'ís transferring 140 dunams of land in the city of Ein Gev in the Galilee in exchange for some 160 dunams of land surrounding Bahá'u'lláh's Shrine. The head office of the land development department was in Tel Aviv and there, on November 12, 1952, at nine in the morning, Leroy signed the contract for the land with the Government.

He continues the story:

I knew the Guardian was extremely anxious about the transfer, so instead of telephoning – it took longer to telephone than to travel to New York – I drove quickly to Haifa and immediately sent a note over to the Guardian that the contract had been signed and we now had possession of the property. One of the provisions of the contract was that we could take immediate possession of the land. The Guardian quickly sent word back that he would come over to the Pilgrim House for lunch. During lunch he asked many questions about the transfer. Are you *sure*, he asked me, that we are the owners of that property? That it is now ours? I said here is the contract, Shoghi Effendi, you can go and do anything you want with that property, right now.

By two o'clock the Guardian was en route to 'Akká. He said, 'Abdu'l-Bahá for fifty years wanted to beautify that Shrine; ever since the passing of 'Abdu'l-Bahá, *I* have wanted to beautify that Shrine as the Master wanted it done, and now that we have the property, I will not lose five minutes in starting the work. He went over and spent four or five days at Bahjí and when he came back he had his plans drawn up and the work was started. It was a formidable task. Now you see it all level* but we had to bring in bulldozers and fill in about two meters of land.

The interesting thing is this: the property on the Sea of Galilee, which 'Abdu'l-Bahá said never to sell because it would become a holy place, has now become the Ḥaram-i-Aqdas, the holy area that surrounds the most holy place in the Bahá'í world, the Shrine of Bahá'u'lláh.

On the same day, the Guardian cabled the news of the formal transfer of the long-desired property to the Bahá'í world, stating it equaled in volume all the Bahá'í endowments purchased in the course of sixty years in the vicinity of the Báb's Sepulcher. He noted the "indefatigable efforts" of Larry Hautz and Leroy Ioas in this "initial stage" of an enterprise which would "eclipse in its final phase the splendor and magnificence of the Báb's resting-place on Mt. Carmel." The embellishment of the approaches to "the holiest spot in the entire Bahá'í world" said the Guardian, was "a prelude to the eventual erection . . . of a befitting Mausoleum enshrining the precious Dust of the Most Great Name."[3]

In his message the following year to the Intercontinental Conference in Chicago, Shoghi Effendi again spoke of this precious land: "The stupendous process of the rise and consolidation of the World Administrative Center has been accelerated through the acquisition, in

* Leroy was speaking in 1962.

the Plain of 'Akká, of a one hundred and sixty thousand square meter area, surrounding the Qiblih of the Bahá'í world, permitting the extension of the Outer Sanctuary of the Most Holy Tomb – to be designated henceforth the Ḥaram-i-Aqdas . . ."[4] This is when the term came into Bahá'í usage.

There is a building alongside the Mansion of Bahjí in which the worst remnant of the Covenant-breakers lived. On one of the Master's darkest days caused by this man's scheming, 'Abdu'l-Bahá told him that he would live to see the collapse of everything he had done. When the Baydún land was transferred, he still lived on as the Master had predicted, nearly one hundred years old, paralyzed, unable to speak, but looking out as the Guardian's handiwork took form: the magnificent gardens, the great park, all of it illuminated at night because the Guardian associated light with the Bahá'í Manifestations.

No other land acquisition during those years compared in importance to this, yet each was a necessary part of the ever-expanding protective zones being created around these sacred places. In March of 1953 Leroy consummated a land purchase for the Guardian of six and a half acres on Mt. Carmel, a property the Guardian had wanted for thirty years, which significantly extended the belt immediately surrounding the Shrine of the Báb. It was finally purchased, at a cost of one hundred and sixty thousand dollars, from the estate of Roy Wilhelm.* The Guardian included this joyous news in his Naw-Rúz cablegram:

INTERNATIONAL ENDOWMENTS SURROUNDING TOMB PROPHET-HERALD FAITH ON BOSOM GOD'S HOLY MOUNTAIN CONSIDERABLY EXTENDED THROUGH ACQUISITION, AFTER THIRTY YEARS EFFORT, OF WOODED AREA OVER TWENTY-THREE THOUSAND SQUARE METERS INCLUDING BUILDING OVERLOOKING SACRED SPOT MADE POSSIBLE THROUGH ESTATE BEQUEATHED FAITH BY HERALD BAHA'U'LLAH'S COVENANT ROY WILHELM RAISING TOTAL AREA WITHIN PRECINCTS PERMANENTLY DEDICATED TO BAB'S SEPULCHER TO ALMOST QUARTER MILLION SQUARE METERS.[5]

---

* A member of both Bahá'í Temple Unity and the National Spiritual Assembly until ill health forced his resignation. He was the trusted conduit of 'Abdu'l-Bahá's messages to the North American believers, the teacher of Martha Root, and was named a Hand of the Cause posthumously by the Guardian.

The years 1954 to 1956 were rich in land purchases, and in acquisition of houses and buildings to be held for future development of the Bahá'í properties. It was of particular concern to Shoghi Effendi, as Israel built rapidly for its swelling population, that no large buildings be constructed overlooking the Shrine. The Guardian wished land to be purchased on the heights above the Shrine on the axis of Carmel avenue (now Ben-Gurion avenue) which leads up to the Shrine. Leroy studied the matter and made contact with landowners, municipal authorities and state authorities. He found a plot of some ten dunams in the desired location. It was owned by the State with the understanding that they would relinquish it to the city for public building purposes.

The Guardian felt they should try to purchase the four dunams of land directly overlooking the Shrine and gardens. Leroy negotiated with the city which, after much discussion, agreed to relinquish its claim on the property if the Bahá'ís agreed to use it for gardens and would lease it to the city for a period of years so that certain of the municipal gardens might be enlarged. The Guardian approved this plan and what Leroy termed "arduous negotiations" ensued. Finally in late October 1954 a contract was signed for the purchase of the four dunams of land. The reason we mention this particular plot of land, of crucial importance in the eyes of the Guardian as it in effect protects the sanctity of the Shrine of the Báb, is that it was purchased and held in the name of the Israel Branch of the National Spiritual Assembly of Iran, the sorely-tried community in the land of Bahá'u'lláh's birth which had never been able to incorporate and therefore to hold property. The pen with which the contract was signed was given to the National Archives of the Bahá'ís of Iran.

One goal of the Ten Year Crusade was construction of a befitting structure to house the priceless relics and archives of Bábí and Bahá'í history. The International Archives building was to be the first of the major edifices that would comprise the world administrative center, the first building to be situated on the newly-designed Arc on Mt. Carmel. But important projects such as this had to be held in abeyance because small parcels of land could not be purchased. One such parcel was a thirteen hundred meter plot owned by a Covenant-breaker of the family of 'Abdu'l-Bahá, who lived in America. It lay near the Shrine, overlooked the tomb of the Greatest Holy Leaf and adjoined the tombs of the brother and mother of 'Abdu'l-Bahá. From neglect it had become an eyesore in those sacred surroundings.

The Guardian had sought for thirty years to purchase this land but what he termed the greed and obstinacy of the Covenant-breaker had prevented it.* Finally, appeal was made to the authorities for expropriation of the parcel and this was concluded on the recommendation of the Mayor of Haifa. Within a few months of its purchase, excavation work began in preparation for the Archives building.

The Guardian often described the sweep of the Arc across Mt. Carmel, and yet the southern tip of the projected Arc lay on property which the Bahá'ís did not own. This piece of land was being held intact for construction of a hotel. Shoghi Effendi asked Leroy to look into its purchase. He reported that it would be very involved as plans for the hotel were already drawn up though construction had not begun. Some time later the Guardian came to dinner and said, I've sent a cable today announcing the building of the Arc and the buildings around it. Then he smiled and said to Leroy, Now you had better buy that land! The Guardian was abroad when it was finally purchased, but he cabled: "Tell Leroy deeply appreciate splendid achievement." Each accomplishment was hailed with similar cablegrams when the Guardian was out of the country. After the four dunams were acquired above the Shrine: "Tell Leroy abiding appreciation outstanding success." When parcels of land were bought at Bahjí and the land expropriated for the Archives building: "Tell Leroy delighted victories." And when the Temple land was acquired: "Tell Leroy loving appreciation achievement."[6]

Another property which the Guardian had been anxious for many years to secure bisected the Bahá'í properties. It was owned by another Covenant-breaker. At one time the Guardian had offered sixty thousand dollars for the land, but the owner refused to sell to him. Then an interesting development occurred. The civil authorities, anxious to preserve green space that would be open to the public, designated a large swath of land on Mt. Carmel as permanent open space on which no one could build. This meant that anyone holding land between that open space and the Bahá'í properties, which were also held as open space, was not permitted to build on his property.

* Leroy had already dealt with this question for the Guardian in earlier years in America.

When this became law, the land in question lost its commercial value and the owner, who had refused to sell to the Guardian, became anxious to rid himself of it. Leroy negotiated the purchase of this land for little more than fifteen thousand dollars, while the owner had for many years borne the expense of land taxes as well as assessments for road improvement. This acquisition was concluded in early July of 1953. It shows what happens, Leroy wrote to an old friend, to those who oppose the divine movement here at the World Centre.

But not all properties needed by the Guardian for future developments were within financial reach of the Bahá'ís. A hotel was for sale on land that ran alongside the Bahá'í properties. When Leroy informed the Guardian that it was available, the Guardian said, We ought to own that property. But we don't have the money. Have you figured out what it would cost? Yes, Shoghi Effendi, about a half million dollars. The Guardian, who would occasionally tease Leroy who took every word of the Guardian with utmost seriousness, remarked: I bring a Hand of the Cause here to Haifa and then he bankrupts the Cause.

Second only in importance to the acquisition of the Baydún land was the purchase of the twenty thousand square meter site for the future Ma<u>sh</u>riqu'l-A<u>dh</u>kár on the crest of Mt. Carmel. "It is truly in an imposing position", wrote the International Bahá'í Council in 1955. "West, the sun sinks into the Mediterranean; south are the rolling hills, the Valley of Askalon, and the coast line; north, across the bay, lies historic 'Akká and Mt. Hermon often crowned with snow; east lies Haifa City and, daintily outlined, the dome and pinnacles of the Báb's Shrine silhouetted against the sky half way up the mountain."[7]

When Jerusalem was captured during the First Crusade in 1099, a large sweep of land on this summit was granted to a newly-created religious order, the Carmelite Order of Discalced Monks, who considered Carmel the Mountain of God and intended to remain there. In the twelfth century they built the monastery known as Stella Maris (Star of the Sea) above the cave of Elijah, but left the rest of the land undeveloped. They no doubt prayed through those eight centuries for the coming of the Lord of Hosts to His holy mountain. It was in the vicinity of the monastery that Bahá'u'lláh pitched His tent and in the course of that visit revealed the Tablet of Carmel which He addressed to the sacred mountain. Shoghi Effendi has described how Bahá'u'lláh chanted the Words of the Tablet with supreme majesty and power: ". . . the forceful tone of His exalted language sounded all around, so that even the monks, within the walls of the monastery, heard every word uttered by Him."[8] Thus did Bahá'u'lláh consecrate that soil.

This was the land Shoghi Effendi wished to acquire as the site of the future Temple. One night he asked Leroy if he thought "we could get this land" to which Leroy replied that he thought it should be possible and would look into it. When once the Guardian decided on a course, as Leroy knew, he went forward as if it were done.

A few days later the Guardian called Leroy over to the Master's house and said he wished to go up and look at the land for the Temple. During their drive up the mountain the Guardian said: This is a historic day because today we are going to select the site for the Temple. He walked over the entire area, indicating which plots were essential and which were not. He chose the most difficult area to acquire, on the highest point of the mountain, and indicated the exact spot where the heart of the Temple should be; Leroy marked it with a large stone. Today a marble obelisk has replaced the stone. They returned to the car and drove back. Now, the Guardian said, you must get busy and buy that land.

It took two years of effort to acquire it. During the protracted negotiations there was not one person who thought it could be done; everywhere he went, Leroy was told it would be impossible. (Shoghi Effendi once asked, What do you think, Leroy, when these people say you cannot have something you want? Leroy answered: When I know Shoghi Effendi wants it, I just don't hear their "no".)

Investigation revealed how involved the question of ownership was. In fact Leroy felt this might facilitate its acquisition, as only God could disentangle such a web. The property had been owned by the Carmelite Order for nine centuries, but during the Mandate the British War Office wanted it for military purposes as it commanded the whole harbor. The Carmelites sold the land to the British with the understanding that they could one day reclaim it. When the Mandate ended, the British agreed to resale of the property but the Carmelites could not pay in hard currency so the contract was never concluded, and both claimed ownership. The State of Israel also claimed ownership through a law that returned to the State any land registered in the name of the British that had not been transferred. Finally, the Israeli defense ministry requisitioned the land stating ownership was immaterial, they needed it, no doubt for the same reasons the British had. In addition to these factors, the city of Haifa had drawn up a town plan to make that land one day the center of an urban development project.

This was the situation when negotiations were started. Leroy began working with many departments of the Government, slowly winning favor for the idea that the Government waive to the Bahá'ís its rights to the land if the Bahá'ís were able to purchase it from the Carmelites. When this favorable attitude became known it aroused heated criticism from the Carmelites, to whom the Government had not agreed to relinquish the land. One high official, however, dismissed the criticism, saying the Carmelites had done nothing to develop the land in nine hundred years and it was now in a highly deteriorated condition. If we give it to the Bahá'ís, he said, in two or three years we will have beautiful gardens there, it will be an asset to us. Then he said, ask the Order what they do with their hard currency, do they bring it into Israel? What do the Bahá'ís do? They carry on their work with hard currency; they bring us what we need. Who is bringing pilgrims here from everywhere in the world? Whose world center is here? At that meeting it was agreed that if the Government had any legal claim to the property it would be waived in favor of the Bahá'ís.

But the defense department occupied the land and difficult negotiations continued with them for many months. One branch of the services was adamantly opposed to relinquishing the land and Leroy requested a meeting in the Defense Minister's office. The Minister was out of town but a brilliant young deputy chaired the meeting, who, as it turned out, had attended a seminar at Harvard University with one of Leroy's long-time railroad colleagues. A warm relationship was immediately established and Leroy left the meeting with a letter of intent favorable to releasing the land to the Bahá'ís. But three persons still objected and it took more lengthy negotiations before they would agree to the release. When it was thought everything had been decided, the official representing the State Domain stood in the way of final settlement, as he would not agree to include the essential plot on which the Guardian had centered the Temple.

Leroy had what he called a "spirited discussion" with him. It centered on two points. One, the suggestion that you put "your building" somewhere other than the area Shoghi Effendi had designated for it.

What is so particular about this spot? he asked; we just will not give it to you. Leroy said this is the spot we must have because it is a holy place. Leroy asked him why they didn't move their Wailing Wall [in Arab-held East Jerusalem] over to New Jerusalem; why didn't they use a wall of the King David hotel? You won't do it, Leroy said, because the Temple of Solomon was built right there and the Wailing Wall is one of the walls of the Temple. This is *our* holy place and we don't move a holy place any more than you do.

Then came the reaction that "because you have dollars" you feel you can buy anything you want, but I am going to prevent the sale of this piece of land to you. Leroy answered that yes, he had dollars, but the Bahá'ís don't use money to force people to do things. What have the Bahá'ís forced you to do? We are building parklands and gardens for you, we are erecting beautiful buildings for you, we use money to serve society. You are a Jew, Leroy said, and if ever a people in history learned what the hand of God can do, it is the Jewish people. I tell you that we are going to have this land because God wants us to have it and no force on earth can stop it.

Negotiations with the Carmelites had in the meantime resulted in a price for the land which was within the amount of a gift made to the Guardian for this purpose (by Hand of the Cause Milly Collins) and a contract was signed. Their land representative in Israel went to Rome to have the sale confirmed but came back two months later to say they could not do business with the Bahá'ís; the property could not be sold to another religious organization. With that decision two years of work were apparently gone. "You can imagine," Leroy wrote to Milly Collins who was out of the country, "how low that made me feel. No one here to discuss the matter with and under pressure from the Guardian not to bother him with anything that is not absolutely necessary . . ." Leroy finally went to the Carmelite with whom he had dealt and said: Father, you know me and I know you. You know we have to have this land and you want us to have it, the State has agreed to let us have it. What can we do about it? You have handled many of these matters, tell me how to do it.

It ended with the Carmelites selling the land to a third party, the attorney for the Bahá'ís, who bought it as a Trustee for the Bahá'ís. An interesting detail is that the State habitually imposed a seven per cent tax on each such transaction. As the property was registered in the name of the British War Office it had to be transferred from them to the Carmelites, who then transferred it to the attorney, who then transferred it to the Bahá'ís. The Government agreed to a single transfer, so the property was finally passed from the British War Office directly to Shoghi Rabbani in a single transaction.

After the land had been acquired Milly Collins one night asked the Guardian if in future the Temple land and the Shrine properties, two kilometers distant, would not be joined together with gardens. The Guardian said yes, and we will have our own road between the two, but we have to purchase the intervening land where houses are now built. A month or two later Leroy was in the office of the Mayor on other business, when the Mayor said, Today I signed a contract with the Carmelites that will interest you – it was a contract whereby they will permit the city of Haifa to make a permanent Open Space of green trees and flowers on their land on the flank of the mountain. Ideally this should be linked up with your lands and gardens, so the entire area would be a Green Place." Leroy immediately told him that the Bahá'ís had every intention of acquiring that linkage when possible. The Mayor added, "You had to build your own gardens around the Shrine, now we will build gardens for you on the front of the mountain."

Some time after the Bahá'ís had taken possession of the Temple land, Leroy asked the Guardian if it were possible that this was the general area where Bahá'u'lláh had revealed the Tablet of Carmel. The Guardian said, I think it is. About a week later Leroy asked the Guardian if it were possible that this was the *exact* spot where Bahá'u-'lláh revealed the Tablet of Carmel and the Guardian replied, Yes, I think it is. Thus when the Mashriqu'l-Adhkár is one day erected, it will be on the very site where Bahá'u'lláh revealed the Tablet of Carmel, the charter for the establishment of the World Centre on that sacred mountain.

# CHAPTER TWENTY-FIVE

# The Queen of Carmel

IN 1942 Shoghi Effendi asked Sutherland Maxwell to begin work on the design of a superstructure with which to embellish the heavy stone edifice built by 'Abdu'l-Bahá on Mt. Carmel to receive the remains of the Báb.

In the evening of His life 'Abdu'l-Bahá would look up at the edifice and say: "The sublime Shrine has remained unbuilt."[1] Shoghi Effendi knew the Master envisaged a dome and an arcade surrounding the building but beyond that he had no knowledge of what the "completed" Shrine should be. He searched the Writings but found no indication of 'Abdu'l-Bahá's wishes.

We have noted that Shoghi Effendi, after the passing of May Maxwell in 1940, invited Mr. Maxwell, the father of Rúḥíyyih Khánum, and a well-known Canadian architect, to live with them in Haifa. Sutherland Maxwell's move to the World Centre was the start of a creative collaboration between the Guardian, who had labored in solitude all the preceding years to beautify the Bahá'í endowments solely through his own highly developed artistic sensibilities, and his gifted father-in-law. In their first two years together Sutherland Maxwell designed innumerable stairways, gates and garden ornaments for Shoghi Effendi. Then he was asked to undertake the major work of his life.

It was Bahá'u'lláh Himself Who had chosen the site on the slope of Mt. Carmel where the Báb should be interred, immediately below a circle of cypress trees planted by one of the German Templer colony, and had instructed 'Abdu'l-Bahá to commence the lengthy move of the remains of the Báb from Persia.* 'Abdu'l-Bahá set about realizing

---

* The dramatic story of the half-century concealment of the remains of the Báb and the

continued on p. 218

the wish of His Father. The desired land was purchased and construction begun on a strong, nine-roomed building of Palestinian stone, the
work being done without adequate roads up the hillside, and at terrible
strain. "Every stone of that building," the Master once remarked,
"every stone of the road leading to it, I have with infinite tears and at
tremendous cost, raised and placed in position."[2] Much of the work
was directed by 'Abdu'l-Bahá from 'Akká to which He was again
restricted by the Commission of Inquiry sent from Constantinople to
investigate His activities.

It is interesting to note, in connection with the surroundings of the
Shrine, that it was two city planners during the Mandate years who
had incorporated into their design for the city a monumental stairway
and cypress avenue leading uphill from the Templer Boulevard on the
plain of the city to the Shrine, providing, as Sir Patrick Geddes, the
Mandate town planner, recalled, "a useful and needed access, and a
beautiful and dignified memorial."[3] 'Abdu'l-Bahá approved the design
and donated land for two roads that were needed.

Only six of the nine rooms were completed by the time of 'Abdu'l-
Bahá's passing, and Shoghi Effendi later added the three remaining
chambers, arduously carving out the mountainside with unspecialized
tools in order to accommodate the additional rooms. It was in these
rooms that he installed the first International Bahá'í Archives, to which
treasures began to flow from the land of the Faith's birth.

For twenty years following the passing of 'Abdu'l-Bahá, Shoghi
Effendi devoted considerable energy to acquiring land around this
stone edifice, surrounding it with gardens, and building terraces
leading up to it. Ugo Giachery notes in his memoirs of Shoghi Effendi
his impression that the Guardian worked from the beginning with a
well-developed plan in his mind, as shown by his call from the start of
his Guardianship for funds with which to purchase land on Mt.
Carmel and by his manner of planting gardens, leaving wide areas on
which future buildings could be constructed.

companion executed with him is told in Shoghi Effendi's history of the first one hundred
years of the Faith, *God Passes By*, pp. 273–4. The remains, which had been thrown into a
moat surrounding the city of Ṭabríz, were retrieved during the night and hidden with
the utmost secrecy in some dozen locations until 1899 when 'Abdu'l-Bahá directed that
they be brought to 'Akká. A number of believers transported them quietly overland to
Beirut from whence they were taken by water to 'Akká and there concealed until 'Abdu'l-
Bahá was freed in 1908 from sentence of imprisonment.

After two years of intensive work by Mr. Maxwell, the plans for the superstructure were completed. A fully realized design was unveiled in Wilmette during the celebration of the centenary of the Declaration of the Báb in 1944. The Guardian had followed each step closely, himself suggesting the octagon shape above the arcade, the eight minarets, the eight columns on each side. (It was said that in the latter days the Throne of God would be built on eight columns. Qu'rán, Sura LXIX, verse 17: ". . . and the angels shall stand upon its borders, and upon that day eight shall carry above them the throne of thy Lord." 'Abdu'l-Bahá always referred to the Shrine as the Throne of God.) It was the Guardian who wished the Letters of the Living to be immortalized through the eighteen lancet windows set in the clerestory. It was he who chose gold for the tiles of the dome with which Sutherland Maxwell crowned the structure. The design was of exquisite beauty.

It was not until 1948 that the Guardian could begin construction of the superstructure. By that year, however, the Mandate was ending and the State of Israel appeared certain to come into being. Many of the excellent Egyptian and Palestinian stone carvers had fled, and supplies of building materials were almost impossible to secure. Therefore the Guardian turned to Italy for the work, detailing Ugo Giachery and Sutherland Maxwell to search out the means, in that war-ravaged country, to assure initiation of the project. The initial contracts were to cover partial construction of the edifice only, as the Guardian lacked the funds to consider completing the work at that time. He intended building just the majestic arcade and the parapet that is seated securely on it like a crown. Indeed, so beautiful were the arcade and the parapet, with its four concave corners bearing the Greatest Name in fire-gilded bronze set on green marble, that many Israelis thought the building completed; early pictures of the work attest to the deeply satisfying harmony and balance of the incomplete building.

However, during this stage of construction Shoghi Effendi realized that interrupting the work might have a devastating effect on the high standard of workmanship and accessibility of supplies, and, encouraged by the response of the Bahá'ís to his calls for sacrifice, he asked that contracts be issued to complete the Shrine – its octagon, pinnacles, eleven-meter-high clerestory and golden dome. It was then that he cabled the Bahá'ís in the United States that they must extend their two year period of austerity – necessitated to complete the exterior ornamentation of the House of Worship – for another two years, and the same austerity must be extended to all parts of the Bahá'í world – this time for completion of an enterprise "transcending in sacredness any collective undertaking launched in the course of the history of the hundred year old Faith".[4]

The first threshold stone, weighing one thousand pounds, was set in place in March of 1949. Ugo Giachery described the material of the Shrine as soft beige marble from Chiampo and, for the columns, magnificent pink granite from Baveno, which the stonemasons felt would last at least three thousand years.[5] Within one year the carved parapet was in position. In the next year the most delicate part of the work commenced: putting piers down to bedrock through the walls of the old building to support the weight of the upper structure and its great dome. The work required cutting through the roof of the old building, in some places eight feet thick. 'Abdu'l-Bahá had indeed built for the ages.

At that particular time, the early spring of 1952, Leroy arrived in Haifa and began at the Guardian's request to supervise work on the Shrine. Ugo Giachery recalls that "erection of the Shrine of the Báb was of paramount importance in his [Shoghi Effendi's] mind; it was a subject which he favoured most and he expressed his ideas with deep conviction and much expectation."[6] The Guardian gave instructions that Leroy was to be in full charge of the construction work on the Shrine and make decisions on the innumerable problems that arose during construction.

Leroy was shortly to learn an important lesson in how the Guardian conducted the affairs of the Cause. There was much discussion at the time of his arrival concerning the work on the Shrine. The Guardian was very upset, feeling the contractors were dishonest in their dealings and he would not continue working with any contractor who was "cheating us". Therefore, much as he wished to see the work progress, he said: "I will not put another stone on that Shrine if I have to deal with these dishonest people and the Báb will praise me for it in the next world". Shoghi Effendi said they could do anything to him, but they could not insult the Cause of God. Leroy was sent on many a mission to see that this standard was upheld.

As we have learned, Ugo Giachery was on an extended visit to Haifa in early 1952 so that the two men collaborated closely for two months in the continuation of the work. That edifice was to be Leroy's major preoccupation during the next year and a half. When not called away by other responsibilities, he went up twice a day to the building site, seeing that each step in the work was accomplished with exactitude, applying his practical mind to problems he had not faced before, technical matters in the resolution of which common sense played a large role, particularly in the absence of sophisticated machinery. He had the experience of nineteen years' trusteeship, with the other National Assembly members, of the House of Worship in Wilmette, which now stood him in good stead, as Shoghi Effendi had foreseen it would. On crucial days he was there from early morning to dusk. Acutely aware of the sacrifices being made everywhere to further the work, he would be there even when ill. One day when Sylvia urged him to stay at home he said, I *must* go to the Shrine, we are working with blood money.

By Naw-Rúz (March 21) of 1952 the Octagon was completed; during the Riḍván period (April 21 through May 2) the balustrade was erected and exquisitely gilded. In June scaffolding was erected for construction of the third unit of the building, the clerestory, which would be crowned by the final unit, the dome.

The Guardian anticipated that work on the dome might begin shortly after the opening of the Holy Year in October. Lengthy and elaborate testings were already being made in the Netherlands to create a gilded tile that would withstand the climatic conditions of Haifa. The start of this last unit on the Shrine, the Guardian presaged, would pave the way for "the fulfilment of 'Abdu'l-Bahá's prophecy, uttered in the dark days of the First World War, envisaging the glory of the resplendent Dome greeting the devout gaze of future pilgrims drawing nigh to the shores of the Holy Land."[7]

But it was not until Naw-Rúz of the next year, 1953, that the first stones of the crown of the dome were put in place. A joyful message from the Guardian announced: ". . . building operations of the final unit of the Báb's Sepulcher commenced" through placement of the first stones encircling the base of the dome. Over a period of sixty years, the Guardian pointed out, evolution of the Shrine had been associated with the festival of Naw-Rúz: it was at Naw-Rúz in 1909 that 'Abdu'l-Bahá laid to rest "the Dust of the Martyr-Prophet", Naw-Rúz of 1949 that the first stones of the superstructure were laid,

Naw-Rúz of 1951 when the delicate excavations were completed for
the piers that would support the three-story superstructure, and Naw-
Rúz of 1952 when the "second crown" – the octagon – of the edifice
was completed.[8]

The time of the second Intercontinental Conference was approaching, termed by the Guardian "certainly the most distinguished" of the
conferences, as it marked at the same time the centenary of the birth
of Bahá'u'lláh's Mission, the inauguration for public use of the
Mother Temple of the West and the first presentation in the West of
the Ten Year Crusade.[9] It was to be held in Wilmette and would be the
crowning event in the history of the House of Worship. Leroy's father
Charles had collaborated on the letter to the Master which requested
permission to build the Temple, and he himself had been closely associated with its construction for most of his adult life. (He commented
to a Chicago journalist visiting Haifa that he knew "just about every
stone that went into the Temple".)

Leroy longed to be present. But as he watched his fellow Hands of
the Cause leave for the United States (Milly Collins as companion to
the Guardian's representative, Rúḥíyyih Khánum), he quietly decided
to remain in Haifa – even though he and Sylvia had received Shoghi
Effendi's permission to attend – so as not to leave the Guardian alone.
He thought to himself, I've been blessed by being there many times; I'll
just remain here.

Later, on the ninth day of Riḍván, a Holy Day, Shoghi Effendi
joined everyone in the Eastern Pilgrim House, as was the custom, for a
spiritual meeting at which he spoke. Leroy had the privilege of sitting
next to him and from time to time the Guardian turned to him and
briefly told him what he was saying to the friends (he was speaking in
Persian). The Guardian then led them to the Shrine and chanted for
them, after which as usual he left and the meeting was ended. As they
walked out of the Shrine that day, the Guardian stopped and said to
Leroy, "You may have thought I had not noticed that you did not go to
Chicago to attend the Conference. I did notice it and I appreciate very
much your staying here to help me with the work." This was recompense in Leroy's view for any sacrifice he might have made.*

* It was not until June of 1958 that Leroy was able to attend his first devotional meeting in
the Temple, at which Sylvia read selections from the New Testament and from *Prayers and
Meditations of Bahá'u'lláh*.

Four months later while working on the Shrine one hot August day Leroy stepped on a board that the workmen had inadvertently left unsecured and fell some eight or nine feet onto the roof of the Inner Shrine. The fall dislocated certain vertebrae in his back necessitating bed-rest of a week or ten days and rest each day for some time thereafter. He did not wish the Guardian, who was away from Haifa, to know of the accident but after a few days decided he should be informed. He immediately received a cablegram: "Distressed fall loving prayers surrounding you cable news health urge complete rest." Sylvia wrote to her daughter: "Daddy knew when the Guardian began praying for him as the pain became easier to bear." Within two days Rúḥíyyih Khánum sent a note to "dearest Sylvia" saying she would not answer "any of Leroy's questions about publicity, etc., until I hear he is better, for it will only start him off working again." She reiterates the Guardian's request for cabled reports of his condition – "so keep us informed".

The nerves of the back were impinged so that for a period of six to eight months Leroy could not raise his arms or lift anything. After completion of the Shrine, when as Leroy wrote to his daughter "some of the pressure is letting up here", the Guardian wished them to have a change before setting in on the numerous new duties of the winter and suggested they go to Europe. While in Paris, Leroy consulted a well-known osteopath and after one treatment the pain began to recede; after three, he could use his arms as before.

In time for the third Intercontinental Conference in Stockholm in August, films had been made of the superstructure of the Shrine as it neared completion. Ugo Giachery, the Guardian's representative at the Conference, wrote to Leroy of the excitement they generated: "We saw the beautiful motion pictures of Haifa and 'Akká, and I cannot believe my eyes. I told the friends what wonderful work you have done in the erection of the Shrine! No one can realize the magnitude of the task, unless, like me, he knows every detail of the building and the tremendous handicaps involved!"

The Guardian, intensely absorbed in the progress of the Shrine, now wished for its speedy completion, and everyone concerned worked vigorously toward that end. Leroy wrote to his daughter: "I have promised the Guardian that we will finish the building during the Holy Year [ending October 1953] and we will do so if we are not held up by the supply of materials, particularly the gold tiles. We have only five thousand of them here out of twelve thousand but hope to have the remainder within the next two weeks. At this tempo we should finish the building by the end of September."

In regard to those golden tiles, Leroy told an amusing story concerning Levi Eshkol, the Minister of Finance (later Prime Minister of Israel), with whom he was on very friendly terms, and who very closely controlled the foreign exchange and gold of the State. On one occasion when he met the Minister, Leroy remarked that he had heard the Minister didn't like the Shrine being built in Haifa. Astonished, the Minister said he found it very beautiful, an asset to the State of Israel. I'm glad to hear it, Leroy said, but the word is that you particularly don't like the dome. More astonished, the Minister said, but why shouldn't I like it . . . what do you mean? Leroy said, they tell me it's because it's the only gold in Israel that you don't control. Laughing, Eshkol said, now don't give me any ideas!

The Shrine was nearing completion. But one thing remained to be done before the tiles could be affixed to the dome and the cupola (a stone lantern which sits atop the dome) could be placed. The Guardian had in his possession a small piece of plaster from the ceiling of the cell in which the Báb had been imprisoned in the Castle of Máh-Kú in northwestern Persia. Shoghi Effendi intended to place it beneath one of the large tiles at the base of the dome. A few of the tiles had been affixed in time for the celebration of the ninth day of Riḍván.

On the morning of the Holy Day Shoghi Effendi called Leroy to his office in 'Abdu'l-Bahá's house, one of only two occasions on which Leroy went to his office during the time he worked for the Guardian. Shoghi Effendi pointed to a small silver box on his desk and asked if he knew what it was. It was the box containing the plaster fragment from Máh-Kú and he said he wished to place it under the tiles that afternoon. Leroy rushed to instruct the workmen to reinstall some of the scaffolding that he had that very morning ordered removed so that the friends could see the first tiles in place on the Holy Day. With the help of a workman, he prepared the location and the cement and made the opening where the silver case would be placed.

That afternoon Leroy wished to precede the Guardian to test the strength of the scaffolding, but the Guardian said, You forget, I am a mountaineer. He then climbed to the base of the dome, followed by

Leroy and Lotfullah Hakim, member of the International Bahá'í Council, and "during the course of a moving ceremony in the presence of pilgrims and resident believers of 'Akká and Haifa" carefully placed the silver box in its niche and sealed the tile. He stooped to kiss the tile and then circumambulated the dome before descending. He sent a cable to the Intercontinental Conference then taking place in Wilmette:

I HAVE PLACED REVERENTLY FRAGMENT PLASTER CEILING BAB'S PRISON CELL CASTLE MAH-KU BENEATH GILDED TILES CROWNING UNIT MAJESTIC EDIFICE CIRCUMAMBULATED BASE DOME PAID HOMAGE HIS MEMORY RECALLED HIS AFFLICTIVE IMPRISONMENT OFFERED PRAYER BEHALF FRIENDS EAST WEST . . . HIS HOLY SHRINE.[10]

The *Jerusalem Post* reported from Haifa, under the headline "Gold Tiles Gleam on Bahá'í Shrine":

The first golden tiles for the dome of the Bahá'í Shrine in the Shrine Gardens here, have been laid, as the building is nearing completion. A small silver case containing plaster from the ceiling of the prison room of Máh-Kú, Persia, where the Forerunner of the Faith, the Báb, was imprisoned in 1847, was cemented into the dome under the first tile, considered the Consecration Stone of the Shrine. Bahá'ís consider it a vindication of the Báb's call for world unity over 100 years ago, for which he suffered and finally was martyred . . . The building will be floodlit at night, and will be a distinguished Haifa landmark, with its gleaming gold dome visible from all parts of the town and far out at sea . . . A feature of the construction work is its surprising cleanliness: though at extra cost and effort, the building is continually being cleaned during construction so that its sanctity will not be desecrated by dust and dirt . . .[11]

Richard St. Barbe Baker, well-known conservationist and "Man of the Trees" who was in Haifa at the time, reported to the friends in England that the dome, removed from its scaffolding, "rose over Haifa like a sun".

The noble structure was a cause of joy to the Guardian and called forth his deepest admiration. Many tributes poured from his pen concerning the noble edifice. . . . "whose site no less than the Founder

of the Faith has selected; whose inner chambers were erected by the
Center of His Covenant with such infinite care and anguish; embo-
somed in so sacred a mountain; on the soil of so holy a land; occupying
such a unique position; facing on the one hand the silver-white city of
'Akká – the Qiblih of the Bahá'í world; flanked on the right by the hills
of Galilee – the home of Jesus Christ, on the left by the Cave of Elijah;
and backed by the plain of Sharon, and beyond it Jerusalem and the
Aqsá Mosque, the third holiest Shrine in Islám. . . ." The believers the
world over, he said, should appreciate the bounty they had received in
being able to sacrifice for the Shrine: ". . . to participate in the erection
of such an edifice is a privilege offered to this generation at once
unique and priceless, a privilege which only posterity will be able to
correctly appraise."[12]

Shoghi Effendi chose the occasion of the fourth and final Intercontinental Conference, convened in New Delhi, India, to announce its
completion. The news electrified the attendants and seemed a fitting
climax of the Holy Year. This was the Guardian's triumphant description of the Holy Sepulcher:

QUEEN OF CARMEL ENTHRONED GOD'S MOUNTAIN, CROWNED GLOWING GOLD,
ROBED SHIMMERING WHITE, GIRDLED EMERALD GREEN, ENCHANTING EVERY
EYE FROM AIR, SEA, PLAIN, HILL.[13]

Bahá'u'lláh's desire, expressed on that scrub-covered, wild mountain,
had been fulfilled; 'Abdu'l-Bahá's trial-laden efforts had borne their
fruit. The Shrine was completed. Those in Haifa were witness to the
joy of the Guardian.

Speaking a number of years later about divine guidance and the
manner in which it passed mysteriously from the Manifestation to
'Abdu'l-Bahá and from the Master to Shoghi Effendi, Leroy recalled
an incident that occurred after completion of the Shrine in 1953.
When the Guardian came to dinner one night, he was extremely
happy. He said: "Last month I received a letter from Mr. Bushrui, one
of 'Abdu'l-Bahá's secretaries.* He said he had found among his papers

* Mírzá Badí' Bushrú'í (referred to by 'Abdu'l-Bahá, Who shaped his life from the age of ten,
  as "Badí' Effendi") spent many years carrying out important projects for the Master. In 1948
  on advice of the Guardian he moved with his family to Alexandria, spending the remaining
  twenty-five years of his life in outstanding service to the Bahá'í community of Egypt.

a diary kept during the days when he served 'Abdu'l-Bahá. He wrote to ask if I'd like to read the diary and I said, of course I want to read it. He sent it to me, and what do you think I found today? I found a talk that 'Abdu'l-Bahá had given, recorded in this diary, in which 'Abdu'l-Bahá explained how the Shrine should be embellished and beautified. And there it is on Mt. Carmel, just as the Master had described it."

The final lighting arrangements planned by the Guardian were not completed until after his departure for Europe in 1957. Sylvia, Leroy and Dr. Lotfullah Hakim went to view the first completed lighting of the Shrine on September 16th, shortly before the Guardian's passing.

It was always 'Abdu'l-Bahá's intention to illuminate the Shrines of both the Báb and Bahá'u'lláh. To that end, He had invited a Bahá'í from America, Curtis Kelsey, to the Holy Land to install three lighting plants sent there by Roy Wilhelm. Dr. Zia Bagdadi of Chicago was the first person to receive news from Haifa of the completion of Curtis Kelsey's work which, alas, 'Abdu'l-Bahá did not live to see; the Shrines were illumined by powerful electric lights for the first time only at Ridván 1922, six months after His passing. But in accordance with His wishes, the Shrines were illuminated simultaneously in a great burst of light. Here are Bagdadi's words:

I [have] never forgot how the Master acted and what He said regarding the illumination of the Blessed Shrine of the Báb. It was the anniversary of the martyrdom of His Holiness the Báb, while all the pilgrims were at the Sacred Shrine. The beloved Master remained silent for a few minutes . . . standing at the Holy Threshold. His silence broke with gushing tears and He cried loudly, saying: "In all the years of imprisonment in Máh-Kú, the Báb spent the nights in utter darkness. Yea, not even a candle was allowed Him . . . Therefore, God willing, I shall illumine His Sublime Shrine with one hundred electric lamps . . ." Now, the news has come that on the last day of the Feast of Ridván the three Blessed Shrines were illumined with electricity and the light is flooding the Bay of 'Akká . . ."[14]

"So grievous was His plight while in that fortress," Shoghi Effendi reiterated in *God Passes By*, his review of the first century of Bahá'í history, "that, in the Persian Bayán, He Himself has stated that at night-time He did not even have a lighted lamp . . ."[15]

One day, after visiting the Shrine with the eastern pilgrims, the Guardian stopped and turned to face them. "Do you know," he asked, "why I immerse the Shrine of the Báb in light every night? It is to compensate for the dark nights of the prison of Máh-Kú where the Blessed Báb was denied even a lantern. . . ." He then firmly added: "Who could imagine that His sacred remains would be transferred to the Mountain of God from the edge of the moat of Ṭabríz? Who could imagine that His Shrine would be erected with such glory and majesty? Such is the power of God. Such is the divine confirmation".[16]

Shoghi Effendi chose the final great Intercontinental Conference to pay tribute to the three Hands of the Cause associated with the super-structure of the Shrine. "Moved", he informed the participants, "request attendants Conference hold befitting memorial gathering pay tribute Hand Cause, Sutherland Maxwell, immortal architect Arcade Superstructure Shrine. Feel, moreover, acknowledgement be made same gathering unflagging labors vigilance Hand Cause, Ugo Giach-ery, negotiating contracts, inspecting dispatching all materials required construction Edifice, as well assiduous, constant care Hand Cause, Leroy Ioas, supervising construction both Drum Dome. To two doors Shrine recently named after first two aforementioned Hands, Octagon Door, now added, henceforth associated with third Hand who con-tributed raising stately, sacred Structure . . ."[17]

# CHAPTER TWENTY-SIX

# Báb-i-Ioas

IT was said that Leroy loved two persons above all others. One was his mother, the other Sylvia. When he left Chicago in 1952, it must have been with the knowledge that he would not see his mother again in this world. Maria Ioas was 87 and in delicate health. In the days and weeks following Leroy's departure, she would weep whenever she spoke of him, but this sorrow at his loss changed to pride as she learned of the services he was being called upon to render the Guardian.

She wrote to her son shortly after he left: "My dear son, I pray daily for God's love and care for you, and to give you wisdom and knowledge to become a true helper to the Guardian in his great work . . ."

Shoghi Effendi comforted her with a tender note appended to a letter acknowledging a contribution to the Shrine of the Báb: "The work in which your very dear and highly esteemed son is now so devotedly and actively engaged is highly meritorious in the sight of God . . . Be happy and confident, for his self-sacrificing labours will be richly rewarded by Bahá'u'lláh."

The dedication of the Temple in Wilmette took place during Riḍván of the following year. Rúḥíyyih Khánum had come to represent the Guardian. Maria was then 88 years of age and confined to bed much of the time. But the final desire of her life was to attend the dedication of the Temple, and for several weeks beforehand she had spoken of the coming event. She felt she would not live to see it, but her daughter Marguerite assured her Bahá'u'lláh would want her to have that great privilege. Readied for the occasion and in her wheelchair, she was able to attend the dedication. Two days later she insisted on going to the Temple again, to view the portraits of the Báb and

Bahá'u'lláh. Her son Paul and son-in-law Clarence Ullrich again took her in her wheelchair and wheeled her to the front of the auditorium on the left side.

Rúḥíyyih Khánum was arranging the covered portraits of Bahá'u-'lláh and the Báb on the table, roses massed around them. A long procession of Bahá'ís started wending its way to the portraits, but it was slow moving. Rúḥíyyih Khánum sent Paul Haney and Edna True to ask that the ushers permit Maria to break into the line. Although she had not walked for several weeks, she insisted on walking up to the portraits, so with Paul Haney and son Paul on either side she approached the table. She wept as she viewed them. When she was helped back to her wheelchair, Rúḥíyyih Khánum went over to her and Maria looked up at her and said in a strong voice: God bless you, God bless Shoghi Effendi, and God bless Leroy. That is when Rúḥíyyih Khánum put her arms around her and kissed her and then walked quietly with her to the door of the Temple. It was a very touching moment, someone wrote to Leroy, and of all the things Rúḥíyyih Khánum has done to endear herself to the people here, this was a most lovely one. Rúḥíyyih Khánum told Sylvia that Maria looked so very, very frail that she felt her spirit was very near to the other world.

Some of the Persian Hands of the Cause were to be in Wilmette and Leroy asked them as a special favor to call on his mother. When the Conference had adjourned, these loving souls (Hands of the Cause Samandarí, Khadem, Varqá, 'Alá'í, and Furútan) went to have dinner with Leroy's family and then to meet with his mother. A few short weeks later she passed away, and Zikrullah Khadem wrote a note to Leroy, filled with that higher understanding of the purpose of life possessed by such a spiritual soul: "How wonderful to live so successfully in this world, having such a wonderful family as hers, all so devoted to the Cause . . . such a wonderful fruit, and to take flight happily and proudly to the Abhá Kingdom. I am so thankful that we had the great honor and privilege to meet Mother one whole night in your home where we had hours of reunion in her presence . . . and to see her again in the Temple which cheered her heart so much to take part in the Temple dedication and gaze at the holy countenances . . . that beautiful and historic day when Mother paid homage to the two Manifestations of God touched everyone's heart – I shall never forget it in my life."

Leroy and Sylvia received two cables on May 25, one asking for their prayers for Maria who had gone into a coma; the second, sent a few hours later, telling of her passing. Sylvia wrote to her daughter that Leroy was "of course very brave and spiritually strong, but none the less stunned by the news". Milly Collins ordered a car and the three went to Bahjí to have prayers for her. Then Sylvia and Leroy went up to the top of Mt. Carmel and walked for a couple of hours. The next day they prayed for her in the Shrines of the Báb and 'Abdu'l-Bahá and Leroy sent a note to Shoghi Effendi asking him to remember her in his prayers.

The Guardian had not intended coming over for dinner that night as he was pressed with urgent work. But he did come and when Leroy greeted him asking, How are you tonight, Shoghi Effendi? the Guardian replied: "I am very sad because of this news we have had." Leroy wondered what he was referring to, and suddenly realized the Guardian was speaking of his mother. The Guardian shook hands with both of them and continued: "You have my deepest sympathy at the passing of your dear mother. I will surely remember her in my prayers. I will pray for her ardently.

"You must not grieve, you must not weep. We have been assured by the Master and Bahá'u'lláh that when we go to the other world, our awareness of things increases – keenness, consciousness, all are increased. You can be sure she is following your services with much greater awareness now than before her death. She follows every detail of your services here at the World Centre and rejoices at them.

"She is very, very happy now, joined with your father, and both of them rejoicing together at the services you and your family are rendering – and watching the progress of you and your work."

When Leroy told the Guardian that Maria was the oldest living Bahá'í in America, in years of Bahá'í service, having become a Bahá'í in 1898, Shoghi Effendi said: "I was not aware of that – that is in itself a station."

The Guardian then told Leroy of a plan he had conceived some time earlier: "You remember on the 29th of April, after the placing of the plaster from the ceiling of Máh-Kú under the golden tile of the dome of His Shrine here, I expressed my appreciation of what you had done? I had a gift and reward for you, which I thought of telling you of then. But I thought I would wait until the Shrine was completed.

"Now I am going to give you that gift and reward now, with the hope that it will lessen your sadness.

"The one remaining door of the Shrine of the Báb will be named after you. You owe this door to Sutherland, who has designed the Shrine in such a way as to have nine doors. There are eight doors on the ground floor and one door, the ninth, in the octagon. It is the door that gives access to the dome of the Shrine, to the portion of the Shrine with which you have been associated. That door will be named after you, because of your services on that section of the Shrine. I am not going to inform the Bahá'í world now, but will when the dome is completed."

Ugo Giachery wrote to Leroy a week later: "The news of the Door, Báb-i-Ioas as it shall be called, has brought me great happiness, because it rewards you in all eternity for all your labors, sacrifices, sufferings and the hundreds of obstacles and difficulties you have met in carrying on the completion of the Shrine. The generosity and recognition of the Guardian, on your behalf, is more than touching and I wish I could be there to thank him from the depth of my heart. . . ."

# CHAPTER TWENTY-SEVEN

# Serving Quietly

IT was not only Leroy who was the recipient of encomiums and honors from the Guardian. Shoghi Effendi also recognized Sylvia's services during her years in Haifa.

From the time of her arrival in the Holy Land in the late summer of 1952 Sylvia looked for ways to be of help in the small closely knit Bahá'í community. She was immediately given certain duties, and her responsibilities grew with the passing months.

Her homemaking skills were put to immediate use in assisting Rúḥíyyih Khánum in the affairs of the household, and when Rúḥíyyih Khánum was absent, the Persian girls who served in the Guardian's house and the Pilgrim House turned to Sylvia for instruction and advice. During the pilgrimage season, when, in Sylvia's words, life "speeded up a thousand fold", she would often take full charge of arrangements for the comfort of the western pilgrims, planning the meals each day, supervising the cooking and giving directions for running the Pilgrim House.

It was not long before she was given the bounty of guiding at the Shrine of the Báb, which was open to the public from nine until one every day other than Bahá'í Holy Days. Though visitors could walk freely in the gardens at all hours of the day, when visiting the Shrine itself each group had to be accompanied by a guide. Sylvia often spent as many as four mornings a week in this service. Leroy wrote to friends in Wilmette in 1954 – who said they could not find people to serve as guides at the Temple – that on the Jewish Sabbath more than one thousand persons visit the gardens and Shrine, on one Saturday reaching a peak of seventeen hundred, and at Bahjí another three to four hundred come each Saturday. The handful of Bahá'ís in Haifa, he said – all overworked – are still able to cope with these crowds, and he suggests that some of the people in Chicago might take inspiration from the way in which those at the World Centre "take on the task and do it".

Sylvia missed the freedom to teach which they had enjoyed before moving to Haifa, but she felt that as she talked with visitors to the Shrine from all over the world she could "start them thinking of something they've never known of before", even though needing to be circumspect. Sylvia was made responsible for the very special task of assuring that fresh flowers were placed in the Shrine each day. Surely there were few pilgrims who did not gather and hold as precious a few of the petals from yesterday's flowers that were scattered each day on the sacred threshold!

She was a frequent companion to the western pilgrims during their visits to the places of pilgrimage, which at that time included the two Shrines, the prison of 'Akká, the house of 'Abbúd where the Aqdas was revealed, the mansion of Mazra'ih (Bahá'u'lláh's first abode outside 'Akká), and Bahjí, where the pilgrims were privileged to spend the night. In Haifa they also visited the house of 'Abdu'l-Bahá (with the peacocks from the days of the Master in the garden) and visited the room where 'Abdu'l-Bahá passed away. After the property was acquired, they visited the site of the future Temple on Mt. Carmel.

This service with the pilgrims was of the greatest importance; the Guardian frequently referred to pilgrims as "the stream of life-blood flowing in and out of the great heart of the Faith here".[1] Sylvia had carefully worked out a text, with Leroy's help, of what the Guardian wished the pilgrims to understand about each site they visited. Isobel Sabri recalled Sylvia's first words to them were those of the Guardian: that they were making a pilgrimage to the Holy Shrines and not to meet him, and Sylvia made sure that they visited the Shrine of the Báb before doing anything else. She herself usually accompanied them on their first visit. When she was free, she remained with them through the day, helping them in every way possible, even to taking them to a post office. (When the number of pilgrims was quadrupled by the House of Justice in 1969, Sylvia recalled what the Guardian had said a number of times: there would in future be a large Pilgrim House on the side of Mt. Carmel where all the friends would be able to be together . . .)

Wherever she traveled in later years, Sylvia would meet and be remembered by pilgrims who associated her with the most spiritually enriching experience of their lives.

As in her earlier years, Sylvia continued to help Leroy in whatever way she could. This included keeping the accounts of the men working on the International Archives building, and typing dozens of letters for him from his rough or handwritten drafts. As there were no computers then, correspondence absorbed many long hours. One pilgrim* said the memory of Leroy which left the greatest impact on her was seeing him "sitting at an old typewriter in one of the anterooms of the Pilgrim House, typing letters. He was a Hand of the Cause, assistant secretary to the beloved Guardian, and yet he did his own typing – a man who had once had many secretaries and typists to call upon, but who had chosen this way to serve his Faith." She often spoke in her later travels in North America of his material sacrifice and of his spiritual gain.

Sylvia did everything to make Leroy's life easier, always traveling with small pictures and objects which would give a sense of home to a hotel room, and he visibly relaxed when he saw these familiar objects appear. Following his heart trouble she was, as someone said, like an angel hovering over him, caring for him, supporting him. As long as the Guardian lived he was able to push this weakness into the background, but afterwards the intense grief seemed to leave him prone to increasing illness. Persevere, the Guardian said, and the Hands of the Cause, Sylvia pointed out, sacrificed themselves in the path of Bahá'u'lláh. With the passing of time, she realized how unique these persons elevated to the rank of Hands of the Cause were, as she watched their work from the vantage point of the World Centre. The Hands are such spiritual people, she wrote to her daughter, when I watch Milly and daddy here, I see that everything they undertake seems to succeed.

When the pilgrim season was closed for the year, Sylvia had some unhurried moments, such as the afternoon when, as she noted in writing to her daughter, she "took Milly for a drive in the afternoon and we picked wild flowers, brilliant red anemones, way up in the hills among the pine trees". From time to time she and Leroy would slip

* Florence Mayberry, later named a Counsellor for North America.

away to the Sea of Galilee which they dearly loved and spend a day together quietly. Sometimes they shared these brief holidays with Dr. and Mrs. Walter Lowdermilk (he was an eminent American land conservationist and adviser to the Government) with whom they had developed a close friendship. Occasionally they accompanied the Lowdermilks on official trips to places such as Eilat, where a government boat took them out on the Gulf of Aqaba to the coral reefs and the border of Egypt and they visited Solomon's mines which the Israelis were at that time planning to re-open.

Sylvia grew and developed in the sacred atmosphere of Haifa, finding depths in her faith and devotion which she had not experienced before. She was quite aware that she was living in a powerful spiritual atmosphere and deeply treasured it.

It is certain that the Guardian remarked the quality of her reverence, for within two years, as Milly Collins became increasingly handicapped by arthritis, the Guardian gave Sylvia an extraordinary privilege, the task of airing the sacred relics of the Báb, Bahá'u'lláh and the Master that were preserved in the Archives. She worked with Dr. Lotfullah Hakim who with Milly had been the only person permitted to render this service. Each of the treasures had to be carefully removed from the Archives – which at the time were still housed in rooms of the Shrine of the Báb and a nearby house – placed out in the sun to air, and then returned to their place among the other treasures.

Shoghi Effendi then bestowed a much higher honor upon her, the first personal honor to come to her. In 1955 he cabled the Bahá'í world that he had appointed her the ninth member of the International Bahá'í Council:

ANNOUNCE NATIONAL ASSEMBLIES NUMBER MEMBERS INTERNATIONAL COUNCIL RAISED NINE THROUGH APPOINTMENT SYLVIA IOAS.[2]

It caused commotion and trepidation in her heart, modest and unused as she was to being in the position of receiving rewards. It is a bounty, she wrote to Marion Hofman, for which I shall be eternally grateful to our beloved Guardian. Her dear friend Honor Kempton saw it as a reward for her entire life of service: "I remember the early days in San Francisco and your steadfastness, your unfailing kindness and hospitality, the hours you spent helping others and entertaining inquirers . . . a

time of absolute service and this has gone on all your Bahá'í life . . .
Well done, Sylvia dear." As for Leroy, he was joyous at the honor that
had come to her and he wrote and cabled many of their close friends
with news of the recognition given her. He wrote to his brother that he
felt the appointment came because of the work in which she was constantly engaged. When the Hands of the Cause called for the election
of the International Bahá'í Council in 1961, Sylvia was one of those
elected, together with Mildred Mottahedeh, Jessie Revell, Borrah
Kavelin, Ali Nakhjavani, Lotfullah Hakim, Ian Semple, Charles
Wolcott, and Ethel Revell.

   In reminiscing about the Haifa years near the end of his life, Ugo
Giachery remarked that "Sylvia was a jewel . . . And as for Leroy,
Shoghi Effendi used to talk with him with golden-winged thoughts.
Together the two formed an unbreakable and solid chain of love for
the Faith and for the extraordinary work done by Shoghi Effendi".[3]

# CHAPTER TWENTY-EIGHT

# The International Bahá'í Archives

SHOGHI EFFENDI attached the greatest importance to archival material. The original Tablets, the relics and possessions of the Founders and heroes of the Faith represent the authoritative history of the Cause and are the authentic research materials for future scholars. This is one reason he chose an Archives building as the first of the edifices that would constitute the administrative center of the Faith on Mt. Carmel. Such a facility was much needed and he foresaw that it would be both the easiest and the least expensive to construct of the World Centre buildings.

The relics which the Guardian had collected for more than two decades had now overflowed the areas allotted to their care – the three rooms added by Shoghi Effendi to the Shrine of the Báb and a small building near the grave of the Greatest Holy Leaf. These were inadequate to the volume of material and unsuitable to its proper care and display.

In October of 1952 the Guardian announced to the Bahá'í world his intention of erecting an International Bahá'í Archives and referred to it as one of the foremost goals of the Ten Year Crusade. But as we have seen, there was a half acre of land essential to its construction whose acquisition had eluded the Guardian for thirty years. When finally able to acquire the property, he cabled the Bahá'í world that "ownership this plot will now enable us locate site, excavate foundations erect structure International Bahá'í Archives . . . which will serve as permanent befitting repository priceless numerous relics associated Twin Founders Faith Perfect Exemplar its teachings ['Abdu'l-Bahá] and its heroes, saints martyrs. . . ."[1]

The Archives building was inspired in its proportions by the Parthenon in Athens, a building greatly admired by Shoghi Effendi who felt that as there is not yet such a thing as Bahá'í architecture, we should use the classical forms instead of new experimental ones. "The Greek style is beautiful", he replied when asked why he chose it, "it has withstood the test of time and has remained beautiful for over two thousand years". The Guardian had never studied art, so he was not limited by conventional thought on the subject, and he freely mixed styles to create quite original designs. As Rúḥíyyih Khánum has noted, he possessed an innate sense of beauty and of that "balance which delights the mind and eye".[2] The International Archives building set the style for the future buildings to be constructed on the Arc.[3]

In the winter of 1952, after deciding on the dimensions of the building, Shoghi Effendi asked the Hand of the Cause Mason Remey, who had studied architecture in Paris at the turn of the century, to make some preliminary drawings. When Leroy visited Paris many months later he paced off and measured the Madeleine church in central Paris, which is a copy of the Parthenon, comparing it with what he knew the Guardian was planning to build in Haifa, and which he knew he would be responsible for building.

After drafting of the plans had begun, drawings were brought to the dinner table each night and hung for inspection. The Guardian would modify and modify, so that the result was a structure which, while using the basic form of the Greek building, is otherwise quite distinctive. Shoghi Effendi preferred the Ionic order for the columns of the building rather than the Doric used on the Parthenon. He filled the large triangular tympanum on the front of the building with an elaborately decorated disc bearing a calligraphy of the Greatest Name, from which radiate nineteen gilded rays of varying length. Above the tall simulated windows, usual in the Greek form, he placed small true windows to light the narrow interior balconies that run the length of the side walls. He inserted an immense window of sixty-eight tinted glass panels into the far wall of the structure, through which light is filtered into the interior. The Guardian confidently made his own rules, the result being a building of great beauty and striking originality.

When the design was completed it was officially unveiled at the New Delhi Intercontinental Conference in October 1953. The Guardian sent Ugo Giachery to the conference with a pen and ink rendering of the building, which was placed each day at the front of the speakers' table. He also sent a message the following Riḍván in which he impressed on the Bahá'ís the importance of the project: "The design of the International Bahá'í Archives, the first stately Edifice destined to usher in the establishment of the World Administrative Centre of the Faith on Mt. Carmel – the Ark referred to by Bahá'u'lláh in the closing passages of His Tablet of Carmel – has been completed, and plans and drawings forwarded to Italy for the purpose of securing bids for its construction immediately after the conclusion of the necessary preliminary steps taken in the Holy Land for its forthcoming erection."[4] Shoghi Effendi turned to Italy for supplies of the same creamy white marble which had been used in much of the superstructure of the Shrine of the Báb. This stone came from a quarry where veins of varying shades exist, so that in order to have finished pieces of a uniform and perfect color, three times as much stone must be quarried as needed. Hundreds of tons of marble were also required from which to cut the fifty-two columns, each seven meters in height, which form colonnades along the sides of the structure. Because of the extreme difficulty of shipping monolithic columns of such height, each was cut into three drums of two metric tons each, and then fluted according to the finished design. Each of the three segments had to exactly match the others so that the completed column would appear seamless, an intricate work carried out with precision and skill. As when the components for the Shrine of the Báb were being prepared, there was available in Italy a veritable army of artisans, sculptors, draftsmen, miners in the quarries, architects of the highest caliber who eagerly worked to produce the completed stone pieces that were shipped overland by rail and then by sea to the port of Haifa, all crates marked "S.E." – initials of the Italian words meaning His Eminence. It took seventeen ships to transport the one thousand tons of carved marble alone. Many more were employed to carry all the other furnishings for the building, down to chain-lifts, drain pipes and nails.

The first contract for stone was signed in Italy in January of 1955. Two months later Shoghi Effendi, always keeping the Bahá'ís informed of activities at their World Centre, cabled them to "joyfully announce the commencement of the excavation for the foundations of the International Archives . . ."[5]

The Archives building was in effect ordered in Italy and then assembled in Israel, a prodigious undertaking involving many problems. Watching the work go forward, Rúḥíyyih Khánum noted how these difficulties taxed "the strength and ingenuity of Mr. Ioas in Haifa and Dr. Giachery in Italy, often to the limit".[6] One day the nephew of the Hand of the Cause Samandarí was watching the head mason and his men working on a problem of construction. Leroy was also watching them. Finally Leroy went over and indicated how it could be done – and then when they could not do it, he did it himself. The young Samandarí told the Guardian that afternoon that the head mason couldn't do it but the Hand of the Cause did it. The Guardian said humorously, Yes, Mr. Ioas is the invisible hand of God.*

The Archives building lay at the western extremity of the Arc whose paths had already been laid out by Shoghi Effendi in the shape of a bow traversing the Bahá'í land on the mountain. The Arc was centered above the graves of Bahá'u'lláh's "consort in all the worlds of God" and two of their children, the saintly young Mírzá Miḥdí who died in the prison of 'Akká, and the daughter known to history as the Greatest Holy Leaf. This saintly figure had been the closest comfort and support of Shoghi Effendi in the first decade of his Guardianship and at her death in 1932 he laid her to rest in the gardens near the Shrine of the Báb. But he knew of her longing to be near her mother and brother, so he transferred their remains from a site outside the walls of 'Akká and with great ceremony and solemnity interred them close to hers.[†] Then he ordered exquisite monuments for the grave sites and made these three graves the spiritual nucleus around which the world administrative center would rise. ". . . these three incomparably precious souls", is his description of them, "who . . . tower in rank above the vast multitude of the heroes, letters, martyrs, hands, teachers and administrators of the Cause of Bahá'u'lláh . . ."[7]

Shoghi Effendi was accustomed to working with the simplest of tools. So when the dimensions of the Archives building had been

* In the sayings of the Muslims they refer to the solution of a difficult problem that no one can solve as being solved by the invisible hand of God and this is what the Guardian referred to.

† The Guardian feels it of the utmost importance, Leroy wrote to his mother, that the Báb, Bahá'u'lláh, 'Abdu'l-Bahá, the Greatest Holy Leaf, 'Abdu'l-Bahá's mother, His wife and younger brother have the most beautiful surroundings to rest in, as they suffered so much all their lives.

decided upon, he went, as he had often done when laying out gardens in Bahjí and Carmel, with white string and pickets and delineated the building on the ground. The Archives was to be a structure thirty-two meters in length and fourteen meters in width, built on a steep hill, which added to the difficulties of construction. The Guardian had at first thought to place it higher on the hill but reconsidered and positioned it near the mountain road running between the Shrine properties and the Arc properties. In the end it appeared to be set upon an outcropping of rock. Most important in its location was its orientation toward the Shrine of Bahá'u'lláh.

Ugo Giachery, who on one of his visits was asked by Shoghi Effendi to verify the delimitation of the area where the building would be constructed, wrote of the extraordinary ingenuity of the Guardian in laying out the plan of the building: "To the countless pilgrims who have since visited the blessed spot on the holy mountain, as well as the endless stream of visitors who daily wander throughout the whole area, the beauty and perfect order may appear the result of skilled engineering calculations done over a number of years. Nothing could be further from the real truth, as the credit beyond all praise goes to the talent, versatility and ingenuity of Shoghi Effendi alone."[8]

In an innovative action, the Guardian started planting gardens and laying out paths, borders, hedges and trees on three sides of the building area. He told Leroy that he would have to build the Archives from the rear, where it backed into the mountain, and make use of the few meters left bare along the sides of the building. The extraordinary result was that on completion two years later the building possessed planted gardens all around it as if the structure had always been there. This was the effect Shoghi Effendi wanted and not an unkempt site that would take years to beautify. The Guardian was wedded to beauty and once said, "I will always sacrifice utility to beauty."[9]

It was the start of two years of intensive work for Leroy. This initial structure on the Arc was dear to him, as he was personally responsible for its construction from inception to completion. So it is well to pause a moment to look at his situation at that time.

Since his arrival in Haifa three years earlier, Leroy had assisted in the completion of the Shrine of the Báb, he was the correspondent for the Guardian in all matters pertaining to the Ten Year Crusade, he had traveled for the Guardian, notably to Uganda and to Europe, he had bought all the lands needed for Bahá'í development and worked to establish the Israel Branches of National Assemblies; he was active at the Guardian's instructions with protection of the Faith in the Holy Land; and he was largely responsible for governmental relations for the International Bahá'í Council. At one point, the Guardian said he did not know what he would have done without Leroy's help.

All these tasks were done simultaneously and under trying conditions: the mixture of the eastern and western way of doing things, the aggressive energy of the Israelis with whom he was constantly dealing, and the conviction that he must succeed with the tasks he was given. (The Guardian once remarked that when he gave Leroy something to do, he never again worried about it, as Leroy took the matter in hand and watched every detail.) He worked through the humid summer each year, which was his busiest time of year as the Guardian was away.

After two years of this demanding and rigorous routine, it became apparent that he was not well. Paying scant attention to his fatigue and curtailing few of his activities, he had continued on. But by so doing he had put a severe strain on his heart. Though he never suffered a heart attack as many Bahá'ís thought, he had neglected the warning signs until his heart was permanently damaged. He was to live from then on with diminished physical resources.

On hearing this news, the Guardian insisted that he go away for a full month and do absolutely nothing. But this was the height of the drive for pioneers and new settlements, and Leroy asked to spend the time somewhere in Europe where he might start a new group or leave a few Bahá'ís behind from his visit. The Guardian said that would not do; he was not to let any Bahá'ís know where he was and he was to see no Bahá'ís, as that would mean meetings and there would be no rest. Leroy later told friends he had always felt he was stealing time from the Faith when he rested, but after that experience he felt less badly when needing to rest. These were the conditions under which he started his part of the work on the Archives building, work for which he had no special training or expertise.

An interesting observation was made by Rúḥíyyih Khánum concerning the construction of the Archives building. It is this: that Shoghi Effendi essentially accomplished the erection of the building with amateurs: "When one recalls that this building and its gardens were realized through the instrumentality of . . . untrained 'gardeners', an

Italian chauffeur [the Guardian's driver] who carried out the instruction of his employer standing directing him, an ex-railway executive, a
doctor of chemistry [Ugo Giachery was trained as a chemist] and an
elderly man who, though an architect, had had little experience in such
undertakings, one bows one's head before the inborn genius and determination of the Guardian."[10]

In August of 1955, just seven months after the initial contracts were
signed in Rome, the first shipment of stone arrived in Haifa. In September Leroy wrote to Milly Collins: "We are working strenuously on
the Archives building. At every turn there has been problem after
problem* but it forges ahead, and some think we are making good
progress. Ugo thinks it is miraculous. The marble work on the north
podium is being completed. Next will come the marble steps and then
the other sections of the podium, before we can begin to set in place
the fifty-two marble columns." In December of the same year the first
magnificent column was placed in position, on the north-east corner of
the podium, facing east toward the Shrine of Bahá'u'lláh.

In his lengthy message to the national conventions the following
April, Shoghi Effendi linked the emergence of this first structure at the
World Centre of the Faith with the continued decline in the fortunes of
the Covenant-breakers, referring specifically to the disappearance "in
miserable circumstances" of a "malignant" enemy of the Cause even
as the Archives rose in all its beauty: "No less than thirty of the fifty-
two pillars, each over seven meters high, of this imposing and
strikingly beautiful edifice have already been raised, whilst half of the
nine hundred tons of stone ordered in Italy for its construction have
already been safely delivered at the Port of Haifa. A contract, moreover . . . has been placed with a tile factory in Utrecht [the same that
produced the golden tiles of the Shrine of the Báb] for the manufac-
ture of over seven thousand green tiles designed to cover the five
hundred square meters of the roof of the building."[11]

The most difficult – and critical – step in building the Archives was
the pouring of the ceiling after the walls were in position. Leroy shares

---

* Many testing Leroy's patience to the limit, such as the unloading by city workmen of a
huge quantity of material from the city dump, ordered as an economy measure to shore
up the Archives building, but left in the wrong place on the building site. Leroy was
furious with them. He was very exacting about service to the Faith even from non-
Bahá'ís.

a few technical details in writing to his brother-in-law, an engineer: The ceiling is ten meters wide by twenty-five meters long, and this creates a problem of strength and of preventing cracks. First, the lower ceiling of six centimeters was poured; then beams thirty-seven centimeters high were poured, and finally the cement slab above it of eight centimeters. Now that it is completed, we see the end in sight and hope the exterior will be finished by Riḍván of 1957.

That hope was realized. The Guardian was able to inform the Bahá'í world in April, the Riḍván period, that "the remaining twenty-two pillars of the International Bahá'í Archives . . . have been erected. The last half of the nine hundred tons of stone, ordered in Italy for its construction, have reached their destination, enabling the exterior of the building to be completed, while the forty-four tons of glazed green tiles, manufactured in Utrecht, to cover the five hundred square meters of roof, have been placed in position, the whole contributing to an unprecedented degree, through its colorfulness, its classic style and graceful proportions, and in conjunction with the stately, golden-crowned Mausoleum rising beyond it, to the unfolding glory of the central institutions of a World Faith nestling in the heart of God's holy mountain."[12]

Exquisite as was the exterior of the building, Leroy thought its interior "even more breathtakingly beautiful". The inner area was a great open space with a stained glass window at the far end made up of rich-hued red, amber and blue panels rising almost the full height of the wall. Oriented toward the west, the panels were struck by the rays of the afternoon sun, flooding the hall with a diffused glow. Six crystal chandeliers manufactured in Bohemia were placed the length of the hall and brilliantly lit the area. The warmth of wood was everywhere in the cabinets and tables holding relics, Tablets, decorative objects of art. Narrow wooden balconies, with balustrades in a design of the 16th century architect Palladio, hung without support along each side of the vast hall, and were also lined with cabinets containing more precious objects of Bahá'í and Bábí history. There is the sword of Mullá Ḥusayn with which the Báb's young disciple cleft in twain tree, soldier and musket.* There is the táj which Bahá'u'lláh wore on His head, the star-shaped Tablet penned by the Báb in exquisite calligraphy with five

---

* A dramatic story told in *The Dawn-Breakers*, an eye-witness account of Bábí history.

hundred verses, all consisting of derivatives of the word "Bahá". There in original Tablets are the evidences of the unsteady penmanship of Bahá'u'lláh following the attempts to poison Him in Adrianople. There on either side of the many-hued window are two cabinets carefully placed at a slight angle inward. They are closed except when the pilgrims come to view, on the one side, the portrait of the Báb, on the other the photograph of Bahá'u'lláh.

One wonders what the followers of the world's religions would give to have even one such object, authenticated as belonging to the Founder of their faith. The archives are a priceless treasure which the Bahá'ís of all generations owe to Shoghi Effendi who initiated this collection just eight years after assuming the Guardianship.

As to the preservation of these precious relics, the Guardian said this is a task left for future generations. "Our task is to do what must be done now; we have neither the time nor the money to do these things." The relics are preserved in the best way possible for the present "and we know," he said, that the finest experts will be involved in future in their lasting preservation." At one time he remarked that the Cause in future would be very rich – so rich they will want to plaster the Shrine of the Báb with jewels!

Shoghi Effendi passed away before the interior of the building was completed, so that he was not able personally to arrange the exhibits as he had anticipated. But he had himself selected the beautiful cabinets in which the relics were to be placed. Many were choice pieces which he and Rúḥíyyih Khánum had purchased, often at minimal cost, during their trips abroad. There were decorative objects – Chinese, Japanese, Persian – the Guardian selected whatever would add to the beauty of the completed Archives. Over a period of several years following his passing, Rúḥíyyih Khánum, with the assistance of the friends in Haifa and of the Hand of the Cause Hasan Balyuzi, lined the cabinets with precious fabrics and arranged the relics as she knew the Guardian had anticipated placing them.

This building, like the Holy Shrines of the Báb and Bahá'u'lláh, is maintained by the believers as a service of loving devotion. The Archives building was opened to Bahá'í pilgrims in the winter of 1961.

A keen observer of the work on the Archives building was Leroy and Sylvia's friend, Walter Lowdermilk who, when he saw the completed edifice, wrote to Leroy, "I want to express, inadequately, my profound congratulations on the completion of the Archives building on the grounds of the Bahá'í Shrine on Mt. Carmel. Such an achievement must give you great satisfaction and we rejoice for you and Sylvia. It is a beautiful building giving a sense of proportion and permanency that arouses a sense of peace in this world of tumult in economics and ideology . . . There is this certainty that it will be there as a mighty boulder; it will stand five hundred years, a thousand years, yea, five thousand years. . . ."

# CHAPTER TWENTY-NINE

# The Ten Year Crusade: The First Five Years

THE last teaching campaign of the Guardian's ministry was the Ten Year Crusade. Its purpose was much broader than anything contemplated under the seven year plans which he initiated in 1937 and 1946. Its goal was to implant the banner of Bahá'u'lláh in the farthest corners of the earth and the remotest islands of the seas. It was to last from 1953 to 1963. It was the first universal, world-wide teaching plan ever to be undertaken by the Bahá'í international community as a whole. Its foundations had been laid by a series of national plans given to the various communities in separate countries: North America's two seven year plans, the Egyptian, German and Canadian five year plans, the Australian six year plan, the four year plan for Persian women, the Central American one year plan, the Indian nineteen month plan, the six year plan of the British Isles, and the two year plan which involved the opening of Africa with the participation of five National Spiritual Assemblies co-ordinated by the National Spiritual Assembly of the British Isles. Together, these all led up to 1953 when the Guardian launched his Ten Year global Crusade, which mobilized the entire Bahá'í world in one "army of light" directed from the Bahá'í World Centre.

The Guardian termed the Crusade a "historic spiritual venture at once arduous, audacious, challenging, unprecedented in scope", a venture that would call upon the twelve National Spiritual Assemblies then in existence to coordinate their work and concentrate their pioneers, funds and expertise on the winning of common goals.

In notes which he left, Leroy made some interesting observations concerning the Crusade:

The ten year global crusade was developed fully by the Guardian long before it was given to the friends. In the summer of 1952 while away from Haifa he formulated the ten year plan. Then he drew it in detail on the world map, with his own hands. Then he decided how it should be presented to the Bahá'ís. It was unfolded to them through cables which he sent to the national communities at the opening of the Holy Year (1952–53) and at special events held during that year, then through Riḍván cables to all the National Conventions, and finally through the release of a statistical book which included his map and outlined the details of the crusade. The Guardian prepared his messages well in advance of their release to assure that they would reach all parts of the world in proper time. He worked over these carefully, changing and revising as necessary.

Thus the focal point of the creative work of the Faith was the Guardian. The spirit operated through him, and he disseminated it. Never in speaking of the teaching plans did he refer to them as "my" plans, even speaking of them as if he personally had nothing to do with them, which indicates to what an extent he was the vehicle of the spirit. The ten year crusade can thus be seen as the Will of God for that period. It came to us through the nerve center, the heart of the Faith.[1]

Leroy assisted the Guardian with a number of the Crusade goals affecting the World Centre: the extension of the International Endowments, the acquisition of land for the Mashriqu'l-Adhkár on Mt. Carmel, embellishment of the lands around the Shrine of Bahá'u'lláh, construction of the International Archives building, and incorporation of seven Israel Branches of National Assemblies. A task specifically given him by the Guardian was to coordinate the work of those carrying out the Crusade, through correspondence with the pioneers and the National Assemblies, to encourage them and transmit the Guardian's wishes and instructions. These early years of the Crusade were the busiest of Leroy's life and Shoghi Effendi was fully aware of it. One summer when leaving for Europe, the Guardian told Leroy he could not put into words his indebtedness to him for his assistance; he said the entire Bahá'í world was indebted to him for all that he was doing at the World Centre.

The Crusade would take the Faith into uncharted waters. The first mariners would perforce have to be the Bahá'ís of the older established

communities. Yet it was these very communities which were not maintaining their spiritual vigor as the Guardian hoped and expected.

Shoghi Effendi viewed the two world wars as God's refining fire, as
purifying agents that would heighten receptivity to the teachings of
Bahá'u'lláh. He said the people of Europe in particular should be ready
to accept the Faith and he fully expected large numbers would come into
the Faith in Europe after the war, particularly in Germany. But it would
depend on the actions of the Bahá'ís. Twice he sent Leroy to Germany
to consult with the National Assembly of this "virile and highly promising" community concerning the pace of their teaching work.

But of greatest concern to him was the slow growth in North
America. He spoke of it at length during Leroy's first evenings in
Haifa, when Leroy asked if he might write to his former National
Assembly to share the Guardian's thoughts on this crucial matter.

The letter which he sent was read to the delegates at the National
Convention and caused quite a stir. The American Bahá'ís were still
under the shock of his departure and the delegates paid close attention
to this first communication from him. They requested copies of the
letter to study and to take home to their communities.

One delegate, John Allen, an old friend who in the next year would
move permanently to Swaziland, expressed the reaction of many when
he wrote that ". . . I am sure every Bahá'í in his heart wants to do what
the Guardian advises and I feel you were the link that pushed everyone
into a decision to act. But I think people are trying to make the job too
difficult . . . they haven't gotten themselves to the point where they are
willing to devote their time and effort to their neighbors and friends
but are thinking of grandiose plans for the multitudes, and from such
plans few Bahá'ís result."

A few lines from Leroy's letter convey the tenor of the Guardian's
thought: "The reason we are not achieving our goals on the home
front is because the friends are concentrating on so many other things
that there is little time for teaching. This must be reversed. The friends
must be consecrated to teaching so that things of lesser importance fall
into their proper place. Consecration is the motive power of the individual in the teaching field. The Guardian said if the friends attain this
ideal condition and arise and act and teach, their actions will become a
magnet attracting the confirmations of Bahá'u'lláh. Every Bahá'í must
teach at all times: it is the source of spiritual life for the giver as well as

for the recipient . . . Such teaching work includes the living of a life of service as well as talking, because one real and genuine act of love and kindness may confirm a soul as readily as his listening or studying the books. The Guardian feels we have more than sufficient materials. What we need is not more materials, not different methods of doing this or that – but *doing*."

The North American Bahá'ís, as the chosen trustees of 'Abdu'l-Bahá's Tablets of the Divine Plan, had been given primacy in the teaching work. It was they who had contributed the bulk of pioneers to the first and second seven year plans. It was they who would be expected to produce an even greater number of pioneers for the global crusade that was taking shape in the Guardian's mind. Indeed, he had written that the North American Bahá'ís must "brace themselves" to play a preponderating role in the impending crusade.

Toward the end of the Crusade – this was after the Guardian's death – Leroy spoke very frankly with a large group of Bahá'ís in San Francisco, saying he felt an obligation to share with them Shoghi Effendi's thoughts on the United States and the Crusade. The Guardian had fully expected many thousands more to be enrolled in the Faith in America than there had been. This hasn't happened, Leroy said. You know it, I know it, the whole Bahá'í world knows it. The Guardian, he said, told you that the citadel of the Bahá'í world is America and if America does not produce more Bahá'ís it will not have pioneers to send out, and our teaching work everywhere will suffer. During the last few years of his life, the Guardian was in fact "greatly disturbed" that the Cause had not grown, and grown more rapidly, in this venerable community.

In Haifa they asked the Guardian why the old established centers appeared to have lost their dynamism. Leroy made note of the Guardian's reply. The condition of the Faith, Shoghi Effendi told them, is affected by two things. The first is the condition of the world at large. In these old established centers all the means of human comfort exist, the people are distracted, they are steeped in material-ism and these material interests are affecting the Faith. The second is the condition of the Bahá'ís themselves. They are not properly conse-crated to the Cause, they are Bahá'ís through the mind; they understand the Faith but do not live it sufficiently. When we dedicate ourselves to the Faith we must do so in accordance with the standards of the teachings and not of the civilization in which we live. If we work simply to cause a renaissance within that civilization, we will have accomplished nothing. But if we strive to establish the Bahá'í way of life, we will be laying the foundation of the Kingdom of God on earth.

During the persecutions in Iran in 1955 the Guardian's Naw-Rúz message to these stalwart believers said that "sorrow and joy always embrace each other". Never since the early days of the Faith, Leroy noted, had there been so much teaching work and so many people coming into the Faith in Persia as during that oppression – people were asking, who are these people who are being persecuted?* The old centers in the west, the Guardian said, are not suffering enough.

In this regard, Leroy often told the story of a new Bahá'í in Laurenco Marquez by the name of Rudolfo Duna. The territory was Portuguese and officially opposed to the Faith. Such was Rudolfo's zeal that after becoming a Bahá'í, he led most of his Methodist church into the Faith. He was a Bahá'í only a few months when he was first arrested. It was a warning. On his second arrest, all his books and translations of Bahá'í texts were taken from him. Then he left for Angola, walking across the continent, formed two Assemblies there and returned to Mozambique. Again he was jailed and his home ransacked. They asked if they now had all his translations and he told them where there were others on which he was working. Finally after lengthy investigation they stamped in his passport the title "Bahá'í Teacher" and with this he was free to travel anywhere; it was in effect a recognition of the Faith. It is this kind of sacrifice, Leroy told people in the west, that is bringing the victories.

As with each of the Guardian's teaching plans, the Ten Year Crusade was revealed in its full scope only gradually as it evolved in his inspired mind. In early cables he mentioned "another seven year plan" after a respite of several years following completion of the separate national teaching plans. But he was to abandon the idea of another seven year plan. He felt "a great restless forward surge among the believers" arising from the remarkable success of the African and European campaigns and the excitement engendered by the growing evidence that they were indeed a world community.

* Efforts to mitigate the persecutions were coordinated from Haifa and Leroy noted that cables and pressure from the United Nations and various governments had forced the Persian Government to realize the universality of the Faith.

Sensing this readiness for continued effort, the Guardian sent the Bahá'ís a long and powerful message in June of 1952. In it he called for the first Holy Year in Bahá'í history, a term they had not heard before. The Holy Year would last from 15 October 1952 to 15 October 1953 and would celebrate the second great centenary of Bahá'í history, the "Year Nine", when, as promised by the Báb, the new Revelation would be born. Shoghi Effendi was educating the Bahá'ís in the history of their Faith, informing them that it was during several days in mid-October of 1852 that Bahá'u'lláh received the intimation of His Mission. This mystic event occurred during His four month confinement "in chains and fetters . . . amidst the gloom and stench of the Siyáh-Chál", a subterranean dungeon in Teheran.[2] Two months later Bahá'u'lláh was released from prison, the purpose of His imprisonment accomplished.

It is in this message that the Guardian first makes reference to a ten year crusade, which he describes as the "grandest crusade thus far launched in Bahá'í history". He informs the believers of the spiritual prerequisites to success in this global undertaking, and summons them in moving language to their "high destiny". He mentions each national community by name, praising the particular talents which it will bring to the great endeavor ahead, and pleads with the believers, in a poignant phrase, "with all the fervor that my soul can command and all the love that my heart contains" to dedicate themselves to the challenges soon to be set before them. The Guardian's theme finds resolution in deeply moving passages which end the message: "I adjure them . . . I adjure them . . . never to flinch, never to hesitate, never to relax, until each and every objective in the Plans to be proclaimed . . . has been fully consummated."[3]

This message of June 30th pierced the hearts of the Bahá'ís. Its beauty, its poignancy, its appeal to their deepest convictions, are almost without equal among the many notable statements sent them by the Guardian. It made clear that difficult and soul-searing years lay ahead of them.

Let us go ahead now to the end of that summer, when Shoghi Effendi returned from Europe with Rúḥíyyih Khánum, and share the atmosphere in which those in Haifa learned of the great new plan. It was the end of summer, 1952.

Leroy recalls what a great stir there was when the Guardian

returned from abroad. The girls who served in the household worked for days to have everything perfect for Shoghi Effendi. Leroy said it was touching to see the expectancy with which his return was awaited.

Leroy had the privilege of meeting the Guardian and Rúḥíyyih Khánum at the airport and being with them during the return trip to Haifa. This time he noted there was something different about the Guardian; Shoghi Effendi was "speaking in a different vein". Leroy thought to himself that something of great moment was at hand.

That evening when the Guardian came to dinner he was very happy and enthusiastic. After dinner he said, I have been very busy this summer. I have worked out a teaching program for the Bahá'ís of the world. I would like to tell you about it and see what you think. (The Guardian often asked what people thought of things and it never ceased to astonish Leroy that the sign of God on earth would solicit anyone's opinion.)

The Guardian outlined his Ten Year Crusade with dazzling clarity and force. "Well, what do you think?", he asked. Those around the table, staggered by what they had heard, said they didn't know what to think, it was overwhelming. Reiterating the various elements of the plan, the Guardian turned to Leroy and asked what aspect of it he thought would be the easiest to accomplish. Leroy said, Shoghi Effendi, I believe the easiest will be to establish the Faith in those one hundred and thirty-one new countries. To be the first Bahá'í in a new place is glamorous and you're going to have many people immediately wanting to do that. What, the Guardian asked, do you think will be more difficult? More difficult, Leroy offered, will be raising all the money you need; the Bahá'ís hold on to their money too long. And what will be the most difficult? Leroy answered without hesitation: the consolidation work you have outlined, Shoghi Effendi, because that is drudgery, just plain drudgery, right on the home front where there's no glory associated with it; that is going to be hard. The Guardian said, "I agree with you, I think it will be like that".

Two months later, on October 8, the Guardian told the Bahá'í world of the Crusade:

FEEL HOUR PROPITIOUS TO PROCLAIM TO THE ENTIRE BAHA'I WORLD THE PRO-JECTED LAUNCHING. . . . [OF] THE FATE-LADEN, SOUL-STIRRING, DECADE-LONG, WORLD-EMBRACING SPIRITUAL CRUSADE . . .[4]

There were at the time twelve national or regional Assemblies representing thirty-six countries; the Guardian had outlined twelve plans, one for each of the Assemblies. Their goal was "the immediate extension of Bahá'u'lláh's spiritual dominion as well as the eventual establishment of the structure of His administrative order in all remaining Sovereign States, Principal Dependencies comprising Principalities, Sultanates, Emirates, Shaykhdoms, Protectorates, Trust Territories, and Crown colonies scattered over the surface of the entire planet."[5]

Rúḥíyyih Khánum summed it up: "Shoghi Effendi lifted the curtain on the arena of the new Plan: Where? Why, everywhere . . . To whom? Why, to all peoples . . ."[6]

Were this crusade a human one, commented the National Assembly of the British Isles to their constituents, such vast expansion might seem an idle dream; but the crusade is a stage in the Plan of God given through 'Abdu'l-Bahá . . . whereby the Glad Tidings of Bahá'u'lláh may be brought to all people.[7]

The Guardian, who loved maps, had drawn a detailed map with all the elements of the twelve plans, showing at a glance how the National Assemblies would work together, crossing all boundaries, in a united effort bringing together all the elements of a world community; the Crusade would involve the simultaneous prosecution of the twelve plans. Leroy was asked to keep detailed listings of pioneer goals throughout the world as they were settled. Always meticulous with details, Leroy in one letter asks Dwight Allen, in Greece with fellow pioneer Amin Banani, to let him know immediately whether Amin's wife and child are with him, so that the lists may be accurate.

In the brief years of the Báb's Dispensation, the new Revelation was known in only two countries; during Bahá'u'lláh's lifetime, in fifteen; by the time of 'Abdu'l-Bahá's passing, it had spread to thirty-five countries. Through means of various teaching plans the Faith gradually spread to one hundred and twenty-eight countries. Now with the Crusade, the Bahá'ís were asked to double that number within a single decade. It is no wonder the Guardian cabled that "the next ten years must see feats eclipsing all the pioneering feats of the previous one hundred and ten years".[8]

When Bahá'u'lláh was living in exile in Baghdad, one of the believers went to a town twenty miles north of the city. Shortly afterwards he wrote Bahá'u'lláh a letter saying "This place is opened to the Faith! As I go about my business I talk to the people about the teachings and one of them is very much interested." Bahá'u'lláh called all the Bahá'ís together in the garden of Riḍván for a feast and said, "Think how wonderful it is, the Cause of God has already spread north of Baghdad!" The Guardian told this story as reports came in to Haifa of the remote territories to which the Faith was spreading.[9]

The Ten Year Crusade was formally introduced to the Bahá'í world at the Intercontinental Conferences which the Guardian had called to celebrate the Holy Year. At each, his representative would present the goals of the Crusade and then raise the call for pioneers. What was needed, the Guardian said, was "immediate, determined, sustained, universal" dispersal throughout the unopened territories.[10] When Leroy asked about the great urgency of dispersal, the Guardian answered: "We must build lighthouses of the Faith through which the Holy Spirit may descend. When the people enter in flocks, if there are ten centers, they will become a hundred. We are making new doorways for the people to enter the Kingdom of God."

The Crusade had four major objectives: to develop the institutions at the World Centre; to consolidate areas under the jurisdiction of regional and national Assemblies; to consolidate all other areas where the Faith had been introduced; and to open the virgin areas of the world to the teachings of Bahá'u'lláh.

The most urgent goal was the last, the settlement by Bahá'í pioneers of one hundred and thirty-one countries and territories where the Faith was not yet established. The Guardian's list of targeted areas included every locality mentioned by 'Abdu'l-Bahá in the Tablets of the Divine Plan, which numbered forty-one in Asia, thirty-three in Africa, thirty in Europe, and twenty-seven in the Western Hemisphere – places such as the Falkland Islands off the southernmost coast of South America, the Galapagos, the territory of Franklin in Canada's Northern Territories, Keewatin, the Hebrides, Tasmania, Malta, Siam, Ceylon, Andorra, the Straits Settlement, Cape Verde, Mauritius, Reunion – names many of the Bahá'ís had never heard and which they could not have located on a map. And yet they began to rise up and go to these places. Iran Furútan Muhájir recounts that when she and her husband, Dr. Raḥmatu'lláh Muhájir,* left Iran to pioneer in the Mentawei Islands, they knew no

* Appointed a Hand of the Cause in 1957 shortly before the Guardian's death.

one in Teheran with any knowledge of Indonesia and they left without knowing the conditions of life there or even what a "tropical climate" in that part of the world meant.

Other major elements of the Crusade were a two-fold increase in the number of Houses of Worship, with the first two to be built in Asia and in Europe; purchase of sites for eleven additional Houses of Worship; acquisition of land on Mt. Carmel for a House of Worship, and extension of the International Endowments on Mt. Carmel and in 'Akká. To house the priceless relics of Bábí and Bahá'í history, an International Bahá'í Archives was to be constructed as the first edifice situated on the Arc on Mt. Carmel. Certain properties of immense historic import were to be acquired: the Garden of Riḍván, the site of the Siyáh-Chál, the site of the Báb's martyrdom in Ṭabríz and of His incarceration in Chihríq. The Shrine of Bahá'u'lláh, the most holy site in the Bahá'í world, was to be embellished, by which the Guardian did not intend the construction of a befitting superstructure – a task which lay in the future – but rather the spiritual "cleansing" of the areas near the Shrine and the creation of the Harám-i-Aqdas (see Chapter 22).

The number of National Assemblies was to be quadrupled and seven additional Israel Branches of National Spiritual Assemblies were to be legally incorporated, two of European Institutions, two of Asian and one each of American, Australian and African bodies. These would hold in their name portions of the International Endowments of the Faith, a right exercised since the early 1930s by the Israel (then Palestine) Branch of the National Spiritual Assemblies of the United States and Canada, and of India, Pakistan and Burma. (By Riḍván of 1954 the Guardian could announce to the Bahá'í world the formation of Branches of the National Assemblies of the British Isles, Persia, Canada, and Australia and New Zealand. By November 1957 the remaining Branches were formed for the separate National Assemblies of New Zealand, Alaska and Pakistan. Into the hands of these nine Branches were confided the sacred properties of the Tomb of Bahá'u'lláh, the Shrine of the Báb, and all other International Endowments.) A Synopsis and Codification of the Most Holy Book of Bahá'u'lláh, the Kitáb-i-Aqdas (His book of laws), was to be made.

The Crusade was to culminate in what the Guardian called the Most Great Jubilee in the year 1963, when he was convoking a world congress in the city of Baghdad, the third holiest city of the Bahá'í world.

The story of the Ten Year Crusade is lengthy and is covered fully in Bahá'í publications (notably *The Bahá'í World*, vol. XIII). Here we will give only a few stories of the settlement of new territories, as there was never any doubt that this had precedence in the mind of the Guardian and therefore of Leroy. At the inception of the Crusade, he said "The most glorious service any Bahá'í can render, regardless of what position he is in or what his station is, is to go into one of these virgin areas of the Crusade." The time is ripe, the Guardian told the Bahá'ís, for them to disencumber themselves of worldly vanities – to unfurl the banner of renunciation – to mount the stead of steadfastness – to flee their homelands.

More than once the Guardian said to those around him, "I must be here in Haifa, at the World Centre. I cannot be elsewhere and I cannot recreate people; that is the work of Bahá'u'lláh. To accomplish the tasks, I must have workers, I must have people in the field." (So great was his longing to be part of this movement that at times he would say he was "deprived" of personal participation.) He further said that no one need any longer worry about the administrative order of the Faith; nothing would happen to it if prominent administrators left for the pioneering field; pioneering was the greatest service.

In a letter to his friend and colleague Elsie Austin, an eminent and distinguished American believer, Leroy wrote that the Guardian had "talked at length about this last night when he read us the cable he is sending to the New Delhi Conference, announcing that some thirty-nine of the virgin areas are already settled". Elsie Austin was one of those who fled her homeland. She, along with four of her fellow members of the National Assembly of the United States, resigned to pioneer in the unsettled areas: Elsie to Morocco, Kenneth Christian to Southern Rhodesia, Mamie Seto to Hong Kong, Matthew Bullock to the Dutch West Indies, and Hand of the Cause Dorothy Baker, who was en route to her pioneering post in Grenada when she was killed in an airplane explosion over the Mediterranean Sea.

Africans such as Enoch Olinga set out from the first Intercontinental Conference in Kampala for their pioneering posts, in his case the virgin area of the British Cameroons. There he taught five new believers who immediately arose and settled in five other virgin areas. Thus he as well as his five converts became Knights of Bahá'u'lláh, which is unique in the history of the Crusade. The Guardian gave Enoch

Olinga the title of Abu'l-Futuh, the father of victories.

At the second Intercontinental Conference, held in Chicago and attended by Amatu'l-Bahá Rúḥíyyih Khánum as the Guardian's representative, many believers were inspired to volunteer for service in the unsettled areas. One evening the Guardian came to dinner filled with enthusiasm. He said, "I have a cable from Rúḥíyyih Khánum in Chicago: they asked for pioneers to go out and settle these one hundred thirty-one countries, and more than one hundred and fifty people arose and offered to leave for these areas. Just think of it", Shoghi Effendi said, "if we send one person to each area we will have all of the countries settled. How wonderful it is, from this one Conference! I did not expect such a response as this." Leroy ventured to remark to the Guardian that as he had chaired the National Teaching Committee for thirteen years, he knew many of these people who had volunteered and he knew the problems in their lives. But Shoghi Effendi interrupted him: "Leroy, you stop it! I don't care how practical you are, I don't care how well you know America; nothing you can say is going to interfere with my joy and happiness tonight!"

The Guardian used the tools given him, as had 'Abdu'l-Bahá before him. One evening he came to dinner with a telegram from the American National Assembly, concerning an elderly lady who was insistent that she pioneer in one of the difficult posts. The Assembly felt that because she was sick, had many problems, and was not an effective teacher, she should not be sent; they had cabled the Guardian for advice. Rúḥíyyih Khánum spoke up and said, Shoghi Effendi, surely you are not going to send this person. I know her very well. She is not a good teacher, she knows nothing about the teaching work, she is sick and will need assistance and will not be able to do anything. Shoghi Effendi said he had cabled the Assembly to send her out at once, not to delay. He said that what you are forgetting is that the leaven of the world today is the Holy Spirit released by Bahá'u'lláh, which quickens the souls of men, and the Holy Spirit is brought to a new area only through a Bahá'í, there is no other way. "If that woman goes to that island and never opens her mouth, she has brought the spirit of Bahá'u'lláh there and the leavening process has begun. If there is even one area", Shoghi Effendi added, "which remains unsettled, that area is deprived of the influence of Bahá'u'lláh."

Many who could not go abroad served the pioneering work in their own, sometimes very modest, way. An elderly American, known to two generations of Bahá'ís as Auntie Victoria (Victoria Bedekian), made drawings for the pioneers with inspirational quotations from the writings, to be used as gifts for seekers or as decoration for the pioneer's home. Leroy wrote to thank her for helping in this way and told her, "I need your prayers, as does everyone here. The tasks are many and often very arduous, but the love and prayers of the friends make them easier. The great reward is lifting some of the burden of the beloved Guardian, whose work has increased many fold since the opening of the Crusade. We are all working harder to absorb more of it for him, so as to give him some relief."

Others who could not go abroad pioneered at home. One of these was the beloved early Bahá'í of New York City and frequent hostess of 'Abdu'l-Bahá, Vaffa Kinney. At the age of seventy, a widow, she moved from her lifetime home in New York City to the small town of River Edge across the Hudson. The Guardian is greatly pleased, Leroy wrote to her, with the devotion and consecration of the friends in River Edge and hopes they will establish a strong and thriving Assembly. Your own devoted services are greatly valued, and he is sure the Master will richly reward you, both here and in the hereafter.

The Guardian's sense of urgency, his insistence that the Bahá'ís act "while there is yet time", arose from the worsening conditions of the world which he clearly perceived. A number of times in speaking of the future, he characterized it as "extremely dark" in the immediate future – because of the dangers facing humanity – but very bright in the distant future. (Leroy was so disturbed by one of these talks that he was wakeful the entire night.) Much, the Guardian said, depends on the extent to which the Bahá'ís exert themselves in spreading the healing message of Bahá'u'lláh, as His teachings will alleviate the suffering ahead.

When Shoghi Effendi returned to Haifa from Europe the following October, Leroy met him as usual at the airport, and the Guardian talked to him as he paced up and down outside the airport awaiting Rúḥíyyih Khánum who was busy with some customs matter. Shoghi Effendi said he had been thinking about the Crusade, and particularly the settlement of the one hundred and thirty-one virgin areas. "We must settle all these areas immediately", he said. "I have been thinking of what we should do to stimulate the Bahá'ís so that they will act quickly. I think we will call the people who settle in the coming year Knights of Bahá'u'lláh." He asked what Leroy thought of that. Shoghi Effendi, it is wonderful, Leroy answered, but this past year you have sent many people to other places in the world and if they had known such an honor was contemplated they might have waited so that they could become Knights of Bahá'u'lláh. The Guardian corrected him by saying that they went by their own decision. Leroy said, Shoghi Effendi, when the Guardian suggests someone go to a particular place, they wish to follow his suggestion. The Guardian said, "Don't worry, God will reward them richly – *richly* – for what they have done."

The next day Shoghi Effendi sent a cable announcing that the individuals who settled in these countries during the coming year would be named Knights of Bahá'u'lláh. 'Abdu'l-Bahá had used a similar term when He referred to "Knights of the Lord". Rúḥíyyih Khánum points out to us that "all the fires the Guardian lit were from the sparks gathered so painstakingly from the writings of his forefathers".[11] Their names were to be inscribed on a scroll, each name within a medallion embossed in gold and decorated with floral designs, bearing the name of the territory. Thereafter, whenever Knights of Bahá'u'lláh came to Haifa on pilgrimage Shoghi Effendi brought out the scroll with their names on it.*

The Guardian's heart was with the pioneers, with those serving out on the front lines. He gloried more in their achievements than in anything else. Whenever he learned of difficulties that befell a pioneer he was depressed and saddened. When news of their successes came to him, he was joyous. If they were forced to leave their posts he was grieved. In a Riḍván message from the Hands of the Cause after the Guardian's passing, they wrote: "It is not possible for us to describe the wistful sadness and the look of concern and care that would pass over his blessed face when he received news that a goal had had to be abandoned and was lacking a pioneer." Rúḥíyyih Khánum tells us of the time when three pioneers had to leave their posts; she watched as the Guardian crossed off two of their names in a small book he carried, but said he could not bring himself to cross off all three at once. Leroy observed many times that when the Guardian was saddened, everyone

---

* Leroy was intensely pleased that three of his family were Knights of Bahá'u'lláh: his nieces Margery Ullrich Kellberg in the Dutch West Indies, Florence Ullrich Kelley in Monaco, and his nephew Charles Ioas in the Balearic Islands.

in Haifa became sad; when he was happy, everyone in Haifa was happy.

One pioneer who went to an island in the Pacific became very discouraged: he could not find work, no one would listen to him, he was opposed by the clergy and oppressed by the government. He wrote to the Guardian asking permission to leave his post. The Guardian instructed Leroy to write back and encourage him to persevere, promising him that "every seed would ripen". Later the man again wrote asking to leave and again the Guardian replied that he should persevere. He wrote again of his desperate financial plight and the Guardian said it must be arranged that his own National Assembly finance him to stay at his post. Then, after some months, the Guardian came to dinner and with great joy shared a cable from this same pioneer. Fifty persons had come into the Faith and the pioneer had formed not only one Assembly but two. The Guardian said if we had let him go home he would not have won those victories. Leroy said, Shoghi Effendi, it is the Guardian who has won those victories; if you had not insisted on his staying he would have left. Leroy was amazed at the Guardian's response – he knew Shoghi Effendi was speaking not solely to those at table but to the Bahá'ís everywhere. Leroy, he said, that is correct, I won those victories; I won them. And I want to say to you that if the Bahá'ís of the world will do what I ask them to do and teach in the way I have asked them to teach, they will be amazed at the victories I will win through them.

Only years later did Leroy realize the full import of this answer, when the spirit of the Guardian was released from its physical confines and could work far more powerfully than when he was in this world. Let me tell you, Leroy said at the time, these extraordinary victories that are being won (in the second half of the Crusade) – Shoghi Effendi is winning them. His spirit is influencing anyone who becomes a proper vehicle for him to work through.

Shoghi Effendi was interested in the service a Bahá'í rendered the Faith and the degree of his devotion, not in exterior traits. One afternoon when Leroy answered the door of the Western Pilgrim House, he found a small man of curious appearance, rather shabbily dressed. The man said he was Charles Dunning, the pioneer from the Orkney Islands. Leroy welcomed him, settled him in his room and later when they were to go to dinner and meet the Guardian – each time it was a special occasion – he asked Charles if he wished to change his clothes before he met the Guardian, and he said yes, yes. When they went downstairs, however, Leroy noticed he had on the same clothes. Yet when Charles entered the room, the Guardian put his arms around him and kissed him – something he rarely did. He sat Charles at the head of the table, next to him, and said, you are a Knight of Bahá'u-'lláh, you deserve to be at the head of the table. What the Guardian saw was the man's devotion to the Cause, his going at the age of sixty-nine to the northern, windswept Orkney Islands where the people were hard, uninterested in religion, looking with suspicion on newcomers. Alone and persecuted, he served in that cold, bleak place – Leroy said many of the people were colder than the weather – under very difficult conditions, and the Guardian knew it. After Charles left Haifa, the Guardian said: He is one of God's heroes.

One evening at the dinner table there was talk of the heroism and sacrifice of such pioneers. "Yes," the Guardian said, "they are hardly to be duplicated. And yet", he said after a pause, "we must remember, they can never duplicate the acts of the Letters of the Living at the time of the Báb. Those are unique and will never be surpassed by any Bahá'í in the world. But the Bahá'ís of today", the Guardian affirmed, "in their services and struggles for the Cause of God, are sacrificing and gaining victories almost as great as those of the eighteen Letters of the Living." Leroy thought to himself – in contact as he was with the people in the field – that their accomplishments will make another book of Acts of the Apostles.

As the Crusade gained momentum a deepening consciousness was clearly developing within the Bahá'ís. The believers everywhere were responding to the challenges with astonishing vigor and clear-mindedness. In Leroy's view this was one of the miracles of the early period of the Crusade.

The Guardian summarized what had been accomplished during the very first year of the Crusade: "The first twelve months of this decade-long enterprise . . . have witnessed the hoisting of the banner of the Faith of Bahá'u'lláh in no less than a hundred virgin territories of the globe. The total number of the newly opened sovereign states and dependencies . . . represents almost seven-eighths of all the territories, exclusive of the Soviet Republics and Satellites, destined to be opened in the course of an entire decade."[12]

The northernmost outpost of the Bahá'í world had pushed beyond the Arctic Circle, its southern limits reached down beyond the Falkland Islands. Posts lying outside the routes of normal travel included Sikkim in the Himalayas, the archipelagos of the North Sea, penal colonies in the Indian Ocean, St. Helena in the center of the South Atlantic, the war-devastated atolls of the Gilbert Islands, and so many others. The Bahá'í world had swelled to two hundred and twenty-eight states and dependencies. And the Bahá'ís themselves had added many supplementary goals.

These achievements brought intense joy to the heart of the Guardian and filled him with enthusiasm. "The developments are coming so rapidly", he said, "I can't keep up with them." He thought of his maps; a second one with the supplementary goals was nearly full. "We will have to get someone to make these maps for us." Yet he continued to keep his maps, finishing the last one, which he called "The Half-way Point of the Ten Year Crusade", the night before he died.

Then came the evening when Shoghi Effendi said to those around him, "Do you realize that we have virtually won the Crusade from the standpoint of settling the new countries? One hundred and two have now been settled, there are sixteen in the Iron Curtain countries which we may not be able to fill because of their particular conditions, we have several islands which are privately owned and very difficult of access and we may not be able to settle them. Then there are a few areas to which people are en route or preparing to go."

"You know," the Guardian repeated, "we have virtually *won* the Crusade, because the most important of the goals is to establish the Faith throughout the world, which was to have been accomplished by 1963."

In choosing the time to launch each of the teaching plans the Guardian had been inspired by the writings of 'Abdu'l-Bahá. The Master, in various Tablets, cited dates by which certain milestones would be reached in the evolution of the Faith. One of these was the date given by Daniel in the Old Testament verse: "Blessed is he who cometh unto the thousand, three hundred and thirty-five days." (12:12.) This prophecy, 'Abdu'l-Bahá said, refers to the centenary of the Declaration of Bahá'u'lláh, 1963, by which time ". . . the teachings of God [will] be firmly established upon the earth, and the Divine Light . . . flood the world from the East even unto the West."[13]

In speaking of this prophecy, the Guardian said: "Think of it! Daniel said it would take until 1963, yet we have practically accomplished it nine years ahead of schedule. Think of it!" The Guardian paused, then said: "Of course, Daniel did not know what kind of Prophet Bahá'u'lláh would be." Everyone laughed, and then Leroy said, Shoghi Effendi, if I may say so, Daniel also did not know what kind of Guardian we were going to have.

In later years Leroy often pondered the question of why "we few poor miserable Bahá'ís" had been privileged to be the channels for the fulfillment of the prophecy of Daniel, which millions of people over the centuries have prayed to see. What have we done to warrant such greatness? he asked. And not only are we alive to witness it, we are actually taking part in its fulfillment.

These initial years of the Crusade were the final years of the Guardian's life. How clearly 'Abdu'l-Bahá had urged the believers in His Will and Testament to assure that "no dust of despondency or sorrow" would stain Shoghi Effendi's radiant nature. The believers did not always guard him nor encourage him nor fulfill the hopes he had for them. Yet during the last five years of his life, as they caught his vision of the Faith of Bahá'u'lláh sweeping triumphantly into the most distant and remote spots on earth, they were at last giving him the victories he had so intensely sought for so many years.

He had in his lifetime – "ahead of schedule" – witnessed the consummation of Daniel's one thousand three hundred and thirty-five days. He had seen achievements far beyond his expectations. "When we started the Crusade five years ago", he said, "I never dreamt [Leroy recalled that Shoghi Effendi used that word] that the Bahá'ís could do what they have done. I never thought they would sacrifice enough, that they would rise up sufficiently to go out and do all the things they have done. Just *think of the victories we have won!*"

"But I want to tell you this," the Guardian continued as he looked into the future, "the second five years of this Crusade will be far more glorious, far more dramatic, far more miraculous than the first five years. The Bahá'ís will perform deeds at which they themselves will be amazed."

In what way, Shoghi Effendi, Leroy asked, will the second half of the Crusade be more glorious than the first – as we had presumed nothing could surpass the settling of the virgin areas. "It will be the beginning of mass conversion", the Guardian answered, "that will be more glorious than the one hundred thirty-one countries." And in what way, Leroy asked, will it be more dramatic. "In the formation of all the National Assemblies; that will be the drama of the second five years."

After each of the great Conferences that took place during the Holy Year that preceded the Crusade, when the Guardian summoned the Bahá'ís again and again to action, he would say: "Now we must see what the friends will do." They had not disappointed him.

# CHAPTER THIRTY

# Ella Bailey

LEROY recalled one night when the Guardian came over to dinner very disturbed, very grieved at news of various matters which he had received, among them the death of Ella Bailey at her pioneering post in North Africa. He pushed his plate aside and though Rúḥíyyih Khánum urged him to eat, he again pushed the plate aside. What do the Bahá'ís think of their Guardian? he asked. I call upon them to go out and teach, and some are in jail, some persecuted, some die in foreign lands. The others at table answered: "But they glory in this privilege, they are proud that the Guardian has urged them to go out as pioneers." The next evening he came over with the text of a cable-gram he had just sent to the American National Assembly. In it he announced that Ella Bailey had attained the station of martyrdom and that he himself intended to build her monument in Tripoli.

Many of the pioneers who settled in new areas of the world during the Ten Year Crusade left their homelands with no thought of return. One of these was Ella Bailey, the oldest American to enter the field of pioneering.

Ella was a cripple from early childhood, having contracted poliomyelitis at the age of three, and she was rarely free of pain throughout her life. Yet she possessed a saintly and submissive counte-nance that was magnetic in its attraction. She earned her living by teaching school and was an active Bahá'í teacher, in spite of the heavy boot-shoe her condition forced her to wear and which slowed her walk and circumscribed her activities.

She heard of the Bahá'í Faith in 1905 after moving to Northern California and subsequently studied its teachings with Lua Getsinger.

Her knowledge of the Faith deepened through her life-long friendships with Helen Goodall and her daughter Ella Goodall Cooper, who tenderly looked after her welfare as long as they both lived. When Berkeley formed its first Spiritual Assembly in 1925, she was elected chairman.

It was with the Goodalls that she traveled to Chicago in 1912 to meet 'Abdu'l-Bahá and it was there that she had several memorable interviews with Him. She recalls that on one of these occasions, 'Abdu'l-Bahá stood for a long time gazing out of the window and then repeated her name several times: *Ella Bailey, Ella Bailey, Ella Bailey . . . I love Ella Bailey.*

"He put into my name," she recalled, "every possible emotion. That was the wonder of it . . . It meant to me as if He had said in plain words, 'My child, you are going to suffer; you are going to have a great deal of sorrow . . .' In those few words He gave me all the emotions of a lifetime – He gave me suffering but with it He gave me faith and strength."

At the start of the world Crusade in 1953 she heard that her close friends in the Berkeley community, Bahia and Robert Gulick, were planning to move as Bahá'í pioneers to Tripoli in North Africa. Secretly she longed to go with them but was too humble to mention her desire. It was they who spoke to her of accompanying them and though she was thrilled, she said it would be selfish of her to go and be a burden to them. The Gulicks, however, felt her presence would be a blessing and they cabled the Guardian for his advice, which came swiftly, "Approve Bailey accompany you."

She was eighty-eight years old and in frail health. But she made ready to leave. In New York she fell ill and was confined to bed at the home of a Bahá'í doctor. The Hand of the Cause Zikrullah Khadem, one of the few persons allowed to visit her, recalls how the New York Assembly was planning her memorial service, when she rose from her bed and left for Tripoli. The three travelers arrived on July 20. But Ella soon fell ill again and passed away on August 26, a month after arriving at her pioneering post. By her move she became a Knight of Bahá'u'lláh.

The Guardian's heart was always with such pioneers and after he had announced Ella Bailey's station and his intention to build her monument, Leroy asked if he might tell Shoghi Effendi a story about her. A few years earlier, he related, when he was Treasurer of the National Assembly, the American Bahá'ís had had to raise one million dollars in two years in order to complete the ornamentation of the Temple. During a business trip to San Francisco he was asked by Ella to come and have tea with her. She said: you need a lot of money for the Temple; I don't have much money. But I have one hundred and fifty dollars for my burial and I want you to take it for the Temple. I will ask in my Will to be buried in a pauper's grave. What good is this body anyway, she said, it has given me pain all my life.

Leroy said: we don't need a hundred and fifty dollars, Ella, we need one million dollars. You keep that hundred and fifty dollars and have a proper burial; you are entitled to that. No, she said, my mind is made up. And she gave him a check for the Fund.

Shoghi Effendi, Leroy concluded, here is a woman who had given up the money for her burial, here is a woman willing to be buried in a pauper's grave, yet who becomes a martyr to the Cause of God, and the Guardian of the Cause, the sign of God on earth, is building her monument. This is surely one of the great sacrificial victories.

The Guardian was deeply moved by this story and at the conclusion of the Holy Year one and a half months later, he paid tribute again to Ella Bailey in a cablegram to the Intercontinental Conference in New Delhi in which he acclaimed her contribution to the world Crusade:

IRRESISTIBLY UNFOLDING CRUSADE SANCTIFIED DEATH HEROIC EIGHTY-EIGHT-YEAR-OLD ELLA BAILEY ELEVATING HER RANK MARTYRS FAITH SHEDDING FURTHER LUSTER AMERICAN BAHA'I COMMUNITY CONSECRATING SOIL FAST AWAKENING AFRICAN CONTINENT.[1]

Leroy wrote to her fellow pioneer, Robert Gulick: "It shows how the Hand of God directs the destinies of man – that one who would sacrifice to this extent and want to be buried in a potters' field, should have her monument erected by the Guardian of the Faith . . . The pioneers are consecrating the soil in many areas and assuring the victory by their sacrifices and death."

Many versions of the story of Ella Bailey's sacrifice have been shared among the Bahá'ís; this is the accurate one.

In March of 1954 when Marion Jack died, the Guardian linked her name with Ella's and other outstanding American pioneers:

. . . TRIUMPHANT SOUL [MARION JACK] NOW GATHERED DISTINGUISHED BAND COWORKERS ABHA KINGDOM: MARTHA ROOT, LUA GETSINGER, MAY MAXWELL, HYDE DUNN, SUSAN MOODY, KEITH RANSOM-KEHLER, ELLA BAILEY, DOROTHY BAKER, WHOSE REMAINS, LYING SUCH WIDELY SCATTERED AREAS GLOBE AS HONOLULU, CAIRO, BUENOS AIRES, SYDNEY, TIHRAN, ISFAHAN, TRIPOLI DEPTHS MEDITERRANEAN, ATTEST THE MAGNIFICENCE PIONEER SERVICES RENDERED NORTH AMERICAN BAHA'I COMMUNITY APOSTOLIC FORMATIVE AGES BAHA'I DIS-PENSATION.[2]

On the elaborate map the Guardian produced of the goals for the Ten Year Crusade, he put a star on the site of Tripoli and said, "This is Ella Bailey".

# CHAPTER THIRTY-ONE

# The Passing of Shoghi Effendi

ONE evening the Guardian came to dinner at the Pilgrim House in a deeply troubled mood. He didn't want to eat. Though Rúḥíyyih Khánum urged him to have some food he pushed the plate aside. He began to speak in an introspective manner.

"You know," he said, "shortly before Bahá'u'lláh passed away the Master went to see Him in Bahjí and found His papers strewn over the sofa. The Master collected them and laid them on the divan next to Bahá'u'lláh. He said, 'Bahá'u'lláh, I have collected your papers, I have put them in order and I have put them here for you.' Bahá'u'lláh said, 'It is of no use to gather them, I must leave them and flee away.'"

The Guardian continued: "Shortly before 'Abdu'l-Bahá passed away they found His papers scattered about His room, and He was very meticulous. His secretaries collected the papers, put them in order and brought them to the Master. But He put them aside and said, 'I am done with the papers, it is finished now. I don't want them any more.' Shortly afterwards He passed away."

Shoghi Effendi then said, "I am getting so tired of my papers, I don't want them any more. I just don't want these papers any more. I am going to throw them away just as Bahá'u'lláh and 'Abdu'l-Bahá did."

Rúḥíyyih Khánum was greatly distressed. She said, Shoghi Effendi, every Bahá'í in the world would do anything to lighten this burden for you. Tell them what to do. And Leroy said, Shoghi Effendi, why don't you give these papers to Rúḥíyyih Khánum and myself? We will digest them for you, we will pick put the salient points and call them to your attention; then you can give us your decisions and we will do this work

And he added, Shoghi Effendi, why don't you stop seeing all pilgrims individually, walking with the Oriental pilgrims, talking with them, spending the whole afternoon with them. Then in the evening you visit with the Western pilgrims, answering their questions, speaking with them. Future Guardians can not do this. But the Guardian said, "No, the time is not yet ripe for these things."

On one rare evening, Shoghi Effendi, weary and pressed from work and not far from the time of his passing, wished to speak only of spiritual matters. "Let us enter the door of heaven," he said to those around him, "and forget for a few moments." He spoke at length – the most beautiful, the most penetrating words Leroy heard from his lips during the six years he had spent in Haifa.

As he escorted the Guardian home that evening after dinner, Leroy hoped that Shoghi Effendi would, as he often did, continue to speak on the theme he had been expounding. But instead, he turned to Leroy and said: "Leroy, you know I have been Guardian of the Cause for thirty-six years. Bahá'u'lláh was the head of the Faith, from the time of His announcement in 1863, for twenty-eight years, and 'Abdu'l-Bahá for twenty-nine years. I have been the head of the Faith for thirty-six years. In the days of the Báb the Cause was established in two countries, in the days of Bahá'u'lláh in eleven and in the days of the Master in thirty-one. Today it is established in two hundred and fifty countries and islands of the world. The responsibilities, the work, the worries are simply weighing on me and I must have some relief." Leroy again asked what he could do to relieve him. I can do much more work, he said, but I will have to have some help. I will have to have someone assist me with all the land matters and the construction work. I can do more, Shoghi Effendi, and that will give you some relief. The Guardian turned to him and said with tears in his eyes: "Only God can give me relief."

This was shortly before the Guardian left for Europe in 1957. His last words to Leroy were that he was "very very proud" of the work he was doing.

It was late afternoon in London when Rúḥíyyih Khánum telephoned Haifa; in the Holy Land it was seven at night. She informed Leroy that the Guardian had died early that morning in his sleep.

Sylvia heard him fall to the floor and ran to him but he had already risen and continued the terrible conversation. A cablegram sent earlier in the day by Rúḥíyyih Khánum had not yet been received in Haifa. It read:

BELOVED GUARDIAN DESPERATELY ILL ASIATIC FLU TELL LEROY INFORM ALL
NATIONAL ASSEMBLIES INFORM BELIEVERS SUPPLICATE PRAYERS DIVINE PRO-
TECTION FAITH.[1]

On finding the Guardian that morning Rúḥíyyih Khánum had immediately called two doctors but they could do nothing; Shoghi Effendi
had died instantaneously and painlessly in his sleep. She turned to her
fellow Hands, Hasan Balyuzi, the Guardian's cousin, and John Ferraby,
who immediately joined her at the hotel. She telephoned Ugo Giachery in Rome who within two hours was on a flight to London. Then, as
she later wrote, unable "to deal the naked blow to the hearts of other
Bahá'ís which she herself had received and had been forced to inflict
on three of the Hands" she sent this first cable to Haifa, hoping to
soften for the Bahá'ís everywhere in the world the unacceptable news.[2]
Leroy carried out her wishes and dispatched the message early on
November 5 from Haifa:

WITH DEEP SADNESS ADVISE BELOVED GUARDIAN DESPERATELY ILL ASIATIC FLU
PLEASE IMMEDIATELY INFORM ALL FRIENDS SUPPLICATE PRAYERS DIVINE PRO-
TECTION FAITH. LEROY IOAS

Shortly all Bahá'í institutions received the second cablegram which
came from London via Haifa:

SHOGHI EFFENDI BELOVED OF ALL HEARTS SACRED TRUST GIVEN BELIEVERS BY
MASTER PASSED AWAY SUDDEN HEART ATTACK IN SLEEP FOLLOWING ASIATIC
FLU STOP URGE BELIEVERS REMAIN STEADFAST CLING INSTITUTION HANDS LOV-
INGLY REARED RECENTLY REINFORCED EMPHASIZED BY BELOVED GUARDIAN.
ONLY ONENESS HEART ONENESS PURPOSE CAN BEFITTINGLY TESTIFY LOYALTY
ALL NATIONAL ASSEMBLIES BELIEVERS DEPARTED GUARDIAN WHO SACRIFICED
SELF UTTERLY FOR SERVICE FAITH. RUHIYYIH[3]

Their world suddenly darkened and empty, feeling lost and alone,
Sylvia and Leroy went over to break the news to Milly, who had
returned twenty-four hours earlier from America and whom Sylvia

had left resting just an hour before. Leroy told her as sweetly and gently as he could but she saw their stricken faces. She was completely crushed and they feared for her as she was so frail. She laid her head on Leroy's shoulder and just wept and wept. But her faith and fortitude were indomitable and she kept saying, God will give me strength; God will give me strength. At eleven that night they went up to the Shrine of the Báb and had many, many prayers, which was the comfort they needed and wanted. Before the dark day of November fourth ended, Leroy and Sylvia sent a cablegram to Rúḥíyyih Khánum: "In Guardian's passing whole Bahá'í world grieved crushed but your personal loss insurmountable. Sylvia myself send deepfelt sympathy love admiration your strong determination assist his released spirit gain even greater victories beloved Faith."

Early the next morning Leroy drove Milly to the airport where she took a flight to London to be with Rúḥíyyih Khánum, to whom she had become like a mother. When the Guardian left in early summer he had taken Milly's hands in his and looked into her eyes. He said: "Don't be sad, Milly, don't be sad." He had never said such words to her before. Those words were of great help to her during the sorrow and sadness of his passing and the turmoil and work of the Hands of the Cause; she tried, she said, to obey him and "not be sad".

Amidst their anguish, those in Haifa did what had to be done. Leroy immediately placed men around the clock at the Holy Places and at the Guardian's residence, assigning two faithful believers to sleep at each Shrine and two at the Guardian's house. The members of the Council who were in Haifa (Leroy, Sylvia and the two Revells), with several husky men, went up to the Guardian's personal living quarters, which had been locked by Shoghi Effendi before he left, verified that they were well secured, and sealed them off. Leroy had one man sleep outside the apartment, another at the foot of the stairs leading up to it. A memorandum of these actions was made and signed by the four Council members (see Appendix 1).

Leroy promptly and befittingly notified the Government of the passing of His Eminence and informed it that an announcement would shortly be forthcoming from the Bahá'í World Centre. Conditions in Haifa were therefore sufficiently calm that Leroy decided he could leave the Holy Land over the weekend to attend the Guardian's funeral in London on Saturday.

*With the Guardian at the funeral of Isfandiar, April 1957. (Photograph by Lotfullah Hakim)*

*Leroy at his desk*

*With Ugo Giachery in Jerusalem*

*The President of the State of Israel*
*Mr. Ben-Zvi(left); the Speaker of the*
*Knesset Mr. Sprinzak(center); Leroy Ioas,*
*1959. The photograph on the wall is of the*
*first President of Israel Chaim Weizmann*

*Leroy presenting Mr. A.-A. Furutan*
*(right) to Mr. Ben-Zvi (left)*

*With an Orthodox clergyman*

*At a ball given by the Italian Consul*
*aboard a ship in Haifa Port, 1953*

*Leroy greeting the Prime Minister of Israel, Mr. Ben-Gurion, 1959.*
*Mr. Sprinzak, Speaker of the Knesset, is on the left*

*Talking to Mr. Ben-Gurion about the Bahá'í Faith*

*Kampala, Uganda, Intercontinental Conference 1953. Greeting the African Bahá'ís on behalf of the Guardian*

*Ten Hands of the Cause of God assembled at the Ḥaẓíratu'l-Quds during the Conference. From left: Músá Bánání, Valíyu'lláh Varqá, Shu'á'u'lláh 'Alá'í, Mason Remey, Horace Holley, Ṭarázu'lláh Samandarí, Zikrullah Khadem, Leroy Ioas, Dorothy Baker, 'Alí-Akbar Furútan*

*At the dedication of the British Ḥaẓíratu'l-Quds, January 1955*

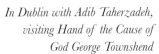

*In Dublin with Adib Taherzadeh,
visiting Hand of the Cause of
God George Townshend*

*Building the superstructure of the Shrine of the Báb:*
*the way it looked when Leroy arrived in Haifa in 1952*

*Leroy with workmen*

*Building the dome*

*Báb-i-Ioas. The ninth door of the Shrine of the Báb, named by Shoghi Effendi*

*When the Arc was first laid out*

*Leroy on the Arc, the Archives under construction, with the completed Shrine of the Báb in the background*

*At the funeral of Shoghi Effendi, Guardian of the Bahá'í Faith, November 1957. Leroy with American Bahá'í Billy de Forge*

*At the beloved Guardian's resting-place five months after his passing, March 1958, with David Hofman*

Hands of the Cause were arriving in London as rapidly as was possible from their posts in farflung corners of the world. Horace Holley was in hospital in America, and 'Alí-Akbar Furútan was asked by the National Spiritual Assembly of Iran to remain there and comfort the believers by attending the memorial meetings planned in Teheran. Ordinary Bahá'ís were also reaching London – the customs men said they had not seen its like, each flight bringing people from everywhere.

Everything was done in London in strict accord with the provisions of the Kitáb-i-Aqdas. The one asked to prepare the body of the Guardian for burial was the Hand of the Cause Dr. Adelbert Mühlschlegel. A peaceful, parkland setting was found at the North London Cemetery for the interment; within a week one of the Bahá'ís had purchased whatever land was available around the burial place of the Guardian. The cemetery chapel – much too small to accommodate the number of grieving Bahá'ís who came to the funeral – was banked with many-hued flowers selected by Rúḥíyyih Khánum and Milly Collins; pure white silk was purchased by them, as well as a large piece of heavy green velvet, the color of the Síyyids from whom Shoghi Effendi was descended through his illustrious ancestor, the Báb. This covered the catafalque during the ceremony and was placed over the coffin before the vault was sealed. The night before the funeral the Hands of the Cause met late at the Ḥaẓíratu'l-Quds arranging the program for the next day. The Hand of the Cause John Ferraby and his wife Dorothy answered hundreds of telephone calls and received and sent cablegrams from the National Centre; Persian ladies worked there to prepare the silk for the Guardian's shroud and the green velvet for the catafalque. On Friday the sealed casket was taken to the funeral home; two Hands of the Cause stood guard throughout the day keeping vigil over the body of the Guardian.

Leroy arrived in London at eight on Saturday, the morning of the funeral, and was met by Rafi and Mildred Mottahedeh. With him he carried the precious items requested by Rúḥíyyih Khánum, a small rug from the innermost Shrine of Bahá'u'lláh, which was placed under the Guardian's casket in the burial vault, giving, as Ugo Giachery noted, "an air of domesticity, like a corner of home, a bit of Persia, a symbol from the cradle of the Faith to receive the great-grandson of Him Who, one hundred and four years earlier, was compelled to leave His native land, never to see it again",[4] and a blue and gold brocade covering which had also rested in that inner Shrine and which was spread over the coffin above the green velvet. He carried with him throughout the hours of plane travel a large bouquet of white jasmine from 'Akká and a box of flowers and petals gathered from the gardens at Bahjí, Riḍván, Mazra'ih and Haifa. Before the tomb was closed Rúḥíyyih Khánum spread the still-fragrant jasmine over the length of brocade covering the Guardian's coffin.

Sixty-five cars left the National Bahá'í Centre in London in the cortege carrying Bahá'ís to the funeral of the Guardian. The brief ceremony consisted entirely of the writings of Bahá'u'lláh with the exception of the first two paragraphs of the Will and Testament of 'Abdu'l-Bahá praising "the blest and sacred bough that hath branched out from the Twin Holy Trees". At its conclusion everyone followed the Guardian's coffin to the gravesite, the Hands of the Cause, their heads bared, following Rúḥíyyih Khánum with Hand of the Cause Amelia Collins beside her. Carpets of flowers lay near the burial site; a single spray of deep red roses, gardenias, lily of the valley and fuchsia covered the Guardian's casket with Rúḥíyyih Khánum's hand-written card: "From Rúḥíyyih and all your loved ones and lovers all over the world whose hearts are broken." A soft rain began to fall as the Bahá'ís quietly filed past the coffin for more than two hours, saying their farewell to the Guardian.

In the message sent by the Hands of the Cause the following Riḍván to the National Conventions of the world, they mentioned the great wave of sympathy that had come from the officials of the State of Israel, who responded and cooperated in every way to protect the interests of the Faith at its international center. The Government instructed its *chargé d'affaires* in London to attend the funeral on its behalf, the sole non-Bahá'í in attendance, and he remained throughout the lengthy and moving farewell of the believers to the Guardian at the gravesite.

That evening, thinking of Sylvia alone in Haifa, Leroy sent a brief cable: "Beautiful service large attendance good burial area Farrukh here joins sending love." What great rejoicing, he kept thinking, there must have been in the Abhá Kingdom when the Guardian was welcomed after his long years of heart-rending service here!

Faithful to the Guardian's love of frankness and openness among the Bahá'ís, Rúḥíyyih Khánum on the day following the funeral shared the following comforting details in a cablegram to the believers world-wide:

BELOVED GUARDIAN LAID REST LONDON ACCORDING LAWS AQDAS IN BEAUTIFUL SPOT AFTER IMPRESSIVE CEREMONY HELD PRESENCE MULTITUDE BELIEVERS REPRESENTING OVER TWENTYFIVE COUNTRIES EAST WEST. DOCTORS ASSURE SUDDEN PASSING INVOLVED NO SUFFERING BLESSED COUNTENANCE BORE EXPRESSION INFINITE BEAUTY PEACE MAJESTY. EIGHTEEN HANDS ASSEMBLED FUNERAL URGE NATIONAL BODIES REQUEST ALL BELIEVERS HOLD MEMORIAL MEETINGS EIGHTEENTH NOVEMBER COMMEMORATING DAYSPRING DIVINE GUID-ANCE WHO HAS LEFT US AFTER THIRTYSIX YEARS UTTER SELFSACRIFICE CEASELESS LABOURS CONSTANT VIGILANCE. RUHIYYIH[5]

On the afternoon of that day, the Hands of the Cause met with the believers who were constantly gathering at the Ḥaẓíratu'l-Quds. Some of the Hands chanted, Paul Haney spoke of the protection of the Faith, Leroy spoke powerful words on teaching as the way to bear witness to one's love for the Guardian. Then Rúḥíyyih Khánum rose, and in spite of her personal grief and with the steel she said the Guardian had instilled in her, spoke fully and intimately to the friends of everything that had happened since that early morning of November 4th. She then assured those present that it would all be written down and diffused to the believers; shortly she and Hand of the Cause John Ferraby accomplished this invaluable task for history.[6]

Shoghi Effendi was sixty-one years of age when he died, so very young and yet as Rúḥíyyih Khánum has said, so exhausted by the relentless work of his thirty-six year Guardianship. No one thought of his dying; indeed, many could not have borne the thought of it. Amidst the shock and confusion of his passing, the Bahá'ís went to their Scriptures and wondered who, in accordance with the Will and Testament of 'Abdu'l-Bahá, would succeed Shoghi Effendi. The text is clear that the Guardian must nominate his first-born son if that son inherited a spiritual character to match his glorious lineage; otherwise the Guardian is enjoined by the Master to choose another of the Aghṣán (the descendants of Bahá'u'lláh). But those who knew Haifa had never heard of an heir, and those who knew the history of the virus of Covenant-breaking wondered what Aghṣán there could be to succeed Shoghi Effendi. In London, the Hands of the Cause decided there must be an immediate meeting in Haifa of the full body of the Hands of the Cause, the Chief Stewards of the Cause as the Guardian had termed them in his final message to the Bahá'ís.

Leroy returned to Haifa the night after the Guardian's funeral. Hundreds of cablegrams had been received during the days since the Guardian's passing, many of them from officials of the Government. One of the first was from the President of Israel, Itzhak Ben-Zvi:

DEEPLY GRIEVED AT THE LOSS OF THE ESTEEMED SPIRITUAL LEADER OF THE BAHA'I FAITH SHOGHI EFFENDI RABBANI PLEASE TRANSMIT MY CONDOLENCES AND THOSE OF MRS. BEN-ZVI TO MADAME RABBANI AND THE BAHA'I COMMUNITY IN ISRAEL.

Three days later Rúḥíyyih Khánum returned, and within a few days all the Hands of the Cause, with the exception of Corinne True who was too frail to travel, arrived at the World Centre, twenty-six in all. A memorial meeting for the Guardian was held in the precincts of the Ḥaram-i-Aqdas and then all repaired to the Shrine of Bahá'u'lláh. Sylvia was overcome to see for the first time all the Hands of the Cause together . . . so stricken, she said, with such sad faces, yet so distinguished and strong through it all . . .

The next day nine of the Hands broke the seals that had been placed on the Guardian's safe and desk (placed there by the five Hands serving in Haifa, immediately after their return from London) and their contents were examined. The nine Hands included those in service at the World Centre, plus Hasan Balyuzi, a member of the Afnan family, Horace Holley representing the believers of the western hemisphere, Músá Banání representing the believers of Africa, and 'Alí Muḥammad Varqá, Trustee of the Guardian representing the Asian continent. Their determination, which they immediately conveyed to their fellow Hands waiting in Bahjí, was that the Guardian had left no will nor any indication of his wishes. They together certified that the Guardian had no heir nor did he find anyone among the Aghṣán to succeed him.

The Hands of the Cause, Rúḥíyyih Khánum has told us, were in "the very abyss of despair".

Meeting through the lengthy days in the great hall of the Mansion of Bahjí, seeking guidance through their prayers in the Shrine of

Bahá'u'lláh, they read the Guardian's messages over and over. Slowly came the realization that Shoghi Effendi himself would have been the first to remind them that Bahá'u'lláh "has quickened those powers and resources of faith within mankind which would achieve the unity of the peoples and the triumph of His World Order".[7] Inspired by Shoghi Effendi's life of service, the Hands accepted the enormity of their role as Chief Stewards of the Faith.

Six days later, on November 25, they issued their "Unanimous Proclamation".* It stated that as the Guardian had passed away without appointing his successor, it had fallen to the Chief Stewards "to preserve the unity, the security and the development of the Bahá'í World Community and its institutions"; and in accordance with the Will and Testament of 'Abdu'l-Bahá they must elect nine of their own number to be at all times occupied in the important services of the Guardian; they therefore had elected those nine to act on their behalf as Custodians of the Bahá'í World Faith . . . "to exercise all such functions, rights and powers in succession to the Guardian as are necessary to serve the interests of the Bahá'í World Faith . . . until such time as the Universal House of Justice, upon being elected in conformity with the Sacred Writings of Bahá'u'lláh and the Will and Testament of 'Abdu'l-Bahá, may otherwise determine."

They thus ensured the unity, the purity and the protection of the Faith of Bahá'u'lláh. At one time a pilgrim had asked the Guardian about the succeeding Guardian. Shoghi Effendi had answered: "The Faith will *always* be adequately protected."

The nine elected to serve as Custodians were Rúḥíyyih Khánum, Hasan Balyuzi, Amelia Collins, 'Alí-Akbar Furútan, Paul Haney, Leroy Ioas, Jalál Kházeh, Adelbert Mühlschlegel and Mason Remey.[8]

From this first Conclave of the Hands of the Cause, a further Proclamation to the Bahá'ís of East and West went out on the same day, November 25, from the Mansion of Bahjí. It reminded the believers of the true legacy of Shoghi Effendi: the establishment of the World Centre on a firm foundation, the spread of the Faith throughout the globe with the simultaneous emergence of the embryonic administrative institutions of Bahá'u'lláh's world order, the translations and masterworks of interpretation from his pen, the institution of the Hands of the Cause and the establishment of the International Bahá'í

* For full text see Appendix 2.

Council, the latter clearly to evolve, as he wrote, through an appointed to an elected body and then into that Universal House of Justice created by Bahá'u'lláh.

The Guardian himself had frequently made a remark, which in retrospect took on extraordinary significance, that his book *The Dispensation of Bahá'u'lláh* "is in reality my Will and Testament, so that after me no differences may occur". In that lengthy "letter" to the Bahá'ís written in 1934, the stations of Bahá'u'lláh, the Báb, and 'Abdu'l-Bahá were stated once and for all and the nature and indissoluble relationship of the Administrative Order to the entire Revelation expounded.

The mission and scope of the Ten Year Crusade had been laid out in detail by the Guardian. He had called for a great Congress to close the Crusade befittingly and when asked by those in Haifa why he used the word Congress which he had never before employed, he said that a Congress is more formal, where formal things will be done. It was clear to the Hands that even without the two institutions intended to give divine guidance to the Bahá'í world (the Guardianship and the Universal House of Justice), they had before them the guidance of the Guardian up to the date of 1963. They therefore set as their goal the accomplishment of every provision of the Guardian's Crusade, without the slightest deviation from his program.

The responsibility was crushing and it would be idle to think that the Hands simply rose above their sorrow. Rather they continued on in spite of it, because of their boundless love for, and fidelity to, Shoghi Effendi. Theirs was the dual burden of losing a leader to whom they were intimately bound and of finding in their hands the reins of the Bahá'í world.

Leroy, who had been associated with Shoghi Effendi on a daily basis in Haifa, was profoundly affected by his death.* He wrote to his friend Bishop Brown, a pioneer in South Africa, that "all the lights went out". Yet, like the others, he carried on – without the presence, the inspiration, the very heart of what had been life for those in Haifa. Sylvia noted how within a short time his hair turned completely white. It hardly seems possible, he wrote poignantly to his family, that we are to

* For those in Haifa "every tree and pebble and flower" reminded them that he was gone (Message from the Hands of the Cause to the Annual Conventions 1958, in *Ministry of the Custodians*, p. 76).

see him no more and that his strong hand of guidance has been removed from us.

It became evident to the Hands of the Cause that these events were God's will. In a letter to friends during these historic occurrences, Leroy wrote: "That the Guardian found no one in the family of Bahá'u'lláh able or qualified to succeed him, and that there were no children, would make it appear that what has happened is a part of the Plan of God . . ."

"We have been through very difficult days here," he wrote in another letter, "the new development which immediately presented itself to us was met [by the Hands] with deep humility and with the assurance that the program that was instituted was one which the Guardian surely had in mind because of his recent writings with regard to the Hands of the Faith being the Stewards of the Bahá'í world commonwealth."

At the memorial meetings in Teheran, 'Alí-Akbar Furútan told the friends: "We trust, with no hesitation or doubt, that the ascension of the beloved Guardian to the Kingdom of Abhá is in conformity with the wisdom of God, and in itself will move the believers to rush to the arena of service, pioneering and sacrifice, to promote the Cause of God."

It was perhaps natural for the Bahá'ís to wonder if Shoghi Effendi had foreseen the time of his death. In retrospect Rúhíyyih Khánum realized that during that last summer he had revisited many of the places that were dear to him. And she recalled their last conversations while he was ill in London and the intensity with which he said he would not continue to do "all these things"; he would return to Haifa, he said, but leave these things to others; he could not go on. She slept little the two nights before his passing, with these words weighing on her heart, so different from the Guardian's usual enthusiasm and dynamism.

During that summer Leroy had received many letters and cable-grams from Shoghi Effendi, detailing work the Guardian wished done before his return, in preparation for further projects which he had in mind. He urged Leroy to hasten the completion of a number of these tasks. It seemed inconceivable to Leroy that the Guardian would have specifically postponed demolition of the house of the Covenant-break-ers if he had the least sense of not returning, for it had been his life-long desire to rid Bahjí of every trace of their presence. Yet he had cabled that the demolition should await his return, as he wished to oversee the work himself. It was of great comfort to the Hands of the Cause to assemble at Bahjí in mid-December, their minds filled with thoughts of Shoghi Effendi, and watch the disappearance of the building, and to see how the Guardian's plan for the gardens could be laid out as if the structure had never existed.

In mid-January Rúḥíyyih Khánum left Haifa for Kampala to fulfill her obligation to represent the Guardian at the first of the five conferences called by Shoghi Effendi for 1958, and to lay the cornerstone of the first Bahá'í Temple to be erected on the continent of Africa.

Two months after Shoghi Effendi's passing, Leroy wrote to William Sears, one of the last-named and youngest Hands of the Cause, that the influence of the Guardian would now be more powerful than before: "The spirit of the Guardian is now released from the limitations of this world – and from the weaknesses of the Bahá'í world – and will be able to work more vigorously through the friends for the accomplishment of his goals."

The comfort of the Bahá'ís would be in activity. "It is increasingly evident," he wrote to Marion Hofman the same month, "that the only solace which the friends will find will be in renewed service to the Cause of God. The true test of devotion to the Guardian is to arise with new zeal to win all the goals of the Ten Year Crusade and to win them as quickly as possible. This will give him real happiness in the realms beyond – when he sees how those whom he loved so much and served so diligently, have now arisen to carry out the work which he began and, moreover, to carry it on their own shoulders."

Certainly England has been truly blessed, Sylvia wrote to her daughters. The Guardian loved England – how often he spoke of England and the English people, and how happy he was last winter when we had many English pilgrims here!

The Hand of the Cause Hasan Balyuzi, who had made his home for many years in London, wrote in a special message to the Bahá'ís of the British Isles:

The sign of God, the beloved Guardian, began his Guardianship in these Isles, and here he laid down his mandate. What Divine mystery is there, we do not know. When I was saying farewell in the Pilgrim House on

Mount Carmel, I was told, 'You are fortunate; you are going from one Holy Land to another Holy Land.' [These had been Leroy's words to him.] For indeed Britain has become a holy land, holding in her bosom, as she does, the sacred remains of Shoghi Effendi. God has blessed this community and raised it high, to have made it the custodian of his shrine. How great is the responsibility, therefore, that this community bears, and how surely must it show its gratitude in deeds! Through the decades and centuries men will come here from the four corners of the earth to pay homage to Shoghi Effendi. We, the Bahá'ís of the British Isles, will be their hosts. May we be truly worthy of this honour and this blessing.[9]

# CHAPTER THIRTY-TWO

# The Beloved Guardian

SHOGHI EFFENDI's leadership extended over such a lengthy period of time that most Bahá'ís had known no other head of the Faith. Their lives were intimately bound up with him, his translations of their sacred scriptures, his lengthy general letters setting a standard for their thought, his personal responses when they wrote to him. His loss was devastating, and they turned to those who had known him, longing to hear of his life and to know more of him as a person.

Several books written in English give glimpses of his life, but the incomparable work on the Guardian is and will remain that of his widow, the Hand of the Cause Amatu'l-Bahá Rúḥíyyih Khánum, which she chose to call *The Priceless Pearl*, a term used by 'Abdu'l-Bahá in His Will and Testament to describe Shoghi Effendi.

Others who worked closely with Shoghi Effendi added priceless memoirs: the Hand of the Cause Ugo Giachery, whose work *Shoghi Effendi: Recollections*, is the account of his meetings with the Guardian during construction of the Shrine of the Báb; Milly Collins, serving as the Guardian's representative to the Intercontinental Conference in Frankfurt nine months after his passing, spoke words of power and beauty concerning his life, which were published as *A Tribute to Shoghi Effendi* by the U.S. Bahá'í Publishing Trust. The early accounts of pilgrims to 'Akká and Haifa include references and observations concerning Shoghi Effendi, as does *Blessings Beyond Measure*, a unique and tender account by Ali Yazdi of his friendship with Shoghi Effendi during their childhood and youth.

Some who were close to Shoghi Effendi left no memoirs but spoke frequently of him; Leroy is one of these. He never tired of speaking of the Guardian – indeed it was a comfort to him – telling the stories over and over, as the Bahá'ís never tired of hearing them. For most, it was the closest they would get to the Guardian.* The Hand of the Cause 'Alí-Akbar Furútan remembers Leroy coming to the Eastern Pilgrim House during the time of the Custodians to speak with the Persian pilgrims. "Leroy", he said, "always spoke about the life of the Guardian, his exalted station, his divine knowledge, his arduous and painstaking work. He showed such love and devotion towards the beloved Shoghi Effendi that all who heard him, young and old, were deeply touched."

When introducing Leroy to a large audience in Wilmette a year after the Guardian's passing, Horace Holley called him "the person closest to Shoghi Effendi" with the exception of Rúḥíyyih Khánum, and Leroy's descriptions of the Guardian revealed how deeply he was affected by this close association. It is touching to note that often when Leroy spoke of the Guardian in later years, it touched chords of grief and love so deep that it would affect his damaged heart, causing him to cough repeatedly from the strain of the emotion.

It was only in the last half dozen years of the Guardian's life that the evidences of success began to appear and gradually surrounded him on all sides, bringing him immense joy. Leroy felt these years were undoubtedly the happiest period of his Guardianship, though Rúḥíyyih Khánum tells us that the happiest years of his entire life were those after 'Abdu'l-Bahá's return from America, when Shoghi Effendi accompanied the Master everywhere. A pilgrim returning to Haifa in 1956 after a lapse of many years asked Leroy what had happened to the Guardian that he was so joyous. Leroy replied that the question was not what had happened to the Guardian, but what had happened to the Bahá'ís that they were at last responding with real vigor to his appeals and fulfilling the tasks he set for them. Many times in later years Leroy told the Bahá'ís they should be eternally grateful that they had given the Guardian so much happiness in his last years.

During Leroy's early days in Haifa many people wrote to him of his "glorious spiritual bounty" in serving the Guardian. Privilege, yes, beyond measure, he would reply, but it would be a mistake to think that "we sit quietly and bask in the rays of the spiritual sun". Some

---

* Donald Witzel, in later years a Continental Counsellor, who listened to Leroy's accounts of the Guardian when on pilgrimage in 1963, wrote to him: "Your stories made me feel so close to Shoghi Effendi that having missed knowing him personally was forgotten."

Bahá'ís even believed Shoghi Effendi to be a quiet person, associating spirituality with quiescence. Little did they know the drive of the Guardian! he said. Everyone and everything in Haifa was in constant motion. Shoghi Effendi told the friends that "the secret of meditation and prayer is action; it is only through action that God can answer your prayer".

The Guardian was the center of spiritual power in the world "and that power continually radiated from him; it was a driving spiritual energy which impelled him forward". To be close to that power, to live near that force, was not an easy thing; it was something to aspire to but he felt "few of us achieved much in the way of nearness to the Guardian's spirit". The Guardian could speak with such power that the very walls of the room seemed to vibrate and at such times "you knew it was more than a man speaking", it was the power of the spirit speaking through him. Leroy thought this even more apparent in the Guardian than in 'Abdu'l-Bahá, as the Master was in His own right a unique and incomparable figure, whereas Shoghi Effendi had through effort achieved the station of evanescence which he possessed.

The unerring guidance of God encompassed Shoghi Effendi at all times, as promised by the Master, and to observe this mysterious process at work was a "tremendous experience". The Bahá'ís wondered if this guidance operated in all matters or only in regard to the Faith. Leroy said he frankly did not know where it began or ended; he had discussed the question with Rúḥíyyih Khánum, who has written that she herself did not know "where Shoghi Effendi ended and the Guardian began". Once Leroy even broached the subject to Shoghi Effendi. The Guardian opened his eyes very wide and looked at him: "Leroy, have you not read the Will and Testament of the Master?" Leroy replied that he had read it many times, and the Guardian said: "Well, what does it say?" Leroy answered that while he knew what was said in the Will, he had been asked to write many letters to Bahá'ís wanting advice on personal matters and Shoghi Effendi almost always advised them to consult experts and follow the advice they received. "Yes," said the Guardian, "that is in accordance with the teachings of Bahá'u'lláh, the Bahá'ís must consult experts at all times." Leroy said this had led him to ask whether the Guardian was guided in all matters or only those relating to the Cause itself. The Guardian replied: "In the Will and Testament, there are no limitations placed on the infallibility of the Guardian." On another occasion the Guardian told Leroy: "Bahá'u'lláh has conferred upon me a power that enables me to know what I need to know."

We don't understand, Leroy said, what this power is which flowed through the Guardian, but we constantly saw it in operation. We do know that when the Guardian decided upon a certain course of action for the good of the Faith, it was because he had been guided to do so. He confirmed this to us many times. Thus his insistence that the Bahá'ís act immediately to accomplish the things he knew must be done.

There were constant small examples of this penetrating power. One night Shoghi Effendi was speaking of the manner in which the Universal House of Justice and the National Assemblies would function together in future. As he spoke, Leroy thought to himself that under certain circumstances what the Guardian was describing would not work, and he made a mental note to ask for further elucidation. When the Guardian had completed his thought, he took a sip of coffee and turned to Leroy: "You wouldn't think this would work under certain circumstances, but I will explain to you how it does."

In another instance the Guardian was deeply concerned with the spirit behind an action taken by the U.S. National Assembly. He turned to Leroy and said, "You were on the Assembly when this was first discussed; tell me what their thinking was." As Leroy gave some details, the Guardian stopped him, saying, "I will tell you what occurred." He then explained what had happened as if he had been at the meeting, and asked whether he was right or wrong. You are exactly right, Shoghi Effendi, Leroy responded, even to the details.

A characteristic that struck Leroy, and others who had dealt with persons of capacity and authority, was the rapidity and precision of the Guardian's mind, far superior to that of the people they had known. The Guardian knew everything that was occurring in the Bahá'í world. He was efficient in everything he did and wished to see results from every undertaking. This was the constant pressure under which they all worked in Haifa. How he truly suffered, Leroy said, from the inefficiency of the Bahá'ís ! Leroy recalled the lengthy letters the Guardian would receive, filled with expressions of devotion but with pages of ill-defined questions. Often the Guardian would hand these to Leroy to determine what their exact questions were so they could be answered. Once he even remarked that the friends could be "oceans of love but mountains of inefficiency".

He would often acquaint pilgrims with developments in their own countries if they were not aware of the facts and figures which he carried in his memory. He was very open in discussing the weaknesses as well as the strengths of the various Bahá'í communities, hoping that in knowing their weaknesses they could overcome them and add to their strengths. The Guardian, Leroy said, considered nothing more wasteful than Bahá'ís of capacity, and communities of capacity, "frittering away their energy on unimportant matters, discussing everything except the all-important issues affecting the development and spread of the Faith throughout the world".

Shoghi Effendi's view was world-encompassing and everyone who heard him was dazzled by his explanations of the future development of the Faith and its interaction with world events. He closely followed what was happening in the world and foresaw how the Bahá'ís would be affected. He saw the approach of the cataclysmic events foretold by Christ, which the Prophets referred to as the great and terrible Day of the Lord. He saw the terrible Day of the Lord approaching and he wanted the roots of the Cause to be spread widely and deeply before it struck. He often had a faraway look, recalled Ugo Giachery,* as though he were seeing something not visible to our eyes . . . He was planning in terms of centuries, not just a few years . . . he was creating a World Centre that would withstand all the storms and conflicts of the world.

Shoghi Effendi was of an infinitely kind and loving nature. Before meeting him, many Bahá'ís, sensitive to his station in the Cause, were fearful. But they were immediately put at ease by his warmth and affection, and shortly, as Leroy noted, one simply loved him and wanted to be near him.

It was a moving experience, Leroy recalled, to see the love and tenderness expressed by the Guardian for others. He was constantly encouraging and complimenting people for what they did, were it the gardeners working on the properties, or the pilgrims, trying to make them happy as 'Abdu'l-Bahá wished them to be, identifying himself with their hurts and sorrows. Given his tender nature, Leroy said, no one will ever know how much he suffered from the treatment of his

---

* Speaking at the Intercontinental Conference in Chicago six months after the Guardian's death.

family. He rarely mentioned this, but one could see how deeply he had been stricken by his own kin turning away from the Faith.

On the final day of pilgrimage the pilgrims were often sad as they prepared to leave the presence of the Shrines and the Guardian for the somber-hued world outside, but the Guardian always assured them that "this is your home; this is your spiritual home".

Leroy recalled the tender consideration paid by the Guardian to the Hand of the Cause Corinne True when she visited Haifa on her final pilgrimage at the age of 89. On the last night of her visit the Guardian said he had a present for her. "This is a billfold which 'Abdu'l-Bahá carried when He was in America", he said in giving it to her, "and I know you will treasure it knowing that it comes from Him." She pressed it to her forehead and tears gathered in her eyes. Then the Guardian said to her, "Open it and see what is in it." Inside, the Guardian had placed a gold coin that had belonged to the Master. He urged her to look at the date on the coin. It was 1907, the date of her first pilgrimage to 'Akká. Leroy marveled that with all that was weighing on the Guardian he had found the time to think of that billfold, to find that coin, to remember the date of that visit.

Another instance among the many which Leroy witnessed occurred during the pilgrimage of a member of the National Spiritual Assembly of Canada. She spoke to the Guardian of their translations for the Eskimo people whom they were trying to reach, and wondered if they might use different similes in some of the references so that the northern peoples, who lived in snow and ice, would have examples familiar to them. When Bahá'u'lláh speaks of the nightingales and the roses could they not refer to the ice flowers which grow in the north? Shoghi Effendi said, "When translating the texts of Bahá'u'lláh, 'Abdu'l-Bahá or the Báb the text must remain the same. But in your explanatory literature you may refer to whatever you wish." On the last night of the pilgrim's visit, the Guardian presented her with a vial of attar of rose made from the roses of Persia which he asked her to use with the members of the National Assembly. Then he drew another vial from his pocket and said: "This is for the Eskimos. When an Eskimo becomes a Bahá'í, anoint him with this, and in that way he may begin to know the roses of Persia about which Bahá'u'lláh wrote." Shoghi Effendi was able to think of such gestures, Leroy said, in the midst of the pressures of his life.

In Leroy's view the most striking characteristic of the Guardian, given the exalted position to which 'Abdu'l-Bahá had raised him, was his profound humility. He never spoke of himself and would deflect praise of himself. When Rafi Mottahedeh was in Haifa on pilgrimage in the late 1940s he attempted in parting to convey to Shoghi Effendi how much the Guardian meant to the Bahá'ís, but the Guardian said simply: "We are all servants of Bahá'u'lláh; I am one of those servants."* Milly Collins remembers how he would "brush aside our adulation and praise, turn everything we wished to shower on him towards the central Figures of the Faith".

The Guardian spoke of the days of the Báb, the days of Bahá'u-'lláh, the days of 'Abdu'l-Bahá, and then – he spoke of the days *after* 'Abdu'l-Bahá. He would never let anyone associate his capacities with those of the Master, and strongly cautioned Leroy one day when he did so. When the Guardian referred to the teaching plans, he never spoke of his part in developing the plans, he never mentioned that they were his plans, rather he spoke of "the tasks which God has given us under the Ten Year Crusade", and he associated himself with the Crusade in concert with his fellow Bahá'ís. He would not allow pictures of himself to be taken or disseminated, he would not permit the Bahá'ís to take note of the date of his birth. In *The Dispensation of Bahá'u'lláh*, he says in referring to the Guardian, ". . . to commemorate any event associated with his life would be tantamount to a departure from those established truths that are enshrined within our beloved Faith."[1]

He never considered himself. Indeed, on his appointment as Guardian of the Cause, he knew with certainty that his life as an individual was over. He knew that he would never lay down his burden as long as he lived. "I was not prepared for what came," he told them in Haifa. "I was overwhelmed when they read the Will of the Master appointing me as the Guardian of the Cause of God. I felt unworthy of it. I wasn't ready for it. I didn't want it . . . that is why I left, that is why I went into the mountains of Switzerland and I fought with myself until I conquered myself, and then I came back and I began my service as Guardian."

* In one of His Tablets, 'Abdu'l-Bahá speaks of the Báb and Bahá'u'lláh, and then affirms: "We are, one and all, servants of their threshold, and stand each as a lowly keeper at their door."(See Shoghi Effendi, *World Order of Bahá'u'lláh*, p. 127.)

"What I have done," he told those around him in Haifa, "you must do, every Bahá'í must do."

The first international survey of the Bahá'í world to appear after the passing of Shoghi Effendi carried this dedication:

To Shoghi Effendi, Guardian of the Bahá'í Faith, this volume is dedicated in love and homage, in pride and sorrow. For thirty-six years of unremitting toil he devoted himself to the establishment of the institutions, the consolidation of the foundations and the translation of the sacred writings and literature of the Bahá'í Faith. He spread its message to 219 new sovereign states, dependencies and major islands. He unified the scattered Bahá'í communities of east and west in one firmly-knit, actively cooperating, dynamic whole. He planted the Banner of Bahá'u'lláh in the farthest reaches of every continent and in the midmost heart of every sea. He subscribed himself, and proved to be, the "true brother" of every Bahá'í.[2]

# CHAPTER THIRTY-THREE

# The Custodians

DURING the five and a half years that separated Shoghi Effendi's death from the election of the Universal House of Justice, Leroy served as one of the nine Custodians of the Faith in Haifa, while at the same time traveling abroad more frequently and for longer periods of time than had been possible during Shoghi Effendi's lifetime when he left only on specific missions.

With the passing of the Guardian, Leroy's tired body began to show its deep weariness. He had momentarily fainted on hearing of the Guardian's death, he developed chest pains almost immediately there-after, and was finally forced to face the worsening condition of his health.

A few months later he went to Europe for medical treatment and stopped in Paris to see his daughter Farrukh. There he recorded a brief, somber talk – no doubt reflective of the mood of the Hands of the Cause – for the attendants at the forthcoming Convention where the first National Spiritual Assembly of France would be elected. He related what had occurred in Haifa when the Hands convened in their first Conclave:

In the Will and Testament of 'Abdu'l-Bahá He has provided that nine Hands of the Cause should be elected by all the Hands of the Cause throughout the world and that these nine should be continuously in the service of the Guardian.

When the twenty-six Hands of the Cause met in the Holy Land after the passing of the Guardian, they consulted very deeply, in a conse-crated manner, with utmost humility, to try to find the pathway which would lead to the unity of the friends throughout the world, and which would ensure the protection, the development and the success of the Ten Year Crusade.

It became evident that the Ten Year Crusade was the mandate of the beloved Guardian to the friends of the world. Therefore it was most logical, and indeed absolutely necessary, that the Hands of the Cause elect that body of nine referred to in the Will of the Master. That is the action which was taken, and the body of the Hands in the Holy Land, now increased to nine, and elected by all of the Hands of the Cause, will be continuously in the service of the beloved Guardian.

It is their hope that they will be helpful to the friends throughout the world in carrying out all the duties and obligations of the Cause and in winning this great and glorious victory which will resound as the greatest spiritual crusade in the history of mankind . . .

The day following Rúḥíyyih Khánum's return to the Holy Land from the funeral in London, the Hands living in Haifa met with and thereafter worked closely with Shoghi Effendi's lawyer, the capable and loyal Dr. Abraham Weinshall. They sought and rapidly received a statement of loyalty to the Custodians from all National Spiritual Assemblies, so that within three weeks they were able to establish with the written approval of the entire Bahá'í World Community, recognition by the State of Israel of their legal position as successors to His Eminence Shoghi Effendi and to receive all properties and accounts to which Shoghi Effendi had had legal title, which were then transferred to them. Leroy went to Jerusalem with a fellow Hand to conclude these transfers and to call on a series of government officials. Bahá'í international lawyer Aziz Navidi was called to Haifa to assist with legal matters, an assistance that was sought (and devotedly given) on many later occasions by the Custodians and the House of Justice.

In addition to the historic Proclamations issued by the Hands of the Cause on November 25th, which defined the new Stewardship of the Faith, two Resolutions were issued. One concerned the operation of the full body of the Hands with the Custodians. The relationship established by the Guardian was maintained, whereby the Hands in the Holy Land acted as the conduit for all information to and from the Hands abroad. The second Resolution set forth the responsibilities of the Custodians (see Appendix 3). A press release in appropriate

language was released, noting for those outside the Bahá'í community
the scope of the work to be undertaken by the nine newly designated
officials.

They were to correspond with Bahá'í National Assemblies on
matters related to the prosecution of the Guardian's teaching plan;
they were to assist National Assemblies in matters involving administrative issues by "citing passages of the Bahá'í sacred literature which
direct the Assemblies to a sound solution"; they were empowered to
"act for the protection of the Faith whenever its teachings or institutions or properties" were assailed by enemies from within or without
the Bahá'í community. They were to administer the many and varied
Bahá'í properties; in the press release this was stated in terms which
honored the Guardian's work: "This body of nine will maintain the
Bahá'í Shrines and Holy Places in 'Akká and Haifa, which His Eminence, the late Shoghi Rabbani, World Head of the Faith, had made
into beauty spots of the Mediterranean area, and continue their
expansion."

Meanwhile the full body of the Hands was to deliberate on the
ways in which the International Bahá'í Council would "evolve through
the successive stages outlined by the Guardian, culminating in the call
to election of the Universal House of Justice . . ." From the start, in
their very first Conclave message, the Hands mentioned the birth of
the Universal House of Justice, and their every effort was focused not
only on accomplishing the goals of the Crusade but on preparing for
the election of the highest legislative body of the Faith. Leroy shortly
turned to Marion Hofman in England, asking her to research the writings of Bahá'u'lláh in English for all references to the House of Justice,
a compilation which she completed and sent to Haifa within four
months of the Guardian's death.

The International Bahá'í Council was now to function under the
direction of the Custodians, who would conduct their relations with
the Israeli Government through the Council, its membership reinforced by the additional Hands assigned to work in Haifa. (It can thus
be seen that all the Custodians could be called upon to assist with the
work of the Council.) Leroy continued as its Secretary-General until
1961 when the Council became an elected body, with the Hands no
longer members, and Charles Wolcott, a newly elected member, was
given this responsibility. During the two year mandate of the elected

Council, Charles accompanied Leroy to meetings with government officials both of the State and of the municipalities of Haifa and 'Akká, with whom Leroy had long-established and close links. Charles said some years later that what impressed him most about Leroy during those years was "his strong and evident desire to protect the Bahá'í Holy Places. I recall vividly his persistence when negotiating about bits of property which would protect the environs of the Shrines, and his uncompromising attitude towards the Covenant-breaking descendants of Bahá'u'lláh who were still living here and causing mischief. Though his health was failing, Leroy's spirit was indomitable. He set an example to follow."

How vivid to the stricken Hands of the Cause were the evidences of the guidance of the Guardian! Not only had he left an instrument, the Chief Stewards, to carry forward his plans, but he had increased the number of Hands shortly before his death through the addition of eight predominantly young members.* As several of the Hands were in poor health the younger members served as fresh recruits for the arduous work which lay ahead and for what proved to be the difficult task of ensuring a quorum of Custodians in Haifa at all times. The Guardian had also planned the holding of five intercontinental conferences in the year 1958. The first was convened within two months of his passing. The Hands recognized with profound gratitude the solace these conferences provided for the believers, rallying points where they could come together, gain inspiration from one another and rededicate themselves to the tasks at hand.

The Hands of the Cause asked Bahá'ís throughout the world to observe a nine month period of mourning for Shoghi Effendi, and to suspend all manner of Bahá'í festivity during that time; the Hands also suspended pilgrimage to the Holy Shrines for one year.

Shortly the work of the Custodians fell into a certain routine. "We meet almost daily to review matters," Leroy wrote to his family, "and we are proceeding very slowly, determined to carry forward all the projects which the Guardian had begun in various parts of the world. . . ." 'Alí-Akbar Furútan, who had moved from Teheran to serve as a Custodian, recalls that "they did each day the same thing, answering letters, consulting. And everyone did everything, no one was made

* All were born in the twentieth century, two after the appointment of Shoghi Effendi as Guardian.

more special or elevated. If something special needed to be done the Hands would assign one of them to do it." Each year in the month of November they held a Conclave bringing together the Hands of the Cause from all parts of the world to review progress made on the teaching plan of the Guardian and to deliberate on the affairs of the Bahá'í world.

The six years ahead (1957-63) were to be a time of back-breaking work, with the Hands crushed under the weight of their immense responsibility and grieving for the lost Shoghi Effendi. Rúḥíyyih Khánum wrote of those years: "It is, I think, impossible for others to understand how hard the Hands in the Holy Land daily worked . . . We could not again pass through even five minutes of the suffering we went through in those years!"[1]

Within a month of Shoghi Effendi's death, Leroy, who was suffering increasing physical pain, consulted a heart specialist in Haifa and on his advice left three months later for treatment at a clinic in Zurich. He had paid little attention the previous year, when he was working on the expulsion of the Covenant-breakers from Bahjí and other vital matters, to the Swiss doctor's warning that he *must* take three months' rest, and the severe strain he was under in Haifa had seriously aggravated his heart condition. Now the pattern evolved that he was to follow for the remainder of his life, faithfully carrying out his obligations while trying to husband his strength, and restlessly seeking in Europe and America treatment that might ameliorate the condition of his damaged heart and give him the strength better to serve.

As every doctor counselled rest, he realized that major changes would have to be made; he must modify his habits to work at a slower pace and to rest between activities. Nonetheless almost everywhere he traveled he gave talks for the Bahá'ís and their friends, gaining spiritual refreshment from his greatest love, the "diffusion of the divine fragrances".* "You can be thankful," he wrote to Marion Hofman in early 1958 while he was still in Haifa, "that you are not here in the Holy Land during these dark days but are out . . . where you can carry forward the creative work of the Faith, which is teaching."

From Switzerland he and Sylvia traveled to England and were taken by the Hofmans for a quiet visit to the grave of Shoghi Effendi. "How wonderful it was to be with you in London," he wrote later to

* Cited by 'Abdu'l-Bahá as one of the two principal duties of the Hands of the Cause.

David, "and to be able to discuss our most important questions with you – and get your clear views of the future development of the Faith. It is apparent that from whatever aspect you look at it, the clearly indicated step now is to arrange for the election of the Universal House of Justice just as quickly as possible. In its wisdom – and under the 'Divine guidance' and 'freed from error'* – it, and it alone, will know what to do. Until then we are just speculating."

They were to be away from the Holy Land for eight months. With the concurrence of the Custodians Leroy went to consult doctors in Chicago where he could rest at the home of his sister Marguerite. But when the news spread that he and Sylvia were to be in America there were many requests for him to speak. He accepted them whenever feasible – meeting with people as he passed through New York and giving talks in Florida, where he rested for several weeks far from the severe winter of Chicago. His effective teaching style was rendered even more potent by his heightened emotional condition since the loss of the Guardian.

In Chicago the doctors' diagnosis, given in late March, was that the main aorta of the heart was hardening due to blockage of the front arteries, and now the body had to open new, smaller arteries to supply the heart with blood; this would occur if proper care were taken. They prescribed six months of total rest and avoidance of stress and strain for two or three years. It was the first complete and understandable diagnosis he had received and it was very difficult news to accept, given the weight on the Hands of the Stewardship of the Faith, and the fact that he was to represent Shoghi Effendi in September at the Intercontinental Conference in Indonesia on the other side of the earth. The Hands in the Holy Land advised him to follow the doctors' orders strictly "to assure your being able to fulfill the mission the beloved Guardian gave you . . . we feel that everything else should be subordinated to the carrying out of this most important assignment". Leroy wrote to them in return, "I wish you to know that I will very definitely fulfill the mission given me by the beloved Guardian . . . Regardless of what may happen to my health, I will attend as his representative and carry out whatever functions may be required of me." He remembered the line that he had chosen as the basis of his talk at the high school Declamation Contest: "I am here by command of now

* Specific promises made by Bahá'u'lláh concerning the House of Justice.

silent lips." Every other task given him by Shoghi Effendi he had completed before leaving Haifa and now *nothing* would prevent him from carrying out the Guardian's last assignment.

He accepted to rest; indeed, he longed to rest. He felt a deep pervasive fatigue. But as Sylvia commented, it was difficult for someone with his active mind to do nothing. She had brought with them the small German dictating machine Milly Collins had given him in the hope that he would record some of the stories of Haifa. Alas, it was little used. He kept in close contact with the work of the Custodians and maintained his large correspondence. With the September mission on his mind, he exchanged a series of letters with the Bahá'ís in Djakarta who were organizing the conference, urging them lovingly but firmly to move ahead rapidly so as to ensure the success of the historic occasion.

As the time for the annual Convention drew near, the U.S. National Spiritual Assembly asked him to attend one of its sessions, which he agreed to do. He chose to speak about the teaching work in America and the urgent needs of the "home front", where there remained one hundred and twenty-five new Assemblies to be formed within five years if the goals of the Crusade were to be met. "Teaching on the home front", he said, "was always on the Guardian's mind, even when the major emphasis was on dispersal." Charles Wolcott, chairman of the National Assembly, warned the attendants that the hardest objectives were still ahead, echoing Leroy's answer in 1953 when the Guardian asked those in Haifa what they thought would be most difficult to accomplish in the Crusade, and Leroy said, the "drudgery" of working in the obscurity of the home front.

The second Intercontinental Conference called by the Guardian followed immediately upon the Convention. Leroy, who was asked with other Hands of the Cause to participate, spoke at one of the sessions. "The Word of God," he said, "while it might be old, is forever new. The words of the Báb are as if given for this conference. He asked the peoples of the world to leave their homes and travel far and wide to spread the Cause of God. Shoghi Effendi laid down the path and the steps we might take to achieve this. May we in this conference enter into the spirit of the Guardian, who was a driving, dominating force who knew only success, and he will guide our path over the next five years."

One hundred and fifty pioneers serving in goal areas of the

Crusade were introduced, and during the sessions one hundred more arose and offered to resettle as homefront pioneers. When they were all presented to the audience, Leroy was asked to make some closing remarks. He said: "It is with no little emotion that I arise to speak. These holy souls who have arisen to carry the banner of Bahá'u'lláh to so many areas bring vivid memories of the Guardian's happiness and enthusiasm when he received news of the success of the pioneers. Those of us who serve in Haifa think how happy Shoghi Effendi would be with this gathering."

For several months he did little but rest and take short walks. He was able to visit quietly with brothers and sisters whom he had not seen for years and with his daughter Anita, who had returned from Indo-China. She commented that they were wonderful days because "for once there was time to talk". After three months of this regime, however, he became restless and made plans to travel to California to see other family members, in particular Sylvia's family. While there he accepted to speak at his beloved Geyserville school, as well as in San Francisco and Los Angeles. Large numbers came out to hear him after these years of separation and on each occasion he spoke to them of Shoghi Effendi and the needs of the plan. Amidst this considerable activity, Sylvia wrote to dear friends whom they could not see: "Roy was not up to very much. The talks he gave were more than the doctors wanted him to do, but they don't know Roy – if he feels the urge to do something for the Cause, his own health is secondary." He stopped in Wilmette on the return trip to Haifa, where Bahá'ís filled Foundation Hall of the Temple to hear him speak of Shoghi Effendi and the Guardianship, and of the work at the World Centre. It was a lengthy and rich talk in which he reminisced and shared his inner thoughts with this community of believers who had been his friends and colleagues of many a spiritual struggle in former years.

He and Sylvia then left for Haifa, to spend a brief week preparing for the trip to Djakarta. Leroy consulted his heart specialist there who disapproved of his going to Indonesia, but Leroy told him he *was* indeed going and what he needed from the doctor was his help to do so. Though quite upset at Leroy's insistence, the doctor finally agreed on condition that Leroy take a sleeper all the way; from Athens it would be a thirty-hour flight. A day or two before leaving, Sylvia and he went to the Shrines and prayed to Bahá'u'lláh that his health might improve and he be given the strength to fulfill his mission. While they were praying, Leroy said he felt a strengthening of his heart: ". . . I could physically feel something happening in my heart and I have been much stronger since; I only hope it is a permanent cure." But he was never to have good health again, only a slow diminution in the seven years that remained to him.

Leaving from Haifa with Leroy and Sylvia was Hand of the Cause Abu'l-Qásim Faizi; at Athens two Bahá'ís from Turkey boarded, at Abadan twenty-one from Persia, in Karachi ten more, including four from Arabia; finally there were thirty-six Bahá'ís on the plane. The Conference was to open the day after their arrival in Djakarta.

During their flight the Indonesian Government revoked the permit for the Conference. The Regional Spiritual Assembly and the Hands of the Cause who had already gathered in Djakarta asked Jamshed Fozdar* to break the news to Leroy. He recalled: "I went to greet him at the ramp and knowing of his heart condition, told him in a casual manner that we were having difficulties holding the Conference in Indonesia due to the political situation. Instead of appearing crestfallen he grasped the matter at once and became like a general in command, planning the next move for the forces of Bahá to triumph over the crisis that had been created."

Though they pursued the matter further, calling on the Prime Minister, Foreign Minister and Minister of Religion, nothing could be done. In an unexpected way the revocation of the permit had a positive effect on the future of the Faith in Indonesia for it lifted the Faith out of obscurity, causing authorities at every level to be aware of its existence. When the Conference convened in Singapore Leroy noted in his opening remarks that there were now three countries where the Faith was known to all echelons of government: Iran, Israel and Indonesia, all, curiously, beginning with the letter "I". The iteration of the letter reminded Leroy of the answer of the Báb when asked by the Persian authorities who He claimed to be: "*I am, I am, I am the Promised One! I am the One Whose name you have for a thousand years invoked . . .*"

The crisis also proved of benefit to the indigenous Bahá'ís of both Indonesia and Malaysia. At the time it was not possible for Malaysian Bahá'ís to obtain visas for Indonesia and the transfer of the Confer-

---

* A member of the outstanding Fozdar family originally of Bombay, and a vigorous pioneer who left his mark in the pioneering field, particularly in Vietnam.

ence to Singapore permitted them to attend. In Djakarta, where three hundred Bahá'ís had poured into the capital from all parts of the archipelago expecting to attend the Conference, the two days spent making representation to the Government permitted them to have in effect a two-day conference just for themselves. The ten Hands of the Cause in Djakarta showered them with love in a much more personal way than would have been possible at a large conference, meeting with them in small groups, Enoch Olinga in particular spending many hours with them. Leroy spoke with them of the Guardian and the great teaching plan which he had given the believers. Some said they had seen pictures of Leroy embracing the African believers in Kampala and they wanted to see for themselves the oneness of mankind. The local Bahá'ís had opened their homes and their national center to house them, and all during the day they brought friends from different parts of the world to meet them.

A room of the Ḥaẓíratu'l-Quds had been quickly emptied and arranged with banks of flowers. There the indigenous believers were invited to view the portrait of Bahá'u'lláh which Leroy had brought from the Holy Land, and each received a few petals from the Holy Shrines. Leroy wrote in his report on the Conference that it was "wonderful and inspiring to see their veneration of Bahá'u'lláh". They went back, Leroy commented, very happy and eager to teach their people at home, accepting as their sacrifice for the Cause that they could not attend the Conference. But, he said, the most important aspect of the Conference, which was to transmit the spirit of the Faith to the indigenous believers, had been accomplished in spite of the Government's abrupt action.

It was decided to convene the Conference in Singapore, and Leroy, together with eight Hands of the Cause, left with the remaining visitors for that city. The Fozdar family had gone ahead with a few others and miraculously made all arrangements for living accommodations and the use of Victoria Memorial Hall. A banner had been extended the length of the building's facade proclaiming the Bahá'í Conference, a banner seen by the Mayor of Djakarta when he arrived in Singapore on an official visit, while his own city was deprived of the bounty of hosting the followers of Bahá'u'lláh.

"Our host at this Conference," Leroy said in his opening remarks, "is Shoghi Effendi himself." He pointed out that this South-East Asian

Conference was unique, because for the first time in Bahá'í history believers of the brown race had gathered together in large numbers. It was distinguished also by having representatives of more races and religious traditions than any previous Conference and "this very gathering together of all the races and religions has fulfilled the precondition for the appearance of the Universal House of Justice".

Leroy spoke movingly and at length of the life and work of Shoghi Effendi, bringing a keen awareness and love of the Guardian to those present. There were many new Asian Bahá'ís in the audience, one of whom, Ho-San Leong of Malacca, left his impressions of Leroy:

There was a very large gathering [at the home of Mrs. George Lee, an early Bahá'í of Singapore, who opened her estate for the use of the Bahá'ís during the Conference] to celebrate the Nineteen Day Feast. I was standing close to the main entrance of the very large room when Mr. Ioas and several of the friends walked in. He turned to me, extended his hand in a firm manner, and said "I am Leroy Ioas and I am from the Holy Land", in such a natural style, warm and friendly. I shook his hand and introduced myself as a new Bahá'í from Malaysia. I had no idea then who he was or what he was doing in the Holy Land . . . He gave the keynote address on the work of the beloved Guardian spanning thirty-six years. The talk was so powerful and with every word and sentence you could sense his great love and devotion to the Guardian. I don't believe there was a dry eye in the audience when he ended. Young and inexperienced as we were, we were taken to new heights of belief and vision of the greatness of this faith of ours, and that we had indeed joined a religion that would one day unite all mankind on this planet. We also saw a glimpse of the services and dedication of those great and self-effacing souls who labored day and night to bring joy and happiness to the Guardian . . .

He was a giant on the stage. He spoke in a powerful voice and in a flowing style, and I do not recall him talking about his achievements, only the achievements and victories that were won, one by one and so painstakingly, by the beloved Guardian. We knew so little then of the Guardian and his mission on earth, but Mr. Ioas in the course of his masterful talk described the Guardian in such vivid detail, it was almost as if Shoghi Effendi was present himself that day in spirit. And he gave us such a vision of the Holy Land . . . In the course of the conference we soon learned who Mr. Ioas was and of his selfless work in the service of the Faith.

The Conference in Djakarta/Singapore was highly significant for Leroy, not only because it was the Guardian's last assignment to him, but because it was his first contact with the Bahá'ís of the Asian region. He knew of the teaching efforts of these comparatively new believers but he knew little of their deep understanding of the Faith or of their attachment to it. Not once but many times after the Conference he remarked that no matter what might happen to the world in future, "these people will be out teaching the Faith". He felt certain that this area of the world would produce heroes and leaders for the Faith. It was an altogether comforting experience for him.

Hand of the Cause Abu'l-Qásim Faizi wrote to a fellow Hand that Leroy, as the Guardian's representative, was "so much surrounded by love" that Faizi believed it improved his health. "He made everyone in the Conference happy. He embraced the Knights of Bahá'u'lláh, hugged the volunteers, cheered the hearts of those who pioneered under terrible conditions, visited the land offered for the Ḥaẓíra, prayed at the grave of the friends in the Bahá'í burial ground, visited the Afnáns who were at the Conference, and then the night before he left, told me: 'That is all. My job is finished.' I told him, No, you must be ready now for your work as a Hand of the Cause in Asia and America and everywhere."

Sylvia commented later that "Leroy was just wonderful. God granted him the strength he needed each day, and he has come through it, tired but very happy. We all felt the Guardian's great spirit with us at all times."

It is fitting, Leroy said in one of his talks at the Conference, that this be the final Conference, because it has brought together the last great group of the world's population and now "all races have become members of the Bahá'í Faith". The Custodians wrote in their message to the Conference: "It is significant to ponder that the first, the opening Conference of this half-way point of the World Crusade, was chosen [by the Guardian] for the heart of Africa, and that the last, the closing Conference, was set midway in the Pacific-Asian region. He did not thus honor the old world and the new. No, he chose the black people and the brown people for this distinction. He visualized the African and the Pacific peoples vying with each other in the spread of the Faith. Each marked increase in membership in one region was relayed by him to the other, with the hope of stimulating a fresh burst of enthusiastic teaching efforts. Much of his joy, during the last years of his life, came from the news of the remarkable progress the Faith was making in these two areas.*

"Who knows", the Custodians continued, "perhaps it is the immediate destiny of our great Faith to be raised on the two wings of the black and brown races through a great wave of mass conversion . . ."[2] When this was read, the faces of the native Bahá'ís turned with the pride and joy of spiritual camaraderie toward the Hand of the Cause Enoch Olinga who represented for them all their brothers in Africa.

The Conference ended in late afternoon with a few words from each of the Hands of the Cause, then as everyone sat in silence, a wreath was laid on behalf of those present at the grave of Shoghi Effendi in London.

With the Conference ended, Leroy and Sylvia made plans to fly to South Africa to rest in Swaziland at the home of their old friends, John and Valera Allen. While waiting in Singapore for their flight, Leroy wrote a ten page handwritten report to the Hands of the Faith in the Holy Land, carefully detailing what had happened to the only Intercontinental Conference that was to have been held in a Muslim country.

The Hands cabled him in Swaziland: "Deeply appreciate conference report. News received here reflects inspiration you conveyed friends outstanding success your mission behalf beloved Guardian."

It was a month of rest for Leroy, filled with satisfying teaching work. "Our visit to South Africa", he later wrote to Eunice Braun in America, "did us great good, as there is so much spiritual vitality there – especially in Swaziland, where the Cause is expanding wonderfully. If something like this could happen in America, the entire continent would be changed."

On the last day of their visit, Leroy arranged an appropriate setting in the Allen's home and then brought out the portrait of Bahá'u'lláh which he was carrying back to Haifa. Valera later wrote to him: I am sure you know just how much that last hour spent in our home meant

---

* It is interesting to note that the first countries to seek consultation with the Universal House of Justice are situated in the Pacific area: the Cook Islands, the Marshall Islands, and Papua New Guinea, whose Deputy Prime Minister wished to consult "on the future role of Papua New Guinea as an emerging nation and on the destiny of the Pacific region".

to us . . . we shall never forget it, and in every way possible we hope we can bring to the Swazi people the spirit of that moment.

The pace of work for the Hands of the Cause – and the Custodians – never slackened. The second Conclave took place in November 1958, an excellent meeting, Leroy said, during which further plans were made for implementing the provisions of the teaching plan. The dramatic news to emerge from the Conclave was the doubling in enrollment among the black and brown races since the previous year, "a triumph which alone would have brought infinite joy to [Shoghi Effendi's] heart". The Hands met once or twice each day and then dealt with the work arising from the meetings, a very full schedule for Leroy but he coped well. It was decided that his health required some modification in their living conditions: an air-cooled bedroom was added to their rooms at the back of the Pilgrim House and a small kitchen and bath made from the former bedroom. The privacy and the possibility of eating upstairs when they were not with the pilgrims or with the Hands permitted him to conserve his energy.

The Hands noted during the second Conclave that progress in achieving the goals of the plan was not sufficiently rapid – three hundred and ninety-four local Assemblies and thirty-eight National Assemblies remained to be formed – and the Bahá'ís needed more encouragement in their teaching efforts. The Hands decided it was imperative that they and their Auxiliary Board members greatly increase their travels, in spite of the general shortage of funds due to the demands placed on Bahá'í monies by the construction of three Houses of Worship.*

"The work has been pressing", the Custodians wrote in a letter to their fellow Hands some months after the Conclave, "and we try very hard not only to keep abreast of current problems and correspondence, but to do creative work, in the spirit of the decisions which we all made last November during our second Conclave . . ."[3] The Hands abroad increased their travels. Ugo Giachery undertook a lengthy trip through Central America; Hermann Grossmann made the first of several far-ranging visits to South America; Enoch Olinga was traveling extensively in West Africa as well as in New Zealand, where a Maori chief asked that a "distinguished Bahá'í" visit their closed area to tell them more of the Bahá'í teachings; William Sears moved to

* Subscriptions to their construction came from all quarters of the Bahá'í world.

North America to assist in the work there; John Robarts retired from business to devote his full time to the work in Africa. A blow to the work that year was the heart attacks suffered by the Hands of the Cause Horace Holley and Adelbert Mühlschlegel, which considerably curtailed their activities.

The third Conclave, in November of 1959, brought decisions of truly historic import. "We had a very wonderful Conclave", Leroy wrote to Zikrullah Khadem who could not attend, "even though it was fraught with many difficulties and was very exhausting. Never in the history of religion were so many important decisions taken, so rapidly and with such unified action. As we look back, we see that history was made."

"They were such strenuous meetings," Sylvia wrote to her daughters, "continuing steadily for thirteen days, so very much to decide and worrying whether they were doing the right thing – but with going to the Shrine of Bahá'u'lláh each morning before meetings and again after lunch, the Hands were surely guided. Great and momentous things have come from this Conclave, as you will see."

At the close of the Conclave, the Hands issued a statement from the Mansion of Bahjí "to the Bahá'ís of East and West". They announced the historic news that a convention was to be held in the Holy Land during the first three days of Riḍván 1963 for the purpose of electing the Universal House of Justice, which the Guardian said "posterity will come to regard as the last refuge of a tottering civilization".[4]

The Hands of the Cause were fully aware, as Leroy often said, that the guidance of the Guardian would continue throughout the period of his Ten Year Crusade. But then they had to consider what steps should be taken to "bring divine guidance back into the Bahá'í world". As two institutions were promised divine guidance in the Writings, the Guardianship and the Universal House of Justice, the logical decision was to elect the House of Justice. This is what the Hands of the Cause voted to do.

"The interesting thing," Leroy said, "is that when 'Abdu'l-Bahá passed away, Shoghi Effendi thought the Master in His Will might have given him the honor of convening the congress to elect the House of Justice. We know that the only world congress ever convoked is the one called by the Guardian for Baghdad in 1963, and the decision has now been made to elect the Universal House of Justice at that time.

*Leroy in the Ḥaram-i-Aqdas. This picture seems to capture the loneliness of those few who carried tremendous responsibilites in the years of the Custodians*

*Second Conclave of the Hands of the Cause, November 1958*

*Leroy with Sylvia at the Chicago International Conference, May 1958*

*Leroy with his daughter Anita, before returning to Haifa after a long stay in the United States*

*At the Singapore Conference, September 1958. Hand of the Cause Raḥmatu'lláh Muhájir, Daood Toeg, Leroy Ioas, Sylvia Ioas, Iran Muhájir*

*In Abadan, traveling to the Djakarta Interconti-nental Conference, September 1958. Hands of the Cause Valíyu'lláh Varqá, far left; Leroy Ioas, third from left; Abu'l-Qásim Faizi, second from right*

*In Djakarta with Hands of the Cause Agnes Alexander and Collis Featherstone and Mrs. Featherstone*

*Hands of the Cause in Djakarta. From left: Raḥmatu'lláh Muhájir, Collis Featherstone (hidden from view), Valíyu'lláh Varqá, Shu'á'u'lláh 'Ala'í, Zikrullah Khadem, Ṭarázu'lláh Samandarí, Leroy Ioas, Agnes Alexander, Enoch Olinga*

*In front of the Eastern Pilgrim house 1960: Hands of the Cause Jalál Kházeh, Leroy Ioas,*
*Amelia Collins and Ugo Giachery*

The International Bahá'í Council, Bahjí, June 1961.

Left to right: Sylvia Ioas, Charles Wolcott, Jessie Revell, Ethel Revell, Ian Semple, Borrah Kavelin, Lutfullah Hakím, Ali Nakhjavani, Mildred Mottahedeh

*Kensington Central Library, September 8, 1961. Leroy Ioas speaking at the Fiftieth Anniversary celebration of 'Abdu'l-Bahá's visit to England*

*With Marian Anderson at the dedication of the Marian Anderson rose garden, at the Temple in Wilmette*

*Talking with Joan and Ernest Gregory at the Irish Summer School, Mourne Grange, 1961*

*Leroy and Sylvia in Luxembourg, 1962*

*At Summer School in Finland, 1962. Hand of the Cause Adelbert Mühlschlegel is seated on Leroy's left, with Joan Gregory next to him*

Little did the Guardian know as a child, when 'Abdu'l-Bahá would place his hand on Shoghi Effendi's head and call him 'My little house of justice', that he would have the responsibility of rearing that House of Justice. Shoghi Effendi initiated its construction and now we are assisting in putting the dome on the building; the Hands in the Holy Land are only the Stewards carrying out the will of Shoghi Effendi."

The night before anyone in Haifa (other than the Hands) knew of this historic decision, Samíhih Banání, who had accompanied her husband Músá Banání to the meetings, had dreamed of Shoghi Effendi. In her earlier dreams of the Guardian, he had always appeared tired and anxious. But in this dream he was very, very happy. Sylvia and Samíhih felt that this decision of the Hands of the Cause had brought him happiness.

In the message issued at the end of the Conclave, the Hands stated that while nothing in the teachings prevented the Hands of the Cause from serving on the House of Justice, and the Bahá'ís were to vote in the election as they wished, the Hands requested that they not be considered for election, so that they could be free to carry out the work assigned to them by 'Abdu'l-Bahá and the Guardian.

Two years had now passed since the Guardian's death, a tumultuous period during which the Bahá'ís had closed ranks to protect the Faith and had rallied with determination to respond to its needs. The Hands noted in their Conclave message that "a great wave of pioneers, unprecedented since the inception of the Crusade, has arisen and is even now beginning to pour out to those goals most urgently in need of settlers and teachers".[5] But to build the National Spiritual Assemblies called for in the plan, many more settlers were needed to reinforce and strengthen the local communities which would support those Assemblies. To assist in the movement of pioneers, the Hands of the Cause for the first time created a joint deputization fund linking the two strongest communities of the Bahá'í world, Iran and America. The intent was for the Persian Bahá'ís, who had the material resources, to assist the American Bahá'ís, who because of their language and citizenship and greater freedom could more easily enter the difficult unsettled areas.

During the Riḍván period of 1959 four additional National Spiritual Assemblies were elected: those of Turkey, Burma and Austria, and the Regional Assembly of the South Pacific. With these new institu-

tions, there were now thirty-one "pillars" to support the Universal
House of Justice.

The Hand of the Cause Hermann Grossmann, who had lived until
the age of ten in Argentina, was traveling in Latin America as bidden
by the Hands. This was the region where the largest number of new
National Assemblies were to be formed, twenty-one in all. Three times
he criss-crossed the vast area, sending back to Haifa from his first visit
such enthusiastic reports of the fervor of the Latin American believers,
that the Hands chose the year 1961, only one and a half years hence, as
the date for the formation of all the Latin American institutions.

Years earlier, when Hermann Grossmann was a pilgrim in Haifa,
the Guardian asked if he would like to return to South America. He
answered that he had now accustomed himself to life in Germany. The
Guardian smiled and said that perhaps one day he would want to
return. When Dr. Grossmann undertook these lengthy and arduous
teaching trips, it was evident how prescient the Guardian's remark had
been.

A far more difficult goal was the formation of eleven National Spiritual Assemblies on the continent of Europe. This would require four
times as many local Assemblies as existed. In spite of all the teaching
work in Europe and the initial successes, response among Europeans
had always been limited and therefore the growth of the Faith was
slow. These were the highly-developed peoples whom the Guardian
praised but nonetheless described as steeped in tradition, skeptical and
self-satisfied. It was difficult terrain for the Bahá'ís. Yet the Hands of
the Cause set the date of 1962 for the election of eleven National
Assemblies. They were aware that nothing but concerted and sacrificial effort would bring them into being. The members of the new
European Assemblies – as well as all other National Assemblies elected
in 1962 – would be the electors of the Universal House of Justice.

Another milestone was reached in the evolution of Bahá'í institutions with the call for election in 1961 of the International Bahá'í
Council, the final stage foreseen by the Guardian in its development.
The Hands wrote that the elected Council would serve a two year term
of office "and cease to exist on the occasion of the election of the Universal House of Justice".

Shortly after the Conclave, the Custodians requested copies of all
letters written by the Guardian to institutions and to individuals

(Shoghi Effendi kept no copies of his letters) so that all possible guidance coming from his pen would be available in Haifa "now that the time is drawing near for the formation of the Universal House of Justice".[6] All preparations were thus going forward leading to the time when the House of Justice would undertake its work. 'Abdu'l-Bahá had written in a Tablet: "The transcription, collection, arrangement, codification and preservation of the Bahá'í Writings is one of the most essential requirements, the very foundation of legislation and the pivot of the religious undertakings of the Universal House of Justice."[7] The dates for the election of the Universal House of Justice, of the International Council, of thirty-two new National Assemblies, a plan of action to complete the Crusade goals, preparatory work to facilitate the work of the future House of Justice – all this came from the historic third Conclave.

Early in 1960 the Hand of the Cause Ṭarázu'lláh Samandarí began the task of identifying the handwriting of some ten thousand Tablets* gathered at the World Centre. Samandarí knew the writing style of both Bahá'u'lláh and 'Abdu'l-Bahá as well as that of their amanuenses. He spent many months going through them and among other treasures found a letter written to the Shah by the eleven-year old Ḥusayn 'Alí (Bahá'u'lláh) in which He offers to answer any questions the ruler may have.†

A few months later, Leroy and Sylvia were struck with another devastating loss, this one highly personal, that of their elder daughter Farrukh. Her rapidly-fatal illness took them to Washington where she was receiving treatment and they remained at her side, Leroy spending many hours reading to her and quietly talking with her, until her passing two and a half months later; this great sorrow occurred within weeks of the marriage of their younger daughter. And it was followed shortly by the astonishing action of one of the Hands of the Cause, Mason Remey, who announced to the U.S. National Assembly that he was the successor to Shoghi Effendi and asked for its allegiance to him.

This extraordinary claim, based on nothing and inherently preposterous given the stipulations of the Will and Testament of 'Abdu'l-Bahá, nonetheless caused perturbation and had to be dealt

* Letters of Bahá'u'lláh or 'Abdu'l-Bahá, which form part of the body of authoritative teachings.

† Bahá'u'lláh was of a noble family with ties to the Court.

with swiftly. On learning of it in Washington, Leroy immediately sent a cablegram to Haifa and then left for Chicago to consult with the National Assembly. The annual Convention was convening the next day and Leroy and other Hands of the Faith spoke to the delegates each day. A cablegram was received from Haifa calling on the Bahá'ís world-wide to join the Hands of the Cause in "complete repudiation this misguided action".[8]

But this attempt at usurpation of the Guardianship was not to die immediately, as around the one making the baseless claim were several determined men who as the weeks passed orchestrated an extensive campaign to make this claim known to all the Bahá'ís and to the Government of Israel. Abu'l-Qásim Faizi was immediately sent to deal directly with those involved in the defection and was treated by them with rudeness and disdain. He had been given full power by the Custodians to do whatever was necessary, and proceeded to dissolve the National Assembly of France on which several of the defectors sat and to visit all communities of that country.

For three months the Hands of the Cause were preoccupied with this matter, during which time the institutions of the Faith were attacked, they themselves condemned, and materials circulated among the Bahá'ís urging them to withdraw all support from the Hands of the Cause. Despite their patience, it became clear that those persisting in these claims and actions had broken the Covenant of Bahá'u'lláh and the decision was taken to put them out of the Faith. This grievous episode reminded the Bahá'ís of the words of 'Abdu'l-Bahá: ". . . Anyone of the Hands who is firm in the Covenant is the genuine bearer of this title."[9] Leroy recalled what the Guardian had once said to him: When a person violates the Covenant, it is as if a veil is drawn down over him; such people lose their good sense and all sense of value, especially spiritual value.

"How Mason could have been so misled," Leroy wrote to David and Marion Hofman, "I don't know . . . but it shows his insincerity when with the Guardian and explains many things that he did and that occurred, which I did not understand. That one who was so highly honored by the Master and by the Guardian should end his days as the outstanding Covenant-breaker of this period is, alas, altogether too sad. How great is the Cause of Bahá'u'lláh that one of Mason's stature and wide field of service should defect and it have such an insignificant response. It shows how well 'Abdu'l-Bahá and Shoghi Effendi have built the structure of the Faith and how deep is the faith of all the friends. It also shows that one must be firmer than a rock and unto the last breath pray for humility and confirmation."

Leroy and Sylvia remained in the United States for some time, seeking comfort with old friends and family, while visiting many of the Bahá'í communities and lecturing at Geyserville. In late August they left for Haifa, consulting with his doctors on the way and making provision for the disposition of their daughter's possessions in Europe. "We are now en route back to the Holy Land," he wrote to Isobel Sabri, "after a trip fraught with happiness, sorrow and distress, not only from the personal standpoint but from the developments in the Faith. Truly this has been a period of mixed joy and sorrow."

The Conclave of October-November 1960 fell in a period of unusually hot and sultry weather in Haifa. "We met for sixteen days steadily," Leroy wrote to his daughter, "and the weather made it all the more difficult." By that date the Crusade had run three-quarters of its allotted span, with only two and a half years remaining. The Hands meeting in Conclave could report many victories in their message to the Bahá'ís: the world-wide community of believers had weathered another severe test; three thousand pioneers had left their homes since the start of the Crusade, a period of seven years of "truly intense service" to the teaching work; the anticipated entry by troops had begun, as evidenced by the rapid adherence to the Faith of large numbers of native peoples in Africa, in Indonesia and among the Indian populations of South America, notably Incan – some thirty thousand since the start of the Crusade, an astonishing twenty thousand of that number in the three years since the Guardian's passing. "The latest word from India", Leroy wrote in a letter to Jalal Nakhja-vani in Tanganyika, "is that there are about eleven thousand new Bahá'ís, while in Bolivia there are some three thousand Indians, in Malaysia about one thousand, in Vietnam the same. The Guardian had set a goal of five thousand new centers to be opened to the Faith during the Crusade; already there are some eleven thousand."*

* In a talk given in Europe in 1962 Rúḥíyyih Khánum remarked that the Guardian rarely spoke publicly of the total number of Bahá'ís anywhere, unless the figures were truly large. He said to do so is not fair as it belittles the power of the Cause. "It is not a true picture, as we have so much more force than we have numerically" was his comment.

Leroy vividly remembered the Guardian citing this rapid growth as one of the two "dramatic achievements" that would occur during the second half of the Crusade, making it "far more glorious" than the first half. The second was to be an astonishing increase in the number of National Spiritual Assemblies. And this also occurred. At the start of the Crusade there were twelve; in the nine years of the plan, forty-four were added, swelling to fifty-six the number that would elect the Universal House of Justice. "Surely these national bodies were not intended to administer a handful of Bahá'ís," wrote the Custodians. They were obviously being reared so that the "troops" could enter.

Another report from the 1960 Conclave concerned the Temple construction. Two of the three Mashriqu'l-Adhkárs foreseen in the plan (those in Africa and Australia) were to all intents and purposes completed. As for the third, the Hands announced "with particular joy" that the cornerstone of the House of Worship in Europe had finally been laid, an event, they wrote, which terminated seven years of "heart-breaking effort" to secure a property. Leroy was close to this effort, going again and again to Germany to consult with the National Assembly. The Bahá'ís had looked at two hundred pieces of land and opened negotiations on thirty-two of them. But they were thwarted in gaining permission to buy and build. In many instances the local authorities looked with favor on their project, but in some cases agricultural usage blocked purchase and in most cases the churches were strongly opposed. One of the arguments was that with many churches unreconstructed since the war this tiny group of people should not be allowed to build a Temple. Finally in October 1957 a contract was signed for twenty thousand square meters of land near the village of Langenhain in a wooded area thirty-five miles from Frankfurt. In November the Bahá'ís applied for permission to build and it was granted, but Leroy notes that "it remained a very complicated struggle for years". The Hand of the Cause Adelbert Mühlschlegel was constantly monitoring these events and keeping the Custodians informed of developments.

During 1960 the Hands of the Cause suffered a grievous loss with the death of the eminent Horace Holley, a giant even among the Hands, an "immemorial figure" in the development of the administrative order, author (with a Bahá'í lawyer) of the documents which set the pattern for the incorporation of Bahá'í institutions worldwide. He it was who titled the lengthy letters of Shoghi Effendi to the West, drawing from the text some apt phrase (*The Promised Day Is Come, The Goal of a New World Order*) and adding sub-titles to facilitate the study of the text. The Guardian fully approved; indeed, Horace's brilliant creative mind was a source of stimulation and comfort to Shoghi Effendi, who once remarked to a close friend of Horace's: he thinks like me, he acts like me.[10] It was his pen, that of a poet, mystic, and man of action, which wrote the Proclamation of the Hands of the Cause in assuming their Stewardship – the last gift of his talented pen to the Bahá'í Faith and "the finest fruit of his knowledge and understanding of its teachings", as Rúḥíyyih Khánum has described it.[11] Horace, though in frail health, moved to Haifa to serve as a Custodian just six months before his death.

With the rapid growth of the Bahá'í world the Hands were traveling wherever the need was most urgent. Leroy was asked to spend several months in 1961 in Europe, visiting as many centers as possible, consulting with each of the twelve local Assemblies of Switzerland and attending several European summer schools. He was to spend the month of September in Great Britain where his visit would be entirely devoted to assisting the British Bahá'ís in honoring the fiftieth anniversary of 'Abdu'l-Bahá's arrival in London in 1911. It was in London that the Master gave his first address before a western audience.*

In April 1961, during the Riḍván period when Bahá'í elections are held, the largest contingent of National Assemblies ever elected at one time came into being. They were the independent national bodies of Latin America, and pursuant to the policy of Shoghi Effendi, eleven Hands of the Cause were asked to attend the twenty-one Conventions. The Assemblies were all duly formed, even in troubled Cuba. Enoch Olinga was able to enter Cuba to represent the World Centre at the Convention.

The Guardian had foreseen only twenty Assemblies in Latin America, as Leroy pointed out to his sister Marguerite who was pioneering with her husband in Jamaica. But due to the rapid

---

* "Never before in pagan or Christian history had the recognized Head of a World Faith come from the East – where all religions have arisen – to stand before and address a western congregation in public . . . 'Abdu'l-Bahá was appearing for the first time before any audience anywhere. He had never given a public talk or preached a sermon." (Balyuzi, *'Abdu'l-Bahá*, p. 142.)

development of the Faith in Jamaica, the Guardian permitted a National Assembly there, the twenty-first. "Thus", he wrote to her, "the National Assembly – on which you are both serving – should be proud of the blessings bestowed on it and it should cause you to redouble your efforts to spread the Faith in all parts of the island. We have heard from [Hand of the Cause] Ala'i and others of the fine work you are doing and I would not worry", he cautions her, "about small matters of local interest, as after all the job now is to teach, not perfect the administrative machinery of the Faith. I think the west has entirely too much administration." (This was one of Leroy's life-long convictions.)

The election of the International Bahá'í Council took place during this same Riḍván period. Any Bahá'í in the world was eligible for membership on the Council, though the Hands of the Cause asked that they themselves not be considered for membership. The Council would assume the two principal duties given by the Guardian to his appointed Council: maintaining links with State authorities and conducting negotiations on matters of personal status. But they would have many other tasks. They were to be the principal assistants to the Hands; they would deal with land matters that were ongoing or incomplete; they would organize the work of guiding at the Shrine of the Báb – ten thousand people each summer; they were to care for the pilgrims;* they were charged with reading and cataloguing the letters of the Guardian which were flowing in to the World Centre; they were to discharge the financial affairs of the World Centre other than the work of the Hands; they were to issue a periodic Newsletter from the World Centre; they were to assist the Hands in planning the International Convention for the election of the House of Justice and the World Congress that would end the Ten Year Crusade.

It was a prodigious amount of work. Those elected to carry it out were the four persons, not Hands, of the outgoing Council, an honor, Leroy felt, indicating that the friends appreciated the work done by those appointed by the Guardian. The five additional members were

---

* The Council later wrote in a trimestrial report to the Bahá'ís of the world: "From the earliest days the spirit of the Faith has been diffused amongst the believers to no small degree by returning pilgrims. Thousands of Bahá'ís have come to the Holy Land since the days of Bahá'u'lláh . . . and returned to their homes fired with new zeal for sacrifice and service."

Borrah Kavelin, Mildred Mottahedeh and Charles Wolcott of the United States, Ian Semple of England, and Ali Nakhjavani of Kampala, all highly gifted Bahá'ís, three, members of National Assemblies and one, an Auxiliary Board member. Ian Semple was able to move to Haifa immediately, others when they had relinquished their former duties. Mildred Mottahedeh spent two months in Haifa and two in New York throughout the period and served as chairman of the committee preparing for the World Congress in London. Borrah Kavelin was appointed a member-at-large.

The Custodians looked forward eagerly to their coming. "Borrah and Charles will be here soon," Leroy writes to Arthur Dahl in June, "and it will be good to welcome them to the Holy Land. We hope the elected Council will be able to render outstanding service to the Cause, and aid in the administrative work here." There was the question of how to announce this new Council and the first step taken by the Hands was to arrange that the newly-elected Council be presented to the President of Israel and Mrs. Ben-Zvi, who recalled their visit to Shoghi Effendi in 1954, and their meeting with 'Abdu'l-Bahá at Bahjí in 1909.

A message of welcome was sent to the Council from the Hands of the Cause: "We extend to you a most loving welcome on the auspicious occasion of your entering upon your historic services to the Cause of God at the World Centre of the Faith. We hope it will be richly rewarding to you and a source of joy to our beloved Guardian. . . ."[12]

The Council convened for its initial meeting on June 25th when its members accompanied the Hands to the Shrine of Bahá'u'lláh, and then met throughout the day at the Mansion of Bahjí. The meetings continued in Haifa through the first week of July, with morning, afternoon and evening sessions. A room had been set aside for the Council meetings; it was the dining room of the Western Pilgrim House where Shoghi Effendi had met with pilgrims and the members of his appointed Council. The initial meetings consisted of thorough discussions with the Custodians regarding the scope of the Council's work. This new Council will have much more to do, Leroy said, than the old one under the Hands, but less than we had in the days of the Guardian.

With the first series of Council meetings completed and its work initiated, Sylvia and Leroy set off for his program in Europe. He went first for treatment to a clinic outside Frankfurt, on the way visiting the site of the future House of Worship and conferring with the National Assembly concerning the use of the interior space of the Temple. The doctor at Bad Nauheim wished him to remain for three months, but he left after three weeks to begin his urgent work in Europe. He did, however, in the interest of his health, modify the plans made for him in the various countries, declining public speeches at non-Bahá'í venues, as these were tiring without directly contributing to his purpose in traveling in Europe, which was to increase the number of Bahá'ís and new Assemblies preparatory to election less than a year hence of National Assemblies in continental Europe. Leroy insisted, however, on doing more than meeting with Bahá'ís. He wished to hold study classes with new believers and meetings with those interested in the Faith. "Actually", he wrote to the British Assembly, "I am more interested in being helpful in the teaching work than anything else. I do want to meet as many of the Bahá'ís as possible, as you have outlined, but I would not feel I had done much toward winning the goals of the Crusade unless I were to help in the actual teaching work." Afterwards he commented that "they kept us too busy and wore me out. But the work went well and the friends were stimulated to new effort. Furthermore they have had a large number of new Bahá'ís recently, which is excellent news."

At the request of the Italo-Swiss National Assembly and the Hands of the Cause living in Europe, Leroy spent several weeks in Switzerland. Adelbert Mühlschlegel had sent the Hands certain statistics concerning the Bahá'í communities on the continent which revealed a serious problem, one that had arisen in the past and would no doubt arise in the future, that of the balance between building institutions and teaching. Leroy saw immediately that the figures confirmed the Guardian's repeated warning that pioneers must reach the native population or communities would be built on shifting sand.

Leroy met with all twelve local Assemblies in Switzerland and held lengthy consultations with delegates of the National Assembly. Speaking in the name of the Hands of the Cause, Leroy told them: We need one hundred and seventy local Assemblies in Europe. We now have one hundred and fifty-three. If all the American and Persian pioneers left and went home, Europe would be left with only fifty-seven Assemblies. In the Italo-Swiss territory we have twenty-four Assemblies. If all the pioneers left their posts, there would be four Assemblies left. The appeal to you from the Hands of the Faith in the Holy Land, the Custodians of the Cause of God, is to concentrate solely on the teaching work and on reaching the native people.

The purpose of the teacher, he said, is not to perfect an administrative structure but to reach the hearts of the local inhabitants. The pioneers should concentrate on making friends among the people, winning their confidence, and then offering them Bahá'u'lláh's teachings. You have come to teach, he repeated, not to build the administrative order and worry over details and issues which stifle activity; throw out seventy-five per cent of your committees and *teach*. The whole purpose of Bahá'í institutions today and in the foreseeable future is to facilitate the teaching work and what is needed is concentration on the task at hand. The purpose, the Guardian has said, is not the maintenance of Assemblies composed of pioneers, but the emergence of Assemblies formed of native believers.

In a letter of thanks one of the American pioneers wrote to Leroy: ". . . you said exactly the words we needed to hear. It was wonderful, and the loving impact of your presence is still with us . . ." And from a Swiss family who had moved to a new locality to implant the Faith: It was not only an honor but also a blessing that you made this sacrifice to come from so far and give us spirit and power from the Holy Land.

The visit to Switzerland was exhausting. "I am taking as easy an approach to this work as possible," he wrote to the Hands in Haifa, "but traveling back and forth, meeting new people and new groups, talking on the needs of the Faith to the Assemblies, and on the teachings to the attracted people and answering their questions – it is not easy." But two weeks of rest near Geneva followed on, when he had the special joy of meeting his two-month old granddaughter, who had been brought from America so that Sylvia and he could be with her. He told a visiting friend that he greatly valued those days as he knew he would never be able to take walks with her.

Then he left for the month-long commemoration in Great Britain. On the anniversary of the very day of the Master's arrival, September 4th, Leroy took part in the special meeting convened at the Northern Irish summer school to celebrate this historic event; he also spoke at three sessions of the school. On September 6th he spoke at a large commemorative gathering in Edinburgh, noting later what a "fine reaction" there was. On the 8th he was present in London at the national celebration of 'Abdu'l-Bahá's visit, which included a reception, dinner and public meeting at the Kensington Central Library, where he shared the platform with Hasan Balyuzi. Adding to the occasion was the presence of Dr. Lotfullah Hakim, the International Council member who had been with 'Abdu'l-Bahá during the entire period of His visit to England fifty years earlier. It is interesting that in publicity surrounding the commemorations, 'Abdu'l-Bahá was referred to as Sir 'Abdu'l-Bahá Abbas, KBE,* His title by virtue of the knighthood which He accepted from the British Government in Palestine in 1920.

The day after the commemoration in London, Leroy was not well and was forced to rest most of the day. He was taken by David Hofman the next day to visit the grave of the Guardian and the City Temple where 'Abdu'l-Bahá gave His first public talk in the West. (Several times during the month David Hofman saw to it that Leroy had the relaxation of drives and sightseeing as a change from the meetings and hotel rooms.) Then Leroy set off to visit seven other communities in England and South Wales. He met with the Bahá'ís and their friends in Bristol, the only city other than London visited by 'Abdu'l-Bahá during His first sojourn in England. In Cardiff, Wales, a home meeting had been arranged which drew Bahá'ís from other parts of Wales. He then returned to London and, having a free evening, took Sylvia to the theater.

When he met with the National Assembly on the morrow he told them how impressed he was by "the spirit which abounds in the British community of love, unity and devotion to the Cause, and by the dynamic will to teach – to translate that love into action." He told the Assembly that with such determination, "backed by the clear vision they had of what they were doing", the goals of their plan would not only be won but in his opinion easily exceeded. The afternoon of the same day he met with the Bahá'ís of the Southern Area of England at a teaching conference.

The following day Leroy left by train for Leicester and more meetings, then to Sheffield where an afternoon home meeting had been planned and an evening meeting at the City Hall. Sylvia and he were then driven to Manchester, a drive which he remembered with keen pleasure because of the beauty of the countryside, and that evening he spoke at a home where the non-Bahá'í spouse had never before con-

* Knight of the Order of the British Empire.

sented to have a Bahá'í gathering. The next evening he spoke at the Manchester Bahá'í Centre and then took the train to Birmingham and the Sutton Coldfield weekend school north of the city, where he again spoke. Following the weekend school, he and Sylvia were driven back to London.

With so many meetings and the travel involved, he was forced to cut short his stay and was not able to journey to the south coast as he had hoped. "I had become very tired", he wrote to the friends in Torquay, "and my health did not permit my carrying on. Furthermore, I had received word from Haifa that it was desirable that I return to the Holy Land as soon as possible. Thus, after the meetings in the Midlands, I left by air for Haifa."

Joan Gregory, a National Assembly member living in Sheffield, sent off a note to Marion Hofman: I just have to write you these few lines, my heart was so torn to see Mr. Ioas during his stay in Sheffield . . . Do we have to wear out our Hands as we did the beloved Guardian? The great bounty to us all of these visits is inestimable, I know, and perhaps this is the answer . . . The spirit diffused by our beloved visitors during their visit to Sheffield was wonderful, most wonderful. I pray that this last weekend in Sutton Coldfield will not prove too much for them.

"It was a special blessing that you could both be with us during the 50th Anniversary Celebrations," the national secretary wrote to him, "and we all have so many precious memories of your visit that the month of September 1961 will shine in our hearts always . . . The National Assembly is deeply appreciative of all that you did to assist the work on the British home front during your visit. It was a great joy for so many of the friends to be able to meet you, and the spiritual bounties poured out during the wonderful month you were here have resulted in an outpouring of new believers . . ."

David Hofman wrote simply: Your trip here has been a very special blessing to me and Marion as well as to the British community.

The Conclave of the Hands of the Cause in 1961 lasted from October 15 to November 5. It was at this Conclave that the decision was taken to change the venue of the World Congress from Baghdad to London, due to conditions affecting the Cause in the Middle East. The Congress would take place during the last five days of the Riḍván period and because it was in the British capital "every believer who plans to be present on this unique occasion . . . will be able to visit the grave of Shoghi Effendi and offer his prayers there as the last, majestic, glorious, globe-conquering Plan of the Guardian draws to its close."[13] In modifying the Guardian's plan, the Hands were comforted by the knowledge that Shoghi Effendi himself had expressed serious doubt toward the end of his life as to the feasibility of holding the Congress in Baghdad.

Only eighteen months now remained before the end of the Crusade and the promises made by Shoghi Effendi were increasingly evident. The rapid entry of large numbers into the Faith continued; twenty-one new National Assemblies had been elected; and two of the three Houses of Worship were completed. It seemed apparent to Leroy, from the vigor and independence with which the Bahá'ís were carrying the work forward, that the condition of the Bahá'ís themselves had changed. Whereas they had been like children, depending on the Guardian, they had now developed deep wells of confidence and strength.

Yet, as the Hands wrote to the Bahá'ís, there were still important areas where much remained to be done. One was the critical lack of funds, particularly as Bahá'í projects requiring financial support were proliferating everywhere in the world. The Hands had asked the Bahá'ís in the previous year to observe a year of austerity; they now felt it necessary to ask that this be extended throughout the Crusade.

A second concern was the slow growth of local communities in some of the oldest centers of the Bahá'í world: the British Isles, the United States, Canada, Australia and Germany. These long-established communities, the Hands wrote in their Conclave message, were among the twelve honored by having the entire planet "entrusted to their care" at the start of the Crusade. It was unthinkable that they who had contributed so much to the work abroad would not achieve their own internal goals. "There can be no doubt", wrote the Hands, "that if each individual believer in these national communities . . . will rise to higher levels of sacrifice in this hour of great need on the home fronts, the victory will be assured."

Third was the challenge to "bring the teachings to the waiting masses". The Hands of the Cause were in the forefront of this work, giving fully of themselves to accelerate the process. The Guardian had promised that once the spirit of mass conversion was released in the world, its momentum would mysteriously increase and would have wide spiritual repercussions. "May not Africa have ignited Indonesia which fired Bolivia which in turn set ablaze India?", the Hands asked in their Conclave message. "That the Guardian's words have already found fulfillment is evident in the astounding flood of teaching victories achieved this year . . ."

Absent from most of the Conclave gatherings that year was one of the pillars and mentors of Leroy's life, the Hand of the Cause Milly Collins. Already frail, she had suffered a fall in her home in Wilmette and had come to Haifa for the Conclave meetings only with the assistance of a faithful friend. But she could attend only one meeting and that for a few hours, and had to be carried in and out. She was very ill, and shortly had to have night and day nurses and few visitors. But, as Sylvia noted, "one day we think she is going to pass on, the next day she is sitting up and quite cheerful, visiting for short periods of time with the friends". This devoted and capable soul, one of the consolations of the later life of Shoghi Effendi, lived only two more months, and passed away in the afternoon of January 1st. Within the hour everyone had assembled in the Shrine of the Báb to have prayers for her. She was buried at 2 p.m. the following day. Leroy said her passing was a great relief for her; she had been suffering intensely, and she "looked forward so longingly to her reunion with the beloved Guardian". After her death, Rúḥíyyih Khánum commented that "now that corner of the house is silent also".*

In early July 1962, the Hands decided to postpone their annual Conclave, always held in late fall, until April 9th of the next year. The purpose was twofold. The teaching work claimed the full time of the Hands (so that the rapid increase in the number of new believers would not slacken), and funds would be conserved by deferring the meetings, as the Hands would in any event be in Haifa at Riḍván for the election of the Universal House of Justice.

A detailed review was now made of the unfulfilled goals of the plan. It showed the astounding results that had been achieved since the previous Conclave. Other than goals which the Guardian himself felt might not be accomplished during the Crusade, only two remained uncompleted: certain numerical goals within the confines of Australia, and the incorporation of certain of the National Assemblies.

The summer of 1962 found Leroy once more out in the teaching

* Milly Collins had been invited some years earlier to live in the Master's house.

field, visiting Europe with its eleven newly-formed National Assemblies. But first he went again to Germany to consult with the National Assembly on problems concerning the House of Worship. The Hands were extremely anxious about this Temple, hoping the generosity of the Bahá'ís would enable them to finish the building by the end of the Crusade,* if it were still physically possible to do so, and they were hopeful that the exterior could be completed and the interior be in condition to hold celebratory gatherings at the time of the World Congress.

Leroy's doctors in Germany again advised him to rest for several months but there was not time; he compromised by remaining for several weeks under their care. That summer he directed his steps to quite another part of Europe, to the northern countries of Scandinavia and Finland, the latter a country which he loved and a people whose qualities he greatly admired. They are firm and steadfast, he said of the Finnish Bahá'ís, once they become believers they do not waver. He made a teaching tour which included the Finnish summer school in Lahti, meetings with the Finnish National Assembly and meetings in Helsinki and Turku.

In Sweden he visited the communities in Stockholm, Uppsala, Goteborg and Malmö, took part in meetings in Copenhagen and met with the Danish National Assembly, visited Bergen, Stavanger and Hetland in Norway and then participated in the summer school for all the Scandinavian countries, which was held near Hälsingborg in Sweden. At one stretch Sylvia noted that he spoke for nine consecutive nights, in addition to the travel. It was exhausting but they both felt great spiritual response from the Scandinavians. He then dropped down to Luxembourg, where the Bahá'ís were holding their first summer school, in the beautiful medieval town of Echternach. Attending this school, in a country where several California friends were pioneering, took his thoughts back to Geyserville and the start of the first summer school in America.

With his Scandinavian program completed, Leroy pondered whether he should go to America with Sylvia. It was the last critical year of the Crusade and all the Hands felt keenly their responsibility to the work. Nonetheless he decided he would spare two weeks to join

* The German Bahá'ís were greatly encouraged when in the final push toward completing the Temple, the National Assembly of Canada in 1961 contributed one-third of its annual budget to the work.

Sylvia to see their grandson who had been born in late August. During the return trip he wrote to his daughter: You have much to be thankful for; may God ever be with you, bestowing his richest blessings. In a note of congratulations on the birth of the child, Marguerite Sears said: These last few months of the Crusade have given everything a quality of feverish activity – and isn't it thrilling to be living at this time!

The winter months running up to 1963 were particularly demanding, with November meetings of the Custodians (which took the place of the postponed Conclave), the crisis caused by the persecutions in Morocco (which we will shortly consider), the work entailed by the final months of the Crusade, and preparations for the International Convention in Haifa and the World Congress in London.

On November 4th, letters had been sent out to all National Assemblies with ballots for the election of the Universal House of Justice and full instructions as to their use. It was suggested in the letter that the Hands of the Faith be left free to discharge the duties of their own institution, and as has been noted in the history of the period, all such decisions were made only after exhaustive consultation and ardent prayers for guidance.[14]

At the conclusion of the Custodians' meetings in late 1962, they sent a long and powerful message to the Bahá'ís. It was a summation really of the Ten Year Crusade, and it focused attention on the turning point in religious history represented by the year 1963 and the events that would occur at that centennial date. Only six months remain, they wrote, until we mark the "greatest of all Jubilees, related to the year 1335, mentioned by Daniel in the last Chapter of his Book, and associated by 'Abdu'l-Bahá with the world triumph of His Father's Faith". They asked the Bahá'ís to pause and contemplate the magnitude of the event and the Words of Bahá'u'lláh referring to it:

> The Scriptures of past Dispensations celebrate the great Jubilee that must needs greet this most great Day of God. Well is it with him that hath lived to see this Day and hath recognized its station.

They pictured the mysterious workings of the spirit which had enabled the Bahá'ís to reach this centenary "laden with the spoils of untold victories". They recalled Shoghi Effendi's enthusiasm at the achievements of the first half of the decade-long Crusade: "The phenomenal advances made since the inception of this globe-girdling Crusade, in the brief space of less than five years, eclipses . . . in both the number and quality of the feats achieved by its prosecutors, any previous collective enterprise undertaken by the followers of the Faith . . ."

The Custodians then reviewed the accomplishments of the second half of the Crusade. Every territory named by the Guardian (other than a few that were inaccessible) had been opened to the Faith. Numerous supplementary goals had been opened. What the Guardian described as an "unprecedented increase in the number of the avowed supporters of the Faith" had indeed materialized, beyond the imagining of the Bahá'ís themselves. Every week brought to Haifa a new record of enrollments in Africa, the subcontinent of India, the Pacific area and Latin America. The three great Temples had been reared. The "roll call of languages" into which the teachings had been translated, tribal and ethnic groups enlisted in the ranks of the followers of Bahá'u'lláh, all far surpassed the numbers originally given by Shoghi Effendi. Fifty-six National Assemblies were now established whose members would constitute the Electoral College of the Supreme Institution of Bahá'u'lláh's world order.

All such victories, the Guardian had written in a memorable statement at the start of the Crusade, are "the earthly symbols of Bahá'u'lláh's unearthly sovereignty".

This message of the Custodians dwells upon the grandeur of the august body, the Universal House of Justice, to be elected "on the first day of the greatest Bahá'í Festival [Riḍván], in the shadow of the Shrine of the Báb." 'Abdu'l-Bahá wrote in His Will and Testament, "unto this body all things must be referred. It enacteth all ordinances and regulations that are not to be found in the explicit Holy Text." Its decisions would be freed from error, as clearly promised by Bahá'u'lláh: "God will verily inspire them with whatsoever He willeth."[15]

The Guardian's Ten Year Crusade was nearing its end. But little did anyone suspect that it was destined to close with a burst of world-wide publicity on a scale the Faith had never before known. The cause was an act of persecution, sudden and unexpected, which took the name of the Faith into the chancelleries of numerous nations and earned the active condemnation of human rights leaders, thinkers, and dispassionate observers.

It began with the imprisonment in early 1962 of fourteen modest

Bahá'ís in an obscure town in the mountains of northern Morocco. The men, all young and most of them young in the Faith, were jailed on a series of charges such as attacks on public security, but from the start it was evident that the charge against them was that they were Bahá'ís. (It is the first time in our history, Leroy wrote to his friend Mark Tobey, that Bahá'ís have been persecuted by Courts of Law for their religion, so it is exclusively a religious persecution . . .)

For nearly five months the men were held with no guidance from outside and virtually no Bahá'í contact except among themselves. At the same time constant pressure was brought to bear on them to renounce their Faith. But they held firm. Then one day a man appeared who greeted them with "Alláh-u-Abhá"* – he was a Bahá'í lawyer with authority to represent them.

They were eventually brought to trial in December in a manner that made a mockery of judicial procedure. Because the charges were never addressed by the prosecution, and defense witnesses were not permitted to appear, the four capable lawyers defending the Bahá'ís refused to plead any further and withdrew from the court. At the end of the trial, nine were convicted, three of them sentenced to death, five to life imprisonment and another to fifteen years at hard labor. The mother of one of them went to prison to persuade him to give up this Bahá'í religion. She returned home and said: "I did not see my son. I saw an angel, and I want to follow in his footsteps and to give my life for this religion too."

From the outset the Custodians wished to obtain justice for the prisoners with as little publicity as possible. But the incident began to attract press attention (starting notably with an article in *Le Monde* of Paris entitled "Inquisition in Morocco"), and the public within the country became increasingly favorable to the accused.

When the verdict was announced the Custodians opened an office in New York City, in the hotel used by 'Abdu'l-Bahá during His visits, and from there launched much of the work of seeking redress. A White Paper was issued and widely disseminated. National Spiritual Assemblies were asked to obtain all possible publicity for the case and to appeal to Secretary-General U Thant of the United Nations for his intervention. They were asked to request the same assistance from United Nations Associations in every country where they existed.

* God is All Glorious, a greeting often used among Bahá'ís.

Appeals were made to thirty-five United Nations delegations to use their good offices under the Genocide Convention which was accepted as international law. Help was solicited from high officials of the U.S. Government while the British Bahá'ís appealed to the Queen. Unasked, scholars and world leaders took appropriate action.

On January 1st the Custodians asked all national and local Assemblies in the world to address a plea for justice to the ruler of Morocco. Leroy hoped there would be a "veritable avalanche" of petitions.

Ironically, the sentence was handed down shortly after a new Constitution for Morocco, guaranteeing freedom of religion, had been overwhelmingly accepted by referendum. And three days before the trial opened, the Government had voted at the United Nations in favor of a draft convention on the elimination of all forms of religious intolerance.

Leroy wrote to his family that the "terrible inquisition" and sentencing of the Bahá'ís "is bringing more favorable publicity than anything in Bahá'í history and has given rise to many opportunities for intensive teaching. It is one of the miracles," he repeatedly said, "that the fate of thirteen unknown Bahá'ís could cause such world-wide repercussions. It shows how God uses all things to the advantage of the Faith."

At one point it was intimated by the authorities that the prisoners would be granted clemency and be given a royal pardon. The Custodians stated that it was "not in the interests of justice that they be given clemency or a royal pardon", as one cannot be pardoned for a crime one has not committed, and nothing but full exoneration would be acceptable.

Appeal was made to the Supreme Court of the country but the case languished there for almost one year. In the meantime the House of Justice had been elected, and it appealed to the Bahá'ís throughout the world to pray on the Feast day of November 23rd that the case be resolved. As it happened, the Supreme Court shortly thereafter called up the case, reversed the decision, and ordered the accused released. They had been held twenty months in close confinement. On being restored to freedom, each received a letter of love and gratitude from the Universal House of Justice.

In a letter to his daughter concerning the case, Leroy says that he did not intend writing at such length "but we have lived with this day to day, directing the activities all over the world, and it is reassuring to see how the Bahá'ís in every part of the world have arisen in defense of the Faith, as that, in reality, is what is being attacked – not these poor unfortunate victims of their hate. These young men are great heroes whose names will resound in history long after their persecutors are forgotten."

One of the last tasks which the Hands of the Cause set for themselves, as they prepared for the election of the Universal House of Justice, was to work out the schema of a nine year teaching plan to be presented to it for whatever use it might wish to make of the document, which was the distillation of the considered opinion of the Hands as to the needs and strengths of the world community. Much of it was based on the vision of Raḥmatu'lláh Muhájir who had been in the forefront of the mass teaching work.

At the end of the Ten Year Crusade, not all the goals as originally conceived had been won. There remained lands that were closed to settlement; the establishment of a Bahá'í Court in the Holy Land did not materialize (in 1959 the Custodians wrote to assure the believers that every effort would be made to establish such a Court before election of the House of Justice, but "we should bear in mind that the Guardian himself clearly indicated that this goal, due to the strong trend towards the secularization of religious courts in this part of the world, might not be achieved"[16]); the World Congress could not be held in the city chosen by the Guardian as the appropriate setting for the centenary of Bahá'u'lláh's Declaration; and goals in Iran and certain other Middle East countries were not possible of achievement. In a talk as late as 1986, House of Justice member Ali Nakhjavani said: "There are many goals yet to be won in the name of Shoghi Effendi."

The Guardian had promised that the last phase of the Crusade would be more glorious than its opening years, with an unprecedented increase of Bahá'ís and Bahá'í institutions in all parts of the world. All of this happened. An immense outpouring of love for their lost Guardian had expressed itself in the remarkable achievements of the believers during the final years of the Crusade. Repeatedly in his last years the Guardian had said: "The Bahá'ís will be astonished at the victories they will win."

"We do not come empty-handed to our Most Great Jubilee," wrote the Hands of the Cause. "By thousands and tens of thousands they have trooped into the Cause of God; behind them already can be seen the shadowy outlines of the hundreds of thousands and millions who are approaching it, tramping nearer day by day."[17]

The last message from the Custodians to the Bahá'ís of the world followed their Conclave in April 1963. They were laying down their burden and passing the baton to Bahá'u'lláh's Supreme Institution. Their message concerned that Supreme Institution:

HANDS CAUSE GATHERED PRECINCTS MOST HOLY SHRINE URGE ALL BELIEVERS WORLD BAHA'I COMMUNITY EITHER INDIVIDUALLY OR IN GROUPS UNITE HEARTS ARDENT PRAYERS BEGINNING SUNDOWN APRIL TWENTIETH FIRST DAY RIDVAN BESEECH BLESSED BEAUTY INSPIRE GUIDE DELEGATES RAISE UP LONG AWAITED AUGUST INSTITUTION FULFILLING GLORIOUS PROMISES SACRED WRITINGS.[18]

# CHAPTER THIRTY-FOUR

# The Universal House of Justice

ONE century had now elapsed since the days in the garden of Riḍván when Bahá'u'lláh revealed the Mission with which He had been entrusted by God. 'Abdu'l-Bahá had promised that by the end of the first century of Bahá'í history ". . . will the teachings of God be firmly established upon the earth, and the Divine Light shall flood the world from the East even unto the West." On this day, He said, will the faithful rejoice.[1]

Specific prophecies of Bahá'u'lláh in the Tablet of Carmel were shortly to be fulfilled. The Ark of the law of God would be launched on the mountain of God, and the "people of Bahá", as Bahá'u'lláh referred to the Universal House of Justice, would appear.

There were many tired warriors scattered throughout the Bahá'í world, but none had more fully merited their fatigue than the Hands of the Cause, raised up by Shoghi Effendi and left with the awesome task, unsuspected until after his death, of guiding the Bahá'í world to the accomplishment of his global teaching campaign.

For them the immediate future would be a time of great change. The reins of authority were passing to others. They, together with their fellow Bahá'ís, would turn to the Universal House of Justice as the source of guidance for the Bahá'í world.

Let us turn now to the joyous days of late April 1963 when Bahá'ís of all countries were coming to the Holy Land for the election of the Universal House of Justice. Rúḥíyyih Khánum had ordered dozens upon dozens of red roses with which to decorate the Holy Places in 'Akká and in Haifa. Sylvia shared with her daughter the sense of excitement: "The day of the arrival of the delegates has come and we have been registering them in all day. The Frankfurt flight arrives tonight, and tomorrow three of us go to the airport to meet the London flight; by Saturday they should all be here. What a day this is!"

The house of the Master was ready. By removing the twelve doors leading into the reception area there would be room to seat the two hundred and eighty-eight delegates (of five hundred and four electors) who were able to attend the historic event in person. 'Abdu'l-Bahá had once said: "This very hall will witness the election of the House of Justice."² Eighteen tellers, all members of National Assemblies, had been selected. Rúḥíyyih Khánum was to open the proceedings.

The delegates were guests of the World Centre while in the Holy Land, though they defrayed their own travel expenses. Several of the National Assemblies arranged that all their members attend, whether or not each individual had the funds; most others ensured that at least one representative was present. Three national communities could send no one because of travel restrictions.

This sacred event would "cast its holy and protective shadow down through the ages" in the words of the Hands of the Cause. To prepare the electors for their role, the Hands in the Holy Land, when sending out election ballots in November of the previous year, had emphasized the spiritual atmosphere in which those who could not attend must vote. It should be done in the presence of their fellow members: "Because of the sacred nature of this historic occasion, and in order that those voting by mail may also partake of the spiritual atmosphere which surrounds this unique and unprecedented election, we urge each National and Regional Assembly to make every effort to meet together in a body on this occasion; not as a part of a National Assembly session, but as a separate and distinct electoral session for the purpose of casting their ballots for the Universal House of Justice."³

To ensure the sacred atmosphere of the International Convention itself, the delegates were invited to arrive on April 18th and to use the three days before the election in spiritual preparation for their unique responsibility. The Shrines of the Báb and Bahá'u'lláh were closed to the public for five days so that the delegates could pray and meditate there at any hour and as often as they wished. The Hands had carefully scheduled periods of time for the delegates to spend in the Shrines and at the Holy Places. On each of the three evenings, designated groups of delegates – this was the greatest mass pilgrimage ever to have been made to the World Centre – would be taken to the International Archives to view the documents and sacred relics preserved there.

On the morning of April 21 the delegates gathered outside the house of 'Abdu'l-Bahá and silently entered the main hall. At 9:30 Rúhíyyih Khánum briefly welcomed them and explained the procedure to be followed. There were prayers, after which the delegates voted in utter silence. The roll call began by country in alphabetical order, Alaska, Arabia, Argentina, Austria . . . to the last, Venezuela. The Universal House of Justice had been elected.

In the atmosphere of joy and relief that followed, one elector stood alone at the bay window of 'Abdu'l-Bahá's house, looking out to the Bay of Haifa. He felt "a rug was being pulled out from under us" and wondered about the Hands of the Cause. He watched as a car drew up and Sylvia alighted and turned to help Leroy cross the street. Even though the House of Justice was just elected and there was much jubilation he was struck that here the Hands were passing. Leroy looked already on his way to the next world.*

The result of the voting was announced at the close of the next morning's session. It was preceded by prayers in a dozen languages – *Glad Tidings! Glad Tidings!* – and one of the first Incan Bahá'ís read 'Abdu'l-Bahá's words: *O Bahá'u'lláh, what hast Thou done!* Weeping at these words, Rúhíyyih Khánum said, It's unspeakably glorious.

Then the chief teller, quoting the Guardian's well-known words to the Bahá'ís at the start of the second Seven Year Plan, said the tellers were "tired but blissful". They had worked the entire night. The names were then announced of those who had been elected to Bahá'u'lláh's Supreme Institution.

Rúhíyyih Khánum invited the members to the platform and after long and sustained applause she introduced them simply:

Charles Wolcott, an American Bahá'í; Borrah Kavelin, an American Bahá'í of Jewish background; Hugh Chance, an American Bahá'í; Amoz Gibson, an American Bahá'í of both Negro and American Indian background; Hushmand Fatheazam, a Persian Bahá'í; Ali Nakhjavani, a Persian Bahá'í; Lotfullah Hakim, a Persian Bahá'í; David Hofman, a British Bahá'í; Ian Semple, a British Bahá'í of Scottish background. Charles Wolcott said a few words for the group. He

* The elector was Douglas Martin, member of the Canadian National Assembly; twenty-five years later he was himself elected to the House of Justice.

spoke of being "newly-born" and gave the promise: "We will do our best to uphold what Bahá'u'lláh, 'Abdu'l-Bahá and the Guardian have established. God bless you all!"

An intermission in the sessions was called; there was too much emotion and everyone needed to share what he was feeling. John Robarts leaned over to Marion Hofman and said: At *last* God has shown His hand! Leroy told her David's election gave him special pleasure.

On the same day the Hands of the Cause shared the joyous news with all communities of the Bahá'í world:

OCCASION WORLDWIDE CELEBRATIONS MOST GREAT JUBILEE COMMEMORATING CENTENARY ASCENSION BAHA'U'LLAH THRONE HIS SOVEREIGNTY WITH HEARTS OVERFLOWING GRATITUDE HIS UNFAILING PROTECTION OVERFLOWING BOUNTIES JOYOUSLY ANNOUNCE FRIENDS EAST WEST ELECTION SUPREME LEGISLATIVE BODY ORDAINED BY HIM IN HIS MOST HOLY BOOK PROMISED BY HIM RECEIVE HIS INFALLIBLE GUIDANCE STOP MEMBERS FIRST HISTORIC HOUSE JUSTICE DULY ELECTED BY DELEGATES COMPRISING MEMBERS FIFTYSIX NATIONAL ASSEMBLIES ARE CHARLES WOLCOTT ALI NAKHJAVANI BORRAH KAVELIN IAN SEMPLE LOTFULLAH HAKIM DAVID HOFMAN HUGH CHANCE AMOZ GIBSON HUSHMAND FATHEAZAM STOP TO JUBILATION ENTIRE BAHA'I WORLD VICTORIOUS COMPLETION BELOVED GUARDIAN'S UNIQUE CRUSADE NOW ADDED HUMBLE GRATITUDE PROFOUND THANKSGIVING FOLLOWERS BAHA'U'LLAH FOR ELECTION UNIVERSAL HOUSE JUSTICE AUGUST BODY TO WHOM ALL BELIEVERS MUST TURN WHOSE DESTINY IS TO GUIDE UNFOLDMENT HIS EMBRYONIC WORLD ORDER THROUGH ADMINISTRATIVE INSTITUTIONS PRESCRIBED BY BAHA'U'LLAH ELABORATED BY 'ABDU'L-BAHA LABORIOUSLY ERECTED BY SHOGHI EFFENDI AND ENSURE EARLY DAWN GOLDEN AGE FAITH WHEN THE WORD OF THE LORD WILL COVER THE EARTH AS THE WATERS COVER THE SEA.[4]

In a talk which he gave in Washington D.C. a few months later Leroy repeated, as he remembered them, certain words of the Guardian concerning the House of Justice: "When the House of Justice comes into being, there will be a new movement within the Faith, there will be a new movement within society; when that universal body comes into existence all the social principles of the Cause and the drive toward the Lesser Peace will increase in momentum."* This was an event which Bahá'ís knew marked a turning point in history.

* The Lesser Peace is Bahá'u'lláh's reference to a political truce to be concluded by nations

(continued on p.333)

To appreciate the joy felt by the Hands of the Cause at this consummation of their Stewardship one need only compare the photograph taken of them during the first Conclave immediately following the Guardian's death, their faces haunted by the events, with the picture taken on the steps of the Master's house just before the International Convention. Both appear in *The Ministry of the Custodians*. In it they appear tired, but it is a triumphant weariness, and all look serene and profoundly happy. The ship had been steered through the storm to port. It will be an infinite burden removed from our shoulders, Rúḥíyyih Khánum had said in Europe some months earlier.

One of the Bahá'ís of Denmark, Egon Kamming, wrote to Leroy that summer: "When my family and I left the cemetery after the funeral of the Guardian, we saw Rúḥíyyih Khánum and yourself sitting together in a car – how terribly bleak and empty the future must have looked to you then, and how heavy the burden resting on your shoulders . . . the friends can never be grateful enough to the Hands for the wise and courageous leadership afforded them."

Seven thousand Bahá'ís gathered in London for the Jubilee, among them jubilant pioneers and numerous members of the races, tribes and peoples newly brought into the Bahá'í family in the concluding years of the Crusade, the harvest of that global effort. There was a sense of exhilaration and deep thankfulness that the House of Justice, so long promised, had now come into being.

Great themes had been chosen by the Hands of the Cause for the five day program; they rolled out like mighty chords from an organ: The Day of Victory, the Mission of Bahá'u'lláh, The Unfoldment of the Divine Plan, The World Centre of the Faith, The Spiritual Conquest of the Planet. A dozen of the Hands of the Cause took part in the programs, bringing the spirit and presence of the Guardian. The last afternoon was given to remembering "Shoghi Effendi, the Sign of God". Rúḥíyyih Khánum was introduced by William Masetlha of Africa,* a continent where she had traveled extensively and the only continent traversed in its entirety by Shoghi Effendi. As she lengthily

of the world "exhausted by war"; the Most Great Peace is the peace program which He offered to the rulers and ecclesiastical leaders of the world in His messages to them in 1867.

* A member of the first National Assembly of South and West Africa, later a Counsellor for Africa.

and movingly recalled his life and his sacrifice of himself, she suddenly stopped and looked down, overcome with emotion. In the ensuing silence there rose the voices of some of the African believers, softly singing "Alláh-u-Abhá" while she recovered her poise and continued.

On the third day the vast hall was tingling with expectancy. The members of the Universal House of Justice were to be presented to the Bahá'ís. A wave of emotion swept over the audience as they rose to their feet in respect and thanksgiving for this blessed body whose protective shadow would lie over the earth for centuries to come. When silence returned, the House of Justice made its first statement to the Bahá'í world, opening with the majestic tribute to God from the Pen of Bahá'u'lláh Himself: "*All praise, O my God, be to Thee Who art the Source of all glory and majesty, of greatness and honor, of sovereignty and dominion, of loftiness and grace, of awe and power. . . .*"[5]

The House of Justice expressed thanksgiving to Bahá'u'lláh for this historic moment which marked not only the centenary of His Declaration, the fulfillment of Daniel's prophecies and the completion of the first phase of 'Abdu'l-Bahá's Divine Plan but the culmination of the Guardian's world-encircling Crusade. For "he it was, and he alone, who unfolded the potentialities of the widely scattered, numerically small, and largely unorganized Bahá'í community . . . He it was who unfolded the grand design of God's Holy Cause . . . and set the ark of the Cause true on its course . . ."[6]

The House of Justice paid a moving tribute to the Hands of the Cause who it said "share the victory with their beloved commander, he who raised them up and appointed them . . . The Universal House of Justice, with pride and love, records on this supreme occasion its profound admiration for the heroic work which they have accomplished. We do not wish to dwell on the appalling dangers which faced the infant Cause when it was suddenly deprived of our beloved Shoghi Effendi, but rather to acknowledge with all the love and gratitude of our hearts the reality of the sacrifice, the labour, the self-discipline, the superb stewardship of the Hands of the Cause of God. We can think of no more fitting words to express our tribute to these dearly loved and valiant souls than to recall the words of Bahá'u'lláh Himself: "Light and glory, greeting and praise be upon the Hands of His Cause, through whom the light of long-suffering hath shone forth, and the declaration of authority is proven of God, the Powerful, the Mighty, the Independent, and through whom the sea of bestowal hath moved, and the breeze of the favor of God, the Lord of mankind, hath wafted."

Leroy was not there to hear their tribute. He was not to savor this shining moment. Though not feeling well, he had attended the opening session of the Congress and the morning session the next day. But then he was too ill to go on, and had to be hospitalized. When the attendants came that evening with a stretcher and asked for the patient, Anita and Sylvia indicated Leroy, pale and leaning heavily against the door jamb, but determined to maintain his dignity and walk through the hotel lobby, crowded with Bahá'ís, to the ambulance.

He had developed what was diagnosed as a fatal pneumonia.

He was to have spoken the next day at the World Congress on a subject dear to his heart: "The Unparalleled Achievements under the Guidance of Shoghi Effendi." Ian Semple, who was announced in his place, pointed out to the startled Bahá'ís "how Leroy's illness brings home the tremendous sacrifices of the Hands of the Cause in recent years. Those on the Council [as Ian Semple had been] also testify to the complete self-sacrifice of the Hands in the Holy Land."

Leroy's life was spared. Was it the prayers of the seven thousand Bahá'ís? Bahá'u'lláh tells us that "*the decree that is impending*" is such that prayer and entreaty can succeed in averting it. When recovery seemed certain a large bouquet of flowers arrived at the hospital with a note: "Beloved friend: The Universal House of Justice was deeply distressed to learn of your illness which deprived you of the bounty of being present at most of the sessions of the World Congress, and it is with relief that we now hear that your condition is improving. We have prayed for a steady recovery so that you may soon resume your labours in the service of the Cause of God . . ."

After several weeks in the hospital, Leroy and Sylvia moved to a small hotel in London so that the doctors could monitor his progress, and he sent a Bahá'í book (*The Renewal of Civilization*) to both the house physician and the cardiologist of the London clinic, who had both inquired about the teachings of the Faith. Leroy was eager to have news of the Congress and Sylvia read him the clippings lovingly gathered by the English friends so that he might have some share in the great event.

I did so much miss the Congress and being with the friends, he wrote to Eunice and Leonard Braun from his convalescence at Bad Nauheim in Germany. But that, he adds with a tone of resignation, is the way of life . . . It was a great climax to ten years of urgent and dramatic effort on everyone's part. It has also given everyone the experience of realizing how universal the Faith is – how it has united so many different peoples of varied backgrounds. The Faith is the only true laboratory of world peace that exists in the world.

In Germany his long-time doctor talked very seriously with Sylvia about his illness. You know, he said, it is literally a miracle that he has come through this – the amount of antibiotics, along with his heart condition and his age – really it is nothing I nor any doctor have done – I tell you it is from a power greater than we are!

While the Hands of the Cause were together in London they met to agree on how they would now operate. They agreed that five Hands of the Cause would live in Haifa to coordinate the international work of the Hands. (During the life of the Guardian five had been associated with the work in the Holy Land.) The five chosen for this were Rúḥíyyih Khánum, 'Alí-Akbar Furútan, Paul Haney, Abu'l-Qásim Faizi and Leroy. In a brief cablegram which they sent to the annual Conventions, they expressed their "loving appreciation heroic dedicated efforts friends everywhere", and said they now wished to return to their own work: "Entire body Hands desirous devote all their efforts protection propagation Faith according functions laid down Holy Texts."[7]

The House of Justice had begun its work already in Haifa, meeting immediately after the announcement of its membership, and held further meetings in London. Its first statement to the Bahá'í world was the brief message crafted for presentation at the World Congress. Then came a message which was sent from London to the Annual Conventions throughout the world.[8] In this lengthy message the Bahá'ís had their first glimpse of the style and direction of the House of Justice.

The great Jubilee in London, the message said, was permeated with a "spirit of such bliss" as could only have been engendered by the outpourings of God. The believers had gained a "heightened awareness of the true and real brotherhood of the human race". The message reaffirmed the tribute made at the World Congress to the Hands of the Cause, "those precious souls who have brought the Cause safely to victory in the name of Shoghi Effendi".

The message informed the Bahá'ís of the initiation of the work of the House of Justice and the arrangements made for establishing the institution in Haifa. It was to have no officers and its communications would be signed UNIVERSAL HOUSE OF JUSTICE over an embossed seal. It stated that the House of Justice would examine, in close consultation with the Hands of the Cause, "the vast range of Bahá'í activity" with the view to preparing a detailed plan of expansion for the whole Bahá'í community, to be launched at Riḍván 1964. Thus the House of Justice within weeks of its election already had in mind plans for the further development of the Faith and gave an immediate objective to the Bahá'ís: "The high intensity of teaching activity reached at the end of the World Crusade . . . must now be increased as the friends everywhere draw on the vast spiritual powers released as a result of the celebration of the Most Great Jubilee and the emergence of the Universal House of Justice."

The Bahá'ís are entering a new epoch in Bahá'í history, wrote the House of Justice: "blessed beyond compare, riding the crest of a great wave of victory produced for us by our beloved Guardian. The Cause of God is now firmly rooted in the world. Forward then, confident in the power and protection of the Lord of Hosts, Who will, through storm and trial, toil and jubilee, use His devoted followers to bring to a despairing humanity the life-giving waters of His supreme Revelation." Confidence, certainty, decisiveness, assurance of divine protection – all are revealed in this first directive to the Bahá'í world from its supreme body.

Three weeks later a brief message came from the House of Justice, the first to issue from its seat in Haifa. Two decisions had been reached which would affect pilgrimage to the Holy Places. As the offices used by the International Bahá'í Council (several rooms in the Western Pilgrim House) were inadequate to the work of the House of Justice, it had decided to take over the entire building at No. 10 Haparsim Street and to terminate all other uses of the building. The pilgrims would henceforth be housed together in one place (as had been anticipated by the Guardian) on Bahá'í property near the Shrine of the Báb.

The Pilgrim House had been Leroy and Sylvia's home for eleven years, so that when Leroy was well enough to return to Haifa one of their first tasks was to find new accommodations. This they did over a period of time and were never rushed in the process.

The Universal House of Justice met for two full days in late May with the Hands living in the Holy Land, after which it wrote to them: "We have been grateful for the consultations we were able to have with you over the past two days, and look forward to others in the coming weeks as the process of our taking over the administrative work of the Cause progresses."

Ten days later, on June 7th, after lengthy discussions between the two institutions concerning the "functions, rights and powers" vested in the Custodians, the House of Justice informed the Hands of the Cause of its decision "that the office of Custodians of the Bahá'í World Faith ceases to exist upon your receipt of this communication". The same day the Hands in the Holy Land drew up a Declaration releasing to the House of Justice all those functions, rights and powers, assumed by them on November 25, 1957, and informing the full body of the Hands of the action they had taken. The period of the Custodians was formally ended.[9]

In a letter to a National Assembly in 1965, the House of Justice wrote of that six year period: "The entire history of religion shows no comparable record of such strict self-discipline, such absolute loyalty, and such complete self-abnegation by the leaders of a religion finding themselves suddenly deprived of their divinely inspired guide. The debt of gratitude which mankind for generations, nay, ages to come, owes to this handful of grief-stricken, steadfast, heroic souls is beyond estimation."[10]

Formal notification was immediately sent by the Hands in the Holy Land to the Government of Israel of the election of the Universal House of Justice, which shortly took steps to strengthen its position with the Government. Still another legal document was drawn up designating the members of the Universal House of Justice as the "members and managers" of the eleven Israel Branches of the National Spiritual Assemblies.

At least once a week the House of Justice met at 10 Haparsim Street with the Hands in the Holy Land to discuss the transition and the relationship between the two institutions and their relation with other institutions of the Bahá'í world. The Universal House of Justice saw the role of the Hands of the Cause as entirely spiritual and took over from them such matters as communication with National Assemblies and the international fund. Many adjustments in working patterns

*Hands of the Cause of God on the steps of the Master's House just before the International Convention, April 1963.*

*". . . they share the victory with their beloved commander, he who raised them up and appointed them. They kept the ship on its course and brought it safe to port. . . . [we] acknowledge with all the love and gratitude of our hearts the reality of the sacrifice, the labour, the self-discipline, the superb stewardship of the Hands of the Cause of God."*

*(The Universal House of Justice, in its first message read to the participants at the First Bahá'í World Congress, May 1963)*

*Top: Leroy with his first granddaughter Catherine; below: Leroy and Sylvia on the balcony of their Haifa apartment*

*Last portraits, taken in
Spring 1964*

*Conclave of the Hands of the Cause of God, October 1964, Bahjí: The Universal House of Justice and the Hands of the Cause of God*

were called for by these decisions. While the House of Justice was constantly seeking the wisdom of the Hands on all these issues and the ramifications arising from them, it was now the Head of the Faith, and made all decisions not directly within the purview of the Hands of the Cause.*

Leroy often spoke of his fascination in watching these young men (the average age of the members was below fifty; he was then sixty-seven), some of them without the lengthy administrative experience of "us older folks", yet who went forward with the utmost assurance. "They make decisions, often of the greatest import, rapidly; they have a definite, positive, almost aggressive manner in approaching all these questions. It augurs well for the future and the unity of the Cause; it is a body in which the Bahá'ís can put all their confidence." As he wrote to his friends Ruth and Bishop Brown in South Africa: "The House of Justice will bring the Faith to everlasting glory!"†

In the dark winter of 1957, there was one issue which the Hands knew they could never resolve. It was the question of the Guardianship. In several lengthy messages to the Bahá'ís they therefore discouraged any speculation on the subject and encouraged the Bahá'ís to put their energies into completing the Crusade. They said the House of Justice in its wisdom would resolve the issue.

Six months into its tenure, the House of Justice did so. The members went to Bahjí and would not leave until they had resolved the question of the Guardianship. They spent one week there. On October 6, 1963, a cablegram was sent to the Bahá'ís of the world:

AFTER PRAYERFUL AND CAREFUL STUDY OF THE HOLY TEXTS BEARING UPON
THE QUESTION OF THE APPOINTMENT OF THE SUCCESSOR TO SHOGHI EFFENDI

---

* An instance of the guidance under which the House of Justice worked was seen by Leroy in one of the goals in its first teaching plan, formation of a National Spiritual Assembly in the Hawaiian Islands. He told the House of Justice of the many letters he had written in which the Guardian advised the Hawaiian Bahá'ís that if they achieved a certain number of Bahá'ís and local Assemblies, he would let them elect a National Assembly. The House of Justice, not knowing of this exchange, was now carrying out the Guardian's intention.

† As the friends came to realize the station of the Hands of the Cause they showed their respect by standing whenever Hands of the Cause entered the room. The Hands themselves, showing their reverence for the institution of the House of Justice, rose whenever the body of its members entered a meeting.

AS GUARDIAN OF THE CAUSE OF GOD, AND AFTER PROLONGED CONSULTATION
WHICH INCLUDED CONSIDERATION OF THE VIEWS OF THE HANDS OF THE CAUSE
OF GOD RESIDING IN THE HOLY LAND, THE UNIVERSAL HOUSE OF JUSTICE FINDS
THAT THERE IS NO WAY TO APPOINT OR LEGISLATE TO MAKE IT POSSIBLE TO
APPOINT A SECOND GUARDIAN TO SUCCEED SHOGHI EFFENDI.[11]

"The news of the decision of the House of Justice", Leroy wrote in a
long letter to Marion Hofman, "was a great heart-rending event. The
Hands in the Holy Land had met with the House of Justice in connection with this grievous matter, but when the announcement of the
decision was made, it tore our hearts to pieces. Sylvia and I left at once
– we had to be alone with our grief, and we went up to Mt. Carmel to
walk. It seemed to us that their decision was the only action possible,
but when it was actually taken it was almost too much. To think that
we can never have another such figure as Shoghi Effendi almost para-
lyzes those who knew him as we did.

"In any event," he continues, "God is watching over His Faith and
as the Guardian said so often, if God's Plan interferes with our plan, it
will result in great good for the Faith. Thus, we go along from day to
day doing our utmost for the Cause. To understand the ways of God is
difficult, nay, impossible. Perhaps in the next world some of these
things will be clear to us. It has been a most historic period in the Faith
– I should say the most historic, beginning in 1937 with the opening of
the united efforts to fulfill the Tablets of the Divine Plan. What a great
bounty it was to have played a part in this great spiritual drama!"

# CHAPTER THIRTY-FIVE

# "You will, I am sure, persevere till the very end."

LEROY reached his full mental and physical stature in the years he spent working for the Guardian. But it was during the last two years of his life that his spirit seemed to blossom, spreading its influence over all whom he met, and his spiritual role as a Hand of the Cause became fully evident. The very resignation with which he bore his physical limitations touched believers and seekers alike.

He had been asked to represent the Hands of the Cause at the annual Convention of his beloved home community in the United States. Knowing this, the National Assembly strongly appealed to him to undertake a teaching trip through the South and Southwest of the country where there were numerous new Bahá'ís. He eagerly accepted to make the trip, though as everyone in Haifa noticed, he walked slowly and looked weaker and weaker as he left on his American trip. This was his last great teaching tour and it was an outstanding success in what he hoped for – the confirmation of the new Bahá'ís and the attraction of new souls to the teachings. He was never so gentle or so loving, as if he had relinquished his struggles with this world.

He traveled to eight areas of the country during the temperate months of late winter and early spring of 1964, speaking throughout the weekend, meeting people privately over lunch and tea and dinner, then traveling to the next place to rest a few days. In this way he met with more than sixteen hundred Bahá'ís. As he began the tour he quickly realized how remote the World Centre seemed to the new Bahá'ís and how unaware they were of the spiritual power emanating from it. And so he spoke to them of the lives of 'Abdu'l-Bahá and

Shoghi Effendi, sharing experiences that showed the need for service and reliance on the Holy Spirit. He spoke of the need and the bounty of pioneering – and many young persons wished immediately to set out but he cautioned them to await the teaching plan of the House of Justice that would shortly be announced – and of the regenerative spiritual influence of the Shrines at the World Centre. He brought them a profound sense of his own love and devotion to 'Abdu'l-Bahá and Shoghi Effendi.

"When Leroy spoke about the beloved Guardian whom he had served so many years and whose call he had answered with such a ready loyalty," wrote the National Assembly of the United States in a tribute to Leroy, "he evoked in the hearts of his listeners a spirit of love and a determination to serve that was not easily forgotten. That he had the power to lift the individual to that spiritual plane and stir him to action in the path of God, in a way that was not only deeply moving but profoundly dignified, was further proof of the capacity of this servant of Bahá'u'lláh to be a channel of His inspiration."[1]

"This [trip] has been the greatest release of spiritual power since the visit of 'Abdu'l-Bahá," wrote an old friend. "Each time I saw him," wrote another, "he seemed to become more openly loving, more detached from the world . . . I felt his soul was reliving those early rugged days when he strove so hard, so indefatigably to awaken people to the call of God and to bring the first teaching plan into triumphant fulfillment. It was a bounty to me to have been a part of his memory of those days." Another friend commented on his unusual power to lift one up when he spoke about 'Abdu'l-Bahá and the Guardian. Leroy retraced the steps of his daughter Farrukh in the Southwest, meeting those she had encouraged in their spiritual search and who remembered her with gratitude and love. He gave freely of himself beyond the limits of his strength. One young Bahá'í remembers how simply and unaffectedly he chatted with him, answering his questions while they sat together in California. Another wrote of "that last quiet summer at Geyserville. We knew of his serious illness and really tried not to impose on him. But whenever he felt like being with us – and it came to be evening after evening – we sat about, listening to him, sharing. It was then that I came to know him as the beloved teacher, gentle and generous, so keenly understanding, so powerful and strong in his physical frailty." A long-time friend remembers visiting him at his sister's home and before she left, he went to the garden, pointing out to his sister which roses to cut, then brought in a large bouquet and said goodbye to her. She knew she would not see him again.

At the close of the tour he told the Hands of the Cause in the United States that two regions of the country were ripe for large scale enrollment: the Atlanta-Greenville (South Carolina) area, and Texas. "These new young Bahá'ís are the real source of power for the rapid spread of the Faith," he observed to the National Assembly, "and nearly all of the new Bahá'ís are young people." By the end of the tour he felt that a deep and dynamic spirit had been tapped. This trip, he said, has been most valuable in making the friends, and especially the new ones, understand the oneness of the Faith and feel the love and spiritual power of 'Abdu'l-Bahá and the beloved Guardian, and to bring them to a better understanding of the unique station and responsibility of the Universal House of Justice.

The annual Convention that year was a somewhat tense and stormy one, with many issues that challenged the friends, and a National Assembly member commented that Leroy was able to "pour into the souls of the friends some of that strength which distinguished him", bringing a higher spiritual vision to their deliberations. Another friend wrote that "Leroy's presence there was provident and enabled us to end on a high note".

The National Assembly was deeply appreciative of his efforts: "We cannot express in words how grateful we are to you and Sylvia for your visit and for the inspiration which you have given to so many hundreds of the newer believers. We know that this difficult itinerary worked a great hardship on you and resulted in a set-back towards your recovery . . . All members send deepest love and join in expressing their highest regard for your illustrious services to Bahá'u'lláh and His Cause, through so many stages of its evolution."

"What a great happiness I had during the teaching trip in the United States," he wrote to Zikrullah Khadem, one of the Hands of the Cause responsible for the work in America. "I could feel the presence of the Master and Shoghi Effendi with me as I spoke; at times, it was as if I was sitting off to one side listening to someone else speaking through me."

A member of the House of Justice recalled that when Leroy returned to Haifa he gave them "a most beautiful and wonderful report full of hope for the American Bahá'í community". The House of Justice is aware, the Hands in Haifa wrote to him, of the great need for the type of deepening in the Faith which you have been able to give the friends in America, particularly the newer believers and the young people who are entering the Faith in such large numbers.

When the tour was over, Leroy's doctor in Chicago told him it had "just about done him in" and he must have complete rest until the October Conclave in Haifa.

It was evident to those who saw him that he was suffering but he constantly made plans – "as soon as I am a little stronger" was a recurrent phrase – "as soon" he would be fully "in service" again. He rented an apartment in Washington to spend two months with his grandchildren, the small people who were the pure joy of his last years. He would sit with the little girl, Catherine, and do crossword puzzles – he always did them in ink and shamed others into doing the same, and for years the child, as she learned to write, would make tiny letters, even when she had a full page of paper. In his enforced inactivity he could not be idle; he had started a stamp collection for his grandchildren and pursued the hobby with all his concentrated energy, gathering exotic stamps, first editions, his mind absorbed and rested by this quiet endeavor. Always planning, always with a goal in mind in his undertakings. He always used his time wisely, said one of his nephews who had observed him over the years.

In Washington he gave a series of classes so powerful that one person called them "absolutely magical – each evening was like free flight over tall mountains". He loved to ask this friend afterwards, how did it go tonight? Was it all right? He knew what was happening and asked the question mostly to get himself back on earth, she said, not for answers. He spent hours preparing for the classes, though as she knew, he possessed the material and had used the outline a hundred times. Yet he prepared carefully and when he began to speak "it was as if he had never spoken on the subject before. It was alive; it was fresh; he cared that everyone understand what he had to say. He was so deeply convinced of what he was saying that his conviction set the stage, and then while he was speaking of spiritual things, his logical mind gave validity to his statements, and one was carried along to the conclusion: certain, sure, positive." "His classes," said another, "were an experience, and at this effulgent period of his life, they were irresistible."

The long periods of convalescence during his last two years gave him time for reflection and floods of memories washed over him. He thought back on the long years of struggle to build communities and develop strength in the believers. He remembered the young Bahá'ís whom he had nurtured and their extraordinary services over the years. He watched as they assumed positions of leadership in the Bahá'í world. He recalled the urgency with which the believers took on the work of the Cause when the Guardian disappeared. He remembered his travels and the long day spent in Dublin with fellow Hand of the Cause George Townshend – whose dearest wish was to meet Shoghi Effendi – when Leroy talked hour after hour about the Guardian and Haifa and led Townshend on a visit to the World Centre right from his sick bed. He recalled traveling to Oxford to visit Balliol College which the Guardian had attended and standing in the library of Manchester College where 'Abdu'l-Bahá had spoken. He remembered the Guardian's love when his mother died and his quiet pride that same evening to learn that the last door of the Shrine of the Báb would be named for him – a gift of his beloved Shoghi Effendi.

He returned to Haifa for the last Conclave of the Hands of the Cause he was to attend. The House of Justice, in its loving solicitude, sent a brief note to Sylvia and him: "We are happy to welcome you back to the World Centre and to express our loving appreciation for the outstanding services you have performed on behalf of our beloved Faith. Please be assured of our prayers for Leroy's recovery."

Happy to be home again in Haifa, after eighteen months living out of suitcases, he entered into the consultations of the Hands and their meetings with the House of Justice. He spent hours with the pilgrims – organizing the pilgrimages was a duty given the Hands by the House of Justice – talking with them, taking them to the Holy sites, lunching with them – the things which the Hands and the Council members had done for twelve years. But shortly, just as he was beginning to feel a part of things again, he developed bronchial pneumonia and was hospitalized for five weeks, leaving him exhausted. After that – it was now early spring 1965 – he again faced a long recuperation. Poor darling, Sylvia wrote to her daughter, he gets so discouraged, he wants to do his work but keeps having to convalesce.

He was more drawn, thinner, now obviously ill. Then it was that the Hands living in Haifa began to go to him for some of their meetings.

He and Sylvia had found a small modern apartment up in the Ahuza district, on the west side of the ridge of Carmel, looking down a canyon to the Mediterranean.

In the months that followed both he and Sylvia suffered greatly. He tried to continue with his activities, writing to a friend in America that "as the faith expands with its growing needs everywhere, the burden is becoming very great on the House of Justice, and to a lesser extent on the Hands . . ." In fact his greatest suffering was not physical. It was that he could not help sufficiently with all the work there was to do. He spoke of this many, many times. In letters, he wrote of the things he *was* able to do, reading reports, writing memoranda, reviewing materials – always insisting on what he could do "while I convalesce".

But he was slowly failing, a prey to every draft and chill, so weak that it depressed him, not understanding what God wanted of him. At times he would pace the floor repeating the Greatest Name, seeking strength, fighting against his condition. "He puts up a good front when visitors come," Sylvia wrote to a friend, "but he is just not well. He tries to keep up, but I know!" She said many times how sad it was to see him deprived of what he wished so much to do, so unable to play his part in the great work to be done. She wrote to Marion Hofman: "Seeing him suffer so much, I can only feel 'God's will be done'. I, too, have always felt Roy was one of the giants of our Faith. His understanding of the teachings is remarkable and his great compassion for those who serve with all their hearts is an example to us all . . . His has been a life of great bounties and great trials, and through it all he has never wavered from his great longing to serve. God bless him!"

He longed to go to Bahjí for the Riḍván Feast, held in the gardens near the Shrine of Bahá'u'lláh. He was so happy to be out and among the friends! But he took a chill, though it was a mild spring day and he wore a sweater and coat. A short time later, after one of the meetings of the Hands in his apartment, Rúḥíyyih Khánum drew Sylvia aside and suggested she might want to ask Anita to come to Haifa to see her father again. So the visit was planned and Leroy looked forward to it. He made plans of what they would do. Perhaps it might be better, he wrote to her, if you come a little later when I will have regained my strength and we will be able to work together on the things I want to write, and you can put them into good English [a touching remark he made several times]. When she arrived with his four-year-old granddaughter, he was sitting on a straight chair within a few feet of the door, eagerly awaiting their arrival. There were five lovely days together and some quiet talks on the small terrace overlooking the sea far below. But on May 30 he had to re-enter Elisha Hospital for medical tests.

He was more gravely ill than he realized and the decline was swift. There were more tests and specialists were called in. The weeks went by, one week the doctor feeling he could not last much longer, then he would rally sufficiently to speak of regaining his health. Then he would sink again and stabilize at a lower level. Sylvia stayed with him in the hospital room, though the doctor felt she should leave at night. But she said she would stay as long as he wanted her there if it was the last thing she did. And he did want her there; the nights were long and restless for him. During one of those days, looking intently at his daughter, he said: "She is an angel! She is an angel!"

Two of the younger Hands of the Cause – Abu'l-Qásim Faizi and Raḥmatu'lláh Muhájir – called to see him just before setting out on lengthy teaching trips. The picture their visit evoked in his daughter's mind, who watched from a corner of the room, was of the young warriors coming to salute the old warrior who lay stricken, and then, stepping over his prostrate form, striding out to continue the battles in which he can no longer join them.

Leroy died shortly past midnight on July 22nd. Some time earlier he had asked Sylvia if she was not tired and she had said she would not mind resting. Then he said, Oh, I'm *so* tired. His heart had been weakening for several hours, and he died quietly a little later.

The next morning a cablegram was sent to the Bahá'í world from the Universal House of Justice:

GRIEVE ANNOUNCE PASSING OUTSTANDING HAND CAUSE LEROY IOAS STOP HIS LONG SERVICE BAHA'I COMMUNITY UNITED STATES CROWNED ELEVATION RANK HAND FAITH PAVING WAY HISTORIC DISTINGUISHED SERVICES HOLY LAND STOP APPOINTMENT FIRST SECRETARY GENERAL INTERNATIONAL BAHA'I COUNCIL PERSONAL REPRESENTATIVE GUARDIAN FAITH TWO INTERCONTINENTAL CONFERENCES ASSOCIATION HIS NAME BY BELOVED GUARDIAN OCTAGON DOOR BAB'S SHRINE TRIBUTE SUPERVISORY WORK DRUM DOME THAT HOLY SEPULCHRE NOTABLE PART ERECTION INTERNATIONAL ARCHIVES BUILDING ALL ENSURE HIS NAME

IMMORTAL ANNALS FAITH STOP LAID TO REST BAHA'I CEMETERY CLOSE
FELLOW HANDS ADVISE HOLD BEFITTING MEMORIAL SERVICES.[2]

Among many deeds done in his name were two which would surely
have given him special pleasure: the building of Leroy Ioas Teaching
Institutes in Swaziland and in Haiti. Two of the persons who loved
him most expressed their feeling in simple words. When Anita telephoned Honor Kempton in Luxembourg with news of Leroy's death,
there was silence, then a burst of soft words: "Oh! I can't *bear* the
thought of the earth without him!" Marion Hofman, when saying
goodbye years later to Anita who was leaving Haifa, said in her deep
musical voice: "Well dear, if I don't see you again in this world, I'll see
you in the next . . . look for me somewhere near your dad." Several
months after his passing, Sylvia received a scroll with an etching of
trees done in the soft golden tones of Jerusalem. It read: A Haifa
citizen has planted twenty-five trees in Jerusalem Forest, in the name of
Mr. Leroy Ioas, in deep appreciation.

Hugh Chance, one of the original members of the House of
Justice, wrote a few years later to Sylvia: Hands of the Cause are
always very precious but this one in particular left his imprint not only
on Bahá'í history but in the history of the early development of the
State of Israel. Everywhere we go we hear his name. One need only
mention that he is a Bahá'í and it brings the immediate response
during his lifetime: "How is Mr. Ioas?" or "How is Leroy?". He is
greatly respected and the instant response of an official we recently
contacted was, "We were so sorry to hear of the passing of Mr. Ioas."
He was indeed a great man and all remember him for this, both high
and low, in Haifa, in Jerusalem, in Tel Aviv, wherever. Nothing we can
say will memorialize his life, for his life itself is his memorial.

One of the last entries in Leroy's diary was on March 8th: "Doctor
says I am doing nicely. Can go out for walks and sit in sun . . . about a
month before I can enter service again." At that late date he had
written to the House of Justice that he thought it better they not share
with the Bahá'í world generally that he was ill, as he soon expected to
be back working again.

How well Shoghi Effendi understood the longing of his heart!:

The Beloved is well pleased with what you have already achieved. You will, I am sure, persevere till the very end.

Your true and grateful brother, Shoghi[3]

Leroy was buried the day following his death in the Bahá'í cemetery at the foot of Mt. Carmel, next to his dear friend Milly Collins. Many years later Abu'l-Qásim Faizi was laid to rest on the other side of his grave.

*Thus ended the life of a man who was blessed as a youth by 'Abdu'l-Bahá, whose qualities of determination, thoroughness, dedication and loyalty were the basis of a heroic life, who devoted himself to a great cause and achieved the highest honor possible in the new religious Dispensation.*

# Statement signed by members of the International Bahá'í Council present in Haifa on 6 November 1957

## *Alláh-u-Abhá*

Haifa, Israel
November 6, 1957

Rúḥíyyih Khánum telephoned me on the evening of November 4th, of the great calamity which had stricken the Bahá'í world, in the passing of our dearly beloved Guardian, in London, during the early morning hours of November 4th.

During our conversation it was decided I would remain in Haifa and take all precautions to protect the Holy Places, the Guardian's apartment, where all his records were kept, and the Faith from attack by the enemies of the Faith here.

The following actions were taken:

1. The Guardian's apartment and office had been locked, so no one could enter it during his absence. We assured ourselves that it was carefully locked, and barriers were placed in front of the door so no one could enter. We then locked and put iron bars across the door to the entrance of the living quarters. These iron bars were padlocked. All the keys to the apartment were then sealed in an envelope, which envelope was signed by Sylvia Ioas, Jessie Revell, Ethel Revell and Leroy

Reprinted from *The Ministry of the Custodians*, p. 25.

Ioas and placed in the safe of my office, in such a way that if the envelope was tampered with in any way, it would be seen immediately.

We then arranged for the Guardian's trusted servant to sleep outside the doors of the apartment and office; likewise another trusted servant to sleep at the foot of the steps, so no one could gain access to the area.

During the daytime, we maintained extra Bahá'ís in the building, so no access could be gained.

2. The Shrine of Bahá'u'lláh was guarded night and day, and one of the Bahá'ís slept in the Shrine each night.

3. The same action was taken with regard to the Shrine of the Báb.

4. The same action was taken with regard to the Mansion at Bahjí.

The sealing of the Guardian's apartment and office was done in the presence of the four members of the International Council here, who have signed this document, in attestation thereof.

The envelope in which the keys to the apartment were sealed, is attached.

Leroy C. Ioas

*[Signed as follows]*
Leroy Ioas
Sylvia Ioas
Ethel Revell
Jessie Revell

# Unanimous Proclamation of the 27 Hands of the Cause of God

Mansion of Bahá'u'lláh
Bahjí, 'Akká, Israel
November 25, 1957

We the undersigned:

Ruhiyyih Rabbani

Charles Mason Remey (who is President of the International Bahá'í Council)

Amelia E. Collins (who is Vice President of the International Bahá'í Council)

Leroy C. Ioas (who is Secretary General of the International Bahá'í Council)

Dr. Ugo Giachery (who is member-at-large of the International Bahá'í Council and Chairman of the National Spiritual Assembly of the Bahá'ís of Italy and Switzerland)

Hasan M. Balyuzi (who is Chairman of the National Spiritual Assembly of the Bahá'ís of the British Isles)

Shoaullah Ala'i (who is Chairman of the National Spiritual Assembly of the Bahá'ís of Iran)

Ali Akbar Furutan (who is Secretary of the National Assembly of the Bahá'ís of Iran)

Reprinted from *The Ministry of the Custodians*, pp. 28–30.

Zikrullah Khadem (who is Treasurer of the National Spiritual Assembly of the Bahá'ís of Iran)

Dr. Ali Mohammed Varqa (who is a member of the National Spiritual Assembly of the Bahá'ís of Iran)

Tarazullah Samandari (who is a resident of Shiraz, Iran)

Djalal Khazeh (who is a resident of Teheran, Iran)

John Ferraby (who is Secretary of the National Spiritual Assembly of the Bahá'ís of the British Isles)

Paul E. Haney (who is Chairman of the National Spiritual Assembly of the Bahá'ís of the United States)

Horace Holley (who is Secretary of the National Spiritual Assembly of the Bahá'ís of the United States)

Abul Qasim F. Teherani

Dr. Adelbert Mühlschlegel (who is a member of the National Spiritual Assembly of the Bahá'ís of Germany and Austria)

Dr. Hermann Grossmann (who is a resident of Neckargemünd, Germany)

Musa Banani (who is a resident of Kampala, Uganda)

William Sears (who is Chairman of the National Spiritual Assembly of the Bahá'ís of South and West Africa)

John Robarts (who is Recording Secretary of the National Spiritual Assembly of the Bahá'ís of South and West Africa)

Enoch Olinga (who is a member of the National Spiritual Assembly of the Bahá'ís of North West Africa)

Agnes Alexander (who is a member of the National Spiritual Assembly of the Bahá'ís of North East Asia)

H. Collis Featherstone (who is Chairman of the National Spiritual Assembly of the Bahá'ís of Australia)

Clara Dunn (who is a resident of Sydney, Australia)

Dr. Rahmatullah Mohajer (who is a member of the National Spiritual Assembly of the Bahá'ís of South-East Asia)

in our capacity as Hands of the Cause of God duly nominated and appointed by the Guardian of the Bahá'í Faith, His Eminence the late Shoghi Effendi Rabbani, assembled this 25th of November, 1957 at the Bahá'í World Centre and constituting the supreme body of the Bahá'í World Community

DO HEREBY UNANIMOUSLY RESOLVE AND PROCLAIM AS FOLLOWS:

WHEREAS THE Guardian of the Bahá'í Faith, His Eminence the late Shoghi Effendi Rabbani, passed away in London (England) on the 4th of November, 1957, without having appointed his successor;

AND WHEREAS it is now fallen upon us as Chief Stewards of the Bahá'í World Faith to preserve the unity, the security and the development of the Bahá'í World Community and all its institutions;

AND WHEREAS in accordance with the Will and Testament of 'Abdu'l-Bahá "the Hands of the Cause of God must elect from their own number nine persons that shall at all times be occupied in the important services in the work of the Guardian of the Cause of God";

We nominate and appoint from our own number to act on our behalf as the Custodians of the Bahá'í World Faith

> Rúḥíyyih Rabbani
> Charles Mason Remey
> Amelia E. Collins
> Leroy C. Ioas
> Ḥasan Balyuzi
> 'Alí-Akbar Furútan
> Jalal Kházeh
> Paul E. Haney
> Adelbert Mühlschlegel

to exercise – subject to such directions and decisions as may be given from time to time by us as the Chief Stewards of the Bahá'í World Faith – all such functions, rights and powers in succession to the Guardian of the Bahá'í Faith, His Eminence the late Shoghi Effendi Rabbani, as are necessary to serve the interests of the Bahá'í World Faith, and this until such a time as the Universal House of Justice, upon being duly established and elected in conformity with the Sacred Writings of Bahá'u'lláh and the Will and Testament of 'Abdu'l-Bahá, may otherwise determine.

*[Signed as follows]*
Rúḥíyyih Rabbani        Zikrullah Khadem        M. B. [Músá Banání]
Charles Mason Remey  Ali Mohammad Varqa   William Sears

Amelia E. Collins       T. Samandari           John Robarts
Leroy C. Ioas           Djalal Khazeh          Enoch Olinga
Ugo Giachery            John Ferraby           Agnes B. Alexander
Hasan M. Balyuzi        Paul E. Haney          H. Collis Featherstone
Shoaullah Alai          Horace Holley          Clara Dunn
Ali Akbar Furutan       Abul Qasim F. Teherani  Dr. R. Mohajer
Hermann Grossmann       Dr. Adelbert Mühlschlegel

# Resolution of the Hands of the Cause of God

Mansion of Bahá'u'lláh
Bahjí, 'Akká, Israel
November 25, 1957

We the undersigned Hands of the Cause hereby record the following action to be taken in unanimous agreement:

1. That the body of nine Hands of the Cause already constituted shall exercise these functions, namely, to correspond with the National Spiritual Assemblies on matters related to the prosecution of the Guardian's Ten Year Plan; to assist the National Assemblies in the solution of administrative problems by citing passages in Bahá'í literature which clarify the nature of these problems; to act for the protection of the Faith whenever its teachings or institutions or properties are assailed by enemies from within the Bahá'í Community or outside its ranks;

2. That the Council shall represent the Faith in all matters related to the Israeli Government and its courts;

3. The nine Hands to reinforce the membership of the International Bahá'í Council through the addition of the five Hands among the nine Hands not already members of the Council;

4. That the entire body of the Hands of the Cause, meeting annually or whenever convened by the nine Hands, shall determine when and how the International Bahá'í Council shall pass through the successive

Reprinted from *The Ministry of the Custodians*, pp. 34–35.

stages outlined by Shoghi Effendi culminating in the election of the Universal House of Justice;

5. That the nine Hands serving at the Bahá'í World Centre shall maintain correspondence with the Hands stationed in the several continents on all matters related to their work of propagating the Faith and defending it from attack, coordinating and encouraging their efforts;

6. That the authority to expel violators from the Faith shall be vested in the body of nine Hands, acting on reports and recommendations submitted by Hands from their respective continents.

7. The Hands of the Cause in the Holy Land may, if necessary, call upon any of the Hands to fill a vacancy temporarily.

*[Signed as follows]*

Rúḥíyyih Rabbani

Mason Remey

Amelia E. Collins

Leroy C. Ioas

Hasan M. Balyuzi

Horace Holley

M. B. [Músá Banání]

A. Furutan

Dr R. Mohajer

Sh. Alai

John Ferraby

T. Samandari

Agnes B. Alexander

[Corinne True by affidavit]

Zikrullah Khadem

A. Q. Faizi

Ugo Giachery

Dr. Adelbert Mühlschlegel

Djalal Khazeh

Hermann Grossmann

John Robarts

Enoch Olinga

Ali Mohammed Varqa

H. Collis Featherstone

William Sears

Paul Haney

Clara Dunn

# In Memoriam: Sylvia Ioas
## 1895–1983

SYLVIA KUHLMAN IOAS was born on September 19, 1895 in Chicago, Illinois. Her mother was Czech, her father's family from Munich. She was reared in a stable loving family.

It was Leroy Ioas who brought the knowledge of Bahá'u'lláh into her life. He was to remain her guide, teacher and companion. She became a Bahá'í shortly before their marriage in Chicago in 1919. Within a short time her immediate family also became Bahá'ís.

Sylvia and Leroy settled in San Francisco, where they spent twenty-eight rich and fruitful years. Both served the Faith vigorously but in quite different ways: Leroy the teacher, the organizer, the speaker; Sylvia the warm hostess, the faithful sustainer. One of her charming characteristics was to feel those she loved could do anything; this surely gave strength to both her husband and the burgeoning communities he labored to build in the Bay Area.

Those years in San Francisco were passed in a life she felt deeply fulfilled by: raising her two daughters, making a home, helping her husband, content to be in the background, with a genuine and unassumed modesty. Her home was the scene of many Bahá'í gatherings, happy evenings that knit the community together. It was the meeting place for the weekend teaching committee meetings that shaped the goals and successes of the first Seven Year Plan. Her cottage in Geyserville was the magnet for the deepening of Bahá'ís and visitors.

* Reprinted from *The Bahá'í World*, vol. XIX, 1983-1986, pp. 611-13, with revisions by Anita Ioas Chapman.

In 1946 Leroy was promoted by the Southern Pacific Railroad; this meant a move to Chicago. It was a difficult decision, but when Shoghi Effendi indicated it would he good for Leroy to be closer to the National Center, they made plans to leave San Francisco.

They settled in Wilmette, close to the House of Worship. The few short years there were a kind of flowering after lean years: Leroy had a fine position, they had a lovely home, Sylvia was able to travel more extensively than she had. She loved activity as she loved people, and to the close of her days was instantly ready to go out, to do, to see. In Wilmette she particularly loved the nearness of the Temple where she could serve as a guide.

Sylvia was alone when the cablegram arrived from Haifa appointing her husband as a Hand of the Cause. She telephoned him at his office; both were stunned by the news. He cabled Shoghi Effendi that he was overcome with a sense of unworthiness. When invited shortly thereafter to move to Haifa, Leroy wondered if he could accept: he was several years from retirement, with family charges. It was Sylvia who said: "Of course you will, Roy!" He later wrote to one of his brothers: "Sylvia has been a tower of spiritual strength, much stronger than I, and the one who has aided me in carrying this through. How God ever gave me such a wonderful wife, I don't know, but thank God He did."

Sylvia perceived the grandeur of the atmosphere she was moving into. Yet the move was traumatic for her, as she rid herself of everything she had gathered over thirty years, and set out with few, very few, possessions. It was in some way her personal world she gave away. And she did it alone, as Leroy went on almost immediately to Haifa. She later wrote to a friend: "I never had to do anything like that before; I didn't know how to begin."

Life in Haifa was not easy. It was a period of great austerity and lack of accustomed privacy. One of the Hands of the Cause paid tribute to the spirit in which Sylvia took up this challenging life: "Very few persons who worked in Haifa in those austere years could display so much poise, dignity and wisdom as dear Sylvia did." And he added: "Sylvia's angelic presence in that Holy Spot made things better for everyone."

Sylvia's learning was intuitive rather than intellectual. In Haifa she was frequently in the presence of Shoghi Effendi; she breathed the holy atmosphere of the Shrines; she came to the knowledge of how the triumphs of the Faith were achieved. Under these influences it was as if she became a new person, developing capacities that had lain dormant. She served tirelessly, cleaning the Shrines with other wives of the Hands of the Cause, helping to run the Pilgrim House where they lived, greeting visitors, spending long hours with Bahá'í pilgrims on visits to Bahjí and Mazra'ih. One of them remembered, and suggests that she touched many lives in this quiet way.

In May of 1955 she was honored by Shoghi Effendi, the first personal honor to come to her. The Guardian appointed her to the International Bahá'í Council, the ninth member of that august body. Leroy was very proud of this distinction that came to her. She was further honored by election to that body in 1961. She worked on it with all the capacity she had. In 1963 when the work of the Council was ended, the members received this tribute: "All the Hands present at our meeting in Bahjí wish to express to the members of the Council their deep appreciation of the services they have rendered the Cause of God . . . collectively and severally they have greatly contributed to strengthening the World Centre of the Faith . . .

During the World Congress, Leroy suffered a pneumonia that was diagnosed as fatal, from which the prayers of the friends in London saved him. He was to live two additional years, years of diminishing physical strength during which he and Sylvia undertook a long teaching trip. He had become, said a friend, spiritually irresistible; the harvest of their travels was rich. For Sylvia, the two years were a time of increasing concern, as she cared for him day and night, and faced step by step the realization of his loss. One afternoon two months before his death, Leroy turned to his daughter and said with a strange intensity: "She's an angel! She's an angel!"

Leroy's death was one of the several great sorrows of her life. In the eighteen years she lived without him, she was valiant and uncomplaining, but not without pain: "I miss him so very much. He was a tower of strength to me, even when sick; he had such loving ideas, so many kind thoughts for everyone." She met her personal tragedies with a quality of faith that was unchanging and without doubts. This caused her prayers to be very powerful.

Though she had to leave Haifa, it always remained home. Her thoughts were there; her energy came from there. When visiting with her family nine years later, she looked down as Lod Airport came into view and said joyously: "Oh, I'm home!"

She lived as a widow first in Wilmette, where loving friends eased the transition to her life alone. She was busy with the Assembly and with guiding. In 1968 she moved to Alexandria, Virginia to be near her three grandchildren. There a close Bahá'í community gave her spiritual support and opportunities for service. She was a member for ten years of the Assembly; she held firesides, she took part in teaching projects, opening areas of southern Virginia; she scrubbed the Bahá'í Center so that a children's school could be opened; she took her grandchildren to summer schools and conferences, to Alaska and Bermuda. But then, she loved to sit down with a *Bahá'í World* volume and just read. Often when one phoned this was what she was doing. Perhaps it took her back. Certainly she brought a breath of Haifa, and the long historic view she acquired there, to all who knew her in those years. She retained her affectionate nature and cheerfulness even as her memory faded in the last years. She passed away on August 24, 1983. She is buried in Washington DC next to her daughter Farrukh.

In a long letter of devotion written to 'Abdu'l-Bahá in 1919, Leroy asked 'Abdu'l-Bahá to remember her: "O my Lord, may Thy blessings and confirmation descend upon my dear wife that she may be of the utmost firmness and steadfastness in the Covenant and Testament, and render always greater service in the Cause."

SADDENED PASSING DEVOTED MAIDSERVANT BAHA'U'LLAH SYLVIA IOAS. HER LONG YEARS SERVICE DIVINE THRESHOLD CONSTANT SUPPORT CLOSE COLLABORATION HER DISTINGUISHED HUSBAND CROWNED BY HER APPOINTMENT BY BELOVED GUARDIAN AS MEMBER INTERNATIONAL BAHA'I COUNCIL AND HER SUBSEQUENT ELECTION SAME HISTORIC INSTITUTION AS ITS VICE PRESIDENT. HER GRACIOUS MANNER CHEERFUL DISPOSITION HOSPITABLE SPIRIT REMAIN AS INDELIBLE IMPRESSIONS HER FRUITFUL LIFE. FERVENTLY PRAYING HOLY SHRINES HER RADIANT SOUL MAY BE RICHLY REWARDED ABHA KINGDOM. URGE NATIONAL ASSEMBLIES HOLD BEFITTING MEMORIAL SERVICES.

*Universal House of Justice*
*25 August 1983*

# BIBLIOGRAPHY

'Abdu'l-Bahá. *The Promulgation of Universal Peace*. Wilmette, Ill.: Bahá'í
 Publishing Trust, rev. edn. 1982.
—*The Will and Testament of 'Abdu'l-Bahá*. Wilmette, Ill.: Bahá'í
 Publishing Trust, 1971. Also printed in full in Taherzadeh,
 *The Covenant of Bahá'u'lláh*, pp. 416–28.
*The Bahá'í Centenary 1844–1944: A Record of America's Response to
 Bahá'u'lláh's Call to the Realization of the Oneness of Mankind.*
 Compiled by the National Spiritual Assembly of the Bahá'ís of
 the United States and Canada. Wilmette, Ill: Bahá'í Publishing
 Committee, 1944.
*Bahá'í Journal*. Monthly magazine published by the National Spiritual
 Assembly of the Bahá'ís of the United Kingdom.
*Bahá'í World, The*. vols. I–XII, 1925–54. rpt. Wilmette, Ill.: Bahá'í
 Publishing Trust, 1980. vol. XIII, 1954–63. Haifa: Bahá'í World
 Centre, 1970.
Bahá'u'lláh. *Gleanings from the Writings of Bahá'u'lláh*. Wilmette, Ill.:
 Bahá'í Publishing Trust, rev. edn. 1983.
— *The Kitáb-i-Aqdas*, Haifa: Bahá'í World Centre, 1992.
— *Prayers and Meditations by Bahá'u'lláh*. Wilmette, Ill: Bahá'í Publishing
 Trust, 1987.
Balyuzi, H.M. *'Abdu'l-Bahá*. Oxford: George Ronald, 1971.
Blomfield, Sara, Lady. *The Chosen Highway*. London: National Spiritual
 Assembly of the Bahá'ís of the British Isles, 1940.
Brown, Ramona Allen. *Memories of 'Abdu'l-Bahá*. Wilmette, Ill.: Bahá'í
 Publishing Trust, 1980.
Busey, Garreta. "Uniting the Americas", in *The Bahá'í World*, vol. IX,
 1940–44. rpt. Wilmette, Ill.: Bahá'í Publishing Trust, 1980.
Collins, Amelia. *A Tribute to Shoghi Effendi*. Wilmette, Ill.: Bahá'í
 Publishing Trust, 1958.

Faizi, Abu'l-Qasim. *Milly: A Tribute to Amelia E. Collins*. Oxford: George Ronald, 1977.

Gail, Marzieh. "California – Host to the Nations", in *The Bahá'í World*, vol. x, 1944–46, p. 679. rpt. Wilmette, Ill.: Bahá'í Publishing Trust, 1980.

— *Dawn Over Mount Hira*. Oxford: George Ronald, 1976.

— *The Sheltering Branch*. Oxford: George Ronald, 1959.

Giachery, Ugo. *Shoghi Effendi: Recollections*. Oxford: George Ronald, 1973.

Holley, Horace. *Religion for Mankind*. London: George Ronald, 1956.

Hollinger, Richard (ed). *Community Histories*. Studies in the Bábí and Bahá'í Religions, vol. 6. Los Angeles: Kalimát Press, 1992.

Ioas, Leroy. "Teaching in North America", in *The Bahá'í World*, vol. ix, 1940–44. rpt. Wilmette, Ill.: Bahá'í Publishing Trust, 1980.

Ishráq Khávarí, 'Abdu'l-Hamíd. *Rahíq-i-Makhtum*. A commentary on a letter of Shoghi Effendi. 2 vols. Teheran: Bahá'í Publishing Trust, BE 103 (CE 1946).

Ives, Howard Colby. *Portals to Freedom*. Oxford: George Ronald, rev. edn. 1969.

Kirkpatrick, Ruth Hyde. "William Miller, student of prophecy", in *The Bahá'í World*, vol. v, 1932–34. rpt. Wilmette, Ill.: Bahá'í Publishing Trust, 1980.

Mathews, Loulie. *Not Every Sea Hath Pearls*. Milford, NH: The Cabinet Press, 1951.

Maxwell, May Bolles. *An Early Pilgrimage*. Oxford: George Ronald, 1969.

Metelmann, Velda Piff. *Lua Getsinger: Herald of the Covenant*. Oxford: George Ronald, 1996.

Momen, Moojan. *Dr. J.E. Esslemont*. London: Bahá'í Publishing Trust, 1975.

— (ed). *Studies in Bábí and Bahá'í History*. vol. 1. Los Angeles: Kalimát Press, 1982.

Morrison, Gayle. *To Move the World: Louis G. Gregory and the Advancemnt of Racial Unity in America*. Wilmette, Ill.: Bahá'í Publishing Trust, 1982.

*The Ministry of the Custodians 1957–1963: An Account of the Stewardship of the Hands of the Cause*. Haifa: Bahá'í World Centre, 1992.

Phelps, Myron H. *The Life and Teachings of Abbas Effendi.* New York: G.P. Putnam's Sons, 1912.

Rabbani, Rúḥíyyih. "The Passing of Shoghi Effendi", in *The Bahá'í World*, vol. XIII, pp. 207–225.

— *The Priceless Pearl.* London: Bahá'í Publishing Trust, 1969.

— *Twenty-five Years of the Guardianship.* Wilmette, Ill.: Bahá'í Publishing Committee, 1948.

Sears, William, and Robert Quigley. *The Flame.* Oxford: George Ronald, 1973.

Shoghi Effendi. *The Advent of Divine Justice.* Wilmette, Ill.: Bahá'í Publishing Trust, rev. edn. 1990.

— *Bahá'í Administration.* Wilmette, Ill.: Bahá'í Publishing Trust, rev. edn. 1968.

— *Citadel of Faith: Messages to America 1947–1957.* Wilmette, Ill.: Bahá'í Publishing Trust, 1965.

— *The Dispensation of Bahá'u'lláh.* 1934. Wilmette, Ill.: Bahá'í Publishing Trust, 1970.

— *God Passes By.* Wilmette, Ill.: Bahá'í Publishing Trust, rev. edn. 1974.

— *Messages to America.* Wilmette, Ill.: Bahá'í Publishing Trust, 1947.

— *Messages to the Bahá'í World 1950–1957.* Wilmette, Ill.: Bahá'í Publishing Trust, rev. edn. 1971.

— *The World Order of Bahá'u'lláh.* Wilmette, Ill.: Bahá'í Publishing Trust, rev. edn. 1955.

*Star of the West.* Rpt. Oxford: George Ronald, 1984.

Stockman, Robert H. *The Bahá'í Faith in America.* vol. I, 1892–1900. Wilmette, Ill.: Bahá'í Publishing Trust, 1985.

Taherzadeh, Adib. *The Covenant of Bahá'u'lláh.* Oxford: George Ronald, 1992.

— *The Revelation of Baha'u'llah.* 4 vols. Oxford: George Ronald, 1974–88.

The Universal House of Justice. *Wellspring of Guidance.* Wilmette, Ill.: Bahá'í Publishing Trust, 1976.

Weinberg, Robert. *Ethel Jenner Rosenberg: The Life and Times of England's Outstanding Bahá'í Pioneer Worker.* Oxford: George Ronald, 1995.

Whitehead, O.Z. *Some Bahá'ís to Remember.* Oxford: George Ronald, 1983.

— *Some Early Bahá'ís of the West.* Oxford: George Ronald, 1976.

Yazdi, Ali M. *Blessings Beyond Measure.* Wilmette, Ill.: Bahá'í Publishing Trust, 1991.

Yazdi, Marion Carpenter. *Youth in the Vanguard*. Wilmette, Ill.: Bahá'í
     Publishing Trust, 1982.

# REFERENCES

## Chapter 1: Charles and Maria

1. Information in this paragraph is cited in Kirkpatrick, p. 604. Miller's lecture was published in 1842 in Boston by Joshua V. Hines; Kelber's pamphlet in 1835 in Stuttgart, Germany.
2. Shoghi Effendi, *God Passes By*, p. 257.

## Chapter 2: Leroy and his Family

1. *Star of the West*, vol. 9, no. 6 (June 24, 1918), pp. 78–9.

## Chapter 3: 'Abdu'l-Bahá

1. Quoted in Blomfield, *Chosen Highway*, p. 64.
2. 'Abdu'l-Bahá, *Promulgation*, p. 323.
3. H.M. Balyuzi, *'Abdu'l-Bahá*, p. 133.
4. ibid., p. 142.
5. Horace Holley, *Religion for Mankind*, pp. 232–3.
6. Shoghi Effendi, *God Passes By*, p. 305.
7. Shoghi Effendi, *Messages to America*, p. 8.
8. Rabbani, *The Priceless Pearl*, pp. 100–101.

## Chapter 5: The Bahá'ís of the Bay Area

1. See May Maxwell, *An Early Pilgrimage*, and Velda Piff Metelmann, *Lua Getsinger: Herald of the Covenant*.
2. Unpublished article, "Mrs.Helen. S. Goodall", ed. Ella Cooper and Bijou Straun, p. 2, Ella Cooper Papers, National Bahá'í Archives, Wilmette, Ill., USA.
3. Letter from Rouhanieh Latimer to Mary Rabb, November 20, 1935, recounting the early history of the Faith in Portland; copy in Ioas personal papers.
4. Quoted in Metelmann, *Lua Getsinger*, pp. 139–40.
5. July 11, 1911; copy in Ioas personal papers.
6. See Ali M. Yazdi, *Blessings Beyond Measure*.

**Chapter 6: Settling In**
1. Ioas personal papers.

**Chapter 7: The Conference For World Unity**
1. *The Bahá'í World*, vol. 1, p. 97.

**Chapter 8: The Geyserville Story**
1. Joyce Lyon Dahl, who began her serious training as a teacher at Geyserville.
2. Letter from Shoghi Effendi to John and Louise Bosch, March 2, 1931; copy in Ioas papers.
3. Letter from Shoghi Effendi to George Latimer, July 23, 1931; copy in Ioas papers.
4. Letter from Shoghi Effendi to Juanita Storch, October 8, 1931; copy in Ioas papers.
5. Letter from Shoghi Effendi to Leroy Ioas, August 5, 1932; Ioas papers.
6. Letter from Shoghi Effendi to John Bosch, July 21, 1932; copy in Ioas papers.
7. Ioas papers.
8. Letter from Shoghi Effendi to Leroy Ioas, September 14, 1936; Ioas papers.
9. Letter from Shoghi Effendi to John Bosch, July 21, 1932; copy in Ioas papers.

**Chapter 13: The First Seven Year Plan 1939–1944**
1. Shoghi Effendi, messages of May 1, 1936; May 30, 1936; and July 28, 1936; in *Messages to America*, pp. 6–7.
2. Cited in Shoghi Effendi, *Bahá'í Administration*, p. 22.
3. Leroy Ioas, report in *Bahá'í Centenary*, p. 169.
4. Ioas papers.
5. Leroy Ioas, "Bahá'í teaching in North America", *Bahá'í Centenary*, p. 171.
6. Shoghi Effendi, *Messages to America*, p. 1.
7. Ioas papers.
8. Letter to Leroy Ioas, November 14, 1935. Ioas papers.
9. Cited in *The Bahá'í Centenary*, p. 170.
10. Letter to Leroy Ioas, November 14, 1935. Ioas papers.
11. ibid.
12. Cable to 1936 Convention, May 1, 1936, in *Messages to America*, p. 6. Cables are quoted in this book as originally received, without linking words; these were added by the editor of *Messages to America*.
13. Letter of May 30, 1936, in *Messages to America*, p. 7.

14. Letter of July 28, 1936, ibid.

15. Cable to 1937 Convention, May 1, 1937, ibid., p. 9.

16. Cable of January 26, 1939, ibid., p. 16.

17. Letter of April 25, 1946, ibid., p. 88.

18. Ioas, "Teaching in North America", report on Seven Year Plan, *The Bahá'í World*, vol. IX, p. 199.

19. ibid., p. 205.

20. Letter to Leroy Ioas, March 14, 1939. Ioas papers.

21. Ioas, "Teaching in North America", p. 207.

22. ibid.

23. Cable to 1942 Convention, April 26, 1942, *Messages to America*, p. 55.

24. Cables of June 17, 1942 and August 15, 1942, ibid., p. 57.

25. Ioas, "Teaching in North America", p. 209.

26. Letter to Leroy Ioas, March 28, 1943. Ioas papers.

27. "Teaching in North America", p. 209.

28. Letter to Leroy Ioas and other committee members, March 28, 1943. Ioas papers.

29. Ioas, "Teaching in North America", p. 213.

30. Letter to Leroy Ioas, December 17, 1943. Ioas papers.

31. Letter of March 28, 1943, in *Messages to America*, p. 62.

32. Ioas personal papers.

33. Letter of January 28, 1939, in *Messages to America*, p. 17.

34. "Teaching in North America", p. 211.

35. Letter of April 2, 1944, in *Messages to America*, p. 69.

36. Rabbani, *The Priceless Pearl*, p. 382.

**Chapter 14: The Republics of the South**

1. Loulie Mathews, *Not Every Sea Hath Pearls*, and *The Bahá'í World*, vol. IX.

2. Garreta Busey, "Uniting the Americas", *The Bahá'í World*, vol. IX, p. 186.

3. ibid.

4. ibid., p. 192.

5. Letter of April 15, 1940, in *Messages to America*, p. 40.

6. Busey, "Uniting the Americas", p. 195.

7. Letter of April 15, 1944, in *Messages to America*, p. 71.

**Chapter 16: The Last Years in San Francisco**

1. 'Abdu'l-Bahá, October 26, 1912, in *Promulgation*, pp. 376–77.

2. Taped memoirs of Isobel Sabri.

3. Published in the *Bahá'í Youth Bulletin of England*, 1948.

4. Ramona Allen Brown, *Memories of 'Abdu'l-Bahá*, p. 88.

5. Letter from National Spiritual Assembly to the Committee on the Bahá'í

Peace Plan, March 19, 1945. Ioas papers.

6. Cited in *The Bahá'í World*, vol. XI, p. 42.

7. Cable of August 10, 1945, in *Messages to America*, p. 82.

8. ibid.

9. Cable of December 31, 1945, in *Messages to America*, p. 85; and letter of December 21, 1945, ibid., p. 84.

10. Cable of February 25, 1946, ibid., p. 86.

11. April 25, 1946, ibid., p. 88.

12. ibid.

13. Cable of June 5, 1946, ibid., p. 89.

14. Cable of August 20, 1945, ibid., p. 84.

15. Cables of August 10 and August 20, 1945; Letter of June 15, 1946; ibid., pp. 83, 84, 93, 94.

## Chapter 17: Return to Chicago

1. Message to 41st U.S. Annual Convention, April 25, 1949, in *Citadel of Faith*, p. 72.

2. Cable of December 24, 1951, in *Messages to the Bahá'í World*, pp. 19–20.

3. Ioas papers.

4. Message to the Bahá'ís of the United States and Canada, February 1, 1948, in *Citadel of Faith*, p. 45.

5. Letter of April 11, 1949, ibid., p. 70.

6. Letter from the National Spiritual Assembly to the Bahá'ís of the United States, November 15, 1948. Ioas papers.

7. Shoghi Effendi, cable of December 24, 1951, in *Messages to the Bahá'í World*, p. 19.

8. Rabbani, *The Priceless Pearl*, p. 251.

9. Cable of January 9, 1951, in *Messages to the Bahá'í World*, p. 7.

10. Cable of March 29, 1951, in *Citadel of Faith*, pp. 91–2.

11. ibid., Further references to this message are on pp. 91—8, passim.

12. Cable of April 25, 1951, in *Messages to the Bahá'í World*, p. 14.

13. Letter from Leroy Ioas writing as N.S.A. Treasurer, May 24, 1951; and letter from Shoghi Effendi through his secretary, to Leroy Ioas, September 28, 1951. Ioas papers.

14. Personal letters, October 4, 1950 and February 18, 1951. Ioas papers.

15. Personal letter, September 28, 1951.

## Chapter 18: Appointment and Departure

1. Taherzadeh, *Revelation of Bahá'u'lláh*, vol. 4, p. 277.

2. Cable of December 24, 1951, in *Messages to the Bahá'í World*, p. 20.

3. Rabbani, *The Priceless Pearl*, pp. 258–9; see also "In Memoriam", *The Bahá'í World*, vol. XIII, p. 834.
4. Unpublished personal communication. Ioas papers.
5. Shoghi Effendi, cable of December 24, 1951, in *Messages to the Bahá'í World*, p. 20.
6. Quotations in the above three paragraphs are from unpublished personal archives, the Ioas papers.
7. Ives, *Portals to Freedom*, Chapter 3.
8. Dr. Mildred Nichols, who taught and confirmed many capable persons in the Faith.
9. Author's personal archives.

**Chapter 20: At the World Centre**
1. *Gleanings*, section XI, p. 16.
2. *Will and Testament*, part one, para. 17.
3. Cited in Balyuzi, *'Abdu'l-Bahá*, p. 135.
4. *Will and Testament*, part three, para. 11.
5. Talk on Shoghi Effendi given at the Frankfurt Intercontinental Conference in 1958, which she attended as the Guardian's representative.
6. Rabbani, *The Priceless Pearl*, p. 94.
7. *Messages to the Bahá'í World*, p. 22.
8. *Message to the Bahá'ís of the East*, BE 108.
9. Rabbani,*The Priceless Pearl*, p. 174.

**Chapter 21: Forging Relationships**
1. Rabbani, *The Priceless Pearl*, Chapter 5.
2. See Shoghi Effendi, *God Passes By*, p. 101.
3. *Messages to the Bahá'í World*, p. 64.
4. Cable of May 4, 1954, in ibid., p. 68.
5. Exodus 3:5.

**Chapter 22: The Hands of the Cause in Haifa**
1. Giachery, *Shoghi Effendi*, p. 17.
2. Bahá'u'lláh, Kitáb-i-Aqdas, verse 174.
3. Cited in Shoghi Effendi, *The World Order of Bahá'u'lláh*, p. 17.
4. October, 1957, in *Messages to the Bahá'í World*, pp. 124–30.
5. Cable of June 11, 1952, ibid., p. 29.
6. *The Bahá'í World*, vol XIII, p. 248.
7. *Messages to the Bahá'í World*, p. 121.
8. September 6, 1957, ibid., p. 124.

## Chapter 23: Representing the Guardian

1. Shoghi Effendi, Message to the Kampala Intercontinental Conference.

## Chapter 24: Land

1. *Messages to the Bahá'í World*, p. 64.
2. Cited in Shoghi Effendi, *God Passes By*, p. 194.
3. Cable of November 12, 1952, in *Messages to the Bahá'í World*, p. 46.
4. *The Bahá'í World*, vol. XII, p. 134.
5. Cable of March 21, 1953, ibid., p. 48.
6. Copies in Ioas papers.
7. Cited in *The Bahá'í World*, vol. XIII, p. 249.
8. Quoted by Giachery, *Shoghi Effendi*, p. 210.

## Chapter 25: The Queen of Carmel

1. Cited in Rabbani, *Priceless Pearl*, p. 235.
2. Cited in Shoghi Effendi, *God Passes By*, p. 275.
3. Balyuzi, *'Abdu'l-Bahá*, p. 447.
4. Cable of March 21, 1951, in *Messages to the Bahá'í World*, p. 9.
5. Talk given by Ugo Giachery at the first European Teaching Conference, 1948.
6. Giachery, *Shoghi Effendi*, p. 100.
7. Cable of June 11, 1952, in *Messages to the Bahá'í World*, p. 29.
8. Cable of March 21, 1953, ibid., pp. 47–8.
9. Cited in Rabbani, *Priceless Pearl*, p. 414.
10. Cited in *The Bahá'í World*, vol. XII, p. 239.
11. *Jerusalem Post*, June 11, 1953.
12. Message of the Guardian to the Intercontinental Teaching Conference, New Delhi, India, in *Citadel of Faith*, p. 96.
13. Cited in *The Bahá'í World*, vol. XII, p. 239.
14. Letter to Spiritual Assembly of New York City, June 8, 1922, cited in "Curtis Kelsey", In Memoriam, *The Bahá'í World*, vol. XV, p. 469.
15. *God Passes By*, p. 18.
16. As recounted by Hand of the Cause 'Alí-Akbar Furútan, *The Story of My Heart*, p. 113.
17. Cited in *The Bahá'í World*, vol. XII, p. 239.

## Chapter 27: Serving Quietly

1. Report of the International Bahá'í Council, July 1952.
2. Cable of May 4, 1955, in *Messages to the Bahá'í World*, p. 86.
3. Conversation between Ugo Giachery and his spiritual son, Mario Piarulli of Lecce.

## Chapter 28: The International Bahá'í Archives

1. Cable of November 27, 1954, in *Messages to the Bahá'í World*, p. 74.
2. *The Bahá'í World*, vol. XIII, pp. 424, 403.
3. Message of the Universal House of Justice, June 1975.
4. Riḍván Message, 1954, in *Messages to the Bahá'í World*, p. 64.
5. Cable of March 20, 1955, ibid., p. 75.
6. *The Bahá'í World*, vol. XIII, p. 422.
7. "The Spiritual Potencies of That Consecrated Spot", in *The Bahá'í World*, vol. VIII, p. 247.
8. Giachery, *Shoghi Effendi*, p. 154.
9. *The Bahá'í World*, vol. XIII, p. 422.
10. ibid., p. 417.
11. *Messages to the Bahá'í World*, pp. 94–95.
12. ibid., p. 108.

## Chapter 29: The Ten Year Crusade: The First Five Years

1. Ioas papers.
2. Letter of June 30, 1952, in *Messages to the Bahá'í World*, p. 34.
3. ibid., pp. 37–39.
4. Cable of October 8, 1952, ibid., p. 41.
5. ibid.
6. Rabbani, *The Priceless Pearl*, p. 423.
7. "The Road to Glory", a statement on the Opening of the Ten Year Crusade, in Ioas papers.
8. Cable of October 8, 1952, in *Messages to the Bahá'í World*, p. 41.
9. Leroy Ioas, pilgrim's note.
10. Cable of May 28, 1953, in *Messages to the Bahá'í World*, p. 49.
11. Rabbani, *The Priceless Pearl*, p. 416.
12. Cable of April 6, 1954, in *Messages to the Bahá'í World*, p. 60.
13. Cited in *The Passing of 'Abdu'l-Bahá*, p. 28.

## Chapter 30: Ella Bailey

1. "In Memoriam", *The Bahá'í World*, vol. XII, p. 688.
2. "In Memoriam" Marion Jack, ibid., p. 674.

## Chapter 31: The Passing of Shoghi Effendi

1. Amatu'l-Bahá Rúḥíyyih Khánum, "The Passing of Shoghi Effendi", in *The Bahá'í World*, vol. XIII, p. 215.
2. ibid.
3. ibid., p. 216.
4. Giachery, *Shoghi Effendi*, p. 182.

5. Rabbani, *Priceless Pearl*, p. 450.
6. "The Passing of Shoghi Effendi", in *The Bahá'í World*, vol. XIII.
7. *Ministry of the Custodians*, p. 36.
8. ibid., p. 30.
9. *Bahá'í Journal*, special issue, January 1958.

## Chapter 32: The Beloved Guardian
1. *Dispensation*, p. 59.
2. *The Bahá'í World*, vol. XIII., p. ix.

## Chapter 33: The Custodians
1. *Ministry of the Custodians*, p. 15.
2. ibid., p. 114.
3. ibid., p. 131.
4. *World Order of Bahá'u'lláh*, p. 89.
5. *Ministry of the Custodians*, p. 167.
6. ibid., p. 171.
7. "Excerpts from 'Abdu'l-Bahá", mimeographed copy, 4 pp., in Ioas papers.
8. *Ministry of the Custodians*, p. 197.
9. Ishráq Khávarí, vol. 1, p. 205.
10. Said to Mildred Mottahedeh during her pilgrimage.
11. *The Bahá'í World*, vol. XIII. p. 857.
12. *Ministry of the Custodians*, p. 285.
13. Message from the 1961 Conclave, in *Ministry of the Custodians*, p. 322.
14. ibid., p. 21.
15. ibid., pp. 378–387.
16. *The Bahá'í World*, vol. XIII, p. 252.
17. *Ministry of the Custodians*, p. 382.
18. ibid., p. 420.

## Chapter 34: The Universal House of Justice
1. Cited in Message to the Bahá'ís of East and West, October 31, 1962, in *Ministry of the Custodians*, p. 379.
2. As recalled by Hand of the Cause Zikrullah Khadem.
3. *Ministry of the Custodians*, p. 390.
4. ibid., p. 425.
5. *Prayers and Meditations*, no. 59; also in many Bahá'í prayer books.
6. *Wellspring of Guidance*, pp. 1–3.
7. *Ministry of the Custodians*, p. 427.
8. May 7, 1963, in *Wellspring of Guidance*, pp. 4–8.
9. *Ministry of the Custodians*, pp. 430, 433.

10. *Wellspring of Guidance*, p. 45.
11. ibid., p. 11.

**Chapter 35: "You will, I am sure, persevere till the very end"**

1. Bahá'í News, August 1965.
2. Wellspring of Guidance, p. 157.
3. Letter of 14 November, 1935, in Ioas papers.

# INDEX

'Abbúd, House of, 234
'Abdu'l-Bahá, 5, 6, 17–28, 86, 96, 143, 148, 153, 159, 167, 182, 208, 221, 313, 317–18
    appoints Hands of the Cause, 153
    buys land at the Sea of Galilee, 207
    Divine Plan of, 27–8, 30, 97, 118
    house of, 234
        site of first election of the Universal House of Justice, 330, 331
    knighthood of, 177, 318
    meets Ben-Zvi, 185, 315
    meets Ella Bailey, 268
    meets Leroy Ioas, ix, 15–16, 22–3
    passing of, 35, 40
    plants a garden at Bahjí, 206
    prophecies of, 135, 137, 329, 330
    relics of, *see* Archives, International Bahá'í
    quotations of, regarding:
        the Benediction, 29
        the Covenant, 18, 310
        Local Spiritual Assembly of San Francisco, 36
        the Mashriqu'l-Adhkár, 11
        peace, 135
        Sylvia Ioas, 361
        teaching, 24
        the Writings, 309
    Shrine of, 163
    Shrine of the Báb, 217, 226
    station of, 18, 25n, 190
    Tablet of, to Charles Ioas, 9
    Tablet of, to Maria Ioas, 10
    visit to Chicago, 19–25
    Will and Testament of, *see* Will and Testament of 'Abdu'l-Bahá
Abraham, 24
Addams, Jane, 20
administration, Bahá'í, 92–3
*Advent of Divine Justice, The*, 110

Adventists, 1
Afnan, Ruhi, 65, 71
Africa, 198–204, 248
Africans, 198, 200–1
Agnew, Arthur, 10, 20, 23
'Akká, 165, 177, 226, 234
'Alá'í, Shu'á'u'lláh, 191, 230, 314, 352, 355, 357
Alaska, 107–8
Alexander, Agnes, 154, 191, 353, 355, 357
Ali-Kuli Khan, 10, 36, 71, 100
All-American Bahá'í Convention, 124
Allen, Dwight, 55, 67, 82, 255
Allen, John, 67n, 90, 250, 304
Allen, Valera, 67, 87, 132, 304
Allen, Dr. Woodson, 33
Angola, 252
Arc, the, 210, 211, 239, 241, 257
Archives, International, 197, 210–11, 218, 235, 236, 238–47, 249, 257, 331, 347
Asadu'lláh, Mírzá, 10
Assemblies, see Local Spiritual Assemblies, Local Spiritual Assembly and National
    Spiritual Assembly
Austin, Elsie, 258
Auxiliary Boards, appointment of, 192–3


Báb, the, 12, 18, 61, 150n, 217, 221, 225, 257, 300
        portrait of, 192, 202, 229–30, 246
        relics of, see Archives, International Bahá'í
        Shrine of, see Shrine of the Báb
Báb-i-Ioas, 231–2, 347
Bagdadi, Dr. Zia, 227
Bahá'í Faith, 203
        attacks on, 190
        centenary of, see centenaries, Bahá'í
        Charles and Marie Ioas learn of the, 4
        condition of, 251–2
        formative age of the, ix, 118
        international representation of, see Bahá'í International Community
        lack of growth in older communities, 320
        persecution of, 252, 324–7
        protection of, 179, 243, 277, 279, 293, 307, 350
        recognized as a non-governmental organization, 138
        spread of, 255, 264
        teaching the, 24, 95–7, 99, 105–6, 277
        World Centre of, see World Centre

Bahá'í International Community, 138
*Bahá'í News*, 19
*Bahá'í Peace Program, The*, 135
Bahá'í Secretarial Bureau, 66
Bahá'í Temple Unity, 12, 20, 39, 96, 98, 209n
Bahá'í youth, *see* Youth, Bahá'í
Bahá'ís,
        African, 198, 200–1
        Black, 79–80
        North American, 251
        numbers, 311
Bahá'u'lláh, ix, 17, 138, 140, 142, 153, 165, 177, 181, 207, 213, 253, 255–6, 264–5, 323, 329
        family of, 169, 193
        letter to S̲h̲áh, 309
        Mansion of, *see* Bahjí
        portrait of, 192, 229–30, 146, 301, 304
        relics of, *see* Archives, International Bahá'í
        selected site for the Shrine of the Báb, 217, 226
        Shrine of, *see* Shrine of Bahá'u'lláh
*Bahá'u'lláh and the New Era* (Esslemont), 129
Bahjí, 163, 165, 178, 185, 188–9, 193–7, 206, 211, 231, 234, 282, 352
Bailey, Ella, 34, 54, 267–70
Baker, Dorothy, 113, 136, 138, 143n, 148, 155, 202, 203, 258, 270
Baker, Richard St. Barbe, 225
Balyuzi, Hasan, 19, 193, 246, 273, 278, 279, 282–3, 318, 352, 354, 355, 357
Banani, Amin, 136, 171, 255
Banání, Músá, 191, 198–200, 278, 353, 354, 357
Banání, Samíhih, 198–9, 307
Baydún family land, 206, 207, 209, 212
beauty, 242
Bedekian, Victoria, 160
Benediction, 29
Benes, Marie, 30
Ben-Gurion, David, 183
Ben-Zvi, President Itzhak, 182, 184–6, 278, 315
Berkeley, California, 71
Bible, 7–8
Bishop, Helen, 57
Blackwell, Ellsworth and Ruth, 86
*Blessings Beyond Measure* (Yazdi), 284
Bolton, Drs. Stanley and Marietta, 131
Bosch, John, 34, 53–8, 62, 63, 70–1
Bosch, Louise, 34, 52–8, 63
Bosch Bahá'í School, 63

Bourgeois, Louis, 11n
Bowman, Amelia, 61, 113
Braun, Eunice, 127, 131, 304, 336
Braun, Leonard, 336
Bray, Joseph, 33
Breitwieser, Professor J. V., 47, 48
British Mandate, 213, 218, 219
Brittingham, Isabella, 34, 35, 37
Brown, Bishop, 280, 339
Brown, Ramona Allen, 33, 137
Brown, Ruth, 339
Browne, Edward G., 6n, 17n, 20
Bullock, Matthew, 258
Burland, Mollie, 37
Busey, Dr. Garreta, 122, 123–4
Bushrú'í, Mírzá Badí', 226–7
business, 73, 181
Byers, Rev. W.J.J., 47, 48


Caen, Herb, 90
Canada, 97, 109–10, 145
Carmelite Order, 212–16
Carpenter, Elizabeth, 36
Carpenter, Howard, 36
Carpenter family, 36
Caswell, Louise, 87
centenaries, Bahá'í, 115, 142, 253
Central America, see Latin America
Chance, Hugh, 331, 332, 348
Chase, Thornton, 4, 10, 20, 21, 34, 35, 35–6, 95
Chicago, 145
         'Abdu'l-Bahá in, 15–16, 18, 19–25
         Bahá'í meetings in, 7
         Bahá'í youth of, 15, 39
"Chief Stewards", see Hands of the Cause
Chile, 123–4
Christ,
         return of, 1–2, 4
Christian, Kenneth, 258
Churchill, Winston, 136
Clark, Mary, 75–6
Coffee, Dr. Rudolph, 46, 47, 48, 49, 130
Collins, Amelia, 27, 60, 132, 152, 156, 160, 162, 163, 169, 191, 216, 222, 231, 235, 244,
         290, 298, 349, 352, 355, 357

appointed Hand of the Cause, 154, 155
association with Geyserville, 57, 59, 62, 66
contributions of, 150–1, 215
illness of, 236, 321
member of International Bahá'í Council, 148, 170, 178
member of National Spiritual Assembly, 91n, 92, 103, 113
member of National Teaching Committee, 104, 113, 134
passing of Shoghi Effendi, 273–4, 275, 276
service as a Custodian, 279, 354
tribute to Shoghi Effendi, 284
Collins, Thomas, 59, 60
Commentary on the Surih of Joseph, 202
Commission of Inquiry, 218
community, Bahá'í, 109
Conclaves of the Hands of the Cause, 278–9, 292–3, 296, 305, 306–7, 308–9, 311, 312, 319, 321, 345
Conference for World Unity, 45–51, 66, 69
consultation, 97
Coolidge, President Calvin, 48
Cooper, Ella Goodall, 33, 34, 40, 41, 46, 48, 50, 54, 62, 66, 69, 128, 148, 268
appointed to the National Teaching Committee, 98
Cosmos Club, 78
Covenant, 68, 83, 145
violation of, 18
Covenant-breakers, 67–8, 131, 169, 187–9, 193–7, 209, 211, 244, 295, 309–11
Crisis, 76
Custodians, ix–x, 106, 193, 279, 292–328, 338
duties of, 293–4, 357
messages of, 303–4, 305, 307, 312, 320–1, 323–4, 327, 328, 330
see also Hands of the Cause


Dahl, Arthur, 73, 78, 315
Dahl, Hilbert, 147–8
Dahl, Joyce Lyon, 51, 54n, 55, 78, 103, 129, 144
Daniel, 264–5, 323
Dawn-breakers, 99, 117
Dawn-Breakers, Nabíl's Narrative of the Early Years of the Bahá'í Revelation, The, 99–100
Dealy, Mrs., 25–6
Dealy, Paul Kingston, 4–5, 25
D'Evelyn, Dr. Frederick, 34, 40, 69
deputization fund, 307
Dispensation of Bahá'u'lláh, The, 280, 290
Divine Plan, 27–8, 30, 97, 118, 334
Djakarta/Singapore conference (1958), 299–304

Dreyfus-Barney, Laura, 145
Duna, Rudolfo, 88, 252
Dunn, Clara, 36, 191, 353, 355, 357
Dunn, John Hyde, 36, 40, 66, 270
Dunning, Charles, 262–3


Egypt, 18–19
Ein Gev, Israel, 207
Elijah, cave of, 212, 226
England, 282
"entry by troops", 198, 312
Eskimos, 289
Eshkol, Levi, 224
Esperanto, 15, 38, 57
Esperanto Association of California, 48
Espinosa, Pedro, 119, 121
Esslemont, Dr John, 50, 84, 169–70
Europe, 108, 139, 148, 250
European teaching committee, 145


Faizi, Abu'l-Qásim, 193, 300, 303, 310, 336, 347, 349, 353, 355, 357
Fatheazam, Hushmand, 331, 332
Featherstone, Collis, 193, 353, 355, 357
fellowship, 78
Ferraby, Dorothy, 275
Ferraby, John, 193, 273, 275, 277, 353, 355, 357
Filipino Association, 69
Filipinos, 69–70
"Fisher, Mother", 87
Formative Age, ix, 118
Fozdar, Jamshed, 300
Frankland, Kathryn, 37, 46, 120
French, Nellie, 91n, 120
Fresno, California, 71
Fujita, Saichiro, 37, 86
funds, Bahá'í, 329
Furútan, 'Alí-Akbar, 155, 230, 275, 279, 281, 285, 295–6, 336, 352, 354, 355, 357


Galilee, Sea of, 207
Geddes, Sir Patrick, 218
Germany, 139, 250, 312, 322
Getsinger, Dr. Edward, 32, 42

Getsinger, Lua, 21, 24, 32, 33, 34, 36, 267, 270
Geyserville Bahá'í School, 51–63, 72, 78–9, 85, 103, 126, 299, 322, 358
Giachery, Ugo, 138, 155, 156, 170, 173–4, 175, 184, 188–9, 191, 197, 223, 232, 237, 239, 273, 275, 284, 288, 352, 355, 357
    travels in Central America, 305
    work on the Archives building, 241, 242, 244
    work on superstructure of the Shrine of the Báb, 218, 220
Gibson, Amoz, 331, 332
*Goal of a New World Order, The*, 121
Golden Gate International Exposition, 129
Goodale, Henry, 10
Goodall, Helen, 33, 34, 35, 36, 268
Greatest Holy Leaf, tomb of, 211, 241
Greenacre Bahá'í School, 55n
Greenleaf, Charles, 25
Greenleaf, Elizabeth, 70, 100
Gregory, Joan, 319
Gregory, Louis, 79, 100n, 113, 123
Gresham, Dean Wilmer, 47
Griffith's Grove, 56
Grossmann, Hermann, 155, 305, 308, 353, 355, 357
Guardian, *see* Shoghi Effendi
Guardianship, 339–40
Gulick, Bahia and Robert, 268, 269

Haddad, Anton, 10, 33
Haifa, ix, x, 165, 214
    *see also* World Centre
Hakim, Dr. Lotfullah, 148, 170, 225, 227, 236, 237, 318, 331, 332
Hands of the Cause, ix–x, 27, 85, 153, 171, 235, 329
    age of, 295
    ask not to be considered for service on the Universal House of Justice, 307, 323
    appointment of, by Shoghi Effendi, ix, 142, 191, 193, 199, 209n
    Conclaves of, *see* Conclaves of the Hands of the Cause
    consultation with the Universal House of Justice, 338–9
    following passing of Shoghi Effendi, 279–80
    duties of, 161, 169, 187–8, 192, 305, 345, 356
    following election of the Universal House of Justice, 333, 336
    messages from, 261, 276, 279, 336, 345
        on election of the Universal House of Justice, 332
    passing of Shoghi Effendi, 273–5, 276, 277–8
    Proclamation of, 352–5
    Resolution of, 356–7

station of, 339n
tribute to, 334, 336
work of, in Haifa, 187–97
*see also* Custodians
Haney, Paul, 148, 191, 230, 277, 279, 336, 353, 354, 355, 357
Hannen, Joseph, 100n
Hannen, Pauline Knobloch, 100n
Ḥaram-i-Aqdas, 194–5, 208, 209, 257, 278
Hatch, Willard, 57
Hautz, Larry, 207, 208
Hayes, Roland, 78
Hearst, Phoebe, 32–3, 57, 66
Hedley, Professor George, 58, 69
Hoagg, Emogene, 32–3
Hofman, David, 126n, 132, 296–7, 310, 318, 319, 331, 332
Hofman, Marion, *see* Holley, Marion
Holley, Doris, 146
Holley, Grace, 37, 54, 71
Holley, Horace, 22–3, 59, 68, 71, 78, 91, 113, 129–30, 138, 143, 148, 169, 275, 278, 285, 313, 353, 355, 357
      appointed Hand of the Cause, 155
      illness of, 146, 306
      passing of, 312–13
Holley, Marion [Hofman], 37, 60, 82, 103, 104–5, 113, 116, 127, 132, 135, 136, 138, 145, 147, 158, 236, 282, 294, 296, 310, 319, 332, 340, 346, 348
Holsti, Dr. Rudolf, 136
Holy Days, 173, 222
Holy Land, *see* World Centre
Holy Year (1952–3), 155, 221, 223, 253
Hoover, Herbert, 48
Ho-San Leong, 302
House of Spirituality, Chicago, 10, 96
House of Worship, *see* Mashriqu'l-Adhkár
Howard, Dr. Clinton, 47, 48
Hull House, Chicago, 20, 22
human rights
      NGO conference on (1948), 138
Ḥusayn, Mullá, 60, 245


Indonesia, 300
Inter-America Committee, 119, 120, 122, 124
intercontinental conferences (1953), 155–6, 222, 256
intercontinental conferences (1958), 193, 295, 298
International Bahá'í Council, 154, 169, 170, 190, 205, 212, 243, 274, 337, 350–1

appointment of, 142, 148–9, 236, 279–81
election of, 237, 294, 308, 314–15
evolution of, 294, 308, 356–7
functioning of, 171–2, 177–86, 314, 315
secretary-general of, 157, 161–2, 294, 347
tribute to, 360
International Convention, 314
Inter-Racial Amity Committee, 65
Ioas, Anita, 41, 128–33, 159, 175, 299, 309, 329, 346–7, 348
Ioas, Arthur, 125, 129
Ioas, Charles (Karl), 1–10, 12, 13, 21, 24, 96, 222
death of, 29
Tablet of 'Abdu'l-Bahá to, 9
Ioas, Charles (nephew of Leroy Ioas), 261n
Ioas, Farrukh (Mary Lorraine), 40–1, 60–1, 128–33, 155, 175, 276, 292, 309, 342, 361
Ioas, Joseph, 8, 10, 12–13, 24, 29
Ioas, Leroy, 5, 352, 355, 357
accidental injuries, 223
account of passing of Shoghi Effendi, 350–1
after passing of Shoghi Effendi, 280–1
appointed to European teaching committee, 145
appointed Hand of the Cause, 154–8, 359
appointed to Inter-America Committee, 119
appointed to National Teaching Committee, 91, 98, 113, 119, 134
appointed to Pacific Coast Teaching Committee, 72
assistant secretary to Shoghi Effendi, 187
attends Djakarta/Singapore conference (1958), 299–303
attends Kampala conference (1953), 180, 191, 198–204, 24
burial of, 349
business connections in Israel, 181
childhood of, ix, 8, 12–16
children of, 40–1, 125–33, 143
church attendance, 13
construction of Archives building, 241, 242–7, 347
correspondence with Shoghi Effendi, 83–5, 101–2, 110, 112–13, 115, 141, 144,
   151, 152, 157, 281, 349
cottage at Geyserville, 60, 61, 358
criticism of, 127
deals with Covenant-breakers, 188–90, 194–7, 295
dreams and visions of 'Abdu'l-Bahá, 26–7, 43
early Bahá'í activities of, 40, 41
family life of, 125–33, 143, 344
favorite prayer of, 14
first contact with Asian Bahá'ís, 303
at first International Convention, 331, 335

given tasks by Shoghi Effendi, 151, 303, 349

grandchildren of, 132–3, 344, 346–7

"Hercules", 171

illness of, 235, 243, 292, 296–8, 300, 305, 316, 318, 322, 335–6, 344–7, 349, 360

impatience of, 127–8

interest in people, 82

letter to 'Abdu'l-Bahá, 38

life in Haifa, 173–5

manages acquisition of land in Israel, 205, 243

marriage of, 30–1, 125

meets 'Abdu'l-Bahá, ix, 15–16, 22–3

meets Ben-Gurion, 183–4

meets Ben-Zvi, 185

meets Shoghi Effendi, 160–4

memories of Shoghi Effendi, 284–91, 345

messages from the Universal House of Justice, 345, 347–8

moves to Chicago, 141, 143, 358–9

moves to San Francisco, 31, 38–9

organizes the Conference for World Unity, 45–51, 66

passing of, 347–8, 360

passing of Shoghi Effendi, 271–82

personality of, 127–8

pioneering, 86–7

quotations of, regarding:

       'Abdu'l-Bahá, 22, 25

       Amelia Collins, 150

       Bahá'í teachers, 43

       the Bosches, 63

       the calamity, 89

       Conclaves of the Hands, 292–3, 306, 311

       Custodians, 295

       economics, 88

       Ella Bailey, 268–9

       Ella Goodall Cooper, 40

       Farrukh Ioas, 132, 158

       funeral of Shoghi Effendi, 276

       Geyserville, 62–3

       grandchildren, 132–3

       Guardianship, 340

       the home, 42

       Jesus, 13

       land transfer in Israel, 207–8

       Louise Bosch, 56

       materialism, 89

money, 89

persecution of Bahá'ís in Morocco, 326–7

pioneers, 117, 316–17

pledging loyalty to Shoghi Effendi, 84

public speaking, 13, 14

race prejudice, 76–7, 79

sacrifice, 150

San Francisco Bahá'í center, 65

Sara Witt, 72

service on the National Spiritual Assembly, 92

service to the Cause, 64, 86, 131, 159

Seven Year Plan, 105, 113, 117

Shoghi Effendi, 162, 176, 260, 271–2, 281, 282, 286, 287, 297, 299, 301, 306–7

Shrine of Bahá'u'lláh, 163

Singapore conference, 302

solving problems, 43

*Some Answered Questions*, 89

spirit of fellowship, 78, 79

Sylvia Ioas, 158, 359, 360

teaching, 15, 39, 65, 71, 72, 87, 89–90, 250–1, 298, 316–17, 343

temple construction, 147

Ten Year Crusade, 249, 260, 282, 292–3, 298, 311, 316

Universal House of Justice, 306–7, 332, 346

Word of God, 298

World Unity Conferences, 49

recreations of, 235–6, 344

residence in the Holy Land, 336, 346

Rotary Club member, 181

sacrifices of, 82

service as a Custodian, 279, 292–328, 354

service on the National Spiritual Assembly of the United States and Canada, 70, 91, 113, 119, 134, 143

services of, to the Cause, 73, 91–4, 143n, 235

services of, to Shoghi Effendi, 172, 229, 235, 285–6

speaking ability, 13, 14, 68–9, 70, 143, 297, 299, 302, 322, 358

study classes conducted by, 42

"teaching letters" of, 86–90

teaching plans of, 43, 45–6, 52

teaching work of, 64, 67–9, 81–90, 107, 143, 341–3, 344

Temple in Germany, 312, 316, 322

Ten Year Crusade goals, 249, 250–1, 255

"train letters" of, 73

travels to Djakarta, 299–301

treasurer of the National Spiritual Assembly, 146

tributes to, 158–9, 342–3, 347–8
unveiling ceremony for the Tablets of the Divine Plan, 28
visits Britain, 317–19
visits Scandinavia, 322
visits Swaziland, 304–5
visits Switzerland, 316
work as secretary-general of International Bahá'í Council, 157, 161–2, 170–3, 179, 188–9, 243, 294, 347
working life of, 14, 41, 72–3, 143, 144, 158
Ioas, Marguerite, 8, 229, 297, 313–14
Ioas, Marie, 3–10, 21, 23, 24, 29, 96, 229–30
passing of, 230–1
Tablet of 'Abdu'l-Bahá to, 10
Ioas, Monroe, 8, 23, 24
Ioas, Paul, 8, 158, 230
Ioas, Sylvia [Kuhlman], 3, 32, 67, 70, 71, 73, 103, 144, 152, 154–5, 156, 162–3, 197, 227, 229, 306, 345–7
after the passing of Leroy Ioas, 360–1
arrival in Haifa, 175
children of, 40–1
describes first International Convention, 329–30
family life of, 125–33, 143, 358
grandchildren of, 132–3
life in Haifa, 173–4, 175, 359–60
marriage of, 30–1, 125
memorial to, 358–61
moves to Chicago, 141, 143, 358–9
moves to San Francisco, 31, 38–9, 358
passing of, 361
passing of Shoghi Effendi, 272–3, 274, 276, 278, 350–1
service on International Bahá'í Council, 236–7, 274, 360
services of, at the World Centre, 233–7, 359–60
spiritual strength of, 161, 173–4, 359
Ioas, Viola, 8, 14, 144
Ioas family, 7–9, 12–13, 24, 29
Iran, persecutions in (1955), 252
Irving, Edward, 1
Irwin, Beatrice, 121
'Ishqábád, 10
Israel, state of, 142, 149, 173, 177–81, 194, 207, 214, 219, 274, 276, 293, 310, 338, 356
Israel branches of National Spiritual Assemblies, 206, 210, 243, 249, 257, 338
Ives, Mabel and Howard, 100, 158

Jack, Marion, 15, 107, 269

Japanese, the, 33, 37, 46
*Jerusalem Post*, 225
Jerusalem Rotary Club, 181–2
Jesus, 13
Jináb-i-Faḍíl, 40, 47, 48, 97, 126
Johnston, Anna, 37
Jordan, Dr. David Starr, 37, 47, 48, 50
Jordan River, 207


Kamming, Egon, 333
Kampala conference (1953), 180, 191, 198–204, 258
Kampala conference (1958), 282
Kavelin, Borrah, 237, 315, 331, 332
Kawasaki, Torao, 47, 48
Kazemzadeh, Firuz, 136
Kelber, Leonard Heinrich, 1
Kellberg, Margery Ullrich, 261n
Kelley, Florence Ullrich, 261n
Kelsey, Curtis, 227
Kemp, Evelyn, 98n
Kemp, Stanley, 98
Kempton, Honor, 60, 107–8, 156, 236–7, 348
Kenny, Sara, 90, 113
Khadem, Zikrullah, 191, 230, 268, 306, 343, 353, 354, 357
Khamsi, Masoud, 187
Kházeh, Jalál, 191, 279, 353, 354, 355, 357
Kheiralla, George Ibrahim, 21
Kinney, Vaffa, 260
Kitáb-i-Aqdas, 190, 234, 257, 275
Kitáb-i-Íqán, 10
Knesset, 182–3
Knights of Bahá'u'lláh, 202, 258, 261, 268, 303
Knobloch, Alma, 100n
Knobloch, Fanny, 100
Kuhlman, George, 30
Kuhlman, Mayme, 30
Kuhlman, Sylvia, *see* Ioas, Sylvia


land, purchases of, 173, 205–16, 238
Latimer, George, 33, 40, 54, 55, 57, 62, 65, 70, 98, 103, 104, 113
Latimer, Rouhanieh, 35
Latimer family, 33
Latin America, 95

first Seven Year Plan, 119–24
Laurenco Marquez, 252
Lee, Mrs. George, 302
Leroy Ioas Teaching Institutes, 348
Lesch, George, 10
Lesser Peace, 138, 332
Letters of the Living, 219, 263
Lincoln Park, 20
Linfoot, Charlotte 'Lottie', 42, 98–9, 103, 104, 113, 134
literature, Bahá'í, 9–10, 33, 122–3
            translations of, 121, 122, 124
Local Spiritual Assemblies
            civil boundaries of, 111
            establishment of, 95, 97, 109, 114, 115–16, 140, 148, 192, 316
Local Spiritual Assembly
            of Chicago, 10
            of Oakland, 42, 68, 70, 84
            of Phoenix, 70
            of San Francisco, 36, 40, 64, 65–6, 82, 135
            of Santa Barbara, 70, 71
Locke, Isobel, see Sabri, Isobel Locke
Lowdermilk, Dr. and Mrs. Walter, 236, 246–7
Lunt, Alfred, 91n


MacNutt, Howard, 100
Máh-Kú, 224, 231
Malaysia, 300–1
Martin, Douglas, 331
martyrs, American, 123, 267
Masetlha, William, 333
Mashriqu'l-Adhkár, 257
            construction of, in Ten Year Crusade, 305, 312, 320, 324
            Germany, 316, 322
            Kampala, 282
            temple land in the Holy Land, 211, 212–16, 234, 249, 257
            Wilmette, 10–12, 15, 20, 25, 74, 96, 145, 191, 221
                        completion of, 103, 112, 140–1, 143, 146–8, 219–20
                        dedication of, 191–2, 222, 229–30
                        guides at, 233–4
Masonic Temple, Chicago, 7, 25
mass conversion, 266, 320–1
Mathews, Edward and Loulie, 120, 121
Maxwell, Mary, see Rúḥíyyih Khánum
Maxwell, May, 34, 57, 71, 72, 90, 98, 100, 123, 149n, 171n, 217, 270

Maxwell, Sutherland, 149, 151, 155
   architect of the superstructure of the Shrine of the Báb, 217–28, 232
Mayberry, Florence, 235
Mazra'ih, 234
McCants, Jack, 81
McCormick, Mr. and Mrs. E.O., 41
McDaniel, Allen, 74, 91n
Meredith, Professor John, 58
Mexico, 120–2
Mihdí, Mírzá, 241
Miller, William, 1
Millerites, 1
Mills, Mountfort, 24, 98
*Ministry of the Custodians, The*, 333
Monon Railroad, 14
Moody, Susan, 100, 270
Morocco, 324–7
Moses, 183–4, 186
Most Great Jubilee, 257, 327, 333, 336–7
Mottahedeh, Rafi, 275, 290
Mottahedeh, Mildred, 138, 237, 275, 315
Mt. Carmel, land purchases on, 209–12, 238
Mozambique, 252
Mudaliar, Sir S. Ramaswami, 137
Muhájir, Iran Furútan, 256–7
Muhájir, Raḥmatu'lláh, 193, 256–7, 327, 347, 353, 355, 357
Muḥammad Tabrízí, 174
Mühlschlegel, Dr. Adelbert, 191, 275, 279, 306, 312, 316, 353, 354, 355, 357
Músá, Mírzá, 207


Nabil, Marzieh [Carpenter Gail], 36
Nakhjavani, Ali, 174, 198–9, 202–4, 237, 315, 327, 331, 332
Nakhjavani, Jalal, 311
Navidi, Aziz, 293
Navváb, tomb of, 241
National Association for the Advancement of Colored People (NAACP), 20, 76, 77–8
National Spiritual Assemblies
   attend first International Convention, 330
   establishment of, 140, 148, 192, 257, 266, 307–8, 312, 313, 324
   European, 308, 316
   Israel branches of, 206, 210, 243, 249, 257, 338
   Latin American, 308
National Spiritual Assembly
   of the British Isles, 202, 248, 318

of Denmark, 322
of Finland, 322
of France, 292, 310
of Germany, 312, 322
of Hawaii, 339n
of Iran, 210
of Jamaica, 314
of the United States, 145–6, 342, 343
    Leroy Ioas elected to, 146
of the United States and Canada, 98
    granted observer status to the United Nations, 138
    Leroy Ioas elected to, 70, 143
    membership of, 113
National Teaching Committee, 91, 95, 97–105, 109, 134
    referred to in *Advent of Divine Justice*, 110
New York City, 18, 42, 96
Ng Poon Chew, 47, 48
Nichols, Dr. Mildred, 141
Nineteen Day Feast, 35
Nine Year Plan, 327, 337
North America, 250–1


Oakland, California, 33, 42, 68, 70, 84
Ober, Harlan, 156
Olinga, Enoch, 193, 201, 258–9, 301, 304, 305, 313, 353, 355, 357
Orkney Islands, 262–3


Pacific area, 304
Pacific Coast Teaching Committee, 72, 77
Palace Hotel, San Francisco, 47, 116
Parsons, Agnes, 45–6, 47
Pereira, Dr. Sarah, 79
persecutions, 252, 324–7
Phoenix, Arizona, 70
pilgrimage, 295, 337
pilgrim house, 234
pilgrims, 179, 221, 233–5, 288–9
pilgrims' notes, x
pioneers, 86–7, 101, 104, 105–6, 107, 108–9, 117–18
    in Africa, 198–9, 201, 204
    difficulty in settling, 111–12, 122
    in Europe, 141, 145
    funding of, 104

Ten Year Crusade, 249, 251, 255, 256, 258, 261–3, 267, 298–9, 307, 311
    youthfulness of, 113
Plans, 248, 264, 327
    *see also* Nine Year Plan, Seven Year Plans *and* Ten Year Crusade
Plaza Hotel, Chicago, 20, 22
*Priceless Pearl, The* (Rabbaní), 284
proclamation campaign, 115


Rabb, Mary, 34
race unity, 65, 75–80
Ralston, Georgia, 34
Ramm, Rev. Charles, 47
Randall, William, 100
Randolph, A. Phillip, 75
Ransom-Kehler, Keith, 100, 123, 270
Reinhardt, Dr Aurelia, 47, 48
religion, 1–2
Remey, Charles Mason, 100, 131, 132, 138, 156, 160, 185, 188, 191, 352, 357
    appointed Hand of the Cause, 155
    claims to be second Guardian, 309–11
    designs Archives building, 239
    member of International Bahá'í Council, 148, 170, 178
    service as a Custodian, 279, 354
*Renewal of Civilization, The* (Hofman), 335
Reno, Nevada, 71, 82
Revell, Ethel and Jessie, 148, 170, 237, 274, 350–1
Rexford, Orcella, 42, 52, 68, 100, 107, 120–1
Riḍván, Garden of, 257
Riverside, California, 144
Robarts, John, 193, 306, 332, 353, 355, 357
Rogers, Dr. Ernest, 34, 51, 57
Root, Martha, 28, 40, 48, 60, 98, 100, 120, 167, 209n, 270
Roosevelt, Franklin D., 136
Rosenberg, Ethel, 84, 169
Rosicrucian Fellowship, 69
Rotary International, 181
Ruhe, David, 81
Rúḥíyyih Khánum, 11, 28, 162, 168–9, 172, 175–6, 179, 185, 186, 217, 222, 223, 229–30, 239, 241, 243–4, 246, 255, 259, 261, 271, 284, 311n, 321, 333, 346, 352, 357
    analysis of the first Seven Year Plan, 118
    appointed Hand of the Cause, 191
    assisted by Sylvia Ioas, 233
    correspondence with Leroy Ioas, 114, 134, 151
    description of Shoghi Effendi, 170

first International Convention, 329, 331
member of International Bahá'í Council, 148–9, 170
passing of Shoghi Effendi, 272–82, 350
residence in the Holy Land, 336
service as a Custodian, 279, 296, 354


Sabri, Hassan, 201
Sabri, Isobel Locke, 60–1, 67–8, 83, 105–6, 126, 145, 201, 234, 311
Sacramento, California, 42, 73, 135, 137
sacrifice, 82, 147
Samandarí, Ṭarázu'lláh, 155, 230, 309, 353, 355, 357
San Francisco, California, 31, 43, 45, 126
        first Bahá'í Center of, 41, 126
        first Spiritual Assembly of, 36, 40
        Leroy Ioas's last years in, 134–41
San Francisco Bay area, 31, 38
        Bahá'ís of, 32–7
*San Francisco Examiner*, 84, 90
San Joaquin valley, 71
Sanor, Sally, 89, 127
Santa Barbara, California, 70, 71, 84
Santa Clara valley, 71
Santa Maria, California, 71
Santa Paula, California, 36
Saunders, Professor Kenneth, 47, 48
Scheffler, Carl, 15, 39, 40, 67
scholars, 238
Schopflocher, Siegfried "Fred", 62, 78–9, 91–2, 113, 191
Sears, Marguerite, 323
Sears, William, 81, 82, 106, 127, 193, 282, 305–6, 353, 354, 357
Semple, Ian, 237, 315, 331, 332, 335
Seto, Anthony and Mamie, 78, 258
Seven Year Plan, first, 58, 85, 88, 95–118, 167
        completion of, 115–17, 124
        in Latin America, 119–24
Seven Year Plan, second, 61n, 108, 113, 140–1, 142, 143, 146, 148
Shaw, Rosa, 78
Shoghi Effendi, ix, 5, 8, 18, 26, 50, 58, 117, 118, 128, 138, 165–72, 176, 284–91
        acquires property for the Faith, 205–16
        appointed Guardian, 290
        appoints Hands of the Cause, ix, 154–5
        chanting of, 173
        constructs Archives building, 238–47
        constructs superstructure of the Shrine of the Báb, 217–28

correspondence with Leroy Ioas, 84–5, 92–3, 101–2, 110, 112–13, 115, 141, 144, 151, 152, 157, 281, 349
Covenant-breakers oppose, 188
dedication to, 291
difficulties faced by, 151, 168–9, 170, 188–90
family of, 174, 288–9
funeral of, 276–7
grave of, 296, 304, 320
humility of, 290
launches Ten Year Crusade, 248–66
leaves no heir, 278–9
Leroy Ioas meets, 160–4
letters of, to be returned to Haifa, 309
love and tenderness of, 288–9
memorial to, at International Convention, 333–4
mission of, 166–7
mourning for, 295
passing of, ix, 27, 196–7, 246, 271–83, 354
quotations of, regarding:
 African Bahá'ís, 200
 American heroines, 270
 architecture, 239
 Archives building, 238, 240, 242, 244, 245
 Báb-i-Ioas, 231–2
 Bahá'ís, 287–8
 beauty, 242
 Black Bahá'ís, 80
 Conference for World Unity, 50
 Corinne True, 289
 Covenant-breakers, 310
 Ella Bailey, 268, 269
 Europe, 139, 140, 141
 Geyserville, 58–9, 61, 62, 63
 Guardianship, 272, 290
 Hands of the Cause, 154
 International Bahá'í Council, 148, 170, 184, 236
 international relief, 139–40
 Israel Branches of National Spiritual Assemblies, 206
 John Bosch, 63
 Knights of Bahá'u'lláh, 261
 Leroy Ioas, 59n, 92, 93, 102, 110, 211, 223, 229
 Letters of the Living, 263
 Marie Ioas, 231
 mass conversion, 266
 *Nabíl's Narrative*, 100

nature of the Bahá'í Faith, 101
Oakland Bahá'ís, 68
passing of Bahá'u'lláh and 'Abdu'l-Bahá, 271
pioneers, 107, 112–13, 199–200, 204, 256, 258, 259, 263, 267
protection of the Faith, 279
purification of the Ḥaram-i-Aqdas, 196
responsibility of the United States, 139
service, 290
Seven Year Plan, first, 102, 103, 113–15, 117–18, 124
Seven Year Plan, second, 140
Shoghi Effendi's work, 167, 168, 286–7
Shrine of the Báb, 149–50, 221, 225, 226–7
Shrine of Bahá'u'lláh, 208–9
spiritual matters, 272
Sylvia Ioas, 236
Tablet of Carmel, 213, 240
teaching, 101
Ten Year Crusade, 202, 248, 253, 254–5, 256, 258, 259, 260–1, 263,
     264, 265–6, 290, 327
translations, 289
traveling teachers, 101
United Nations Conference, 188
Universal House of Justice, 306, 332
Western Bahá'ís, 84
work to be done, 172
standards of, 220
uses term "pioneer", 101
work of, 167–8
*Shoghi Effendi: Recollections* (Giachery), 284
Shrine
     of the Báb, 163, 164, 165, 173, 186, 191, 217–18, 351
          construction of superstructure of, 142, 149, 166, 178, 217–28
          doors of, 232, 347
          guides at, 233
          land surrounding, 205, 208, 209, 216, 218
          lighting of, 227
          Leroy Ioas's work on, 162
     of Bahá'u'lláh, 163, 185, 188, 193–6, 205, 206, 208, 249, 257, 351
          visitors to, 233–4
Singapore conference (1958), 300–1
Siyáh-Chál, 253, 257
Sobel, Julia, 15
soldiers, Bahá'í, 139
*Some Answered Questions*, 89
South America, *see* Latin America

Southern Pacific railroad, 41, 72, 73, 75, 111, 141, 144, 358
southern states (United States), 109
Sprague, Phillip, 146
Stanford University, 34, 36–7, 50
*Star of the West*, 67
Steiner, René, 86
Stella Maris monastery, 212–13
Stewart, Frances Benedict, 120, 121–2, 124
Stratton, Professor G.M., 47
Surat-ul-Hykl (Súriy-i-Haykal), 10
Symposium of Living Religions, 69
Swaziland, 304–5


Tablet of Carmel, 165, 167, 213, 216, 240, 329
Tablets of the Divine Plan, 28, 102, 120, 167, 256
teachers, Bahá'í, 106
teaching, *see* Bahá'í Faith, teaching the
teaching committees, regional, 111
Temple, *see* Mashriqu'l-Adhkár
Temple land, *see* Mashriqu'l-Adhkár
Ten Year Crusade, ix, 78n, 99, 158, 162n, 169, 172, 191–3, 198, 202, 210, 222, 238, 242,
    248–66, 323, 334
        after passing of Shoghi Effendi, 280, 356
        major objectives of, 256–7
        pioneers in, *see* pioneers, Ten Year Crusade
        victories of, 311–12, 320, 321, 324, 327
        virgin areas of, *see* virgin areas
terraces, to Shrine of the Báb, 218
Theosophical Society, Chicago, 20
tiles, golden, 219, 224–5, 231, 244
Tobey, Mark, 88, 325
Townshend, George, 154n, 155, 159, 164, 345
translations, 121, 122, 124, 289
traveling teachers, 100–1
        to Latin America, 119
*Tribute to Shoghi Effendi, A* (Collins), 284
True, Corinne, 18, 20, 91, 143, 191, 278, 289, 357
True, Edna, 143, 145, 148, 230
True, Dr. Katherine, 159
Truman, Harry S., 136, 137
Tsao, Dr. H., 88
Tudor-Pole, Wellesley, 19
Turner, Robert, 32

Uganda, 198–9
Ullrich, Clarence, 230
Union of Sleeping Car Porters, 75
United Nations, 252n, 325–6
    Charter of the, 136, 137
United Nations Associations, 325
United Nations Conference, San Francisco, 135–7
United States, 341–3
unity, 78–9
    race, 65, 75–80, 84
Universal House of Justice, 27, 165, 166, 174, 294, 302, 324
    consultation with the Hands of the Cause, 338–9
    election of, ix, 86, 279, 306, 321, 326, 357
        preparations for, 309, 323, 327, 330
    first International Convention to elect, 329–33
    functioning of, 337, 338–9
    members of, 331, 332, 339
    messages of, 336–7, 338
        concerning Guardianship, 339–40
        on passing of Leroy Ioas, 347–8
    presentation of, at World Congress, 334
    prophecies of Bahá'u'lláh concerning, 329

Vail, Albert, 15, 39, 71, 76
Vambéry, Arminius, 129
Vambéry, Dr. Rustum, 129–30
Vancouver, Canada, 71, 77, 97

Varqá, 'Alí Muḥammad, 191, 278, 353, 354, 357
Varqá, Valíyu'lláh, 155, 230
virgin areas
    of first Seven Year Plan, 106, 109, 111, 112, 114
    of second Seven Year Plan, 140
    of Ten Year Crusade, 256, 258, 260, 265
Visalia, 37, 54, 71

Wagner, Henrietta, 71
Wailing Wall, 215
Waite, Shahnaz, 29, 54, 98
war, second world, 111
Ward, Dr. Forsythe, 103
Ward, Janet, 103n

Weinshall, Dr. Abraham, 293
Weizmann, Dr. Chaim, 179–80
Western Pilgrim House, 174, 337
Wilhelm, Roy, 91n, 113, 127, 134, 209–10, 227
Will and Testament of 'Abdu'l-Bahá, ix, 97, 151, 154, 166, 167, 168, 169, 265, 276, 277, 279, 292
Will and Testament of Bahá'u'lláh, 190
Wilmette, Illinois
    the Ioases move to, 145
Windust, Albert, 10, 30, 40, 159
Witt, Sara, 72
Witzel, Donald, 285n
Wolcott, Charles, 237, 294–5, 298, 315, 331–2
Women's Christian Temperance Union, 69
World Centre, 142, 186, 341–2
    institutions at, 148–51
    land, purchase of, at, *see* land, purchase of
    Leroy Ioas invited to, ix, 128, 157
    life at, 172, 173–4
    pilgrims to, 179
    services of Leroy Ioas at, 141, 157, 161–2, 170–2
    Shoghi Effendi's mission to develop, 166–7
    temple land at, 211, 212–16
World Congress (1963), 280, 314, 315, 319–20, 327, 333–5, 360
*World Order* magazine, 59
World Parliament of Religions, 6n, 20–1
world unity dinners, 65–6


Yamamoto, Kanichi, 33
Yazdi, Ali, 36, 73, 284
Yazdi, Marion Carpenter, 34, 36
youth, Bahá'í, 15, 19, 129


Zamenhof, Lidia, 139
Zikrullah, 207

## ABOUT THE AUTHOR

A native of San Francisco and a third-generation Bahá'í, Anita Ioas Chapman is the daughter of Leroy and Sylvia Ioas whose lives are told in these pages. A graduate of Stanford, she has worked as a writer/broadcaster on Voice of America and Radio Free Europe. She has lived in Indochina, Canada, Luxembourg, Belgium and France, and has served on Bahá'í institutions in France at the national level, and in Paris, Laos, Edmonton, Luxembourg, and Washington DC where she makes her home. She is active in speaking and teaching about the Bahá'í Faith and has also served the Bahá'í community in its Office of External Affairs in Washington, and on the Boards of a ballet company and a scholarship fund for African women. She is married to a former U.S. diplomat and has three children.